KEY ISSUES IN
A-LEVEL LAW
CRIMINAL LAW

CLAIRE STRICKLAND

LONGMAN

Pearson Education Limited
Edinburgh Gate
Harlow
Essex CM20 2JE, England

Printed in Singapore

ISBN   0582 34024 1

The Publisher's policy is to use paper manufactured from sustainable forests.

Contents

List of Figures

Table of Cases

Table of Statutes

Other Materials

Preface

This text on criminal law is the second title in the series *Key Issues in A – Level Law*, following on from *The English Legal System*. As such it aims to be student friendly and to allow interactivity. The chapters at the beginning and end of the book provide the student with an overview of the whole of the criminal jutice system, while the central chapters, covering the substantive law, follow a uniform structure. Such an approach should foster familiarity with the text and enable students to settle quickly into each new area of substantive law.

The 'Statutory Provisions' section is included so that students can read the law at source and see how many of the problems in the substantive law stem from badly drafted statutes.

The 'Setting the Scene' section of these chapters has been designed to allow students to feel their way into each topic, and to prevent students becoming overwhelmed when faced with each new area of law to learn.

In the 'Key Points', students are introduced to leading case law on each topic and are encouraged to think about the application of principles to cases in the 'You Decide Cases'.

The overall aim has been to cover the key points of each area of substantive law in an accessible way, avoiding too much black letter law by making use of flow diagrams, grids and 'You Decide' cases. In addition, the text of some key cases is included to help students see how cases are argued and how previous cases are followed or distinguished.

This book improves on other student texts by including in each substantive law chapter a section on 'Applying principles to examination questions'. Students are given the opportunity to apply their newly acquired knowledge to typical A-level examination questions and are provided with tips on how to approach them. To avoid confusion when studying topics for the first time, these questions match the topics covered in each chapter; the aim here is to consolidate students' learning. In the two Consolidation chapters, ten and thirteen, questions incorporate several topics and allow students

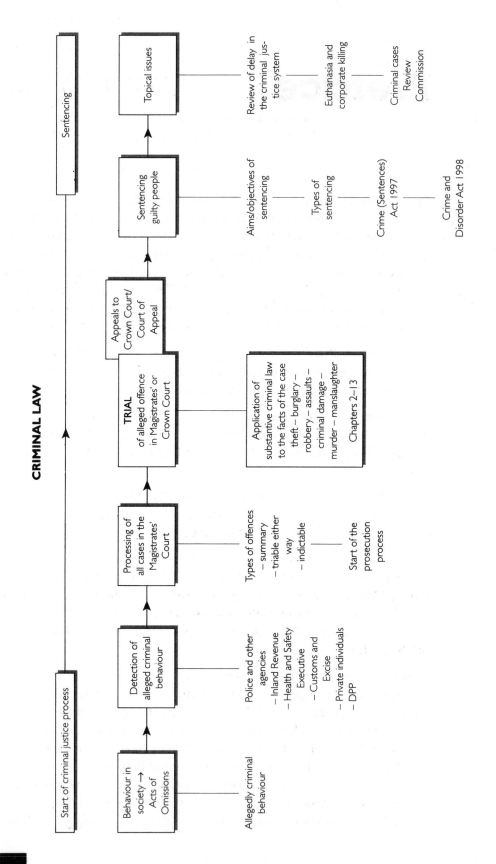

CRIMINAL LAW

Start of criminal justice process

Sentencing

Behaviour in society → Acts of Omissions

Detection of alleged criminal behaviour

Processing of all cases in the Magistrates' Court

TRIAL of alleged offence in Magistrates' or Crown Court

Appeals to Crown Court/ Court of Appeal

Sentencing guilty people

Topical issues

Allegedly criminal behaviour

Police and other agencies
– Inland Revenue
– Health and Safety Executive
– Customs and Excise
– Private individuals
– DPP

Types of offences
– summary
– triable either way
– indictable

Start of the prosecution process

Application of substantive criminal law to the facts of the case
theft – burglary – robbery – assaults – criminal damage – murder – manslaughter
Chapters 2–13

Aims/objectives of sentencing

Types of sentencing

Crime (Sentences) Act 1997

Crime and Disorder Act 1998

Review of delay in the criminal justice system

Euthanasia and corporate killing

Criminal cases Review Commission

to progress to a greater level of difficulty. Suggested answers to all questions are also provided .

Finally, each chapter outlines proposals for reform. In some chapters this is a big area of study while in others it is only a minor one. Nevertheless, knowledge of such proposals is essential to enable students to make informed comment in introductions and/or conclusions to essays.

Progression through the text

Most full-time students study the English Legal System as Module One during their first year of study and then move on to their chosen A2 Module or Modules in the second year. Thus, by the time students embark on a study of the criminal law they should have developed reasonable essay-writing skills. However, their problem-solving skills are usually still undeveloped. This text aims to develop such skills in a progerssive manner. For this reason, in the first substantive law chapters students are not only given tips on how to approach the question posed, but also a translation of such tips into essay format. Students are advised to work through the text in the order in which it is presented in order to gain full benefit from such progression.

As well as developing problem-solving skills throughout the text, students are gradually introduced to concepts of the criminal law which may be difficult to understand if presented all at once. Thus, for example, Chapter 4, on theft, introduce an understanding of the indictment and counts on the indictment.

Data and stimulus-response techniques and statistics

Questions on A-level law examination papers, from whatever syllabus, are increasingly incorporating data and stimulus-response techniques. To develop such techniques the 'Setting the Scene' part of the substantive law chapters incorporates questions which involve students in either data or stimulus response. Thus, some questions may be answered from the data supplied in the text, while others require thought beyond the text and may even require student research. Answers to all questions are supplied to enable students to see what sort of answers they should be giving. In addition, the text offers statistical data and graphs which allow students to develop interpretative skills.

Conclusion

This text has been designed specifically for A-level law students studying criminal law as the A2 Module. It incorporates development of all the skills required to approach this module with confidence, and has comprehensive coverage of the substantive law and related topics, making this an essential student text.

The start of the criminal justice process

The following topics are covered in this section:

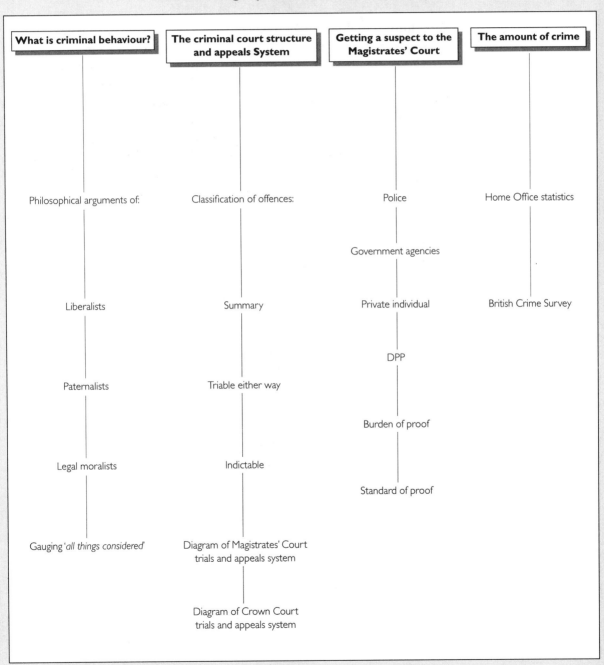

What is criminal behaviour?	The criminal court structure and appeals System	Getting a suspect to the Magistrates' Court	The amount of crime
Philosophical arguments of:	Classification of offences:	Police	Home Office statistics
		Government agencies	
Liberalists	Summary	Private individual	British Crime Survey
Paternalists	Triable either way	DPP	
Legal moralists	Indictable	Burden of proof	
		Standard of proof	
Gauging *all things considered*	Diagram of Magistrates' Court trials and appeals system		
	Diagram of Crown Court trials and appeals system		

1 The criminal justice process

In addition to detailed analysis of the substantive criminal law, such as the law of theft, the law of homicide and so forth, some A-level students are also required to consider the philosophical arguments which underpin such substantive law. This is particularly true of students studying the AEB syllabus. This section therefore begins with a consideration of some of these arguments. However, as this topic may seem somewhat abstract during the early stages of the study of criminal law, it is recommended that it should be considered after the study of some of the areas of substantive criminal law, for instance, after study of the section on offences against property (see page 78).

What is criminal behaviour?

What type of behaviour, by individuals, or groups of individuals, in society attracts the attention of the criminal law? Is it only 'morally wrong' conduct which is regarded as criminal or is other behaviour regarded as criminal? Indeed, some morally wrong behaviour may not be regarded as criminal. Several philosophical arguments can be put forward to justify the labelling of certain types of behaviour as criminal. The types of behaviour they extend to may be the same in some respects but may greatly differ in other respects. Some of these philosophical arguments are considered below.

However, apart from the philosophical arguments, what characterises the type of behaviour that is deemed to be criminal? It can only be said that criminal behaviour is behaviour which attracts the attention of the criminal justice system. As such, it is behaviour which is:

▶ deemed to be an act against the state itself, not just against a victim;
▶ adjudicated against by the state in the criminal courts;
▶ punished by the state;
▶ regarded with social stigma by the rest of society.

Philosophical arguments underlying the criminalisation of behaviour

A discussion of the philosophical arguments underlying the criminal law is to be found in the Law Commission's Consultation Paper 'Consent in the Criminal Law' (Law Com. Consultation Paper No 139) Appendix C. This discussion is the work of Paul Roberts of the University of Nottingham and it will be used as a framework for this part of the text. A good approach to this topic is found in paragraphs C18–20 of the consultation paper.

C18　*In order to determine whether a particular form of conduct should be criminalised it is always necessary to pose two quite separate questions:*

(1)　Is there a good (moral) reason to justify extending the criminal law to this particular conduct?

(2)　Should this conduct be criminalised all things considered (with particular reference to other moral principles and the pragmatics of law enforcement)?

C19　*Only if there is an affirmative answer to both these questions has a case for criminalisation been made out. Moreover, it is of the first importance that the two questions, and the arguments that are deployed to answer them, are kept quite separate and that they are addressed independently. The two inquiries must never be conflated because they stand in an hierarchical relationship to one another. Only if the answer 'yes' can be given to the first Question (1) do we even go on to consider Question (2). On the other hand, no reply to Question (2), no matter how strong or cogent it may be, can ever compensate for a failure to respond adequately to Question (1).*

C20　*A simple example will help to illustrate this point. Suppose that a case is made for criminalising a particular form of injury, by putting forward moral arguments to support its prohibition, that is by providing a 'yes' to Question (1). Suppose also that the prohibition will be virtually impossible to enforce, because the conduct in question is conducted only in private by secretive groups of individuals who never inform on each other. This is the type of argument that might lead one to answer 'no' to Question (2), and therefore to oppose criminalisation* all things considered. *But the inverse does not hold. The fact that it would be very easy to prohibit a particular form of conduct is, of itself,* absolutely no reason whatsoever *in favour of its criminalisation. In determining the moral limits of the criminal law, the considerations addressed to Question (2) only make sense against a background of affirmative answers to Question (1). Nobody would try to argue that wearing a hat in public should be criminal simply because it would be an easy prohibition to enforce. Debates about criminalisation are littered with just this sort of category mistake, albeit in forms that seem more plausible at face value, and which are all the more insidious and misleading on precisely that account. The only way to guard against these category mistakes is to adopt a rigorously logical, step by step approach to the investigation.*

Roberts then considers what he regards to be the three main competing philosophical perspectives which seek to demarcate the *moral limits* of the criminal law:

i liberalism;
ii paternalism;
iii legal moralism.

These will be considered in turn.

Liberalism

With regard to the criminal law, liberalism takes the view that only the 'harm principle' or the 'offence principle' can ever provide a good reason to support criminal legislation. The harm principle was stated by John Stuart Mill as:

The sole end for which mankind are warranted, individually or collectively, in interfering with the liberty of action of any one of their number is self-protection ... The only purpose for which power can be rightfully exercised over any member of a civilised community, against his will, is to prevent harm to others. His own good, either physical or moral, is not a sufficient warrant.

The harm principle would appear to be a good basis on which to base the criminal law but its flaw is that it presupposes a background of moral values and ideals to which not everyone will necessarily subscribe. The harm principle can only be used as a basis for determining criminality when it is given certain concrete maxims or base points to which most people would subscribe. Thus, most people would agree that it is justifiable for the criminal law to be invoked against those who carry out *serious* harms which interfere with the ability of others to pursue their 'welfare interests' of continued life, health, sustenance, shelter, procreation, political liberty and so forth. By the same token, most people would not expect to be able to invoke the criminal law against *trivial* interferences with these interests. Also, most people would agree that the criminal law should be able to be invoked against those people who indulge in behaviour which carries a *high risk* of causing harm to others.

The offence principle defends the criminalisation of behaviour if it is such that it causes serious offence to others and could effectively be prevented by criminalisation.

At the heart of the liberalist ideal is the notion that an individual is at liberty (free) to choose how to lead his or her life – each individual thus has autonomy. For this reason, liberalists prefer minimal state intervention in their lives. Thus, they find state intervention, by means of the criminal law, very offensive, especially as such intervention is backed up with a range of state punishments (prison, community sentences, fines and so forth). However, the liberalist position is modified by the realities of living in modern society. They do not strive for absolute (one hundred per cent) liberty, only *the maximum liberty that is compatible with similar liberty for all*. This is a common sense approach and sits correctly with the harm principle as made more applicable with its concrete maxims. Thus, liberalists support both the harm principle and the offence principle. However, they only support the offence principle sparingly as it is possible that every single activity in society could give offence to someone and on this basis everything could be made criminal! Thus, they only support the offence principle where the offence caused to often unwilling bystanders is extreme. It is highly unlikely, therefore, that liberalists would support the criminalisation of, say, unnatural and consensual sexual intercourse carried out behind locked doors in private. Who would be offended by this?

With regard to whether or not an individual should be able to consent to harm being inflicted upon themselves, the liberalists' position is that an individual who is sufficiently mature and who has adequate mental capacity to lead an autonomous life, should be able to consent to the infliction of harm upon himself or herself. Thus, liberalists aim to protect children and others whose ability to make a genuine consent is impaired. Liberalists do not qualify this ability to consent to harm and so they regard it as part of the autonomy of an individual to be able to consent to their own death. They thus support the legality of both suicide and voluntary euthanasia and would also support the legality of the infliction of actual and grievous bodily harm upon oneself.

Paternalism

Paternalists believe that behaviour may be justifiably criminalised when it is probably necessary to do so in order to prevent harm (physical, psychological or economic) to the actor himself. In other words, the paternalists advocate what the liberalists deny; that the *state may interfere with an individual's choice of actions* in order to safeguard the individual's well-being. The state will intervene not on the basis of what *it believes* to be in the best interest of the individual, but on the basis of what *is in fact* in the best interest of the individual.

When marking out the moral limits of the criminal law, it is not always easy for paternalists to explain why the state should interfere in people's life choices when such interference necessarily takes away individual freedom of choice. This is a difficult task in England because the notion of individual freedom is deeply ingrained into English culture. Sometimes the paternalist approach may seem an appropriate basis on which to justify criminalising behaviour. For instance, it seems appropriate to make it an offence not to wear a seat belt in a car or not to wear a crash helmet when riding a motor bike. In these instances, the state is sending out the message that *it is in fact safer* for people to take such precautions although freedom of choice in such matters is taken away. However, taken to its extreme limits, paternalism becomes less attractive as behaviour such as smoking, sky-diving, mountaineering and other risky pursuits could all be criminalised. Indeed, in paragraph C63 of the Law Commission Consultation Paper it states:

> *In principle, the paternalist seems to be committed to using the criminal law to turn us all into super-fit, clean-living 'spartans', whether we like it or not.*

The paternalist could allow a person to consent to the infliction of bodily harm when such bodily harm *is* in the best interests of the actor, such as when a person consents to surgery. Such an argument could even extend to a chronically ill person consenting to death when this would be in their best interest to relieve suffering. But how does the paternalist explain why behaviour such as smoking, which damages health, is not made more extensively the subject of criminal law? How does paternalism relate to morality and the criminalisation of immoral behaviour? Whereas the liberal would not use the criminal law to enforce morality, as this would limit the freedom of the individual, the paternalist would not use the criminal law to enforce morality because such a course of action would only be in the best interest of the actor if the actor had, in fact, chosen to live a moral life. For those who have chosen to live a less moral life, imposition of a moral life on them would *not* be in their best interests.

Legal moralism

The legal moralist would criminalise behaviour which is intrinsically evil or immoral. Such evils may be said to 'float free' of human interests and could include such things as sexual immorality, evil or impure thoughts, wanton killing of a fly or spider, diminishing good manners and so forth. Thus, whereas the liberalist would only criminalise immoral behaviour if such criminalisation could be justified on the harm and offence principles, the strict legal moralist would criminalise *all* immoral behaviour whether or not it caused harm or offence to anybody. For the liberalists, such a course of action would interfere too significantly in the lives of people. Furthermore, how would one agree on what behaviour is immoral?

Under the legal moralist philosophy, to what extent can a person consent to harm? This ultimately depends on which behaviour is, or is not, regarded as immoral. In paragraph C86 it states:

> *If fornication, adultery and homosexual sex are immoral, they remain immoral even when (especially when?) those who engage in such activities are willing and eager participants.*

The strict legal moralist would use the criminal law to criminalise the infliction of varying levels of harm on a person, even if that person consents, if it is immoral for a person to suffer varying levels of harm. However, it cannot be immoral, for instance, for a person to consent to a surgical operation. In paragraph C91 it is concluded that the moralist case is at its strongest when it advocates the criminalistion of conduct that *most people agree is immoral*, and it is at its weakest when it advocates the criminalisation of conduct which many people see as either morally equivocal or justified, such as prostitution, recreational alcohol and drug use, or 'deviant' sexual practices. A leading liberalist thinker, Feinberg, summarises the liberal case against criminalisation according to the moralists' way of thinking in these terms:

> *The free-floating evils do not harm anybody; they cause no injury, offense, or distress; they are not in any way unfair. At most, they are matters for regret by a sensitive observer. To prevent them with the iron fist of legal coercion would be to impose suffering and injury for the sake of no one else's good at all. For that reason the enforcement of most non-grievance morality strikes many of us as morally perverse.*

How to gauge '*all things considered*' in the criminalistion process

We have noted that even if proposed criminalisation of behaviour is supported by one of the philosophies described above, nevertheless, such behaviour should only be criminalised '*all things considered*'. Roberts lists several requirements to determine whether criminalisation is appropriate '*all things considered*':

i   *criminal legislation is the least coercive means that will be effective in combating the conduct in question* – if some other form of state action, short of criminalisation, might be effective in controlling or eradicating the behaviour in question, then the liberalists, paternalists and moralists are united in advocating that such alternatives (such as advertising, licensing, taxation, civil law remedies and so forth) be pursued first;

ii *the new legislation will not produce side-effects that are morally worse than the conduct to be prohibited* – such as the subjection of groups of individuals or communities to additional surveillance, the arrest and pre-trial detention of innocent people, the growth in back-street abortions if abortion was illegal, the growth in underground trade if alcohol was banned and so forth;

iii *the new legislation will not be inconsistent with the Rule of Law*;

iv *the new legislation will in fact be effective* – because its successful operation is consistent with the limitations on criminal justice resources and the priorities of investigators and prosecutors;

v   *the new legislation is consistent with the existing law and with other law reform priorities.*

Conclusion

In paragraph C109 the Law Commission states:

Much of the exposition has proceeded in the form of a debate between liberalism and its critics. This is not merely coincidental. The liberal values of autonomy, liberty, tolerance and pluralism strike many people as attractive, and their influence on the development of the common law is all-pervasive ... Those who advocate criminalisation from a paternalistic or moralist perspective must overcome powerful and widely accepted liberal counter-arguments.

The criminal court structure and appeals system

A detailed consideration of the criminal courts structure, appeals system and the classification of offences is provided in *Key Issues in A – Level Law: The English Legal System*. What follows here is a brief summary.

Criminal offences are classified as either summary, indictable or triable either way (TEW). Summary offences are less serious offences which can only be tried in the Magistrates' Court. Indictable offences are more serious offences which can only be tried in the Crown Court. TEW offences are those offences which may be tried in either the Magistrates' Court (as if they were summary offences) or in the Crown Court (as if they were indictable offences) depending on which venue for trial is elected during the mode of trial hearing.

Whatever the classification of an offence, all offences *start* their progress in the Magistrates' Court. Summary offences are tried in the Magistrates' Court and from here appeals may be made to either the Crown Court or the Queen's Bench Division (Divisional Court) of the High Court (see Figure 1.1). Indictable offences are tried in the Crown Court and until the Crime and Disorder Act 1998 they only got there after being processed through the Magistrates' Court. Suitable cases were committed for trial at the Crown Court. Criticism of this requirement to process indictable offences through the Magistrates' Court is found in a Home Office Report, *'Review of Delay in the Criminal Justice System'* which is considered in detail in Chapter 16. Since the Crime and Disorder Act 1998, by s.51, committal proceedings for indictable only offences have been abolished. Appeal from the Crown Court is to the Court of Appeal, Criminal Division, as shown in Figure 1.2.

The procedure for appeals is considered in detail in Chapter 15, in conjunction with a discussion of the work of the newly formed Criminal Cases Review Commission which has been established to refer possible miscarriage of justice cases back to the Court of Appeal.

Getting a suspect to the Magistrates' Court

So far in this chapter we have looked at how behaviour can be criminalised and at the courts which exist to deal with those who transgress the criminal law. In this section we will look at how a suspect is brought before the Magistates' Court.

Figure 1.1
Magistrates' Court 'trials' for summary offences, showing appeals hierarchy

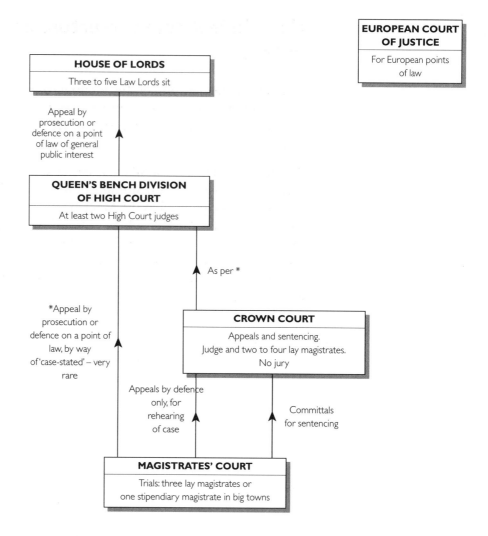

The most common way in which a suspect is brought before the Magistrates' Court is via the police. If the offence in question is an arrestable offence (as defined in the Police and Criminal Evidence Act 1984) then the suspect can be arrested and taken to the police station where he will be charged by the custody sergeant, sometimes after consultation with the Crown Prosecution Service. The charge sheet will usually detail when the suspect has to attend court. In the period between charge and appearance in court the suspect will either be given police bail or remanded in police custody. If the offence in question is not an arrestable offence or if other arrest conditions are not satisfied, then the procedure is that the police officer to whose attention the offence has been brought will apply to the Magistrates' Court for the issue of a summons. This summons will be sent to the suspect, detailing the alleged offence and when the case is to be heard in court.

Figure 1.2
Crown Court 'trials' for 'indictable' offences, showing appeals hierarchy

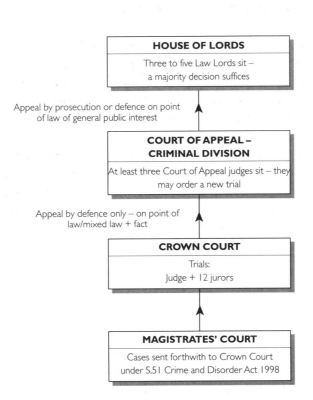

EUROPEAN COURT OF JUSTICE

For European points of law

HOUSE OF LORDS

Three to five Law Lords sit – a majority decision suffices

Appeal by prosecution or defence on point of law of general public interest

COURT OF APPEAL – CRIMINAL DIVISION

At least three Court of Appeal judges sit – they may order a new trial

Appeal by defence only – on point of law/mixed law + fact

CROWN COURT

Trials:
Judge + 12 jurors

MAGISTRATES' COURT

Cases sent forthwith to Crown Court under S.51 Crime and Disorder Act 1998

There are, however, other government agencies which have the authority to apply to the Magistrates' Court for the issue of a summons, such as the Health and Safety Executive, the Inland Revenue, Customs and Excise, Trading Standards, and so forth. It is also possible for an individual to apply to the Magistrates' Court for the issue of a summons to commence a private prosecution, most notably when the Crown Prosecution Service declines to prosecute a case. Finally, a prosecution can also be brought by the Director of Public Prosecutions (DPP) for very serious cases.

When the police or DPP initiate the proceedings, the prosecution is conducted by the Crown Prosecution Service. In the other instances, the prosecution is conducted by the individual concerned (or his lawyer) or by a lay officer of the agency concerned. The DPP can take over these prosecutions if it is deemed appropriate.

In a criminal trial, the prosecution usually carries the burden of proof. That is, they have to prove that the accused committed the offence and, as such, the accused is presumed innocent until proven guilty. The standard to which the prosecution have to prove their case is known as the standard of proof which is 'beyond all reasonable doubt'. This is a high standard of proof.

The amount of crime

Finally, before embarking on an analysis of the substantive criminal law, it is worth mentioning the incidence of crime. How much crime is there in England and Wales? It is impossible to answer such a question definitively as not all crimes are reported. The Home Office is a major source of criminal statistics which are published annually. Figure 1.3 shows the Home Office statistics for notifiable offences recorded by the police for 1996. Another major source of criminal statistics is the British Crime Survey (BCS) which provides a different analysis of criminal activity in England and Wales because it attempts to provide statistics based on the number of *victims* of crime rather than on the number of reported crimes. The BCS was first conducted in 1982, with further surveys in 1984, 1988 and thereafter every two years. In order to gather victim information, a random selection of the population is asked to complete a lengthy questionnaire which asks the participants, among other things, whether they have been the victim of a crime or crimes and, if so, whether or not they reported the crime or crimes. There are many reasons why someone might not report a crime to the police and therefore the statistics provided by the Home Office only reflect part of the criminal activity which actually exists in society. The BCS also has its own set of defects, however, such as the fact that it is based on only a fraction of the total population of England and Wales and that it is possible that people will exaggerate the truth. The topic of criminal statistics receives further discussion in Chapter 6.

Figure 1.3
Notifiable offences
recorded by the police

Key points

Recorded crime

- 5.0 million notifiable offences were recorded by the police in 1996, a fall of 1.2 per cent or 63,700 over 1995. This was the fourth consecutive annual fall.

- 4.6 million or 92 per cent of these offences were against property (including burglary, theft, criminal damage and fraud).

- Vehicle crime fell by 2 per cent to 1.3 million, the fourth consecutive annual fall

- Burglary fell by 6 per cent to 1.2 million.

- Violent crime rose by 11 per cent. This is the largest increase in recorded violent crime since 1989. The 344,800 offences (of violence against the person, sexual offences and robbery) accounted for 7 per cent of all notifiable offences.

- Within violent crime, offences of violence against the person rose by 13 per cent, robberies rose by 9 per cent and sexual offences by 4 per cent.

- 28 of the 43 police force areas recorded fewer crimes in 1996 than in 1995. Seven of the eight metropolitan forces recorded falls.

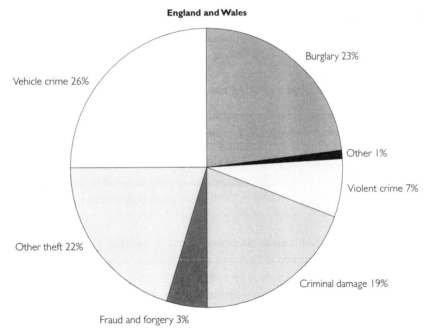

England and Wales

Burglary 23%

Vehicle crime 26%

Other 1%

Violent crime 7%

Criminal damage 19%

Other theft 22%

Fraud and forgery 3%

5,036,553 offences

Source: Home Office, 'Criminal Statistics England and Wales 1996'

SECTION TWO:
The ingredients of a crime

The following topics are covered in this section:

Actus reus	Mens rea	Strict liability

Key cases

Kay v. Butterworth (1945)
R v. Charlson (1955)
Broome v. Perkins (1987)
R v. Larsonneur (1933)
Winzar v. Chief Constable of Kent (1983)
R v. Parking Adjudicator, ex parte Wandsworth B.C. (1996)
R v. Dytham (1979)
R v. Pittwood (1902)
R v. Instan (1893)
R v. Stone & Dobinson (1977)
R v. Miller (1983)

Key cases

R v. Moloney (1985)
R v. Hancock & Shankland (1986)
R v. Nedrick (1986)
R v. Scalley (1994)
R v. Woollin (1997)
R v. Cunningham (1957)
MPC v. Caldwell (1981)
Elliott v. C (a minor) (1983)
McCrone v. Riding (1938)

Key cases

R v. Densu (1997)
Sweet v. Parsley (1970)
Pharmaceutical Society of Great Britain v. Storkwain (1986)
Sherras v. De Rutzen (1895)
Alphacell Ltd v. Woodward (1972)
Gammon (Hong Kong) Ltd & others v. A G of Hong Kong (1954)

The common theme of contempt of court is covered in this section:

Common law contempt
In re de Court (1997)
R v. Schot and R v. Barclay (1997)

Statutory contempt
Contempt of Court Act 1981

2 *Actus reus and mens rea*

OVERVIEW

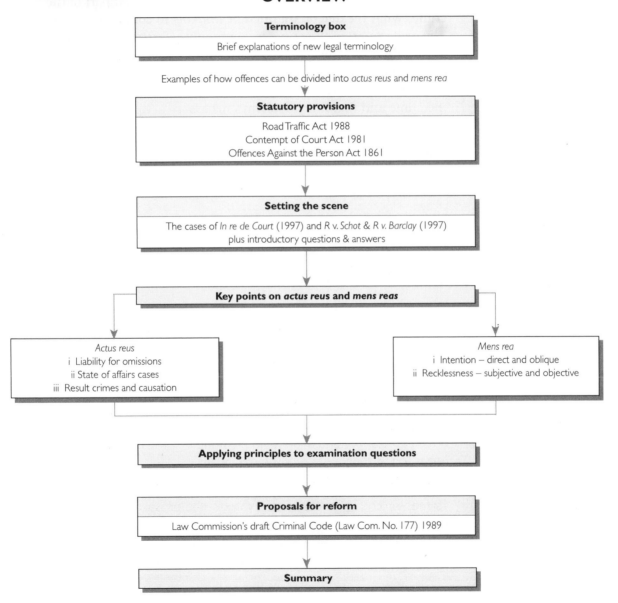

Terminology box

Brief explanations of new legal terminology

Examples of how offences can be divided into *actus reus* and *mens rea*

Statutory provisions

Road Traffic Act 1988
Contempt of Court Act 1981
Offences Against the Person Act 1861

Setting the scene

The cases of *In re de Court* (1997) and *R v. Schot & R v. Barclay* (1997)
plus introductory questions & answers

Key points on *actus reus* and *mens reas*

Actus reus
i Liability for omissions
ii State of affairs cases
iii Result crimes and causation

Mens rea
i Intention – direct and oblique
ii Recklessness – subjective and objective

Applying principles to examination questions

Proposals for reform

Law Commission's draft Criminal Code (Law Com. No. 177) 1989

Summary

Some crimes are still defined by the common law, such as murder, assault and battery, although most crimes nowadays are defined in statutes. One would expect to find some degree of conformity and clarity in the definitions of crimes, especially statutory ones, but in fact this is not the case. When academics and lawyers look at such definitions and try to make sense of them, they tend to analyse them in terms of the *conduct* part of the crime (generally, what the defendant must *do* to commit the crime) and the *fault* part of the crime (what the defendant must be *thinking* to commit the crime). The *conduct* part of the crime is commonly referred to as the *actus reus* of the crime and the *fault* part is commonly referred to as the *mens rea* of the crime. We shall see that it is not always easy to determine which parts of a crime belong to the *actus reus* or *mens rea* elements of the crime and that it is not always necessary or appropriate to analyse a crime in this way.

Brief explanations of some of the new terminology in this chapter are given in the box below.

TERMINOLOGY: *Actus reus* and *mens rea*

Actus reus
This refers to the conduct part of a crime. It is not accurate to say that it refers to the *guilty act* of the defendant as it has to cover those situations where the defendant fails to act (an omission) and those situations where the defendant is merely the subject of a prevailing 'state of affairs' (no positive criminal act by the defendant). These are discussed in more detail below.

Mens rea
This refers to the fault part of the crime. Generally, a crime consists of both an *actus reus* and a *mens rea* element. The *mens rea* element refers to the mental state of the defendant. In criminal law only the mental states of intention, recklessness and negligence are relevant.

Strict liability
Crimes which can be committed without the prosecution having to prove *mens rea* are referred to as crimes of strict liability. The prosecution only have to prove the *actus reus* part of the crime to secure a conviction. This is dealt with in more detail in Chapter 3.

Example

How offences can be divided into *actus reus* and *mens rea*

2

At this stage it is probably helpful to give some examples of actual offences and how they can be divided into *actus reus* and *mens rea*.

1 Common law definition of murder

Murder is the unlawful killing of a human being during times of peace, with malice aforethought.

Note that murder is not defined in a statute. This definition is adapted from one put forward by Chief Justice Coke in the seventeenth century. In this definition it is easier to work out which part of it refers to the *mens rea* element of the crime and then, by a process of elimination, determine that the rest of the definition refers to the *actus reus* element of the crime. The *mens rea* element is 'malice aforethought'. Just what is meant by malice aforethought is dealt with at length in Chapter 12, on homicide. Thus, the *actus reus* element of the crime is comprised of the 'unlawful killing of a human being during times of peace'.

2 Statutory definition of theft

Theft is defined in section 1(1) of the Theft Act 1968 as follows:

A person is guilty of theft if he dishonestly appropriates property belonging to another with the intention of permanently depriving the other of it.

The *mens rea* element of the crime is twofold as it consists of 'dishonestly' and 'with intention of permanently depriving the other of it'. Thus, the *actus reus* element of the crime consists of 'appropriating property belonging to another'.

3 Statutory definition of criminal damage

Criminal damage is defined in section 1(1) of the Criminal Damage Act 1971 as follows:

A person who without lawful excuse destroys or damages any property belonging to another intending to destroy or damage any such property or being reckless as to whether any such property be destroyed or damaged shall be guilty of an offence.

The *mens rea* element of the crime is threefold as it refers to 'without lawful excuse', 'intending to destroy or damage any such property' and 'being reckless as to whether any such property be destroyed or damaged'. The *actus reus* element of the crime is 'destroys or damages any property belonging to another'.

As you progress through this book you will see how closely words used in definitions of crimes are scrutinised by lawyers and that it does not really matter whether a word is put into the *mens rea* or *actus reus* category as these are only used for ease of reference.

Statutory provisions

Road Traffic Act 1988

1 Causing death by dangerous driving

A person who causes the death of another person by driving a mechanically propelled vehicle dangerously on a road or other public place is guilty of an offence.

2 Dangerous driving

A person who drives a mechanically propelled vehicle dangerously on a road or other public place is guilty of an offence.

2A Meaning of dangerous driving

(1) For the purposes of sections 1 and 2 above, a person is to be regarded as driving dangerously if (and, subject to subsection (2) below, only if):
    (a) the way he drives falls far below what would be expected of a competent and careful driver; and
    (b) it would be obvious to a competent and careful driver that driving in that way would be dangerous.

3   Careless, and inconsiderate, driving

If a person drives a mechanically propelled vehicle on a road or other public place without due care and attention, or without reasonable consideration for other persons using the road or place, he is guilty of an offence.

7   Provision of specimens for analysis

(1) In the course of an investigation into whether a person has committed an offence under section 4 or 5 of this Act a constable may, subject to the following provisions of this section and section 9 of this Act, require him:
   (a) to provide two specimens of breath for analysis by means of a device of a type approved by the Secretary of State; or
   (b) to provide a specimen of blood or urine for a laboratory test.

(6) A person who, without reasonable excuse, fails to provide a specimen when required to do so in pursuance of this section is guilty of an offence.

168   Failure to give, or giving false, name and address in case of dangerous or careless driving or inconsiderate driving or cycling

Any of the following persons:
(a) the driver of a motor vehicle who is alleged to have committed an offence under section 2 or 3 of this Act; or
(b) the rider of a cycle who is alleged to have committed an offence under section 28 or 29 of this Act,
   who refuses, on being so required by any person having reasonable ground for so requiring, to give his name or address, or gives a false name or address, is guilty of an offence.

Contempt of Court Act 1981

8   Confidentiality of jury's deliberations

(1) Subject to subsection (2) below, it is a contempt of court to obtain, disclose or solicit any particulars of statements made, opinions expressed, arguments advanced or votes cast by members of a jury in the course of their deliberations in any legal proceedings.

Offences Against the Person Act 1861

23   Maliciously administering poison etc. so as to endanger life ...

Whosoever shall unlawfully and maliciously administer to or cause to be administered to or taken by another person any poison or other destructive or noxious thing, so as thereby to endanger the life of such person, or so as thereby to inflict upon such person any grievous bodily harm, shall be guilty of an offence, and being convicted thereof shall be liable ... to imprisonment for any term not exceeding ten years.

Setting the scene

In order to set the scene for the study of *actus reus* and *mens rea*, which may seem somewhat abstract at the moment, consider the two case studies below. These concern the *actus reus* and *mens rea* of contempt of court and other matters with which you probably feel more familiar, such as the court hierarchies, the role of judge and jury in the Crown Court and judicial precedent. You should note at this point that since the Contempt of Court Act 1981 there are now two broad categories of contempt of court – statutory contempt of court, as created by the 1981 Act, and common law contempt of court. The case studies below both concern common law contempt of court for which both *actus reus* and *mens rea* have to be present.

Case study I – *In re de Court* (1997)

Read the case *In re de Court* (1997), shown on page 21, which was reported in *The Times* on 27 November 1997, and then answer the questions which follow.

Questions

These questions are a mixture of data-response and stimulus-response questions. Thus, for some of them you will find the answer in the text, while for others you will have to research the answer.

1 Why is the case reported as *In re de Court*?

2 What is the definition of contempt of court?

3 Why was the case heard in the Chancery Division of the High Court?

4 How did the Vice Chancellor, Sir Richard Scott, differentiate the case in hand from the case raised by Miss Rich, as precedent, that interference with the purely administrative actions of court officials did not constitute contempt?

5 What constituted the *actus reus* of contempt of court in this case?

6 How was the *mens rea* for contempt of court satisfied in this case?

7 What is the normal sentence for contempt of court?

8 Why was Mr de Court not imprisoned?

9 What punishment was Mr de Court given instead of imprisonment?

Assault on working court official is contempt

In re de Court

Before Sir Richard Scott, Vice-Chancellor

[Judgment November 18]

A physical assault on a court official while he was engaged in official business in the administration of justice was a contempt of court.

Sir Richard Scott, Vice-Chancellor, so held in the Chancery Division after an applicant, Mr Graham de Court, of Waltham Cross, spat at a court official. His Lordship had stood the matter over for the Official Solicitor to make inquiries into Mr de Court's medical condition.

Mr Robert Engelhart, QC, as amicus curiae; Miss Barbara Rich for the Official Solicitor.

THE VICE-CHANCELLOR said that two weeks previously Mr de Court had spat into the face of the Chancery Clerk of the Lists when he was dissatisfied with the clerk's response to his application for a date to be fixed for a hearing.

A medical certificate stated that Mr de Court was not a person responsible for his actions in the way that was normally expected of individuals. He should be regarded as a person under a disability under Order 80, rule 2 of the Rules of the Supreme Court.

Miss Rich submitted that interference with the purely administrative actions of court officials did not constitute contempt. She referred, inter alia, to *Borrie & Lowe on The Law of Contempt* (third edition (1996) p433) and *Weston* v *Central Court Administrator* ([1977)] QB 32) in which Lord Justice Bridge had held that a discourteous and abusive letter written to a court official in respect of his conduct of the purely administrative business of the court was not a contempt.

His Lordship respectfully agreed with that statement but thought that a physical assault on the Clerk of the Lists while he was engaged in official business in the administration of justice was a contempt of court.

The administration of justice depended not just on judges and counsel in court. It also depended upon court officials, members of the court service, discharging essential functions for the purpose of enabling cases to come to court.

In his Lordship's judgment, a physical interference with officers of the court who were conducting their duties in the administration of justice, such as writ issuers, listing officers and process servers, was a contempt of court; how serious would depend on the nature of the case.

There was no doubt that what Mr de Court did constituted the actus reus of contempt of court.

His Lordship, however, was troubled, in view of the medical evidence, that he might not have had the necessary mens rea. But counsel had satisfied him that since he intended to do what he had done and did it consciously, the requisite mens rea existed despite his medical infirmity.

As to punishment, it would be quite inappropriate to deal with the case in what would be the normal way, namely a sentence of imprisonment. But the court's function was not just to pronounce a suitable sentence but was also to protect the officers of the court from repetitions of the incident.

It was no surprise, given the medical evidence, that Mr de Court had expressed no contrition. He had so far made over a hundred attempts at instituting ridiculous and incomprehensible legal proceedings based on documents which were gibberish.

When court officials declined to entertain them or treat them seriously he became angry with the consequence of the sort of incident that had taken place.

His Lordship had a duty to provide protection to court officials not just in the High Court but also in any court where Mr de Court might seek to institute proceedings. He had an inherent power and duty to take those steps as a judge and Vice-Chancellor of the Chancery Division and as far as the county courts were concerned as the head of civil justice.

In the exercise of that power he would make an order in two parts: First to restrain Mr de Court from pursuing any action in court except by a next friend who could act for him; second, to restrain him from entering any civil court premises save as necessary to answer court subpoenas.

The order would be served on Mr de Court and communicated to relevant courts.

Answers

1   Most criminal cases are heard in the criminal courts and are reported as *R* v. *Bloggs*, *Attorney-General* v. *Bloggs* or *DPP* v. *Bloggs* but in this case the criminal offence of contempt was heard in the Chancery Division of the High Court which was exercising its inherent authority to deal with a contempt of court. Most cases in the Chancery Division are reported in the format *In re Bloggs* or *Re Bloggs* and so forth as many of them concern wills and probate matters (where the executors or administrators dealing with the matter are not really parties to a case) and cases concerning company law or minors. This case was heard in the Chancery Division and so was reported as *In re de Court*.

2   First, it must be noted that a person can be accused of contempt of court in either the criminal or civil processes of the administration of justice. Wherever the contempt occurs, in either the criminal or civil sphere, it is regarded as a criminal wrong. Criminal contempt can be committed by means of insulting behaviour in the face of the court or by conduct which interferes with the proper administration of justice. Civil contempt can also be committed by conduct which interferes with the proper administration of justice and, in addition, can be committed by failure to respond to judgments or orders of a civil court. Contempt of court is punishable by imprisonment and/or a fine or by the granting of an injunction to restrain a repetition of the behaviour which amounted to a contempt.

3   In this scenario Mr de Court was interfering with the proper administration of civil justice and, in particular, the administration of the Chancery Court. Where it is necessary for the contempt to be punished immediately the court concerned can deal with the contempt itself and so it was possible for the Vice Chancellor to deal with this case in the Chancery Division. You should note at this point that courts regarded as superior courts for the purposes of contempt of court (the House of Lords when sitting in judicial capacity, the Court of Appeal, the High Court, Crown Court, Restrictive Practices Court and Employment Appeal Tribunal) can punish contempt with a term of imprisonment of up to two years and can impose an unlimited fine. Inferior courts (County Court and Magistrates' Court) can only impose a term of imprisonment up to one month and can only impose a fine up to £2,500.

4   Miss Rich raised the case of *Weston* v. *Central Court Administrator* (1977). The Vice Chancellor, however, distinguished the case in hand because whereas the *Weston* case only involved a discourteous and abusive letter written to a court official, the case in hand concerned a physical assault on the Clerk of the Lists. The Vice Chancellor

determined that physical interference with officers of the court who were conducting their duties in the administration of justice, for example, as writ issuers, listing officers and process servers, was a contempt of court.

5 In this case the *actus reus* of contempt consisted of Mr de Court spitting into the face of the Chancery Clerk of the Lists.

6 The *mens rea* of Mr de Court was established by counsel who satisfied the Vice Chancellor that Mr de Court had *intended* to do what he did and he did it consciously.

7 The normal sentence for contempt of court is imprisonment. (Refer back to the answer to question 3 for the range of sentencing options open to a court for contempt.)

8 Mr de Court was not imprisoned as such a punishment was felt to be inappropriate because it would not protect the officers of the court from repetition of bad behaviour by Mr de Court.

9 The Vice Chancellor made an order in two parts: first, to restrain Mr de Court from pursuing any action in court except by a next friend who could act for him; and second, to restrain him from entering any civil court premises save as necessary to answer court subpoenas.

Case study 2 – *R* v. *Schot* and *R* v. *Barclay* (1997)

This case study is presented in three sections to aid clearer understanding. The data-response and stimulus-response questions which follow relate to all three sections.

The facts of the original trial on 17 February 1997

On 17 February 1997 a trial commenced in Knightsbridge Crown Court before Judge Cooray. There were five defendants in the case, who were charged with having custody or control of a counterfeit note. On 19 February 1997 a jury was sworn in to try the case and the trial proceeded. On 12 March 1997 the jury retired to consider its verdict.

Some time later the jury sent a note to the judge which read: 'We are unable to come to any decisions owing to some jurors' conscious beliefs. Please advise.' The judge brought the jury back into court and asked them to clarify what was meant by 'conscious beliefs' by sending another note to him via the foreman of the jury. The foreman delivered such a note which read: 'Some members of the jury cannot bring themselves to make a true judgment due to our beliefs, not religious but personal. At the beginning of the trial, before we took the oath we felt that we could not stand up in the court and stress this fact. We thought that our feelings may change over time. After retiring we have found that we still feel the same and cannot give a true verdict to these defendants.'

The judge then asked the jury to write down the names of those jurors to whom this second note applied. After this was done, he discharged the whole jury. The jurors to whom the second note applied, Bonnie Schot, aged 20 years, and Carol Barclay, aged 30 years, were told by Judge Cooray to return to the court on 24 March 1997 to show why they should not be fined for contempt of court.

Crown Court hearing for contempt of court on 24 March 1997

At this hearing Judge Cooray found the two women guilty of contempt of court and sentenced them to 30 days' imprisonment. They spent 24 hours in Holloway Prison before being released on bail pending their appeal to the Court of Appeal, which was heard on 12 May 1997.

Court of Appeal hearing on 12 May 1997

The appeal was heard by Lord Justice Rose, Mr Justice Forbes and Mr Justice Keene, and Lord Justice Rose gave the judgment of the court. The appeal was allowed, that is, the findings of contempt of court were quashed. Lord Justice Rose said that Judge Cooray had fallen into a sequence of errors including the following:

i he should not have asked for clarification of the first note and should not have asked for the names of the jurors concerned as such actions imposed on the secrecy of what goes on in the jury room and this in itself could amount to contempt of court;

ii in any event, he need not have ordered a retrial as he could have discharged the two jurors concerned and then let the trial proceed;

iii while it was possible that conduct such as that demonstrated by the two women jurors could amount to the *actus reus* of contempt, the issue of *mens rea* was more difficult to establish. He said that the *mens rea* of [common law] contempt had to be established by showing an '*intention* to impede or create a real risk of prejudicing the administration of justice'. He said that this could be established by '*foreseeability of consequence*' but did not think that the two jurors could have foreseen what did happen as a consequence of their conduct and, as such, their *mens rea* for contempt of court was not proven.

Questions

1 Explain the process by which a jury is empanelled for a Crown Court trial.

2 What is the age range for jurors?

3 What do jurors promise to do when they are sworn in under oath?

4 Can you see any 'danger' for justice in Judge Cooray hearing the contempt of court case?

5 By what conduct could Judge Cooray be said to have committed the *actus reus* of contempt of court?

6 How did Lord Justice Rose define the *mens rea* of contempt of court?

7 In determining that the two jurors did not have the *mens rea* for contempt of court, Lord Justice Rose said that he did not think that they could have foreseen the consequence of their actions; why not?

Answers

1 The empanelling of juries is governed by the Juries Act 1974. An official at the Crown Court concerned summons a randomly selected number of people from the electoral register, which may be done electronically or manually. Some of these people may, in fact, be ineligible to serve, be excused or be disqualified from serving. Once these people are eliminated the potential jurors may be subjected to 'vetting' and, once in court, to 'challenge'. Those people who then comprise the jury are sworn in.

2 The age range for jurors is 18 years to under 70 years on the day the jury service commences.

3 The jurors swear under oath that they will 'faithfully try the defendant and give a true verdict according to the evidence'.

4 In this case Judge Cooray could be described as the *victim* of the contempt of court and, as such, he should not really be hearing the case, especially as he had demonstrated bias against the two women on 12 March 1997. He could have referred the contempt hearing to another senior judge at that court or at another court.

5 Judge Cooray could be said to have committed the *actus reus* of contempt by asking for clarification of the first note and by asking for the names of the jurors concerned as such actions imposed on the secrecy of what went on in jury deliberations. (In fact, such contempt

is statutory, as provided for by section 8(1) of the Contempt of Court Act 1981.)

6   Lord Justice Rose defined the *mens rea* of contempt of court as the '*intention* to impede or create a real risk of prejudicing the administration of justice', which could be established by showing that the contemnors (those committing the contempt) were able to *foresee the consequences* of their actions.

7   It was unlikely that the two jurors could have foreseen that by their actions it would be necessary to abort the trial and order a re-trial. The judge could have discharged the two jurors and let the trial continue or could have instructed the jury to return a majority verdict.

Key points on *actus reus* and *mens rea*

Actus reus

▶   *Actus reus* and *mens rea* are only labels used by academics and lawyers for ease of reference when talking about offences.

▶   The definitions of most offences include words which can be categorised as belonging to either the *actus reus* or *mens rea* elements of the offence. Those offences which are only defined in terms of an *actus reus*, and for which the court imports no requirement for *mens rea*, are called absolute or strict liability offences. These are dealt with in detail in Chapter 3.

▶   The *actus reus* element of an offence (the conduct part of the offence) is often referred to as the external element of the offence, whereas the *mens rea* element of the offence (the fault part of the offence) is often referred to as the internal element of the offence.

▶   The *actus reus* element of an offence generally refers to *positive* conduct on the part of the defendant, that is, the defendant has to have *done* something. However, this is not always the case. Criminal liability can be imposed where the defendant:

i has *omitted* to do something; or
ii is found in a certain *state of affairs*.

These situations are dealt with in more detail below.

▶ The *actus reus* element of an offence has to have been fulfilled *voluntarily* by the defendant. Thus, if A was driving home from work and suddenly suffered a heart attack so that he lost control of his car which mounted the pavement and injured B, could A be convicted of dangerous driving contrary to section 2 of the Road Traffic Act 1988? (See the statutory provisions on page 18.) You will notice that the section 2 offence is defined only in terms of the conduct of the defendant, that is, in terms of the *actus reus*, which means that it is a strict liability offence. Has A fulfilled the *actus reus* of this offence? If he has, then he will be guilty of the offence. The answer is here, however, is no. When the car mounted the pavement and injured B, A was not acting voluntarily and so the *actus reus* was not satisfied.

What if A had been feeling drowsy and had fallen asleep while driving the car which then mounted the pavement and injured B; could A then be convicted for dangerous driving? A could argue that his acts were not voluntary but the court is likely to hold that his criminal liability stems from the fact that he voluntarily got into the car while drowsy and voluntarily drove and continued to drive while drowsy. (See the 'You Decide' cases on page 31.)

> When the defendant's actions are totally involuntary, the defendant is said to be suffering from non-insane automatism and this will afford him a defence to a criminal charge.

▶ Although it might appear that any defendant could argue non-insane automatism as a defence to a criminal charge and say that he did not act voluntarily, in fact the courts only allow this defence in limited circumstances.

> The defendant usually has to show that he lost *total* control of his actions and that the automatism was caused by a unique, external event which is not likely to happen again, such as a blow to the head or an attack by a swarm of bees.

Moreover, in *Bratty* v. *Attorney-General for Northern Ireland* (1963) Lord Denning said that non-insane automatism was confined to 'acts done while unconscious and to spasms, convulsions and reflex actions'. (See the 'You Decide' cases which follow.) Thus, in the example above, where A suffers a heart attack while driving his car and the car mounts the pavement, if this is the first time A has suffered a heart attack then, as stated, the defence of automatism might apply. However, if A had suffered a previous heart attack and/or had felt severe pains before the heart attack the defence of automatism might not apply as A would have voluntarily driven/continued to drive.

▶ Some offences can be described as 'conduct crimes' and some can be described as 'result crimes'. What is the difference between them? For a conduct crime the prosecution need only prove that the accused's conduct was as prohibited by the crime in question. For example, by section 2 of the Road Traffic Act 1988 a person is guilty of dangerous driving when they drive a mechanically propelled vehicle dangerously on a road or other public place. It is not necessary to prove that *by so doing* something else happened, for example, that someone was injured or some property was damaged or destroyed. For a result crime the prosecution have to prove that the accused carried out the prohibited conduct and that a certain result followed. For example, by section 1 of the Road Traffic Act 1988 a person is only guilty of causing death by dangerous driving if their dangerous driving caused the death of another person. Thus, the issue of *causation* only arises in relation to result crimes, such as murder.

Mens rea

▶ There is a presumption of statutory interpretation that all statutory offences require the prosecution to prove that the defendant was at fault, that he had the necessary *mens rea* for the offence. Sometimes it is difficult to determine from the definition of the offence what type of *mens rea* has to be proved. For some offences the courts have decided that no *mens rea* is required as the offence is one of strict liability (see Chapter 3), while for others they have decided that negligence at least is required. Such problems commonly occur in relation to road traffic offences under the Road Traffic Act 1988.

▶ The *mens rea* of the accused works on a sliding scale of blameworthiness or fault, ranging from intention at the top through recklessness and negligence to strict liability at the bottom where the accused has no *mens rea*. Crimes which are regarded as the most serious and which attract the most severe punishments require the prosecution to prove that the accused was very blameworthy, that he acted intentionally. Crimes which are regarded as less serious can be fulfilled by a lesser level of blameworthiness. This is discussed in detail below and shown in Figure 2.1.

▶ It must be noted that, generally, *mens rea* is different to motive which is irrelevant when determining whether or not the accused had the *mens rea* for the crime in question. Thus, on a murder charge it is irrelevant that a husband suffocated his wife with a pillow because she was terminally ill and in great pain; if he intended to kill her he will be guilty of murder.

▶ Different parts of the *actus reus* of an offence can be the subject of different levels of *mens rea*. Thus, it may be necessary to prove intention in relation to one part of the *actus reus*, while recklessness may suffice in relation to another part of the *actus reus*.

▶ Children aged under 10 years are presumed to be incapable of forming the *mens rea* for criminal liability. Thus, even if a child carries out what would be the *actus reus* of an offence, they cannot be prosecuted as the law regards them as incapable of forming the *mens rea* to go with the *actus reus*. They are presumed to be *doli incapax*, that is, incapable of crime.

▶ For most offences, which require the prosecution to prove both the *actus reus* and *mens rea* of the offence, it is also necessary to prove that these two elements of the offence were present *at the same time*. Usually this is not a problem as it is clear from the evidence that the two elements were present at the same time. In cases where it could be problematic, to the extent that an accused might not be convicted of the offence in question, the courts tend to adopt a somewhat *flexible* approach to ensure that a conviction is secured. This topic is the subject of the 'You Decide' cases on page 33.

▶ If A intends to kill B and shoots at B with a gun but misses and shoots C, who dies, can A be guilty of murdering C? The answer is yes. A had the *mens rea* (the malice) to kill B and this malice can be transferred to the *actus reus* that actually occurred, which was the death of C. However, if A intended to injure B and threw a punch at B which missed and broke a window, A could not be charged with criminal damage on the basis of transferred malice. A had the *mens rea* (the malice) for assault and this cannot be transferred to criminal damage. However, A might be charged with criminal damage for breaking the window without the concept of transferred malice if it can be proven that A was reckless as to whether the window was broken. (See the discussion on objective recklessness, below.)

▶ Before progressing to consider *actus reus* and *mens rea* in more detail, students should refer to Figure 2.1 which should help to put the topic into perspective.

Figure 2.1
Actus reus
and *mens rea*

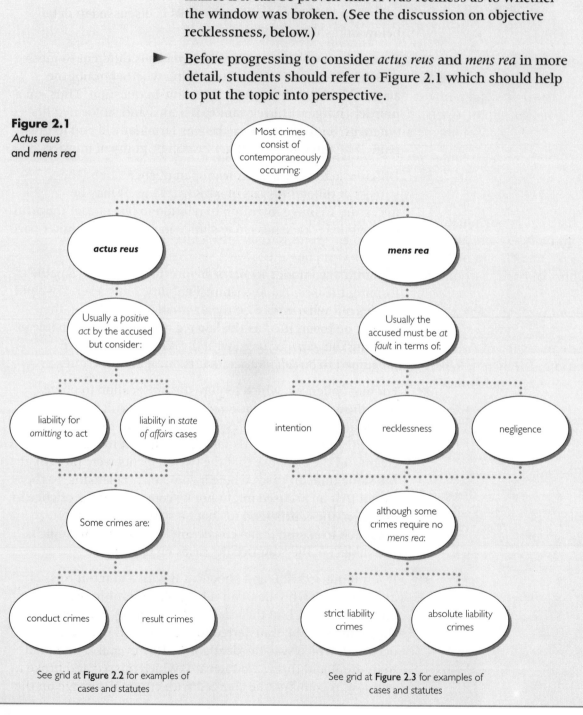

See grid at **Figure 2.2** for examples of cases and statutes

See grid at **Figure 2.3** for examples of cases and statutes

YOU DECIDE

Consider the cases below, which concern non-insane automatism, and answer the questions.

1 Kay v. Butterworth (1945)

In this case the defendant had completed his night shift and was driving home. Despite the fact that he felt drowsy he continued to drive and fell asleep. As a result he drove into a group of marching soldiers.

Do you think the defendant could be convicted of driving without due care and attention and dangerous driving given that he had not driven into the soldiers voluntarily?

2 Broome v. Perkins (1987)

In this case the defendant, a diabetic, had driven home from work and, on arriving home, noticed damage to his car. He reported this to the police fearing he might have had an accident on the drive home because he could remember nothing of the journey. Also, his wife thought he was suffering from hypoglycaemia. Eye witnesses said that he had been driving erratically and, while he had crashed into a parked mini, he had managed to avoid hitting a van.

Could the defendant be convicted of driving without due care and attention – was he acting voluntarily?

3 R v. Charlson (1955)

In this case the defendant hit his son over the head with a hammer and threw him into a river for no apparent reason. He was suffering from a brain tumour which would make him susceptible to impulsive outbursts of violent behaviour over which he would have no control.

Do you think the defendant could rely on the defence of automatism, that is, that his acts were not voluntary?

Answers

1 The defendant was so convicted. He had voluntarily continued to drive when feeling drowsy and so was responsible for what occurred after he fell asleep.

2 The defendant was convicted of driving without due care and attention. The defendant was not in a state of automatism as, although his mind was not in control of his limbs at all times during the journey, nevertheless, at some stages in the journey his mind did react to external stimuli and had control over his limbs. At such times the defendant was driving and so was guilty of driving without due care and attention. He had not lost 'complete' control of his actions.

3 In this case the defendant was acquitted on the basis of automatism, that is, at the time he injured his son he was not acting voluntary and had lost total control of his actions. This case is now generally held to have been decided incorrectly – the proper defence should have been insanity according to the *M'Naghten* rules. This is because the defendant should have been regarded as suffering from a disease of the mind which was prone to result in *recurring outbursts of violence*. Moreover, the outburst of violence was due to an *internal* factor. Refer to Chapter 9, on general defences, and read the 'You Decide' cases of *R* v. *Hennessy* (1989), *R* v. *Sullivan* (1984) and *Quick* (1973) which show how epilepsy and *hyperglycaemia* are regarded as insanity (as caused by internal factors), while *hypoglycaemia* is not (as caused by external factors).

YOU DECIDE

Consider the cases below, which highlight the problems of proving that the *mens rea* and *actus reus* of an offence occurred contemporaneously, and answer the questions.

1 *Fagan* v. *Metropolitan Police Commissioner* (1969)

In this case the accused accidentally drove his car onto a policeman's foot. However, when the policeman told him that the wheel of the car was on his foot, the accused turned off the car's ignition and then restarted the car and drove off the policeman's foot.

Could the accused be convicted of assaulting a police officer in the execution of his duty? Did the actus reus and mens rea of the offence occur at the same time?
(The *actus reus* of such an assault, which actually amounted to a battery as the victim was touched, is the infliction of unlawful personal violence which can be satisfied by mere touching, and the *mens rea* is that the accused inflicted such personal violence either intentionally or recklessly.)

2 *Thabo Meli* v. *R* (1954) (A Privy Council case)

In this case the appellants had taken the victim to a hut and struck him over the head intending to kill him. They then rolled his body over the edge of a cliff so that his death would look like an accident. In fact, the victim was not killed in the hut nor did he die of rolling off the cliff. Medical evidence showed that he actually died of exposure. The appellants were convicted of murder and appealed to the Privy Council.

You decide the appeal.
(Note that for murder the *actus reus* is the killing of a human being and the *mens rea* is doing so with intention to kill or cause serious bodily harm.)

3 *R* v. *Le Brun* (1991)

In this case a husband and wife were arguing in the street and the husband hit his wife on the chin knocking her unconscious. He then started to drag her along the pavement into the house presumably to conceal his assault on her. In the course of this the wife banged her head on the pavement and fractured her skull, from which injury she died. The husband was convicted of manslaughter and appealed.

You decide the appeal.
(Note that for this type of manslaughter the *actus reus* is the killing of a human being by commission of an unlawful and dangerous act and the *mens rea* is regarded as the same for the unlawful and dangerous act in question.)

Answers

1 It would appear that the *actus reus* and *mens rea* occurred at different times as when the accused committed the *actus reus*, the act of driving onto the policeman's foot, he had no *mens rea*; it was an accident. When the accused turned off the ignition, however, he formed the *mens rea* for the assault and so the *mens rea* occurred after the initial assault. However, the Queen's Bench Divisional Court held that the accused was guilty of an assault because the assault in this case was **a continuing act** (the continued presence of the car on the foot) and so long as *mens rea* was formed at some time during the act then the offence was committed.

2 The convictions for murder were upheld. Although the appellants did not carry out the *actus reus* of murder when they had the *mens rea* for murder (in the hut), and they did not have *mens rea* for murder when they rolled the body over the cliff as they thought the body was a corpse by then, the Privy Council held that *actus reus* and *mens rea* could be regarded as contemporaneous because the conduct of the appellants was really **one series of acts** which were **part of an antecedent plan** and *mens rea* had been formed during these acts.

3 The conviction for manslaughter was upheld. The Court of Appeal noted that this case differed from *Thabo Meli* in that there was no antecedent plan and the appellant did not drag his wife along thinking she was already dead. Lord Lane C.J said:

> 'It seems to us where the unlawful application of force and the eventual act causing death are **part of the same sequence of events**, the same transaction, the fact that there is an appreciable interval of time between the two does not serve to exonerate the defendant from liability.'

In this case the *mens rea* was in the initial unlawful assault and the *actus reus* was the dropping of the head onto the pavement.

Details on *actus reus*

We will now consider *actus reus* in more detail in terms of:

  i liability for omissions;
 ii the state of affairs cases;
iii result crimes and causation.

Liability for omissions

Most offences are defined in such a way that criminal liability only arises when the accused has carried out some *positive act*, such as damaging or destroying property (criminal damage), killing a human being (homicide) or appropriating property belonging to someone else (theft) and so on. Criminal liability does not usually arise in situations where the accused has failed to act. The classic example is where adults see a child drowning in a river and do nothing (fail to act) to try to save the child and the child drowns. If the adults have no relationship at all to the child, they will not incur criminal liability in this situation. However, in certain limited circumstances the accused may incur criminal liability for failing to act, that is, for an omission, as shown below.

a *Where statute has created an offence which is committed by omission* – this most frequently occurs in relation to road traffic offences. For example, by section 7(6) of the Road Traffic Act 1988 (RTA 1988) a person may commit an offence by *failing* to provide a specimen when required to do so and by section 168 of the RTA 1988 a person may commit an offence by *failing* to give his correct name and address when required to do so. (See the statutory provisions on page 19.)

b *When the accused is under a duty to act* – as deemed to exist either by statute or by the common law. In *R* v. *Dytham* (1979) a police constable nearing the end of his shift failed to intervene when a man was kicked to death by a 'bouncer' outside a night club. He was charged and convicted of the common law offence of misconduct while acting as an officer of justice in that he neglected to act to protect the victim or apprehend the assailant.

c *When the accused is contracted to act and fails to do so* – in the leading case of *R* v. *Pittwood* (1902) the accused was contracted to operate the gates at a railway level crossing. He failed to close the gates when a train was approaching and a man was killed on the level crossing. The accused was convicted of manslaughter for failing to carry out his contractual duty. It mattered not that his contract was with the Railway Board and not with members of the public. His contract was such that he had a duty to protect members of the public.

d *When the accused has voluntarily assumed responsibility for someone* – and then fails to fulfil such responsibility. In *R* v. *Instan* (1893) the accused was convicted of the manslaughter of her aunt when she had taken responsibility for her but had then failed to feed her properly or call in medical help, with the result that the aunt died. In *R* v. *Stone and Dobinson* (1977) Stone and Dobinson were convicted of the manslaughter of Stone's sister who came to live with them. The sister was anorexic and Stone and Dobinson were of low intelligence and generally ineffective, for instance, they could not even use a telephone. However, the Court of Appeal held that by taking her some food they had assumed responsibility for the sister when she became bedridden. By the same reasoning, if a passerby stops to help someone who is injured in a road accident, they probably voluntarily assume some responsibility for the injured person. What do they have to do to fulfil this responsibility? When does it come to an end? It is not always easy to determine such matters but the responsibility probably ends when professional medical services arrive.

e *When the accused has created a dangerous situation and then fails to avert the danger* – in *R* v. *Miller* (1983) the accused was a squatter in a house who, on return from a public house one night, lay on a mattress and lit a cigarette. He fell asleep while smoking the cigarette but awoke to find that it had set fire to the mattress, at which point he simply got up and went to sleep in another room. In the fire which ensued a lot of damage was done to the property and Miller was charged with arson (criminal damage by fire) under the Criminal Damage Act 1971. His conviction was upheld in the House of Lords where it was held that when Miller became aware of the dangerous situation he had created, it was his duty or responsibility to act to avert the danger and he had failed to do so. Just what he would have been required to do would depend on the stage of development of the fire when he became aware of it. It is unlikely that he would have been expected to tackle a large fire but he could have attempted to douse a small fire or could have telephoned for the Fire Brigade.

State-of-affairs cases

In state-of-affairs cases the accused persons do not voluntarily carry out the *actus reus* of the offences in question. Neither do they have the *mens rea* for the offences. Thus, they are convicted when neither of the two ingredients of most offences are satisfied. In this way such offences are *absolute liability* offences which differ from strict liability offences in that for strict liability offences, while the prosecution do not have to prove *mens rea*, nevertheless, they have to prove that the accused voluntarily carried out the *actus reus* of the offence in question. (See Chapter 3, on strict liability.)

Certain road traffic offences can be described as state-of-affairs or absolute liability offences. For example, by section 1 of the Road Traffic Act 1974 it is conclusively presumed that the owner of a car was the driver of the car at the time of an alleged offence such as illegal parking. Thus, the owner of a car can become liable to pay parking tickets if the car is parked illegally by someone else driving the car with their consent. The severity of such laws is clearly shown in the case of *R v. Parking Adjudicator, ex parte Wandsworth London Borough Council* (1996) shown in the newspaper extract below. In this case liability for illegal parking was attributed to the owner of the car despite the fact that the garage having possession and control of the car had carried out the illegal parking. This type of liability is said to exist for reasons of administrative efficiency, to ensure that parking fines are actually paid.

Other state-of-affairs cases exist in relation to statutory offences which have the words *'being found'* in them. Thus, in *R v. Larsonneur* (1933) a French woman, who had been required to leave the UK and who had gone to Eire, was deported from Eire back to the UK against her will. On arrival back in the UK she was charged under the Aliens Order 1920 in that *'being* an alien to whom leave to land in the UK had been refused, she was *found* in the UK'. Her conviction was upheld on appeal on the basis that it was irrelevant that she had not acted voluntarily. In *Winzar v. Chief Constable of Kent* (1983) the accused had been taken to hospital and then discharged as being drunk. When he was found in a hospital corridor the police were summoned and they took him outside into the street. They then charged him with *'being found* drunk on the highway' under section 12 of the Licensing Act 1872, despite the fact that he had not voluntarily gone into the street. Note that in all of these cases criminal liability is imposed on the accused by application of the literal rule as it applies to statutory interpretation. This is most clearly demonstrated in the case of *R v. Parking Adjudicator, ex parte Wandsworth London Borough Council* (1996) as shown opposite. It it an example of a state-of-affairs or absolute liability offence demonstrating the literal approach to statutory interpretation.

Result crimes and causation

We have already noted that offences can be divided into conduct crimes and result crimes. For result crimes to have been committed the conduct of the accused (which may be an act or omission) has to have caused the prohibited consequence part of the *actus reus*. Thus, to secure a conviction for murder the prosecution have to prove that the conduct of the accused (the stabbing, the shooting, the kicking or the poisoning, etc. of the victim) caused the death of the victim (the prohibited consequence). To secure a conviction for causing death by dangerous driving the prosecution have to prove that the dangerous driving (the conduct of the accused) caused the death of the victim (the prohibited consequence).

Car owner liable for illegal parking by garage

Regina v Parking Adjudicator, Ex parte Wandsworth London Borough Council

Before Lord Justice Stuart-Smith, Lord Justice Morritt and Sir John May

[Judgment November 1]

The registered owner of a vehicle at the time a penalty charge notice was fixed to it under the Road Traffic Act 1991 and not the garage then having the care of the vehicle was liable for the charge.

The Court of Appeal so held, allowing an appeal by the applicant, Wandsworth London Borough Council, from the refusal by the Queen's Bench Divisional Court (Lord Justice Schiemann and Mr Justice Brian Smedley) (*The Times* July 22, 1996) of judicial review of a parking adjudicator's decision. On October 18, 1995 he allowed an appeal by Jane Francis against two penalty charge notices which had been served on her under Schedule 6 to the 1991 Act. At the relevant times the vehicle was in a garage for repairs and had been parked by the garage.

When the garage returned the vehicle to Ms Francis no mention was made of the notices and they remained unpaid. After inquiries to the Driver and Vehicle Licensing Agency, the council served the notices on Ms Francis as the registered owner of the vehicle. She appealed.

Section 66 of the 1991 Act provides: "(2) A penalty charge is payable with respect to a vehicle, by the owner of the vehicle, if – (a) the vehicle, has been left – (i) otherwise than as authorised by or under any order relating to the designated parking place ..."

Section 82 provides "(2) ... the owner of a vehicle shall be taken to be the person by whom the vehicle is kept.

"(3) In determining ... who was the owner of a vehicle at any time, it shall be presumed that the owner was the person in whose name the vehicle was at that time registered..."

Paragraph 2 of Schedule 6 provides: "(I) Where it appears to the recipient [of a penalty charge notice] that one or other of the grounds mentioned in sub-paragraph (4) below are satisfied, he may make representations to that effect to the London authority who served the notice on him ...

"(4) The grounds are – (a) that the recipient – (i) never was the owner of the vehicle in question; (ii) had ceased to be its owner before the date on which the alleged contravention occurred; or (iii) became its owner after that date ..."

Mr Alan Wilkie, QC and Mr Ranjit Bhose for the applicant; Mr Richard Gordon, QC, for the parking adjudicator.

LORD JUSTICE STUART-SMITH said that the "owner" of a vehicle, for present purposes, was defined by section 82(2) as the person by whom the vehicle was kept, and that person, by section 82(3), was presumed to be the person in whose name the vehicle was at the time registered under the Vehicle Excise and Registration Act 1994.

The approach of the parking adjudicator to the case was to regard the question of who was the owner as one of fact and degree. In the circumstances, the adjudicator reached the conclusion, which was upheld by the Divisional Court, that the garage, and not Ms Francis, was the owner liable for the penalty charge.

Mr Wilkie submitted that the presumption of ownership in section 82(3) of the 1991 Act could only be rebutted in the ways mentioned in paragraph 2(4)(a) of Schedule 6 to the Act. In his Lordship's view, that was the correct approach.

Accordingly, a garage which accepted a vehicle for repair was not its owner within the meaning of section 82(2) of the Act. His Lordship would allow the appeal.

Lord Justice Morritt and Sir John May agreed.

Solicitors: Mr M. B. A. Walker, Wandsworth; Charlotte Axelson, Haymarket.

Likewise, to secure a conviction for criminal damage, the prosecution have to prove that the conduct of the accused (the throwing of the stone, the battering with a stick, the setting alight, etc.) caused the damage to, or destruction of, the property in question (the prohibited consequence).

Points on the behaviour of the accused	Examples	Comments
1 Does the behaviour of the accused amount to criminal behaviour? Is there a statute or common law provision which criminalises the behaviour?	Theft Act 1968 Murder	For theft, was 'property belonging to another appropriated'? For murder, was a 'human being killed in the Queen's Peace'?
2 Was the behaviour carried out 'voluntarily' or was it due to 'non-insane automatism'?	Kay v. Butterworth (1945) R v. Charlson (1955) Broome v. Perkins (1987)	The automatism must be due to a unique, usually external, event such that the accused lost total control of his actions.
3 If the behaviour was not voluntarily, can the accused ever be responsible criminally? Yes – consider the state of affairs cases.	R v. Larsonneur (1933) Winzar v. Chief Constable of Kent (1983) R v. Parking Adjudicator ex Parte Wandsworth Borough Council (1996)	These are cases of absolute liability where neither the voluntary actus reus nor the mens rea has to be proved by the prosecution. There is thus no 'fault' at all on the part of the accused. Should these offences exist?

Points on omissions

| Can the accused be responsible for 'failing to act', i.e. for omissions?
Generally no, but sometimes yes:
 i by offences of omission;
 ii when the accused is under a duty to act;
 iii when the accused is contracted to act;
 iv when the accused has voluntarily assumed responsibility for someone;
 v when the accused has created a dangerous situation then failed to avert the danger. | Road Traffic Act 1988
R v. Dytham (1979)
R v. Pittwood (1902)
R v. Instan (1893)
R v. Stone & Dobinson (1977)

R v. Miller (1983) | i For example, by section 7(6) – failing to provide a specimen for analysis.
ii Police constable failed to intervene to prevent a crime/effect arrest.
iii Employee failed to close level crossing gates – a death ensued.
iv Manslaughter convictions resulted where the accused voluntarily assumed responsibility for; then neglected, someone who died.
v Miller started a fire accidentally and failed to avert the danger. |

Result crimes and causation

| Do intervening events ever break the chain of causation between the actus reus and the resulting consequence, for example death? especially in cases involving medical treatment? | R v. Armstrong (1989)
R v. Pagett (1983)
R v. Jordan (1956), R v. Smith (1959)
R v. Cheshire (1991), R v. Malcherek (1981),
R v. Blaue (1975) | For a detailed discussion of this topic and the cases shown, refer to Chapter 12, on homicide |

Figure 2.2 *Actus reus*

Usually it is obvious whether or not the conduct of the accused caused the prohibited consequence, though the issue can be contentious, especially in murder cases. As discussion of the contentious nature of this topic is quite complex and as the issue usually arises in cases concerning murder, it will be dealt with in Chapter 12, on homicide. However, the same principles apply generally for all result crimes.

Details on *mens rea*

Most offences consist of an *actus reus* and *mens rea*. The *mens rea* part of the offence relates to the mental state of the accused which has to be proved by the prosecution. *Mens rea* exists on a sliding scale of blameworthiness with intention at the top as the most blameworthy state of mind. (Refer to Figure 2.3.) Some offences are defined such that intention *has* to be proved as the *mens rea* for the offence; proof of recklessness will not suffice, as is the case for murder. These offences are the most serious offences for which severe penalties exist and thus it is the duty of the state to require proof of a high state of blameworthiness.

The next level of blameworthiness is represented by recklessness. In fact, most offences require the prosecution to prove that the accused acted *either* intentionally or recklessly and, as such, these offences are not regarded as seriously as those where only intention will suffice as the *mens rea*. An example of such an offence is criminal damage.

The next level of blameworthiness is represented by negligence which may be described as the mental state required of the accused in some minor road traffic offences and for gross negligence manslaughter.

Below negligence is strict liability. Offences of strict liability impose criminal liability on the accused when the accused is not necessarily blameworthy at all because he may have no mental state with regards to the *actus reus* of the offence in question: strict liability is the subject of Chapter 3. In this chapter we will discuss negligence and the problematic areas relating to intention and recklessness. Problems exist in this area of the criminal law because of the variety of words used in the common law and in statutes to describe the required mental element of an offence. For instance, the common law definition of murder includes the phrase 'with malice aforethought' to describe the *mens rea*. Statutory provision has also been ambiguous, as demonstrated by the use of the words 'malicious' or 'maliciously' in the Offences Against the Person Act 1861 to describe the *mens rea* for the section 20 offence. As we shall see, even when the words

Types of *mens rea*	Subjective or objective test	Difficulty in proving	Blameworthiness	Examples of offence	Severity of sanction	Cases to note
INTENTION	Subjective	Difficult	Very blameworthy	i Murder ii Theft iii section 18 OAPA 1861	i Life sentence ii Max. sentence 7 years iii Max. life sentence	*R v. Moloney* (1985) *R v. Hancock & Shankland* (1986) *R v. Nedrick* (1986) *R v. Scalley* (1994) *R v. Woollin* (1998)
RECKLESSNESS	a) Cunningham (1957) i.e. subjective test	Quite hard	Blameworthy	i section 18 OAPA 1861 ii Assault and battery iii Rape	i Max. life sentence ii 6 months/level 5 fine iii Max. life sentence	*R v. Cunningham* (1957)
	b) Caldwell (1981) i.e. objective test	Not as hard as (a) above	Not necessarily blameworthy at all	i Criminal damage ii Statutory/regulatory offences, for example, road traffic offences	i Either max. of 10 years or life depending on offence ii As per offence – usually a low penalty.	*MPC v. Caldwell* (1981) *Elliott v. C* (1983)
NEGLIGENCE	Objective	Relatively easy	Not necessarily blameworthy at all	Careless driving contrary to section 3 of Road Traffic Act 1988	Level 4 fine plus an endorsement	*McCrone v. Riding* (1938)
STRICT LIABILITY OFFENCES	No *mens rea* required	Very easy indeed	Not necessarily blameworthy at all	Driving when under the influence of drink/drugs contrary to section 4 of Road Traffic Act 1988	6 months and/or level 5 fine	See Chapter 3

Figure 2.3 *Mens rea*

'intention' or 'recklessly' are used in statutes, their meanings have caused considerable debate.

Sometimes offences are described as either *basic intent* offences or *specific intent* offences. What is the difference between these? Unfortunately, there is no straightforward answer to this question. It is probably true that offences for which recklessness (whether *Cunningham* or *Caldwell* recklessness) is the *mens rea* can be described as basic intent offences. It would be very convenient if it were possible to say that offences for which intention is the *mens rea* could be described as specific intent crimes. However, this is not absolutely true. Whether or not an offence is a specific intent offence is particularly relevant in relation to whether or not intoxication may be pleaded as a defence. This is because it has been held (*DPP* v. *Majewski* [1977]) that intoxication may only be a defence to offences of specific intent. Students should refer to the topic of intoxication as a defence in Chapter 9, on general defences, where offences of specific and basic intent are listed.

Intention

Intention is the *mens rea* which denotes the most blameworthy state of mind in an accused. This is the *mens rea* which has to be proved beyond all reasonable doubt for the most serious offences, such as murder, wounding with intent contrary to section 18 of the Offences Against the Person Act 1861, theft contrary to section 1(1) of the Theft Act 1968 (TA 1968), robbery contrary to section 8 of the TA 1968, burglary contrary to section 9 of the TA 1968, and so forth. In most cases before the court, it will be obvious whether or not the accused intended the consequences of his actions because of the evidence that is brought out in court. However, in some cases the circumstances of the alleged commission of the offence will be such that it is not obvious whether or not the accused actually intended the consequences of his actions. It is this type of case which has produced the case law in which the issue of intention recieves prolonged consideration. Such cases invariably involve murder, probably because the penalty on conviction for murder is a mandatory life sentence, and so this discussion on intention will focus on murder cases. The principles arising from these murder cases do, however, apply equally to other offences which have intention as the *mens rea*.

Before we consider intention in the leading murder cases it is necessary to clarify the difference between the substantive law for murder and the evidential law as regards the judge's direction to the jury on *mens rea* for murder.

Substantive law for murder

The substantive law relates to the definition of the offence in question. Murder is defined by the common law as 'the killing of a human being in the Queen's Peace with malice aforethought'. We have already noted that the *mens rea* part of this definition is the phrase 'with malice aforethought'. This means that the accused either:

▶ intended to kill the victim; or
▶ intended to cause the victim serious bodily harm.

The key mental element for murder is thus *intention*.

Evidential law

When a jury is faced with a relatively straightforward murder case (and we are led to believe that most murder cases are straightforward), for instance, where the accused has directly attacked the victim, the judge need only direct the jury as to the requisite *mens rea* which has to be proved to the extent that the accused had to have intended to kill the victim or cause the victim serious bodily harm – a simple direction.

However, when the case is less straightforward, for instance, when the actions of the accused are very dangerous but not directly inflicted on the victim (and the accused denies intention to kill or cause serious bodily harm) but, nevertheless, death results from these actions, the judge may need to give the jury a more involved direction to help them determine the issue of *mens rea* for murder. It is in such cases that problems have occurred with regard to the *mens rea* for murder as highlighted below:

i some judges have been reluctant to define intention in terms of the substantive law;

ii some judges have confused the substantive law *mens rea* for murder with the concepts discussed in the evidential law as regards their directions to the jury;

iii the judges have been grappling with concepts such as foreseeability of consequences, high degree of probability and virtual certainty in deciding on how to direct the jury on the circumstances from which they might *infer* that the accused intended to kill or cause serious bodily harm;

iv the denial by judges that if the consequences of the accused's actions are *virtually certain* to happen, this *can be equated* to or regarded as the same as *intention*. Instead, the judges regard the virtual certainty of results happening as one of many circumstances in the case from which the jury may *infer* that the accused intended to kill or cause serious bodily harm.

It is for these reasons that directions from the judges to the jury have served only to make the issue of determining the mental state of the accused in murder cases even more obscure. It would be better for the criminal law if intention was defined; students should refer to the proposals for reform on page 57 for further discussion on this.

To help you analyse these concepts in simple terms, consider the following situations and the suggested type of direction the judge might give the jury.

A is angry with B, pours petrol over B and then sets light to B with a match. B dies. This would surely be a straightforward case when only a simple direction would be required to the effect that the *mens rea* for murder is intention to kill or cause serious bodily harm, as it was A's *purpose* to kill B or cause B serious bodily harm. (This is sometimes referred to as 'direct' intent.)

A is angry with B, locks B in a wooden garden shed, pours petrol in through the shed window and sets light to the shed with a match. B dies. A denies intending to harm B claiming that he just wanted to scare B. (This is sometimes referred to as 'oblique' intent.) Here the judge might feel that he needs to direct the jury as to the mental state of A, in which case he should direct them that the *mens rea* for murder is intention to kill or cause serious bodily harm and then he should direct them as to what they are entitled to *infer* from A's actions. Some judges have directed the jury to the effect that they can infer intention if death or serious bodily harm was *'foreseeable as a moral certainty'* (as in *R v. Moloney* [1985]) following the accused's actions, while other judges have directed the jury to the effect that they can infer intention if death or serious bodily harm was *'foreseeable as highly probably'* (as in *R v. Hancock & Shankland* [1986]) following the accused's actions. It is difficult to see the difference between these two tests and no one has yet really answered the question.

The problems associated with directing the jury on *mens rea* in complicated murder cases can be considered by consideration of the case of *R v. Nedrick* (1986).

R v. *Nedrick* (1986) Court of Appeal

Facts of the case

In this case the appellant had poured paraffin through the letter box of a woman's house and set fire to it. He said that he did not intend to kill anyone, rather, he just wanted to frighten the woman. As a result of his actions a fire ensued which killed a child in the house. He was convicted of murder and appealed because the judge had directed the jury to the effect that *foresight of consequences* was the *same as intention*.

This is obviously a case which requires a direction from the judge to the jury because the appellant denied intention to kill or cause serious bodily harm and, on the facts presented, his mental state is not obvious.

Lord Lane C.J. gave the judgment of the court:

That direction [of the trial judge] was given before publication of the speeches in the House of Lords in R v. Moloney *[1985] and* R v. Hancock *[1986]. In the light of those speeches it was plainly wrong . . .*

What then does a jury have to decide so far as the mental element in murder is concerned? It simply has to decide whether the defendant intended to kill or do serious bodily harm. In order to reach that decision the jury must pay regard to all the relevant circumstances, including what the defendant himself said and did.

In the great majority of cases a direction to that effect will be enough, particularly where the defendant's actions amounted to a direct attack upon his victim, because in such cases the evidence relating to the defendant's desire or motive will be clear and his intent will have been the same as his desire or motive. But in some cases, of which this is one the defendant does an act which is manifestly dangerous and as a result someone dies. The primary desire or motive of the defendant may not have been

to harm that person, or indeed anyone. In that situation what further directions should a jury be given as to the mental state which they must find to exist in the defendant if murder is to be proved? . . .

*Where the charge is murder and in the rare cases where the simple direction is not enough, the jury should be directed that they are not entitled to infer the necessary intention, unless they feel sure that **death or serious bodily harm was a virtual certainty** (barring some unforeseen intervention) as a result of the defendant's actions and that the defendant appreciated that such was the case.*

Where a man realises that it is for all practical purposes inevitable that his actions will result in death or serious harm, the inference may be irresistible that he intended that result, however little he may have desired or wished it to happen. The decision is one for the jury, to be reached upon consideration of all the evidence.

The appeal was allowed; the conviction for murder was quashed and a conviction of manslaughter was substituted. The significance of this is in the sentence. On conviction for murder the sentence is automatic life imprisonment, whereas on conviction for manslaughter the sentence is anything up to a maximum of life imprisonment. We can see some of the problems of defining intention in terms of the substantive law in this extract when the notions of the defendant's 'desire' and 'motive' are mentioned. If the definition of intention was equated to desire or motive then, in a case such as this, the defendant would not have intended death or serious bodily harm as this was not his desire or motive. Nevertheless, it could be argued that either death or serious bodily harm were virtually certain consequences of his actions.

In the case of *R* v. *Scalley* (1994), which also involved the death of a child following the setting fire to a house by pushing a lighted paper through the letter box, the conviction for murder was quashed and one of manslaughter substituted because the Court of Appeal held that while the trial judge had correctly made use of the principles in *Nedrick* with regard to what the jury might infer from the circumstances, nevertheless, he had not made it sufficiently clear that this was an inference which still had to be applied to the substantive law of murder. The jury should have been told that the *mens rea* for murder was intention to kill or cause serious bodily harm and that their inferences from the circumstances had to be applied to this.

In the case of *R v. Woollin* (1998) the appellant had thrown his three-month-old son four or five feet across the room towards his pram so that he fractured his skull and died. The Court of Appeal quashed the appeal so that the conviction for murder was upheld by supporting the direction of the judge to the jury that they could infer intention where they were satisfied that the defendant *foresaw more than a slight risk of serious harm* to the victim. This would have lowered the seriousness threshhold of the accused's actions from which the jury might infer intention. However, Woollin appealed and the House of Lords quashed the conviction for murder, substituted a conviction of manslaughter and remitted the case to the Court of Appeal for sentencing. The House of Lords held that the recorder at the original trial at Leeds Crown Court should not have departed from the *Nedrick* direction. Lord Steyn said:

> By using the phrase 'substantial risk' he had blurred the line between intention and recklessness and hence between murder and manslaughter. The misdirection had enlarged the scope of the mental element required for murder. It had been a material misdirection. In the circumstances of the case, the conviction of murder was unsafe and was quashed. Lord Lane's judgment in Nedrick had provided valuable assistance to trial judges. The model direction was by now a tried and tested formula. Trial judges ought to continue to use it . . .

Comment on these difficult cases

These difficult cases all stem from the fact that intention is not defined in the substantive law, leaving judges the task of framing directions to juries to help them determine, on the facts, whether or not the *mens rea* of the accused amounts to intention. It is submitted that the most satisfactory approach to date was taken by Lord Lane C.J. in *R v. Nedrick* (1986) where the concept of *virtual certainty* was used and, indeed, this was reinforced by the House of Lords in *R v. Woollin* (1998). Until intention is defined in terms of the substantive law it is likely that there will continue to be cases which go to appeal on the basis of the judge's direction to the jury. As such, the criminal law can only be improved by the accident of litigation.

Recklessness

As a state of mind recklessness can be enough to make someone guilty of a criminal offence although it is regarded as a less blameworthy state of mind than intention. Recklessness involves risk taking on the part of the accused, which is regarded as unjustifiable by the criminal law. We have already considered the problems which exist in relation to the lack of definition of intention and must now consider whether recklessness causes any problems of definition. To understand fully the discussion which follows it is necessary to grasp the difference in meaning between the subjective and objective way of looking at the mental state of the accused, as recklessness may be regarded as either subjective recklessness or objective recklessness.

The subjective approach to recklessness

When the mental state of the accused is looked at subjectively, the subject, that is the accused, is regarded as a unique person with all sorts of attributes, both positive and negative. The question to be asked is whether or not *this person*, with all his personal characteristics (such as low intelligence), was reckless with regard to the consequences and/or circumstances of his actions. The personal attributes of the accused may be used to demonstrate that he was not reckless. Thus, it is generally quite difficult for the prosecution to prove that the accused was subjectively reckless.

The objective approach to recklessness

When the mental state of the accused is looked at objectively, the accused is not regarded as a unique person and his personal foibles are ignored. The question to be answered is whether or not *the ordinary and prudent man*, in the same circumstances as the accused, could be said to have acted recklessly. Thus, it is generally easier for the prosecution to prove that the accused was objectively reckless, as ordinary and prudent men are not prone to taking risks. In some cases this can seem very unfair to the accused (see *Elliott* v. *C* [1983] below.)

Do the courts apply the subjective or objective test to recklessness?

There has been some confusion in this respect, which can be explained by consideration of the two leading cases on recklessness:

i *R* v. *Cunningham* (1957), the leading case for subjective or 'Cunningham recklessness';
ii *MPC* v. *Caldwell* (1982), the leading case for objective or '*Caldwell* recklessness'.

i *Cunningham* or subjective recklessness

This case involved prosecution under section 23 of the Offences Against the Person Act 1861 (see statutory provisions on page 19) where the *mens rea* part of the offence is described by the words *unlawfully* and *maliciously*. The *actus reus* part of the offence involves the administering to, or causing to be administered to, another person of a noxious substance so as to endanger life. The accused went into the cellar of a house and ripped the gas meter off the wall so that he could steal the money out of it. In doing so gas escaped and seeped into the house next door where a woman was asleep. She inhaled a lot of the gas and became seriously ill so that her life was endangered. The accused was convicted at trial but appealed on the basis that the trial judge had directed the jury that *maliciously* meant *wickedly*. In the Court of Appeal it was agreed that the appellant had acted unlawfully, but had he acted maliciously? The Court held that maliciously should not be equated with the old notion of wickedly but should be understood in the way suggested by Professor Kenny in his *Outlines of the Criminal Law*, published in 1902 and 1952. As such, malice should mean either that the accused *intended* to do the harm that was done or that the accused was *reckless* as to whether such harm would result. Reckless means that *the accused has foreseen* that the harm might be done and yet goes on to take the risk of it happening. Thus, the test for recklessness is a subjective one as it considers what the actual accused foresaw as a risk. The appeal was allowed and the conviction quashed as the Court of Appeal could not say without doubt whether or not a jury, properly directed as to the meaning of maliciously, would have convicted the appellant.

The *Cunningham* case was in 1957 and the *Caldwell* case was in 1982. In between these two cases the Criminal Damage Act was enacted in 1971. Liability for criminal damage (whether basic, aggravated or arson) involves proof of *mens rea* in terms of either intention or recklessness. (See the earlier part of this chapter for the definition of criminal damage under section 1(1) of the Act.) When cases came to court it became necessary to interpret the word recklessly and initially it was interpreted subjectively following on from *Cunningham* and because throughout the work leading up to the enacting of the Act, the Law Commission had viewed recklessness in subjective terms. Thus, it seemed clear that whenever the word reckless or recklessly appeared in an offence, it was to be regarded subjectively. However, when the *Caldwell* case reached the House of Lords in 1982 all of this was to change as their Lordships held that, for criminal damage, recklessness was to be regarded in objective terms.

2

ii Caldwell or objective recklessness

In this case the accused, while drunk, set fire to some curtains in a hotel because he bore a grudge against the owner of the hotel. Not much damage was done as the fire was soon discovered and the accused was charged with various counts of criminal damage under the Criminal Damage Act 1971. (For an understanding of a 'count' students should refer to Chapter 4, on theft). The accused appealed against his conviction for aggravated criminal damage (where life is endangered) and, while most of the appeal concerned the issue of whether intoxication was a defence, nevertheless, their Lordships took the opportunity to consider the meaning of recklessness within the Criminal Damage Act 1971. Lord Diplock referred to the definition of recklessness as put forward by Professor Kenny, and to cases since the Criminal Damage Act 1971 in which recklessness had been given the subjective meaning. He noted that the Criminal Damage Act 1971 had replaced the Malicious Damage Act 1861 and that cases since 1971 had *assumed* that the *mens rea* for criminal damage, as described by the words intention or reckless, meant the same as described by the word *maliciously* as used in the 1861 Act. Lord Diplock said that this was a false assumption to make as the 1971 Act was meant to *revise* the old law not merely to restate it. He formulated his view of recklessness as follows:

> ... to decide whether someone has been 'reckless' whether harmful consequences of a particular kind will result from his act, as distinguished from his actually intending such harmful consequences to follow, does call for some consideration of how the mind of the **ordinary prudent individual** would have reacted to a similar situation ...
>
> In my opinion, a person charged with an offence under section 1(1) of the Criminal Damage Act 1971 is 'reckless as to whether or not any property would be destroyed or damaged' if:
>
> (1) he does an act which in fact creates an obvious risk that property will be destroyed or damaged; and
>
> (2) when he does the act he either has not given any thought to the possibility of there being any such risk or has recognised that there was some risk involved and has nonetheless gone on to do it.
>
> That would be a proper direction to the jury; cases in the Court of Appeal which held otherwise should be regarded as overruled.

This is an important *ratio decidendi* as it comes from the House of Lords which means it is a binding precedent from the highest court in the land. This two-part direction for the jury had to be used in subsequent cases involving the *mens rea* of recklessness. The case of *Elliott* v. *C* (*a minor*) (1983) demonstrates how harsh this new objective test for recklessness could be. In this case the accused, a 14-year-old girl who was in a remedial class at school, went into a garden shed and, having poured white spirit onto a carpet in the shed, she set fire to it. The shed was destroyed in the fire and she was charged with criminal damage contrary to section 1(1) of the Criminal Damage Act 1971. At trial she was acquitted because the magistrates took a subjective approach to recklessness and decided that, to this particular girl, with all her attributes, the risk of damage to the shed was not obvious. The prosecution appealed and the appeal was allowed, that is, the girl was to be convicted. Lord Justice Goff said that despite the fact that it seemed very inappropriate to find this girl guilty of criminal damage, nevertheless, he did not think that he could qualify the case in any way to depart from the objective test as put forward by Lord Diplock in the House of Lords.

To an ordinary prudent man, in these circumstances, the risk of damage from setting light to white spirit in a wooden garden shed would have been obvious and, as such, the conduct of the girl was to be regarded as reckless.

How do the courts know whether to apply the subjective or objective test to any particluar offence?

There is no clear-cut answer to this question. However, it is generally held that:

▶ *Caldwell* or objective recklessness applies to:

   i criminal damage offences under the Criminal Damage Act 1971;
   ii statutory offences which are probably regulatory with minor penalties, such as offences under the Road Traffic Acts.

▶ *Cunningham* or subjective recklessness applies to:

   i offences requiring proof of *malice*, as in sections 18 and 20 of the Offences Against the Person Act 1861;
   ii common law offences against the person, that is, assault and battery;
   iii rape.

This position has been established in numerous cases since the *Caldwell* case in 1981, and in *R* v. *Reid* (1989) the majority view was that the term recklessness had a variable meaning depending on the context. It is thus not true to say (as Lord Roskill said in *R* v. *Seymour* [1983]) that the objective test should be applied to all offences using the word reckless unless Parliament had otherwise ordained. It would now appear that objective recklessness has been confined to

2

criminal damage and offences which have a small penalty. This restriction of the application of objective recklessness is probably a good thing because the underlying ethos of criminal liability is that the *accused* was blameworthy. It is not so appropriate to attach criminal liability to the accused by importing to him the mental state of a fictitious 'ordinary and prudent man'.

Negligence

Negligence is really a civil law notion. However, it does feature in the criminal law in that it is used as the basis for liability in relation to:

▶ some statutory road traffic offences;
▶ common law gross negligence manslaughter.

Negligence resembles the objective or *Caldwell* test for recklessness discussed above as it sets an objective standard for liability based on how the reasonable or prudent man would have behaved. With regards to manslaughter, only gross negligence is sufficient to incur criminal liability. This is discussed in Chapter 12, on homicide.

Because of the general notion that a person has to be at fault to incur criminal liability, there are not many offences for which negligence is a sufficient mental state to impose criminal liability. As we saw with objective recklessness, it is difficult to say that a person is at fault according to such an impersonal test and the same applies with negligence. With regards to road traffic offences the object is to provide a highway system which is as safe as possible given the inherently dangerous nature of the highway. In pursuit of this aim some road traffic offences impose criminal liability on the basis of an objective standard of negligence. As with objective recklessness, demonstrated by the case of *Elliott* v. *C (a minor)* (1983), basing criminal liability on negligence can seem unfair. This is demonstrated in the case of *McCrone* v. *Riding* (1938) which involved careless driving contrary to section 3 of the Road Traffic Act 1988 under which it is an offence to drive a vehicle on a road or other public place without due care and attention or without reasonable consideration for other persons using the road or public place. The key phrases are 'without due care and attention' and 'without reasonable consideration'. These are standards of conduct which are measured in terms of the reasonable and competent driver. In *McCrone* v. *Riding* the driver was a learner driver who had been driving without due care and attention. The court held that the fact that the driver was a learner driver was irrelevant; if the driving fell below the standard of a reasonable and competent driver then the learner driver would be guilty of careless driving. This seems grossly unfair to the learner driver but the safety of all users of the highway has to be considered.

Applying principles to examination questions

Most A-level law syllabuses require students to study the English legal system for paper one and then to choose one or possibly two subjects to study for paper two, including criminal law. The questions on paper one are predominantly essay-type questions, although, increasingly, data- and stimulus-response type questions are being used. Questions on the criminal law papers are usually a mixture of problem-solving questions and essay-type questions which may take the data/stimulus-response format. Thus, the student of criminal law has to learn a new technique for paper two in terms of answering problem-solving questions. Throughout this book much attention will be given to developing this technique, especially in this part of each chapter. At this stage, rather than presenting students with a purely problem-solving question, a question has been selected which is devised in such a way that it combines essay writing with problem-solving skills. As such, it is a perfect introduction to the criminal law paper.

Consider the question posed opposite and note down any key points which spring to mind. Then look back through the chapter to elicit further points and key cases/statutory provisions. Attempt to write the answer to this question and then consider the suggested approach which is given on pages 55–56.

Consider all of the following situations:

i Nurul, who is driving an open-topped sports car, is stunned by stings from a swarm of bees. The car veers to the wrong side of the road and collides with a parked car.

ii Diana, who has had an exhausting day, falls asleep as she is driving. Her car collides with a stationary lorry.

iii Pippa, who is mentally ill, is driving on the motorway when she begins to think that the car ahead of her is being driven by the Devil. She decides to try to force it off the road and deliberately drives into the side of it.

In each case a charge of driving without due care and attention is brought. Section 3 of the Road Traffic Act 1988 states that:

If a person drives a motor vehicle on the road without due care and attention or without reasonable consideration for other persons using the road, he is guilty of an offence.

No further knowledge of the Road Traffic Act is expected or required for this question.

Compare, contrast and comment on the issue of criminal liability in these three situations.

(25 marks)

(Source: NEAB Law Advanced Paper II, June 1995)

Tips on how to approach such a question

Open-topped car is not an offence.

Is the collision relevant?

She voluntarily got into her car and drove while drowsy.

Is the insane delusion a defence? She *intentionally* drives into the other car.

Quote the cases of *McCrone* v. *Riding* (1838) and *Elliot* v. *C (a minor)* (1983). This is a 'conduct' crime.

Highlight the similarities and differences of the three situations.

Consider all of the following situations:

i Nurul, who is driving an open-topped sports car, is stunned by stings from a swarm of bees. The car veers to the wrong side of the road and collides with a parked car.

ii Diana, who has had an exhausting day, falls asleep as she is driving. Her car collides with a stationary lorry.

iii Pippa, who is mentally ill, is driving on the motorway when she begins to think that the car ahead of her is being driven by the Devil. She decides to try to force it off the road and deliberately drives into the side of it.

In each case a charge of driving without due care and attention is brought. Section 3 of the Road Traffic Act 1988 states that:

If a person drives a motor vehicle on the road without due care and attention or without reasonable consideration for other persons using the road, he is guilty of an offence.

No further knowledge of the Road Traffic Act is expected or required for this question.

Compare, contrast and comment on the issue of criminal liability in these three situations.

(25 marks)

Does he try to brush the bees away? Or is his mind blocked with shock? Can he plead non-insane automatism? Consider voluntariness of *actus reus.*

Is the collision relevant? Quote the case of *Kay* v. *Butterworth* (1938).

The test for liability is objective not subjective

This offence is known as careless driving – the courts have decided that the mental test for liability is negligence – an objective test – what would the reasonable and competent driver do?

Tips on how to translate such notes and jottings into a comprehensive answer

This is the format which will be used in each chapter to develop your technique for answering problematic-type questions. In this first substantive law chapter such side notes and jottings will be translated into a comprehensive answer to give you an idea of what you are aiming to achieve. As this is a hybrid question it is necessary to remember all of your essay-writing skills from paper one and then use these to apply your knowledge to the situations presented. You have to impart a good deal of knowledge but in the right places and at the right time; it is no good spotting what you think is the main subject of the question and just writing on this subject at length. Consider the approach suggested below.

Consideraton of key words in the question posed	Be sure to identify what the question is. In this case you are asked to compare, contrast and comment on the issue of criminal liability in these situations. Which are the key words?

Compare and contrast — Highlight the similarities and differences of the three situations.

Comment — Talk about the three situations generally – explain and critically analyse them.

Criminal liability — What is this? It is usually imposed when the accused has acted in a prohibited manner with some degree of fault. Does harm need to occur? Not necessarily.

To attempt this question you should know that section 3 of the Road Traffic Act 1988 (RTA) imposes liability for *negligent* behaviour.

Introduction	Explain that this is the statutory offence commonly referred to as careless driving where the *mens rea* is not explicitly given by use of words such as *intentionally* or *recklessly*. The *actus reus* is the driving of the motor vehicle on a road. It could be said that the two phrases *'without due care and attention'* and *'without reasonable care'* describe the *mens rea* but, equally, it could be said that these phrases merely describe the *actus reus* part of the offence. Note that it is a conduct crime as opposed to a result crime as it is not necessary to show that any damage was caused as a result of the careless driving.

Commentary	Comment on this type of statutory offence which is one of the few criminal offences for which negligence could be described as the *mens rea*. Explain that the test for liability is an objective one so that liability will be imposed on those whose driving falls below the standard of driving of the *reasonable and competent driver*.

Quote the case of *McCrone* v. *Riding* (1938) to demonstrate the apparent inequity of this. Explain that you will now apply this section to the three situations.

Nurul	Has Nurul driven the car without due care and attention on a road? The car is being driven on a road (the potential *actus reus*) but was it being driven negligently? Would a reasonable and competent driver have behaved as Nurul did in these circumstances? The *actus reus* of an offence must usually be carried out *voluntarily*. The exceptions are the state-of-affairs cases – quote the cases of *R* v. *Larsonneur* (1933) and *Winzar* v. *Chief Constable of Kent* (1983). Was Nurul acting voluntarily? It is likely that the magistrates would say

that Nurul was not acting voluntarily as he was suffering from non-insane automatism at the time of the incident. His mind was not controlling his limbs – the car veers and hits another car as a result of either a reflex action to brush the bees away or a mental block induced by the attack. It is probable that a reasonable and competent driver would have acted in the same manner, in which case Nurul should not be prosecuted.

Diana

It could also be argued that Diana did not commit the *actus reus* of the section 3 offence voluntarily as she was asleep. However, it is unlikely that the magistrates would take this approach as Diana would be regarded as having voluntarily continued to drive while feeling drowsy. Quote and explain the case of *Kay* v. *Butterworth* (1945). Thus, it is probable that Diana would be found guilty of the section 3 offence.

A comparison of Nurul and Diana's situations

In both these situations there was a collision with a parked vehicle which is actually irrelevant for the purposes of section 3 as it is not necessary to show that any damage was caused by the careless driving. Also, in both situations, neither Nurul nor Diana *intended* to drive carelessly. It is also likely that neither of them was *subjectively reckless*; certainly Nurul was not. However, Nurul would have a defence to the charge of careless driving because his actions were *totally* involuntary, brought about by a unique and external set of circumstances over which he had no control. In contrast, Diana voluntarily got into the car while drowsy and voluntarily continued to drive while drowsy. She could have chosen not to get into the car and not to drive or she could have stopped the car once she became very drowsy.

Pippa's liability and a comparison with Nurul and Diana's liability

In contrast to the situations of Nurul and Diana, Pippa *intentionally* collides with a vehicle which is also being driven on the road. As such she has a mental state which is the most blameworthy in the criminal law. It was her *purpose* and desire to crash into the other vehicle. As above, the fact that she damaged the other vehicle is irrelevant for the purposes of section 3. Thus, it seems that Pippa would be guilty of the section 3 offence. However, could she raise the defence of insanity, that due to her *personal attributes* she should not be held liable under section 3? Remember that the test for this offence is that of the reasonable and competent driver, an objective test. A reasonable and competent driver would not have deliberately driven into another vehicle, nor is such a driver insane. The test to be applied is universal and fixed and, as such, it is highly probable that Pippa would be convicted under section 3. Insanity can only be a defence to negate *mens rea* in the proper sense of *mens rea*, that is, to negate intention or recklessness. Moreover, in section 3 it could be argued that the phrases *without due care and attention* and *without reasonable consideration* merely describe the *actus reus*, in which case Pippa's mental state has no bearing. This line of argument is probably given weight by consideration of such cases as *McCrone* v. *Riding* (1938) and *Elliott* v. *C (a minor)* (1983) where the objective test was applied to section 3 RTA 1988 and section 1(1) of the Criminal Damage Act 1971 respectively, with strict adherence to the principles of objectiveness. If Pippa is prone to such insane delusions she should not have voluntarily got into her car and driven it.

Conclusion

All three people got into their cars voluntarily and drove them voluntarily. All three people were involved in accidents. Only Nurul has a defence, that of non-insane automatism. Diana and Pippa would probably be convicted for voluntarily putting themselves into a dangerous situation from which they could have withdrawn.

Proposals for reform

In the Law Commission's draft 'Criminal Code' (Law Com. No.177, 1989) the *mens rea* of an offence is described as the *fault element* consisting of intention, knowledge and recklessness, unless Parliament states to the contrary. This is an attempt to reduce the number of words which can be used in statutes to describe the *mens rea* for offences. In doing so, it follows that there should be more clarity, understanding and certainty in the criminal law, and thus, in theory, less time should be spent (wasted) in court grappling with diffucult concepts. The *actus reus* of an offence is described as the *external element* of the offence.

CHAPTER Summary

In this chapter we have noted how the division of offences into *actus reus* and *mens rea* is really an artificial one but one which is very popular. It is not totally accurate to say that the *actus reus* of an offence refers to the guilty act of the accused as the *actus reus* may be fulfilled by an omission or by a state-of-affairs. Thus, it is more accurate to think of the *actus reus* in terms of the conduct of the accused. It is in relation to the *mens rea* of an offence that the law is particularly in need of reform as several words are used in statutory provision and in the common law to describe the *mens rea* for an offence. Thus, *mens rea* may be described by the words 'intentionally', 'recklessly', 'maliciously', 'with malice aforethought', 'without due care and attention', 'knowingly' and 'wilfully'. 'Knowingly' describes the *mens rea*, for example, under section 22 of the Theft Act 1968 where it is an offence to handle stolen goods knowing or believing them to be stolen goods. 'Wilfully' may be interpreted as intention or recklessness. 'Negligence' has been discussed in this chapter on *mens rea* although some academics do not regard it as a type of *mens rea* because it involves measuring the accused's behaviour against an impersonal, objective standard of behaviour. However, could not the same be said of *Caldwell*-type recklessness? Also, as the division of offences into *actus reus* and *mens rea* is an artificial one, in order to prove that the accused committed an offence the main concern should be to match the facts (what actually occurred) with the law (the definition of the offence).

Strict liability offences

OVERVIEW

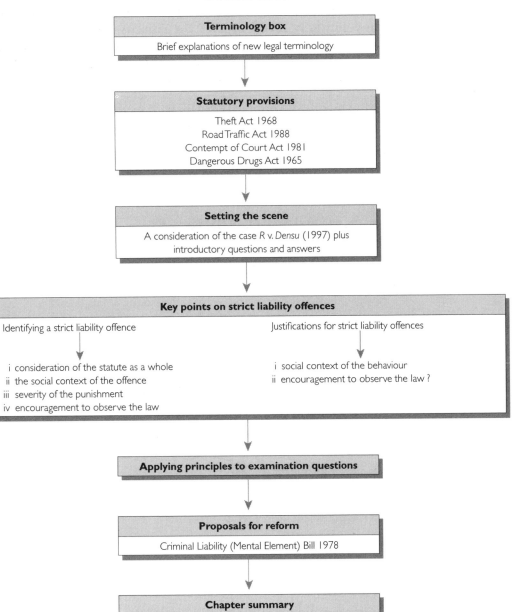

Terminology box

Brief explanations of new legal terminology

Statutory provisions

Theft Act 1968
Road Traffic Act 1988
Contempt of Court Act 1981
Dangerous Drugs Act 1965

Setting the scene

A consideration of the case *R* v. *Densu* (1997) plus
introductory questions and answers

Key points on strict liability offences

Identifying a strict liability offence

  i consideration of the statute as a whole
 ii the social context of the offence
iii severity of the punishment
iv encouragement to observe the law

Justifications for strict liability offences

 i social context of the behaviour
ii encouragement to observe the law ?

Applying principles to examination questions

Proposals for reform

Criminal Liability (Mental Element) Bill 1978

Chapter summary

In the previous chapter it was noted how most offences consist of a conduct element (*actus reus*) and a fault element (*mens rea*), both of which have to be proved by the prosecution beyond all reasonable doubt in order to secure the conviction of the accused. It was also noted that for some offences the prosecution need only prove that the accused *voluntarily* carried out the *actus reus* of the offence. Such offences are known as strict liability offences. These have to be differentiated from offences of absolute liability for which the accused may become liable even if the *actus reus* of the offence was not carried out voluntarily. (See Chapter 2 for a discussion of state-of-affairs cases.) In this chapter strict liability offences will be considered in terms of how the judges in court decide that an offence is a strict liability offence, and in terms of how this can be justified.

In the box below brief explanations of new words are given to aid a clear understanding of the rest of the chapter.

TERMINOLOGY: Strict liability offences

Strict liability	Describes an offence where the prosecution only have to prove beyond reasonable doubt that the accused voluntarily committed the *actus reus* of the offence; the *mens rea* of the accused is totally irrelevant.
Absolute liability	Describes an offence where the prosecution only have to prove that the accused committed the *actus reus* of the offence, even if done so involuntarily; the *mens rea* of the accused is totally irrelevant.
Presumption	An acceptance that a certain situation/state of affairs exists. Such presumptions can be rebutted, that is, shown not to exist.
Stigma	Most convicted criminals carry the stigma or social condemnation of being a criminal. A stigma thus marks society's disapproval of the behaviour in question.
Riparian	Means 'on the river bank', so a company can be described as riparian if it is situated adjacent to a river.

Statutory provisions

3

Theft Act 1968

1 Basic definition of theft

(1) A person is guilty of theft if he dishonestly appropriates property belonging to another with the intention of permanently depriving the other of it ...

Road Traffic Act 1988

3 Careless and inconsiderate driving

If a person drives a mechanically propelled vehicle on a road or other public place without due care and attention, or without reasonable consideration for other persons using the road or place, he is guilty of an offence.

4 Driving, or being in charge, when under the influence of drink or drugs

(1) A person who, when driving or attempting to drive a mechanically propelled vehicle on a road or other public place, is unfit to drive through drink or drugs, is guilty of an offence.

5 Driving or being in charge of a motor vehicle with alcohol concentration above a prescribed limit

(1) If a person:
   (a) drives or attempts to drive a motor vehicle on a road or other public place, or
   (b) is in charge of a motor vehicle on a road or other public place,
   after consuming so much alcohol that the proportion of it in his breath, blood or urine exceeds the prescribed limit, he is guilty of an offence.

Contempt of Court Act 1981

1 The strict liability rule

In this Act 'the strict liability rule' means the rule of law whereby conduct may be treated as a contempt of court as tending to interfere with the course of justice in particular legal proceedings, regardless of intent to do so.

2 Limitation of scope of strict liability

(1) The strict liability rule applies only in relation to publications, and for this purpose 'publication' includes any speech, writing, ... or other communication in whatever form, which is addressed to the public at large or any section of the public ...

(2) The strict liability rule applies only to a publication which creates a substantial risk that the course of justice in the proceedings in question will be seriously impeded or prejudiced.

(3) The strict liability rule applies to a publication only if the proceedings in question are active within the meaning of this section at the time of the publication.

Dangerous Drugs Act 1965

5 If a person:

(a) being the occupier of any premises, permits those premises to be used for the purpose of smoking cannabis or cannabis resin or of dealing in cannabis resin (whether by sale or otherwise); or

(b) is concerned in the management of any premises used for any such purpose as aforesaid; he shall be guilty of an offence against this Act.

Misuse of Drugs Act 1971

8 A person commits an offence if, being the occupier or concerned in the management of premises, he knowingly permits or suffers any of the following activities to take place on those premises, that is to say: . . .

(d) smoking cannabis, cannabis resin or prepared opium.

Setting the scene

In order to set the scene for the topic of strict liability, consider the case of *R* v. *Densu (1997)* which is shown below, and answer the questions which follow. Some of those will require research and some are pure data response. The case was reported in *The Times* on 10 December 1997.

3

Ignorance of nature of weapon no excuse

Regina v. Densu
Before Lord Justice Henry, Mr Justice Gage and Judge Tucker, QC

[Judgment November 7]
Where an accused person was charged with having an offensive weapon in a public place, a claim that he did not know that the article in question was an offensive weapon could not amount to the defence of reasonable excuse within the meaning of section 1(1) of the Prevention of Crime Act 1953.

The Court of Appeal, Criminal Division, so held in a reserved judgment dismissing an appeal by Felix Densu against his conviction on a plea of guilty to having an offensive weapon contrary to section 1(1) of the 1953 Act, after an adverse ruling by Judge Pratt on January 31, 1977, at Croydon Crown Court. He was conditionally discharged for two years and ordered to pay £75 costs.

Section 1 of the 1953 Act provides: "(1) Any person who without lawful authority or reasonable excuse, the proof whereof shall lie on him, has with him in any public place any offensive weapon shall be guilty of an offence..."

Mr Andrew Evans, assigned by the Registrar of Criminal Appeals, for the appellant; Miss Sally Thompson for the Crown.

MR JUSTICE GAGE, giving the judgment of the court, said that the appellant had been involved in a road traffic accident to which the police were called.

They found on the floor beside the driver's seat of the appellant's car a metal telescopic extendible baton. It was common ground that that baton, known as an asp, was an offensive weapon per se. The appellant's explantion was that he had found the baton in a car which he had valeted and was told that it was an aerial. He had used it as a lever for his trolley jack but had not seen it in its extended form and did not know that it was a weapon. On those facts the judge had ruled that he had no defence.

Their Lordships were unable to accept counsel's submissions that lack of knowledge was a matter capable of founding a reasonable excuse defence. The defence of reasonable excuse only arose once it was accepted and proved that a defendant was in possession of an offensive weapon.

The question then for the jury was whether the defendant had a reasonable excuse for having with him that offensive weapon. As a matter of principle it could not be possible for a defendant to argue, once found to have had with him an offensive weapon, that he did not know it was an offensive weapon.

The Act was aimed at eradicating the carrying of dangerous weapons in public. The whole purpose of the Act was to provide strict liability in respect of objects regarded as dangerous.

To allow lack of knowledge to be raised as a reasonable excuse defence defeated the purpose of imposing strict liability in respect of the possession of such a weapon, where the object was an offensive weapon per se. It was not permissible to combine lack of knowledge with an explanation for use of the weapon so as to provide a reasonable excuse.

Solicitors, Crown Prosecution Service, Croydon.

Source: *The Times*, 10 December 1997

Questions

1 What is the maximum punishment under section 1(1) of the Prevention of Crime Act 1953 following:
   a) summary conviction;
   b) conviction on indictment?

2 What is the definition of 'public place' and 'offensive weapon' for the purposes of this Act?

3 What is meant by the phrase 'an offensive weapon per se'?

4 What did Mr Justice Gage say was the aim and purpose of the Act?

STRICT LIABILITY OFFENCES

5 In light of the maximum punishment available on conviction on indictment, do you think it is 'fair' to impose criminal liability on an accused without proof of *mens rea*?

Answers

1 The maximum punishment under section 1(1) of the Prevention of Crime Act 1953 following:

a) summary conviction is imprisonment for a term not exceeding six months or a fine not exceeding the prescribed sum or both;

b) conviction on indictment is imprisonment for a term not exceeding two years or a fine or both.

2 'Public place' and 'offensive weapon' are defined in section 4 of the Act as follows:

public place

– includes any highway and any other premises or place to which at the material time the public have or are permitted to have access, whether on payment or otherwise; and

offensive weapon

– means any article made or adapted for use for causing injury to the person, or intended by the person having it with him for such use by him [or by some other person].

3 In his judgment, Mr Justice Gage said that the baton which was found in the appellant's car was known as an asp which is 'an offensive weapon per se'. This means that the baton is an offensive weapon in its own right, in itself, without the need for adaptation or modification.

4 Mr Justice Gage said that the Act was aimed at eradicating the carrying of dangerous weapons in public and that the whole purpose of the Act was to provide strict liability in respect of objects regarded as dangerous.

5 It would be a defence under section 1(1) of the Act to show that you were carrying the offensive weapon with either lawful authority or with a reasonable excuse. In this case, the appellant was trying to argue that he had a reasonable excuse as he did not actually know that the asp was an offensive weapon. Mr Justice Gage did not accept this line of reasoning because he said that to allow it would be to defeat the whole purpose of imposing strict liability in relation to the possession of such a weapon. Thus, criminal liability was imposed on this defendant by virtue of his commission of the *actus reus* of the offence without *mens rea*. Such strict liability goes against the usual requirement for the imposition of criminal liability, that the prosecution must prove that the accused committed the *actus reus* of the offence in question with the requisite *mens rea*. The reason for this is that when someone is convicted of committing a criminal offence the punishment which may be imposed by the court may be very severe, i.e. loss of liberty, and the person also bears the social stigma of being a convicted criminal. How then can strict liability be justified as it seems grossly unfair to the accused? Possible justifications for the existence of strict liability offences are discussed below in detail. When you have read these you will be able to make up your own mind on the 'fairness' of such liability.

3

Key points on strict liability

▶ While there are a few common law offences of strict liability, such liability usually occurs as provided for in statutes.

▶ Unfortunately, despite the fact that strict liability mainly exists as a statutory creation, it is not always clear whether or not the particular offence is one of strict liability. This is because the drafters of such statutes have not usually explicitly stated that the offence is a strict liability offence. The notable exception to this is the Contempt of Court Act 1981 which specifically refers to the strict liability rule. (See the statutory provisions on page 61.) The problem of whether or not an offence is one of strict liability becomes an issue when the definition of the offence in question does not contain any *mens rea* type words such as 'intentionally', 'recklessly', 'maliciously', 'wilfully', 'knowingly', and so forth. In such a situation how does the magistrate or judge decide whether or not the offence is one of strict liability? They do this according to several factors which are discussed in detail below.

▶ Justifications for the existence of strict liability offences are also discussed in detail below.

Details on strict liability: The factors to be considered in determining whether an offence is a strict liablity offence

Figure 3.1
Identifying a strict
liability offence

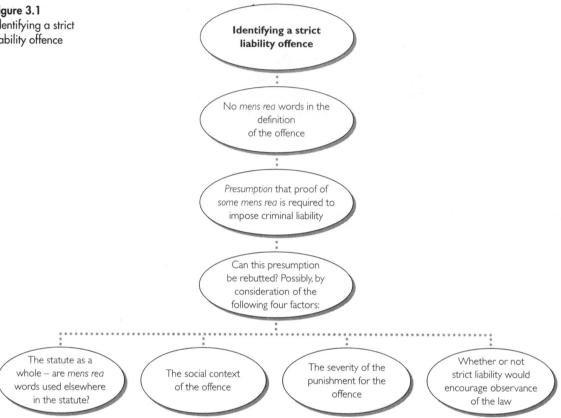

Presumption that proof of some *mens rea* is required to impose criminal liability

If the words in the statute do not explicity state the *mens rea* for the offence in question, magistrates and judges should not automatically presume that the offence is a strict liability offence; rather, they should presume that at least some *mens rea* is required to convict the accused. This was demonstrated in the case of *Sweet* v. *Parsley* (1970). In this case Miss Sweet was convicted of an offence contrary to section 5(b) of the Dangerous Drugs Act 1965, in that she was concerned in the management of premises which were used for the purpose of smoking cannabis. (See the statutory provisions on page 62.) She could not be convicted under section 5(a) of the Act as the smoking of cannabis had taken place in a farmhouse occupied by students who rented rooms from Miss Sweet who lived somewhere else. As such, she was not the occupier of the premises. Nevertheless, she was concerned in the management of the premises. There are no *mens rea* words in section 5(b) of the Act and so the magistrates had to determine whether or not the offence was one of strict liability and they decided that it was. This decision was upheld by the Queen's Bench Divisional Court, but on appeal to the House of Lords the conviction was quashed, as it was held that was not a strict liability offence. Lord Reid stated:

> ... *If this section means what the Divisional Court have held that it means, then hundreds of thousands of people who sublet part of their premises or take in lodgers or are concerned in the management of residential premises or institutions are daily incurring a risk of being convicted of a serious offence in circumstances where they are in no way to blame. For the greatest vigilance cannot prevent tenants, lodgers or inmates or guests whom they bring in from smoking cannabis cigarettes in their own rooms. It was suggested in argument that this appellant brought this conviction on herself because it is found as a fact that when the police searched the premises there were people there of the 'beatnik fraternity'. But surely it would be going a very long way to say that persons managing premises of any kind ought to safeguard themselves by refusing accommodation to all who are of slovenly or exotic appearance, or who bring in guests of that kind. And unfortunately drug taking is by no means confined to those of unusual appearance.*
>
> *Speaking from a rather long experience of membership of both Houses, I assert with confidence that no Parliament within my recollection would have agreed to make an offence of this kind an absolute offence if the matter had been fully explained to it ...*

NB: The Dangerous Drugs Act 1965 was replaced by the Misuse of Drugs Act 1971. The ambiguity created by section 5 of the former Act is avoided in the latter Act because, under section 8 the word 'knowingly' is used as follows: 'a person commits an offence if, being the occupier or concerned in the management of any premises, he *knowingly* permits or suffers any of the following activities to take place on those premises, that is to say – ... (d) smoking cannabis, cannabis resin or prepared opium.'

Consideration of the statute as a whole

Are *mens rea* words used in the statute? They may be used throughout the statute, for example, as in the Theft Act 1968, or they may generally be absent from the statute, for example, as in the Road

Traffic Act 1988 which creates a whole string of strict liability offences. Very rarely the statute will specify that the offence in question is one of strict liability, for example, as in the Contempt of Court Act 1981. The problem for judges and magistrates thus occurs when some sections of an act use *mens rea* words and other sections do not. How should the latter sections be interpreted? The obvious conclusion here is that if the drafters of the statute were mindful to include *mens rea* words in some sections of the statute, then presumably they deliberately left *mens rea* words out of other sections of the statute in order to create strict liability offences in these sections. This was the line of argument used in the case of *Pharmaceutical Society of Great Britain v. Storkwain Ltd* (1986). In this case it was held that section 58(2)(a) of the Medicines Act 1968 did create an offence of strict liability due to the absence of any *mens rea* words, as other sections in the Act did use *mens rea* words. Thus, the pharmacist concerned was guilty of supplying prescription-only drugs to people who had presented him with forged prescriptions (thus the drugs were, in effect, supplied without a prescription) despite the fact that he was in no way at fault as he believed the prescriptions to be legitimate. However, this is not always the approach taken by the courts and it is possible for judges and magistrates to determine that in such circumstances the offence in question does require some type of *mens rea*, as happened in the case of *Sherras* v. *De Rutzen* (1895). In this case a publican's conviction under section 16(2) of the Licensing Act 1872, for unlawfully supplying liquor to a constable on duty, was quashed on appeal. Although other sections of the Act contained *mens rea* words and section 16(2) did not, nevertheless, it was held that some form of *mens rea* was required in order to convict the publican.

Consideration of the social context of the statute

One has to remember that *mens rea* is usually an ingredient of an offence because when someone is convicted of an offence not only do they receive a punishment under the criminal law, but they also have the *stigma* of being labelled a criminal. Such stigma can be devastating for an individual. In this respect, how can the criminal law ever justify the existence of strict liability offences? A way around this problem is to regard some offences as less criminal than others, to regard them as '*quasi-crimes*', for which hardly any stigma is likely to be attached to the convicted person. Such quasi-crimes are typified by road traffic offences where little or no stigma attaches to those found guilty. What is the point of creating such quasi-crimes? If no

3

stigma attaches to the guilty person as the behaviour in question is not really regarded as criminal, why make such behaviour criminal in the first place? It would seem that certain types of behaviour are made quasi-crimes in order to deter such behaviour due to the social consequences of it. Thus, it is for the benefit of society as a whole if road users are encouraged to use the roads responsibly. While there may be little stigma attached to road traffic offences, nevertheless, the threat of accumulation of penalty points on a driver's licence may act as a deterrent to prevent irresponsible driving.

How do the courts determine which offences are to be regarded as quasi-crimes and so suitable for the imposition of strict liability? The courts use two broad tests. First, if the offence applies to specific groups of people only as opposed to everyone in society, then it is more likely that the offence will be regarded as a strict liability offence. Thus, as motoring offences only apply to those who choose to drive, they can be regarded as strict liability offences. Likewise, business people often find themselves subject to strict liability offences concerning the sale of food, the sale of liquor, the sale of drugs or concerning general business practices, as seen in the case of *Pharmaceutical Society of Great Britain* v. *Storkwain* (1986). Second, if the offence exists in an attempt to prevent social danger, then the courts are more likely to regard the offence as a strict liability offence. So, again, motoring offences are generally strict liability offences, as are offences involving the sale of food, drugs and alcohol. Offences concerned with pollution are also regarded as strict liability offences and so, in *Alphacell Ltd* v. *Woodward* (1972) a company was found guilty of *causing* polluted matter to enter a river under section 2(1)(a) of the Rivers (Prevention of Pollution) Act 1951 despite the fact that the company did not know of the pollution. Thus, in this case, the word *causing* did not import any *mens rea*. The words *cause*, *allow* and *permit* are quite often interpreted by the courts as not requiring proof of *mens rea*, particularly as regards road traffic offences, but this is not a definitive state of affairs.

In the *Alphacell* case Lord Salmon said:

> ... *It seems to me that, giving the word 'cause' its ordinary and natural meaning, anyone may cause something to happen intentionally or negligently or inadvertently without negligence and without intention. For example, a man may deliberately smash a porcelain vase; he may handle it so negligently that he drops and smashes it; or he may without negligence slip or stumble against it and smash it. In each of these examples, no less in the last than in the other two, he has caused the destruction of the vase ... The appellants clearly did not cause the pollution intentionally and we*

must assume that they did not do so negligently. Nevertheless, the facts so fully and clearly stated by my noble and learned friend Viscount Dilhorne to my mind make it obvious that the appellants in fact caused the pollution.

Consideration of the severity of punishment for the offence

If the punishment for an offence is not too severe, then it could be argued that this is an indication that the offence is one of strict liability because the offender is not to be regarded as really criminal, only quasi-criminal. On the other hand, if the punishment is quite severe, maybe with a maximum of two to five years' imprisonment, this can also be an indication that the offence is one of strict liability so that it acts as a deterrent to those who are in a postion to cause great social dangers. In other words, the severity of the punishment for an offence cannot be considered in isolation from the other factors which might rebut the presumption of *mens rea*.

Consideration of whether the imposition of strict liability would encourage observance of the law

It is generally the case that strict liability will only be imposed when to do so might encourage others to observe the law. Thus, road traffic offences are strict liability offences as their existence might encourage others to observe the law. In *Alphacell Ltd* v. *Woodward* (1972) the imposition of strict liability on the company might encourage other businesses to take more steps to prevent pollution of rivers. In this case Lord Salmon said:

It is of the utmost public importance that our rivers should not be polluted. The risk of pollution, particularly from the vast and increasing number of riparian industries, is very great. The offences created by the Act of 1951 seem to me to be prototypes of offences which 'are prohibited under penalty' ... If this appeal succeeded and it were held to be the law that no conviction could be obtained under the Act of 1951 unless the prosecution could discharge the often impossible onus of proving that the pollution was caused intentionally or negligently, a great deal of pollution would go unpunished and undeterred to the relief of many riparian factory owners. As a result, many rivers which are now filthy would become filthier still and many rivers which are now clean would lose their cleanliness. The legislature no doubt recognised that as a matter of public policy this would be most unfortunate. Hence section 2(1)(a) which encourages riparian factory owners not only to take reasonable steps to prevent pollution but to do everything possible to ensure that they do not cause it.

It has now been shown that in order to rebut the presumption that some form of *mens rea* is required in an offence when no *mens rea* words are used, the above four factors have to be considered and weighed against each other. While one factor may lead to the offence being an offence of strict liability, another factor might lead to the offence requiring proof of *mens rea*. It is left to the courts to determine.

3

YOU DECIDE

Consider the case below and decide the appeal in light of the foregoing discussion on strict liability offences.

Gammon (Hong Kong) Ltd and Others v. Attorney General of Hong Kong (1954) Privy Council

This case concerned the potential contravention of building regulations in Hong Kong. Under the Hong Kong Building Ordnance, section 40 provides for, among other things, at subsection (2A)(b), prosecution for 'material deviation from an approved plan' and prosecution for 'carrying out works in a manner likely to cause risk of injury or damage'. It has to be remembered that Hong Kong has limited land surface and that buildings tend to be very tall and built close together. During the course of constructing a building, part of it collapsed and it was discovered that this was due to the fact that it was being constructed in a manner which was different (thus a deviation) from the original plans which had been submitted for approval. The construction company was charged under subsections (2A)(b) and (2B)(b), while the project manager and site engineer were charged under subsection (2B)(b). They were convicted at trial on the basis that the offences were strict liability offences and appealed to the Privy Council. On appeal, Lord Scarman, who delivered the judgment of the board, noted the common features of the two subsections. First, they both appeared in section 40 which created several offences; for some of these offences the words made it clear that full *mens rea* was needed but for others it was not clear. Second, each had a maximum penalty of a fine of $250,000 and imprisonment for three years.

Decide the appeal and give reasons for your decision.

Answer

The appeal was dismissed, the convictions upheld. Lord Scarman said:

. . . the only situation in which the presumption [that mens rea must be proven] can be displaced is where the statute is concerned with an issue of social concern; public safety is such an issue; . . . even where a statute is concerned with such an issue, the presumption of mens rea stands unless it can also be shown that the creation of strict liability will be effective to promote the objects of the statute by encouraging greater vigilance to prevent the commission of the prohibited act . . . [and] . . . the legislature by enacting . . . section 40 of the ordnance clearly took the view that criminal liability and punishment were needed as a deterrent against slipshod or incompetent supervision, control or execution of building works. The impostion of strict liability for some offences clearly would emphasise to those concerned the need for high standards of care in the supervision and execution of work. The view that their Lordships have reached, after the thorough review of the ordnance and history . . . is that, . . . it is consistent with the purpose of the ordnance in its regulation of the works to which it applies that at least some of the criminal offences which it creates should be of strict liability. It is a statute the subject matter of which may properly be described as – 'the regulation of a particular activity involving potential danger to public health [and] safety . . . in which citizens have a choice whether they participate or not . . .'

He also said that while the severe maximum penalties appeared to present a 'formidable argument' against strict liability, nevertheless, severe penalties were not, in this instance, inconsistent with strict liability.

Justifications for strict liability offences

Is it acceptable to have quasi-crimes? As previously mentioned, behaviour which may amount to a quasi-crime is not really *criminal* behaviour in the true sense. Surely such quasi-crimes can only be justified if:

i they achieve the desired result;

ii there is no alternative way to achieve the desired result.

What is the desired result? Why do we have these quasi-crimes? The justification for these strict liability offences can be considered in light of two of the previous headings used to decide if the presumption of *mens rea* can be rebutted, that is, the social context of the behaviour in question and whether the imposition of strict liability encourages observance of the law.

Social context of the behaviour

Here the imposition of strict liability is said to be justified in order to protect society from social dangers. Thus, society has to be protected from the social dangers of dangerous motorists, shop keepers selling unhygienic foodstuffs, companies polluting the environment during their manufacturing processes, and so forth. Does this argument stand up to close scrutiny? Maybe not. One problem centres on the fact that the prosecution only have to prove the *actus reus* of the offence concerned, as the *mens rea* is irrelevant. However, the *mens rea* *should* be relevant. While one accused may have been totally blameless (for example, the company which had taken all reasonable precautions to prevent pollution of nearby rivers), another accused may have been very blameworthy (for example, the company which totally disregarded the dangers of polluting nearby rivers . The latter company is unlikely to be worried about a conviction for a criminal offence if the offence carries no social stigma (as trade will not suffer) and carries a relatively small penalty (a fine) which may well be regarded as one of the costs of production. On such reasoning, strict liability offences do not achieve their aim of protecting society from social dangers. The same reasoning can be applied to the other groups targeted by strict liability offences, such as motorists and shop keepers. The existence of the strict liability offence cannot help to protect society from a danger which results *despite* the endeavours of the conscientious person to avoid such a danger. Some aspects of human behaviour cannot be avoided.

Do strict liability offences encourage observance of the law?

Many strict liability offences are regulatory in nature, for instance road traffic offences and those concerning food on sale and display in shops/restaurants, and these often carry low penalties. As such, it is unlikely that these offences deter people from committing them, especially as the chances of being detected are low. How many times do you see motorists speeding or going through red traffic lights, or food displayed uncovered on counters in shops? If such behaviour is to be deemed criminal then surely it would be more appropriate to include an element of *mens rea* in the offence?

While this seems obvious, nevertheless, the practicalities of life take over. There are millions of motorists in the UK and it would be impractal to take every offending motorist through the criminal courts if the prosecution had to prove the *mens rea* part of the offence. The courts simply could not cope with such a workload. Thus, for the sake of administrative efficiency, and as these are regarded as regulatory offences, the requirement of proving *mens rea* is dispensed with. It is a strange argument: the behaviour needs to be discouraged, but it is too expensive to the criminal justice system to make the behaviour a full crime, thus the behaviour is regarded as a quasi-crime, usually with a low penalty for which there is little or no social stigma. The net result is often the paying of a fine by the convicted individual.

With regards to the Alpahcell case, Lord Salmon stated his hope that the strict liability offence in question would *'encourage riparian factory owners not only to take reasonable steps to prevent pollution but to do everything possible to ensure that they do not cause it'*. However, the lack of stigma and the lack of real penalty will not deter those companies who put profitability before pollution of the environment.

Thus, it would appear that the usual justifications for strict liability offences have severe weaknesses. The offences do not always achieve their aim and it is possible to think of alternatives. For instance, it might be more appropriate to import some *mens rea* into these offences, if only that of negligence, as for careless driving under section 3 of the Road Traffic Act 1988.

Applying principles to examination questions

The topic of strict liability is not particularly exciting and examination questions tend to be essay-type questions which ask for a critical analysis of whether there should be offences of strict liability. In order to avoid such a mundane approach, consider the hypothetical statute shown below and answer the question. Note down your initial thoughts and add to these after you have looked back through the chapter, adding cases where appropriate. You should then consider the suggested approach to this question which follows before you attempt to write your essay. By considering the topic in this manner it is hoped that you will be able to remember the information more readily for the examination.

Should judges interpret sections 4 and 5 below as offences requiring proof of *mens rea* or as offences of strict liability?

EARTH (INTEGRITY) ACT 2020

An act to preserve the integrity of Earth by restricting the access of non-terrestrials

1–3 Words, words, words

4 A being from outer space (henceforth 'alien') which lands on Earth without permission shall be guilty of an offence.

5 An alien which causes pollution of Earth shall be guilty of an offence.

6–24 Words, words, words.

25 An alien which knowingly transmits unauthorised messages from Earth shall be guilty of an offence.

26 An alien guilty of an offence under section 4 or section 5 of this Act shall, on conviction on indictment, be liable to imprisonment for a term not exceeding 10 years.

Tips on how to approach such a question

Should judges interpret sections 4 and 5 below as offences requiring proof of *mens rea* or as offences of strict liability?

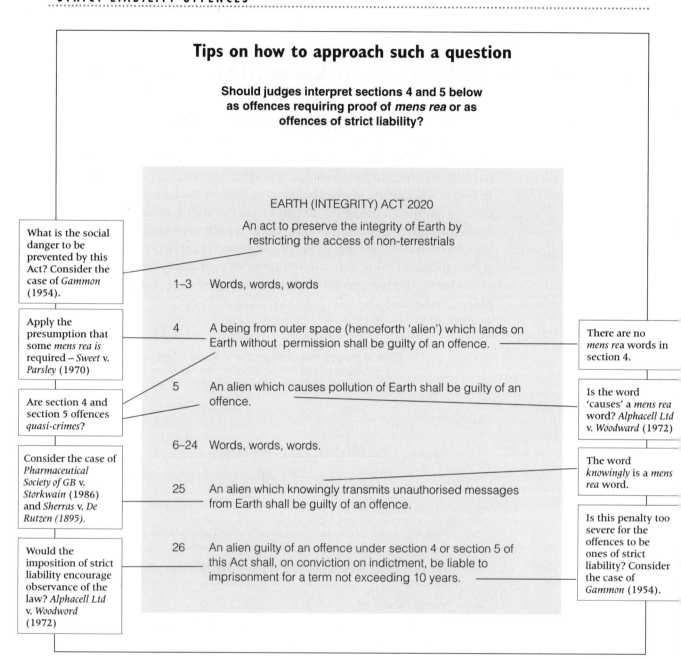

EARTH (INTEGRITY) ACT 2020

An act to preserve the integrity of Earth by restricting the access of non-terrestrials

What is the social danger to be prevented by this Act? Consider the case of *Gammon* (1954).

Apply the presumption that some *mens rea* is required – *Sweet* v. *Parsley* (1970)

Are section 4 and section 5 offences *quasi-crimes*?

Consider the case of *Pharmaceutical Society of GB* v. *Storkwain* (1986) and *Sherras* v. *De Rutzen* (1895).

Would the imposition of strict liability encourage observance of the law? *Alphacell Ltd* v. *Woodword* (1972)

1–3   Words, words, words

4   A being from outer space (henceforth 'alien') which lands on Earth without permission shall be guilty of an offence.

5   An alien which causes pollution of Earth shall be guilty of an offence.

6–24   Words, words, words.

25   An alien which knowingly transmits unauthorised messages from Earth shall be guilty of an offence.

26   An alien guilty of an offence under section 4 or section 5 of this Act shall, on conviction on indictment, be liable to imprisonment for a term not exceeding 10 years.

There are no *mens rea* words in section 4.

Is the word 'causes' a *mens rea* word? *Alphacell Ltd* v. *Woodward* (1972)

The word *knowingly* is a *mens rea* word.

Is this penalty too severe for the offences to be ones of strict liability? Consider the case of *Gammon* (1954).

Proposals for reform

In *Crime and the Criminal Law (2nd ed, 1981)* Baroness Wootton suggested that all offences should be made strict liability when she said:

> ... *If, however, the primary function of the courts is conceived as the prevention of forbidden acts, there is little cause to be disturbed by the multiplication of offences of strict liability. If the law says that certain things are not to be done, it is illogical to confine this prohibition to occasions on which they are done from malice aforethought: for at least the material consequences of an action, and the reasons for prohibiting it, are the same whether it is the result of sinister malicious plotting, of negligence or of sheer accident.*

However, this is not the usual view of how the criminal law should be developed as the criminal law is concerned not only with the occurrence of prohibited conduct, but also with the blameworthiness of the accused. Indeed, in 1978 the Law Commission proposed a Criminal Liability (Mental Element) Bill in which it was stated that for all Acts enacted after the passing of the Bill there would be a presumption that offences had to have *mens rea* and if Parliament intended an offence to be one of strict liability or negligence then this should be expressly stated. This would avoid the necessity of judges and magistrates having to determine whether or not an offence was one of strict liability as they do, only not particularly consistently, at present. In other words, there would be more certainty in the law.

CHAPTER Summary

In this chapter the notion of strict liability has been considered in terms of when such offences are deemed to exist and their justification. The topic is best studied after consideration of Chapter 2, on *mens rea*. Most examination questions on strict liability take the form of essay questions which require the student to explain and comment on the existence of such offences. There is sufficient material in this chapter to prepare students for such questions.

Offences against property:

The following topics are covered in this section:

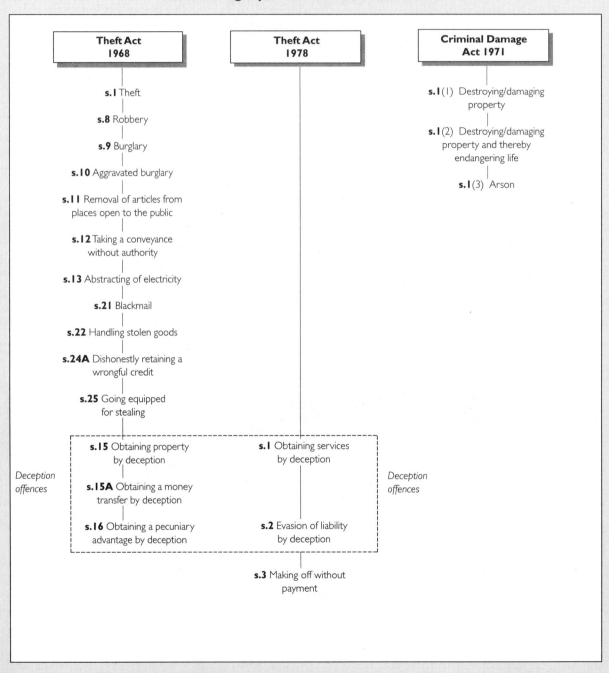

Theft Act 1968	**Theft Act 1978**	**Criminal Damage Act 1971**

Theft Act 1968

s.1 Theft

s.8 Robbery

s.9 Burglary

s.10 Aggravated burglary

s.11 Removal of articles from places open to the public

s.12 Taking a conveyance without authority

s.13 Abstracting of electricity

s.21 Blackmail

s.22 Handling stolen goods

s.24A Dishonestly retaining a wrongful credit

s.25 Going equipped for stealing

Deception offences

s.15 Obtaining property by deception

s.15A Obtaining a money transfer by deception

s.16 Obtaining a pecuniary advantage by deception

Theft Act 1978

s.1 Obtaining services by deception

Deception offences

s.2 Evasion of liability by deception

s.3 Making off without payment

Criminal Damage Act 1971

s.1(1) Destroying/damaging property

s.1(2) Destroying/damaging property and thereby endangering life

s.1(3) Arson

Theft and Related offences

OVERVIEW

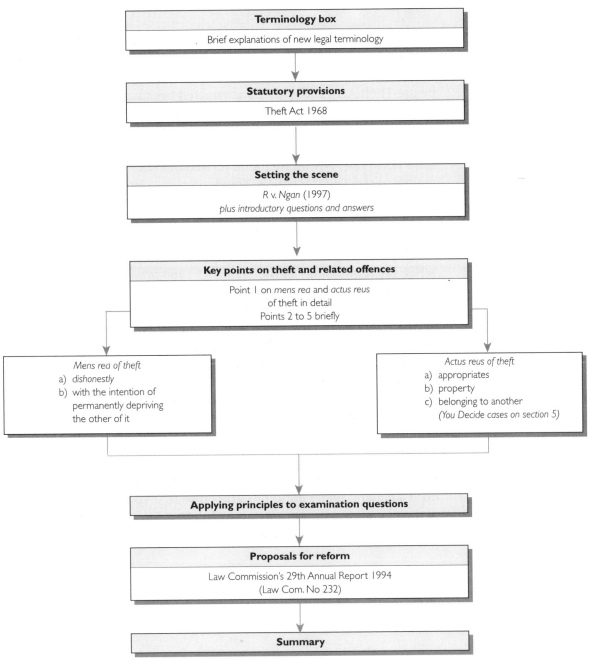

Terminology box

Brief explanations of new legal terminology

↓

Statutory provisions

Theft Act 1968

↓

Setting the scene

R v. Ngan (1997)
plus introductory questions and answers

↓

Key points on theft and related offences

Point 1 on *mens rea* and *actus reus*
of theft in detail
Points 2 to 5 briefly

Mens rea of theft
a) dishonestly
b) with the intention of
   permanently depriving
   the other of it

Actus reus of theft
a) appropriates
b) property
c) belonging to another
   (You Decide cases on section 5)

Applying principles to examination questions

↓

Proposals for reform

Law Commission's 29th Annual Report 1994
(Law Com. No 232)

↓

Summary

Having considered the general notion that most crimes comprise two main elements, *mens rea* and *actus reus*, you are now ready to look at substantive crimes in detail. We will start with theft as most people have a reasonable understanding of what amounts to theft, and the statutory definition of theft lends itself to division into *actus reus* and *mens rea*. The aim of this chapter is to help you understand the basic offence of theft. Later we will revisit theft at a more advanced level by incorporating other factors such as defences, accomplices and attempts.

The Theft Act 1968 was intended to codify the law regarding most property offences and also to improve on the law in this area as provided for by the Larceny Acts of 1861 and 1916. It was followed by the Theft Act 1978 which was enacted because of problems with section 16(2)(a) of the 1968 Theft Act. The 1978 Act, which created two new deception offences and another offence, is only three pages long so, arguably, its provisions could have been inserted into the 1968 Act. Thus, law on theft and related offences is to be found mainly in the Theft Act 1968. The deception offences included in the 1968 Act and in the 1978 Act will be considered in a separate chapter.

(NB: the Theft Acts 1968 and 1978 do not cover forgery or criminal damage.)

While the terminology in the Theft Act 1968 may appear to be straightforward and not too technical, a lot of time is taken up in the criminal courts arguing over the interpretation of words. This stems from the fact that many of the words and underlying concepts in theft are based on 'civil' law notions. (For example, how can you say that someone has stolen something from someone else unless you can show that the wronged person actually owned or possessed the thing in the first place?) There is also a tendency for judges to leave some words in the Act for the jury to interpret (which means that from case to case, there is less chance of consistency in meaning to be attributed to a word).

In the terminology box I have included those words of which you will need a general understanding early on so that you can make the most of the rest of the chapter. Read the brief explanations now and refer back to the box as you progress through the chapter.

T E R M I N O L O G Y: Theft

Property   You have probably come across this word with reference to some tangible item (such as a textbook) which 'belongs' to you – it is your property, you 'own' it. In the course of this chapter you will find that it is also possible to own things which are intangible, such as a right to draw money out of a bank account. The Theft Act 1968 section 4 provides a definition of what amounts to property for the purposes of the Act. (See below.)

Real property   Is mentioned in the Theft Act 1968 section 4(1). Real property essentially refers to the ownership of land and any buildings on the land.

Personal property   Is also mentioned in the Theft Act 1968 section 4(1). Personal property refers to property other than real property; thus, it covers tangible property such as your jacket or school bag, and it also covers intangible property such as your *right* to draw money out of your bank account. Intangible personal properties are referred to as 'things in action' or 'choses in action'. This is because you are unable to possess them physically; the only way you can protect them is by bringing a legal action in court; for instance, you might sue someone for a debt owed to you.

Appropriates   In ordinary usage one would say that appropriation means to take something or to take something away. In the Theft Act 1968 the word 'appropriates' means much more than this.

Title   When someone is said to have title in something, it means that they own the thing in question.

Proprietary right   If you own, say, a shop, you are known as the proprietor of the shop. Thus, if you have a proprietary right to something, you have the rights of the owner with regards to the 'something'.

4

Statutory provisions

The statutory provision in this chapter is quite lengthy and should be consulted as required when studying the appropriate topic within the chapter.

Theft Act 1968

Basic definition of theft

1 Statutory provisions for theft as per sections 1–7

1 (1) A person is guilty of theft if he dishonestly appropriates property belonging to another with the intention of permanently depriving the other of it; and 'thief' and 'steal' shall be construed accordingly.

(2) It is immaterial whether the appropriation is made with a view to gain, or is made for the thief's own benefit.

(3) The five following sections of this Act shall have effect as regards the interpretation and operation of this section (and, except as otherwise provided by this Act, shall apply for purposes of this section).

Dishonestly

2 (1) A person's appropriation of property belonging to another is not to be regarded as dishonest –

(a) if he appropriates the property in the belief that he has in law the right to deprive the other of it, on behalf of himself or of a third person; or

(b) if he appropriates the property in the belief that he would have the other's consent if the other knew of the appropriation and the circumstances of it; or

(c) (except where the property came to him as trustee or personal representative) if he appropriates the property in the belief that the person to whom the property belongs cannot be discovered by taking reasonable steps.

(2) A person's appropriation of property belonging to another may be dishonest notwithstanding that he is willing to pay for the property.

Appropriates

3 (1) Any assumption by a person of the rights of an owner amounts to an appropriation, and this includes, where he has come by the property (innocently or not) without stealing it, any later assumption of a right to it by keeping or dealing with it as owner.

(2) Where property or a right or interest in property is or purports to be transferred for value to a person acting in good faith, no later assumption by him of rights which he believed himself to be acquiring shall, by reason of any defect in the transferor's title, amount to theft of the property.

Property

4 (1) 'Property' includes money and all other property, real or personal, including things in action and other intangible property.

(2) A person cannot steal land, or things forming part of land and severed from it by him or by his directions, except in the following cases, that is to say –

(a) when he is a trustee or personal representative ....; or

(b) when he is not in possession of the land and appropriates anything forming part of the land by severing it or causing it to be severed, or after it has been severed; or

(c) when, being in possession of the land under a tenancy, he appropriates the whole or any part of any fixture or structure let to be used with the land.

(3) A person who picks mushrooms growing wild on any land, or who picks flowers, fruit or foliage from a plant growing wild on any land, does not (although not in possession of the land) steal what he picks, unless he does it for reward or for sale or other commercial purpose. For the purpose of this subsection 'mushroom' includes any fungus, and 'plant' includes any shrub or tree.

Belonging to another

5 (1) Property shall be regarded as belonging to any person having possession or control of it, or having in it any proprietary right or interest (not an equitable interest arising only from an agreement to transfer or grant an interest).

(3) Where a person receives property from or on account of another, and is under an obligation to the other to retain and deal with that property or its proceeds in a particular way, the property or proceeds shall be regarded (as against him) as belonging to the other.

(4) Where a person gets property by another's mistake, and is under an obligation to make restoration (in whole or in part) of the property or its proceeds or of the value thereof, then to the extent of that obligation the property or proceeds shall be regarded (as against him) as belonging to the person entitled to restoration, and an intention not to make restoration shall be regarded accordingly as an intention to deprive that person of the property or proceeds.

With the intention of permanently depriving the other of it

6 (1) A person appropriating property belonging to another without meaning the other permanently to lose the thing itself is nevertheless to be regarded as having the intention of permanently depriving the other of it if his intention is to treat the thing as his own to dispose of regardless of the other's rights; and a borrowing or lending of it may amount to so treating it if, but only if, the borrowing or lending is for a period and in circumstances making it equivalent to an outright taking or disposal.

Theft

7 A person guilty of theft shall on conviction on indictment be liable to imprisonment for a term not exceeding seven years.

2 Statutory provisions for the removal of articles from places open to the public as per section 11:

11 (1) Subject to subsections (2) and (3) below, where the public have access to a building or part of it, or a collection or part of a collection housed in it, any person who without lawful authority removes from the building or its grounds the whole or part of any article displayed or kept for display to the public in the building or that part of it or in its grounds shall be guilty of an offence. For this purpose 'collection' includes a collection got together for a temporary purpose, but references in this section to a collection do not apply to a collection made or exhibited for the purpose of effecting sales or other commercial dealings.

(3) A person does not commit an offence under this section if he believes that he has lawful authority for the removal of the thing in question or that he would have it if the person entitled to give it knew of the removal and the circumstances of it.

3 Statutory provisions for taking a motor vehicle or other conveyance without authority as per section 12:

12 (1) Subject to subsections (5) and (6) below, a person shall be guilty of an offence if, without having the consent of the owner or other lawful authority, he takes any conveyance for his own or another's use or, knowing that any conveyance has been taken without such authority, drives it or allows himself to be carried in or on it.

(2) A person guilty of an offence under subsection (1) above shall be liable on conviction to a fine not exceeding level 5 on the standard scale, to imprisonment for a term not exceeding six months, or both.

(6) A person does not commit an offence under this section by anything done in the belief that he has lawful authority to do it or that he would have the owner's consent if the owner knew of his doing it and the circumstances of it.

(7) For purposes of this section –
    (a) 'conveyance' means any conveyance constructed or adapted for the carriage of a person or persons whether by land, water, or air . . .

4 Statutory provisions for the abstraction of electricity as per section 13:

13 A person who dishonestly uses without due authority, or dishonestly causes to be wasted or diverted, any electricity shall on conviction on indictment be liable to imprisonment for a term not exceeding five years.

5   Statutory provisions for handling stolen goods as per section 22:

22 (1) A person handles stolen goods if (otherwise than in the course of the stealing) knowing or believing them to be stolen goods he dishonestly receives the goods, or dishonestly undertakes or assists in their retention, removal, disposal or realisation by or for the benefit of another person, or if he arranges to do so.

(2) A person guilty of handling stolen goods shall on conviction on indictment be liable to imprisonment for a term not exceeding fourteen years.

6   Statutory provisions for going equipped for stealing as per section 25:

25 (1) A person shall be guilty of an offence if, when not at his place of abode, he has with him any article for use in the course of or in connection with any burglary, theft or cheat.

(2) A person guilty of an offence under this section shall on conviction on indictment be liable to imprisonment for a term not exceeding three years.

(3) Where a person is charged with an offence under this section, proof that he had with him any article made or adapted for use in committing a burglary, theft or cheat shall be evidence that he had it with him for such use.

4

Setting the scene

Read the case overleaf and answer the questions which follow. Read all of the case before you attempt to answer the questions.

Appropriation outwith jurisdiction

July 24 1997
Court of Appeal
Regina v. Ngan
Before Lord Justice Leggatt, Mr Justice lan Kennedy and Mr Justice Collins
[Judgment July 11]

A person who, knowing that money had been mistakenly paid into her bank account in England, signed blank cheques on that account and sent them to her sister in Scotland, did not in so doing commit an act of appropriation within the jurisdiction.

She was, however, guilty of an offence against English law when one of the cheques which necessarily drew upon the mistaken credit balance was brought back to England and presented for payment there. The act of theft was the presentation of the cheque.

The Court of Appeal, Criminal Division, so held when allowing in part the appeal of Sui Soi Ngan against her conviction by a majority on December 19, 1996 at Southwark Crown Court (Judge Laurie and a jury) of three counts of theft.

Conviction on two of the counts, relating to cheques which were presented in Scotland, were quashed. Her appeal against conviction on the third count, which related to a cheque presented for payment in England, was dismissed. Her appeal against a sentence of two years detention in a young offender institution was allowed and a sentence of 15 months was substituted.

Section 3 of the Theft Act 1968 provides: "(1) Any assumption by a person of the rights of an owner amounts to an appropriation, and this includes, where he has come by the property (innocently or not) without stealing it, any later assumption of a right to it by keeping or dealing with it as owner."

Ms Lauren Soertsz, assigned by the Registrar of Criminal Appeals, for the appellant: Mr Peter Gray for the Crown.

LORD JUSTICE LEGGATT, giving the reserved judgment of the court, said that the outcome of the appeal depended upon whether or not, as an ingredient of the thefts, the appellant had committed an act of appropriation within the jurisdiction.

As a condition of her employment she opened an account on August 11, 1995 with a London branch of Barclays Bank. The account number allocated to her had previously been that of a debt collection agency.

Several payments intended for the agency were paid into the account by mistake, amounting to a total of £77,767.25p. Payments were also made for the credit of the account from the appellant's employers and small withdrawals were made from time to time not exceeding the latter credit balance.

Between September 25 and October 9, 1995 cheques were presented for payment in the respective sums of £29,000, £16,000 and £10,000. They were paid because the mistake was not discovered until November 8, 1995.

The appellant when interviewed said that she had signed the blank cheques and sent them to her sister in Glasgow, who had known that she had received the extra money. Two cheques had been presented for payment in Glasgow and the third in Peterborough.

The trial judge rejected a submission of no case to answer made on the ground that no offence had been committed within the jurisdiction.

He viewed the thefts as a joint enterprise between the appellant and her sister and regarded the appropriation as having taken place in this country because the account, the chose in action and the paying bank were all situated in England. However, his reason for that conclusion was wrong: see *R v Governor of Pentonville Prison, Ex parte Osman* ([1990]1 WLR 277).

On each of the three counts the appellant was charged with stealing a chose in action, namely a credit balance belonging to the debt collecting agency. Since it could not be disputed that the appellant had acted dishonestly, it was common ground that she was guilty of theft if the offence had been committed within the jurisdiction.

The question therefore was a simple one: was there any act within the jurisdiction which amounted to an assumption by the appellant of the rights of the owner?

Applying the principle set out in *Osman* (at p294) to the present case, the act of theft was the presentation of the cheque. Until then no right as against the bank had been exercised.

All that had occurred beforehand, including the signing of the cheques. had been preparatory acts. She who supplied the signed, blank cheques, which she knew were to be used to steal from the debt collecting agency, was an aider and abettor of the thefts, even though she was in England when the cheques were presented in Scotland.

As such, she would be liable to be convicted as a principal in relation to a substantive offence committed in Scotland, Viewed as a joint enterprise, that was where it was effectuated. If would not be enough to give the English court jurisdiction that her part in the theft was carried out in England: compare *R* v. *Tomsett* ([1985] Crim LR 369).

When the appellant sent the cheques in blank to her sister, she intended to appropriate such sums as her sister proved to insert into any of the cheques that she used. The appropriation was inchoate.

In their Lordships' judgment, no right was assumed to the part of the appellant's credit balance that was not hers until a cheque was presented for payment in a sum which necessarily drew upon the mistaken credit balance. That represented an assertion of a right adverse to the debt collecting agency to have the cheque met by the bank.

The result was that on the two occasions that a cheque was presented in Scotland no offence was committed within the jurisdiction, but an offence was committed when the third cheque was presented in Peterborough.

When section 2(1) of the Criminal Justice Act 1993 came into force it would render irrelevant where any act occurred proof of which was required for conviction of theft. Meanwhile the appellant was acquitted on counts 1 and 2 of the indictment and her appeal dismissed in relation to count 3.

Solicitors: Crown Prosecution Service, Southwark.

Source: *The Times* 24 July 1997

Questions

1   How many legal systems are there in the United Kingdom?

2   Which one are you studying for A-level law?

3   Why is a crime committed in Scotland not within the jurisdiction of the English courts?

4   Where and when was the case originally tried? Which judge was presiding?

5   Approximately how much time elapsed between the commission of the offences and the original trial?

6   Approximately how much time elapsed between the original trial and the hearing of the appeal?

7   Sui Soi Ngan was originally convicted of 'three counts of theft'. What is meant by a 'count' of theft?

8   Why were her convictions on two of the counts quashed on appeal?

9   Why was the conviction on the third count upheld?

10   What is a 'reserved' judgment of the Court of Appeal?

11   In the case report it says that the appellant was charged with stealing a 'chose in action'. How is this explained in the case?

12 Lord Justice Leggatt said, *'The question therefore was a simple one; was there any act within the jurisdiction which amounted to an assumption by the appellant of the rights of the owner?'* With relation to the Theft Act 1968, why is this an appropriate question to address?

13 Does this mean that Sui Soi Ngan has 'got away' with the theft of money from the debt collection agency with regard to the cheques presented in Scotland by her sister?

(When you have studied Chapter 7, on accomplices, re-read this case, paying particular attention to the last two paragraphs in the third column and on page 86, dealing with the issues of aiding and abetting and principal offenders.)

Answers

1 There are three legal systems within the United Kingdom: one for England and Wales, one for Scotland and one for Northern Ireland.

2 For A-level law you are studying the English Legal System which only applies to England and Wales.

3 A crime committed in Scotland is not within the jurisdiction of the English courts because, generally, English courts only have jurisdiction (authority to deal with an issue) in respect of matters which arise within England and Wales. A crime committed in Scotland will have to be dealt with by the Scottish courts.

4 The case was originally tried in Southwark Crown Court and the verdict was returned on 19 December 1996. The presiding judge was Judge Laurie.

5 The offences were committed between September 25 and October 9 1995 but they were not discovered until November 8 1995. Thus, there was approximately one year between the commission/detection of the crimes and the first trial. What does this tell us about the speed of the criminal justice process? Surely, in the interests of justice, alleged wrongdoers should be brought to trial as soon as possible after the commission of the alleged offence. Then if the person is found guilty, the punishment will follow soon after the crime and the offender can relate the punishment to the crime. On the other hand, if the alleged wrongdoer is eventually found to be not guilty is it appropriate that he has had a cloud of doubt over his head for such a long time? Students should refer to Section Seven which deals with the review of delay in the criminal justice system.

6 We are told that the judgment of the Court of Appeal was given on 11 July 1997 which means that there was a delay of approximately seven months between the original trial and the appeal hearing. Such a length of time delays the criminal justice process even further.

7 When a case is to be heard before the Crown Court the matters which are to be considered are presented on a document called an indictment, hence the phrase 'trial on indictment'. The offence or offences with which the defendant has been charged are listed on this indictment as 'counts'. Thus, the indictment may contain one or several counts. In the case of *R* v. *Ngan* (1997) the indictment would probably have looked something like the one shown in Figure 4.1.

4

Figure 4.1

INDICTMENT

No ....

The Crown Court at Southwark

The Queen v. SUI NGAN

SUI NGAN is charged as follows

COUNT ONE

Statement of Offence

THEFT contrary to Section 1(1) of the Theft Act 1968.

Particulars of Offence
Sui Ngan, on the 25th day of September 1995, stole a credit balance
of £29,000 from the debt collection agency by presentation of a
cheque for payment.

Date: November 1995   An Officer of the Crown Court

COUNT TWO

Statement of Offence

THEFT contrary to Section 1(1) of the Theft Act 1968

(*and so on*)

---

8   Her conviction on the two counts relating to theft by presentation of cheques in Glasgow by her sister was quashed because it was decided that the thefts took place at the moment the cheques were presented for payment. As these two cheques were presented in Glasgow, the crime of theft was committed in Scotland and English courts do not have jurisdiction to deal with matters which arise outside of England and Wales.

9   The conviction on the third count was upheld because this related to the cheque which was presented in Peterborough which is within the jurisdiction of the English Courts.

10   When the Court of Appeal gives a reserved judgment this means that the judges retired to consider the appeal and the judgment was delivered later.

11   In the case report, in column three, the chose in action is described as the credit balance belonging to the debt collecting agency; this is what Sui Ngan was alleged to have stolen.

12   This is an appropriate question to address because, as stated in column one of the case report, section 3 of the Theft Act 1968 provides:

> *'(1) Any assumption by a person of the rights of an owner amounts to an appropriation, and this includes, where he has come by the property (innocently or not) without stealing it, any later assumption of a right to it by keeping or dealing with it as owner.'*

13   The fact that acts in Scotland are outside the jurisdiction of the English courts does not necessarily mean that Sui Soi Ngan has 'got away' with a crime. She will probably be dealt with under the Scottish criminal justice system as an aider and abettor. (Her sister actually presented the cheques and so stole the credit balance but Sui Ngan aided and abetted this crime – see Chapter 7, on accomplices.)

Key points on theft and related offences

The topics covered in this chapter are:

Theft Act 1968:

▶ Theft, section 1;

▶ Taking a motor vehicle or other conveyance without authority, section 12;

▶ Abstracting electricity, section 13;

▶ Handling stolen goods, section 22;

▶ Going equipped for stealing, section 25.

▶ Theft is defined in section 1, Theft Act 1968 as follows: '*A person is guilty of theft if he dishonestly appropriates property belonging to another with the intention of permanently depriving the other of it …*'. The *actus reus* of theft comprises the 'appropriation' of 'property' which 'belongs to another' and these three aspects will be dealt with in detail below. The *mens rea* of theft comprises 'dishonestly' and the 'intention of permanently depriving the other of it' and these two aspects will also be dealt with in detail below.

▶ Taking a motor vehicle or other conveyance without authority, as set out in section 12 of the Theft Act 1968, is aimed at 'joyriding', whereby a conveyance, usually a car, is taken, usually by youths, for a ride and then abandoned. If the car is abandoned it is usually possible for it to be recovered and given back to the owner and this makes it difficult to convict the taker of theft as it is difficult to prove that he intended to permanently deprive the owner of it; he would argue that he only intended to deprive the owner of it temporarily. Note that it is not only the original taker of the car who may be liable under this section. If someone knows the car has been taken without authority and subsequently drives it or allows himself to be a passenger in it, then he may also be liable. If someone merely uses the car to sleep in or to shelter from the weather, then they are not liable under this section as they have not actually 'taken' the car anywhere, they have just 'used' the car while stationary. It is not only vehicles for use on roads that can be taken as boats and aircraft may also be taken without authority.

▶ Under section 13 of the Theft Act 1968 a person may be guilty if he dishonestly 'uses' any electricity without authority, such as cooking on a neighbour's cooker when the neighbour is away, or if he dishonestly causes any electricity to be wasted or diverted. In the latter case the offender does not necessarily benefit from the wasting or diversion; the purpose might be to divert electricity for the benefit of someone else or to waste the electricity of someone else, for instance, by leaving the lights on in a building when the owners are away.

▶ In section 22(1) of the Theft Act 1968 an attempt is made to differentiate between the actual thief who steals goods and the person who handles the stolen goods. This is done by inclusion of the phrase in brackets, 'otherwise than in the course of the stealing'. It is of course possible for a thief to be a handler as well if, after the theft, he then handles the goods according to the definition in section 22(1). What you must note in such a case is that the retention, removal, disposal or realisation of the stolen goods must be for the benefit of another person.

▶ If a person has a crow bar under his jacket and has it there to assist in the commission of a burglary, theft (which includes taking a conveyance without consent for this section) or cheat (a deception offence under section 15 of this Act), then so long as that person is not at his place of abode, he may be liable under section 25 of the Theft Act 1968 for going 'equipped for stealing'. A crow bar is possibly an obvious example of an 'article' which might be used in connection with a burglary etc., but less obvious articles can fall under this section. The test would seem to be whether or not the person has the article with him only because he is going to use it to commit, or in connection with, a burglary etc. Thus, a ladder could be an article for this section, as could a pair of gloves which might be used to avoid leaving fingerprints, or a piece of lead piping. A person's place of abode probably includes his garage, shed and garden so, once he goes beyond these areas, he could fall within the scope of this section. (See the 'You Decide' cases which follow.)

YOU DECIDE

Study the three cases shown below and decide whether or not the appellant would have his appeal against conviction for going equipped to steal, contrary to section 25 of the the Theft Act 1968, allowed or dismissed. The answers are shown below.

4

1 *R v. Ellames* (1974)

After a robbery had taken place, E disposed of a bag containing articles used in the robbery, including a sawn-off shotgun and ammonia in spray containers. He was charged under section 25, Theft Act. The judge directed that the fact that the theft was over did not prevent him from having the articles for the purpose of theft. E was convicted and appealed.

You decide the appeal.

2 *R v. Goodwin* (1996)

In this case the defendant used Kenyan 5 shilling coins to play gaming machines in an amusement arcade. These coins are the same shape, size and weight of a British 50 pence piece and are worth about half as much. He was convicted of going equipped to steal under the Theft Act and appealed.

You decide the appeal.

3 *R v. Lester and Byast* (1955)

L and B were convicted of being found by night having in their possession implements of housebreaking. Most of the implements were found in the boot of a car owned and driven by B, but some were found on B's person. L was a passenger in the car. The police had seen both L and B in the act of stealing petrol from another car, but there was no evidence of joint participation on their part in any enterprise of house-breaking. Both were convicted (of the equivalent of going equipped to steal) contrary to section 28 of the Larceny Act 1916* and appealed.

You decide the appeal.

Answers

1 Appeal allowed; conviction quashed; the articles found on a person must be intended for use in the course of or in connection with some future burglary, theft or cheat.

2 Appeal dismissed; conviction upheld.

3 Byast's appeal was dismissed; conviction upheld but Lester's appeal was allowed; conviction quashed as there was not enough evidence to show that he was *in possession* of the articles, he was merely a passenger in a car in which there were house-breaking articles.

* The Theft Acts 1968 and 1978 replaced the Larceny Act 1916; for more details see proposals for reform on page 114.

A detailed look at theft

Theft can be analysed in terms of *actus reus* and *mens rea* as shown below:

▶ *Actus reus*
   i appropriation of
   ii property
   iii belonging to another

▶ *Mens rea*
   iv dishonestly
   v with the intention of permenently depriving the other of it

In order to find someone guilty of theft the prosecution has to prove all five aspects of the *actus reus* and *mens rea* of the crime. Thus, while a person may have appropriated an item belonging to someone else, the appropriation will not amount to theft of the item unless all the other four aspects of the crime can also be proved. Despite the fact that the Theft Act 1968 helps with the definition of these five aspects of theft, nevertheless, there is considerable case law which elaborates on the definitions. We will look first at the *actus reus* of theft and then at the *mens rea*. The grid below will help you to identify some of the leading cases for each part of the crime.

Figure 4.2

Part of theft	Important cases
Actus reus	
i Appropriation	Gomez (1993) which clarifies the position as regards the Lawrence case (1972) and the Morris case (1984) R v. Gallasso (1993) R v. Atakpu (1993)
ii Property	R v. Ngan (1997) R v. Kohn (1979) Oxford v. Moss (1978)
iii Belonging to another	R v. Turner (No. 2) (1971) R v. Meredith (1973) R v. Hall (1973) Davidge v. Bunnett (1974) Lewis v. Lethbridge (1987)
Mens rea	
iv Dishonesty	R v. Ghosh (1982)
v With intention to permanently deprive	R v. Lloyd (1985) R v. Downes (1983) R v. Bagshaw (1988) DPP v. Lavender (1994)

Details on *actus reus*

i. Appropriation

The leading case on the meaning of appropriation under the Theft Act 1968 is *R* v. *Gomez* (1993) which reached the House of Lords. Two previous cases were also considered at length as they offered different interpretations of appropriation. These cases were *Lawrence* v. *Metropolitan Police Commissioner* (1972) and *R* v. *Morris* (1984). As will be shown in the detailed consideration of these three cases which follows, the *Gomez* case upholds the meaning of appropriation as given to it in the *Lawrence* case.

4

R v. Gomez (1993)
House of Lords

Facts:

In this case the assistant manager of an electrical goods shop (the accused) agreed to exchange two stolen building society cheques from another person for goods from the shop which were worth over £16,000. The two were acting dishonestly. The assistant manager asked his manager to authorise the sale and falsely told the manager that the cheques 'were as good as cash'. Based on this information, the manager authorised the handing over of the goods to the other person in exchange for the two cheques which bounced when presented for payment.

Thus, when the accused was charged with theft, the question arose of whether or not there was an appropriation for the purposes of the Theft Act 1968; was it pos-sible for the accused and his accomplice to 'steal' the goods from the shop when the manager of the shop had *consented* to the goods being taken?

Progress of the case through the courts:

Initial trial   ⟶   convicted of theft

Appeal to Court of Appeal Criminal Division   ⟶   appeal allowed, i.e. conviction quashed

Appeal to House of Lords (on a point of law of general public importance)*   ⟶   appeal allowed, i.e. conviction restored

*Appeal to the House of Lords on a point of law of general public importance

---

In the House of Lords:

Lord Keith of Kinkel stated that two previous decisions of the House of Lords in the cases of *Lawrence* v. *Metropolitan Police Commissioner* (1972) and *R* v. *Morris* (1984) had to be considered in the appeal in hand because they offered different approaches to the meaning of appropriation under the Theft Act 1968.

Commenting on the *Morris case*, Lord Keith stated that while the final decision of the House of Lords had been correct (the conviction for theft was upheld), nevertheless, it had been wrong to indicate in the decision that when the owner expressly or impliedly *consented* to an act, then that act could *never* amount to an appropriation under the Theft Act 1968.

Commenting on the *Lawrence case*, Lord Keith said:

> *Lawrence makes it clear that consent to or authorisation by the owner of the taking by the rogue is irrelevant. The taking amounted to an appropriation within the meaning of section 1(1) of the Theft Act. Lawrence also makes it clear that it is no less irrelevant that what happened may also have constituted the offence of obtaining property by deception under section 15(1) of the Act ...*

> *The decision in Lawrence was a clear decision of this House upon the construction of the word 'appropriate' in section 1(1) of the Act, which has stood for twelve years when doubt was thrown upon it by obiter dicta in Morris. Lawrence must be regarded as authoritative and correct, and there is no question of it now being right to depart from it ...*

Thus, the *Gomez* case fully supports the *Lawrence* case.

In the Gomez case, after the Court of Appeal (Criminal Division) had quashed the conviction for theft, it allowed an appeal to the House of Lords by granting a certificate under section 1(2) of the Administration of Justice Act 1960 (because a point of law of general public importance was involved in the decision of the court) involving the following two certificated questions:

Certificated questions	Answers
When theft is alleged and that which is alleged to be stolen passes to the defendant with the consent of the owner, but that has been obtained by a false representation, has	
(a) an appropriation within the meaning of section 1(1) of the Theft Act 1968 taken place, or	*Yes*
(b) must such a passing of property necessarily involve an element of adverse interference with or usurpation of some right of the owner?	*No*

In the Morris case, Lord Roskill had stated that it was the *combination* of the actions of the switching of price labels on goods and the removal of the goods from the shelf which, *together*, evidenced adverse interference with or usurpation of the rights of the owner and so appropriation of the goods.

In the Gomez case, Lord Keith criticised this view when he said:

> ... But there are observations in the passage which, with the greatest
> possible respect to my noble and learned friend, Lord Roskill, I must
> regard as unnecessary for the decision of the case and as being incorrect.
> In the first place, it seems to me that the switching of price labels on the
> article is in itself an assumption of one of the rights of the owner,
> whether or not it is accompanied by some other act such as removing the
> article from the shelf and placing it in a basket or trolley. No one but the
> owner has the right to remove a price label from an article or to place a
> price label upon it.

Thus, for the purposes of the Theft Act 1968, the *mere switching of price
labels on goods is an appropriation* without the need for adverse
interference or usurpation of the rights of the owner. Note also that it
is only necessary to show that the accused has assumed *one* of the
rights of the owner, *not all* of the rights of the owner. Thus, only the
owner of a wallet can touch it and should anyone else touch it then
this touching could amount to an appropriation.

Facts of the cases:
(Taken from the case of R v. Gomez 1993*)*
**Lawrence v. Metropolitan
Police Commissioner
(1972)**

The appellant was convicted on December 2,1969, of theft
contrary to section 1(1) of the Theft Act 1968. On Septemeber
1, 1969, a Mr Occhi, an Italian who spoke littleEnglish,
arrived at Victoria Station on his first visit to this country. He
went up to a taxi driver, the appellant, and showed him a piece
of paper on which an address in Ladbroke Grove was written.
The appellant said that it was very far and very expensive. Mr
Occhi got into the taxi, took £1 out of his wallet and gave it to
the appellant who then, the wallet being still open, took a further £6 out of it. He then drove Mr Occhi to Ladbroke Grove.
The correct lawful fare for the journey was in the region of
10s 6d. The appellant was charged with and convicted of the
theft of the £6.

Progress of cases through the courts :

Initial trial   ⟶   convicted of theft

Court of Appeal   ⟶   appeal dismissed, i.e.
(Criminal Division)   conviction upheld

House of Lords   ⟶   appeal dismissed, i.e.
                 conviction upheld

Notes: The view of appropriation in this case was supported in *R v. Gomez* (1993).

> There was still an appropriation from the wallet
> despite any implied consent from Mr Occhi that the
> taxi driver could take money out of it.

R v. Morris (1984)

Morris involved two cases of price label switching in a supermarket. In the firstcase the defendant had removed the price
label from a joint of meat and replaced it with a label showing
a lesser price which he had removed from another joint. He
was detected at the check-out point before he had paid for the
joint and later convicted of theft contrary to section 1(1) of the
Theft Act.In the second case the defendant had, in similar
manner, switched price labels on goods in a supermarket but
was not arrested until after he had passed the check-out point
and paid the lesser prices for the goods. He was charged with
two counts of theft contrary to section 1(1) an done count of
obtaining property by deception contrary to section 15(1).

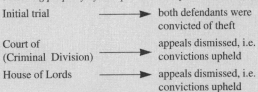

Initial trial   ⟶   both defendants were
                 convicted of theft

Court of   ⟶   appeals dismissed, i.e.
(Criminal Division)   convictions upheld

House of Lords   ⟶   appeals dismissed, i.e.
                 convictions upheld

Obiter dicta comments in this case concerning appropriation
were rejected in *R v. Gomez* (1993) by Lord Keith of Kinkel.

> In supermarkets the appropriation of goods takes place
> as soon as the goods are touched and so a person could
> be apprehended for theft (if all other ingredients are
> present) at this point; the fact that most people sus-
> pected of theft are apprehended outside the supermar-
> ket is for evidential purposes only.

Other cases on appropriation:

R v. Gallasso (1993)

In this case, which was dealt with in the Court of Appeal on the same day as the speeches were delivered in the House of Lords in the *Gomez* case, the court took a different view of appropriation, holding that mere touching of items belonging to someone else did not amount to an appropriation. It is generally held that this case was wrongly decided so that mere touching of someone else's propety does amount to an appropriation. You have to remember that theft will only be proved if all the other ingredients of the *actus reus* and *mens rea* are satisfied and so if you touch a tin of beans on the supermarket shelf and then decide you would rather have spaghetti, while you have appropriated the tin of beans, you have not stolen it because you were not acting with any dishonesty, you did not have the *mens rea* of theft.

In this case a nurse, who was looking after a group of mentally handicapped adults, was entrusted with looking after their financial affairs so that she could buy them the things that they needed. When one of the patients was sent a cheque for £1,800 the nurse opened a cash card account in his name, the implication being that she would draw on the account for her own purposes. She was convicted of theft of the cheque for £1,800 at trial but appealed and on appeal the conviction was quashed because it was held that she had not appropriated the cheque. However, applying *Gomez*, she would have been guilty of theft of the cheque, even though she had not drawn any money out, because by paying in the cheque she had assumed one of the rights of the owner, and at this point she had the requisite *mens rea*. It was totally irrelevant to the issue of appropriation that the patient concerned had impliedly consented to her actions.

R v. Atakpu (1993)

In this case the defendants had hired cars abroad and brought them to England with the intention of modifying them in order to sell them in England. They were arrested as they imported the cars and were charged with conspiracy to steal the cars; at trial they were convicted and appealed.

The Court of Appeal in this case followed the decision in *R v. Gomez* (1993) by stating that the appropriation of the cars had taken place abroad; the cars were first touched when they were hired and this touching is what amounted to the appropriation for theft. Since the defendants planned to keep the cars to sell on at this point, they had the *mens rea* for theft abroad and so the ingredients of theft were fulfilled abroad. This meant that the English courts did not have jurisdiction to deal with the case; the offence was committed abroad and so the convictions were quashed. In this case the fact that the hire company had consented to the touching would have been irrelevant following the cases of *Gomez* and *Lawrence*.

Transfers of money by computer from one country to another

If we look at the problem of a computer operator in England dishonestly transferring money from a bank account in England to his own bank account in America, where has the theft occurred? When he effects the transfer he has *mens rea* in England and by dealing with the account he is assuming one of the rights of the owner and so could be said to have appropriated the money. At the same time, the transfer of money actually takes place in America. J.C. Smith, in his book, *Smith & Hogan, Criminal Law*, 8th edition, says, '*The current position appears to be that where a computer operator in country A makes dishonest dispostions of property in country B, he commits theft in both countries.*'

ii Property

If you look back to the statutory provision section on page 83, you will see that the definition of property for the purposes of theft is provided for in section 4 of the Theft Act 1968. For ease of reference and to highlight some of the key points, see Figure 4.3.

Figure 4.3

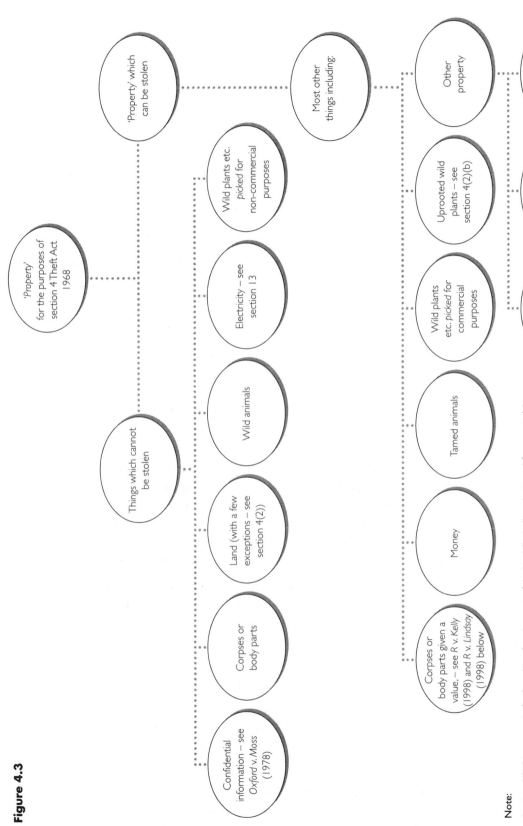

Note:

Section 4(2)(b) covers theft of anything forming part of the land (including plants and flowers etc.) by severance , i.e. total removal of the thing from the land, such as when a plant is dug up or uprooted.

Section 4(3), by contrast, covers situation where wild plants etc. are *picked* from the land, implying that the roots of the plant are left in the ground so that the plant is not severed.

*See the Terminology box on page 81

Bank accounts, cheques and confidential information

The position as regards bank accounts and cheques can seem confusing. The passage below, which is taken from Elliott & Wood's *Case and Materials on Criminal Law 8th edition*, might help to clarify the issue:

> *Lord Goddard C.J. in* R v. Davenport *(1954) 1 All E. R. 602,603:*
> *Although we talk of people having money in a bank, the only person who has money in a bank is the banker. If I pay money into my bank, either by paying cash or a cheque, the money at once becomes the money of the banker. The relationship between banker and customer is that of debtor and creditor. He does not hold my money as an agent or trustee ... When the banker is paying out, whether in cash or over the counter or whether by crediting the bank account of someone else, he is paying out his own money, not my money, but he is debiting me in my account with him. I have a chose in action, that is to say I have a right to expect that the banker will honour my cheque, but he does it out of his own money.*
>
> *If a customer A has a credit of £500 in bank B, the only property is the chose in action, the right to call on B to honour cheques up to that amount. There is no particular sum in the bank vaults over which this right operates.*

The leading case with regards to bank accounts and cheques is *R v. Kohn (1979)*.

In this case a director of a company had the authority to draw cheques against the bank account of the company for the purpose of paying bills and so forth. However, the director drew cheques against the account for himself. At trial he was convicted of theft of the *things in action* (the right to draw against the bank account) and he appealed against his convictions. In the Court of Appeal it was held that:

i   when a cheque was presented for payment at the bank when the bank account was in credit, a *thing in action* existed which could be stolen;

ii   when a cheque was presented for payment at the bank when the bank account was overdrawn but within an agreed overdraft limit, a *thing in action* existed which could be stolen; but

iii   when a cheque was presented for payment at the bank when the bank account was overdrawn beyond an agreed overdraft limit, a *thing in action* did not exist and so there was no property to be stolen.

Thus, the director's convictions for theft of a *thing in action* under conditions (i) and (ii) above were upheld, but his conviction for theft of a *thing in action* under condition (iii) above was quashed.

With regards to bank accounts, cheques and *things in action*, students should refer back to the case of *R* v. *Ngan* (1997) on page 86–7 which also confirms the fact that the appropriation of the *thing in action* takes place when the cheque is presented for payment.

The position as regards confidential information can be seen in the case of *Oxford* v. *Moss* (1978) in which a university student acquired a copy of an examination paper which he read and then returned. He was charged with the theft of confidential information but the charge, was dismissed by the stipendiary magistrate. When the prosecutor appealed to the Queen's Bench Division of the High Court, the appeal was dismissed; it was held that it was not possible to steal confidential information as it did not fit into the definition of property as provided in section 4 Theft Act 1968. It would have been possible for the student to have stolen the examination paper itself, but he returned it and so never intended to appropriate it permanently.

Corpses and body parts

In *R* v. *Kelly and Lindsay* (1998) the Court of Appeal upheld the appellants' convictions for the theft of approximately 35 human body parts from the Royal College of Surgeons. While Lord Justice Rose accepted the 150-year-old common law rule that there was no property in a corpse of part thereof, he also accepted the exception to that rule in *Doodeward v. Spence* (1908) that if a corpse, or part thereof, had been altered for the purpose of medical or scientific examination, it thereby acquired some value and became property which could be stolen.

iii Belonging to another

You may think that this part of the definition of theft is not necessary and that it is obvious that to steal something a person must steal it from someone else who actually *owns* it. However, as will become apparent, the phrase 'belonging to another' encompasses people who do not actually *own* the thing stolen. The phrase is defined in section 5 of the Theft Act 1968 and its range is demonstrated by the fact that the section has five subsections. It is a good idea to take a look at this section as shown in the statutory provisions part of this chapter, pages 82–3.

Note that for section 5(1) property shall be regarded as belonging to *any* person having:

i   possession of the property;
ii control of the property;
iii a proprietary right or interest in the property.

It is not theft to take property which has been abandoned but the taker of property has to be sure that the property has been abandoned and not just lost. Thus, when golf balls are lost on the golf course, the person who has lost them still has a proprietary interest in them and so they can be stolen. Rubbish placed in dustbins has been placed there for the local authority to take away; it has not been abandoned. Thus, anyone taking things out of a dustbin steals from the local authority.

Look at the 'You Decide' section which follows. The cases which are outlined here demonstrate the application of section 5 and you will notice that some of the cases seem to contradict each other. It would be a good idea to discuss such cases with your tutor.

YOU DECIDE

The following cases demonstrate the application of section 5 of the Theft Act 1968

1 R v. Turner (No. 2) (1971)

T took his car to a garage to have it repaired. The repairs having been practically completed, the car was left in the road outside the garage. T called at the garage and told the proprietor that he would return the following day, pay him, and take the car; instead he took the car, using his spare key, without paying for the repairs. Later he lied about the matter to the police. He was convicted of theft of the car and appealed.

You decide the appeal.

2 R v. Meredith (1973)

M's car was impounded by the police while he was at a football match and removed to the police station yard, where it was left locked. When M went to the police station, he found it crowded and so, rather than wait, he took his car away from the yard without contacting any policeman. He was charged with stealing the car.

You decide the outcome.

3 R v. Hall (1973)

H, a travel agent, received money from certain clients as deposits and payments for air trips to America. He paid the money so received into his firm's general account. None of the projected flights materialised and none of the money was refunded. He was convicted of theft. He appealed on the ground that he had not, within the meaning of section 5(3), been placed under an obligation to retain and deal with the sums paid to him in a particular way.

You decide the appeal.

4 Davidge v. Bunnett (1974)

D shared a flat with A, B and C, the expenses being shared. The gas bill having become due, A, B and C gave D cheques for their shares, payable to D's employer, because she herself had no bank account. D cashed the cheques, paid some of the bill, but spent most of the money on Christmas presents.

You decide the verdict.

5 Lewis v. Lethbridge (1987)

In this case A received £54 in sponsorship money for running in the London Marathon. The money should have been paid to a charity but was not. A was convicted of theft of the money and appealed.

You decide the appeal.

Answers

1 The appeal was dismissed; conviction upheld; Lord Parker C. J. said, 'The words "belonging to another" are specifically defined in section 5 of the Act ... This court is quite satisfied that there is no ground whatever for qualifying the words "possession or control" in any way. It is sufficient if it is found that the person from whom the property is taken ... was at the time in fact in possession or control.'

2 The Crown Court judge decided that there was no case to answer; the police had authority to remove the car for causing an obstruction and Meredith could have recovered his car from them by paying £4; however, Meredith could not steal his car from the police yard as the relevant regulations did not allow the police to withhold the car from the owner.

3 The appeal was allowed; the conviction was quashed; Edmund Davies L.J. said, '...what was not here established was that these clients expected them "to retain and deal with that property or its proceeds in a particular way," and that an "obligation" to do so was undertaken by the appellant ... Cases could, we suppose, conceivably arise where by some special arrangement (preferably evidenced by documents), the client could impose on the travel agent an "obligation" falling within section 5(3).

4 D was guilty of theft; D was under an obligation as per section 5(3) to use the proceeds from cashing the cheques in a particular way, that is to pay the whole of the gas bill.

5 The appeal was allowed; the conviction for theft was quashed; the charity had not specified that the actual money collected had to be handed over nor had it specified that a separate fund had to be set up for the money; thus, A was only a debtor to the charity and mere failure to pay a debt was not theft; the result might have been different if the money had been collected in a special box provided by the charity.

Details on *mens rea*

iv. Dishonesty

We can approach the question of whether or not the accused was dishonest for the purposes of theft by asking a series of *negative* questions. This is due to the fact that in section 2(1) of the Theft Act 1968 dishonesty is only partially defined and this is done in negative terms. (Look back to the statutory provisions on page 82.) Thus, the Theft Act 1968 does not list types of behaviour which should be regarded as dishonest. This stems from the fact that it is felt that dishonesty is a concept which almost *'speaks for itself'* and one which can readily be left to the jury. If the accused's mental state does not fall within the scope of section 2(1) this does not necessarily mean that he will have acted dishonestly. In such cases the jury will decide whether or not the accused acted dishonestly as directed by the judge either according to the two tests as laid down in the leading case of *R* v. *Ghosh* (1982) or without mention of the two tests. Figure 4.4 should help you understand this.

We will now look at the leading case of *R* v. *Ghosh* (1982). In this case the accused was a surgeon who was convicted of obtaining money by deception contrary to section 15 of the Theft Act 1968 (see Chapter 5). In this case it was determined that dishonesty for the purposes of section 15 was to be dealt with in the same way as it would be dealt with for theft under section 1. The accused appealed against his conviction and his appeal was dismissed. Below are extracts from the case. You will see that, according to the two tests to be applied, the test of dishonesty is a mixture of a subjective approach and an objective approach. This two-tier test has come under much criticism, especially from the point of view that it is too complicated for a jury to understand and apply. What do you think? Do you understand it?

Figure 4.4

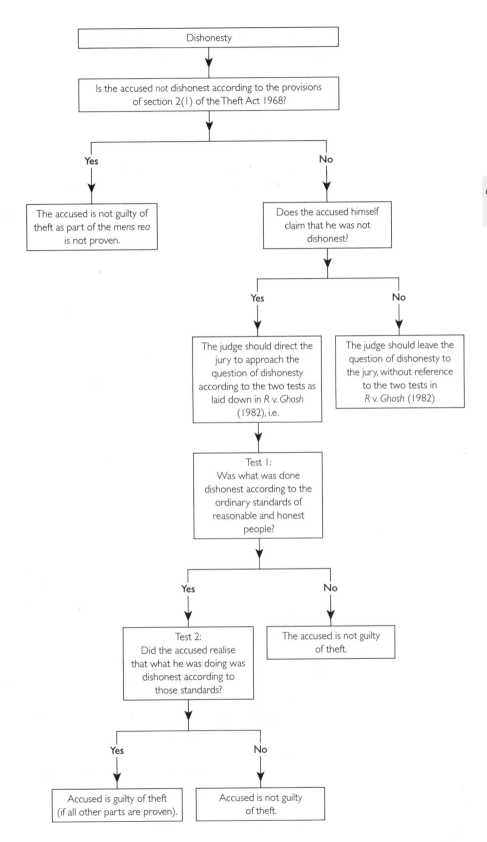

Lord Lane C.J.:

The law on this branch of the Theft Act 1968 is in a complicated state and we embark upon an examination of the authorities with great diffidence. When R v. McIvor *(1982) ... came before the Court of Appeal there were two conflicting lines of authority. On the one hand there were cases which decided that the test of dishonesty for the purposes of the Theft Act 1968 is, what we venture to call, subjective – that is to say the jury should be directed to look into the mind of the defendant and determine whether he knew he was acting dishonestly ... On the other hand there were cases which decided that the test of dishonesty was objective ... In* R v. McIvor *the Court of Appeal sought to reconcile these conflicting lines of authority. They did so on the basis that the subjective test is appropriate where the charge is conspiracy to defraud, but in the case of theft the test should be objective ... We feel, with the greatest respect, that in seeking to reconcile the two lines of authority in the way we have mentioned, the Court of Appeal in* R v. McIvor *was seeking to reconcile the irreconcilable. It therefore falls to us now either to choose between the two lines of authority or to propose some other solution ...*

Is 'dishonestly' in section 1 of the Theft Act 1968 intended to characterise a course of conduct? Or is it intended to describe a state of mind? If the former, then we can well understand that it could be established independently of the knowledge or belief of the accused. [i.e. an objective test]*. But if, as we think, it is the latter, then the knowledge and belief of the accused are at the root of the problem* [i.e. a subjective test].

Take, for example, a man who comes from a country where public transport is free. On his first day here he travels on a bus. He gets off without paying. He never had any intention of paying. His mind is clearly honest; but his conduct, judged objectively by what he has done, is dishonest. It seems to us that in using the word 'dishonestly' in the Theft Act 1968, Parliament cannot have intended to catch dishonest conduct in that sense ... So we would reject the simple uncomplicated approach that the test is purely objective, however attractive from the practical point of view that solution may be.

There remains the objection that to adopt a subjective test is to abandon all standards but that of the accused himself, and to bring about a state of affairs in which 'Robin Hood would be no robber' ... This objection misunderstands the nature of the subjective test. It is no defence for a man to say, 'I knew what I was doing is generally regarded as dishonest; but I do not regard it as dishonest myself. Therefore I am not guilty.'

NB: *Author's comments appear in square brackets.*

What he is however entitled to say is: 'I did not know that anybody would regard what I was doing as dishonest' ...

In determining whether the prosecution has proved that the defendant was acting dishonestly, a jury must first of all decide whether according to the ordinary standards of reasonable and honest people what was done was dishonest. If it was not dishonest by those standards, that is the end of the matter and the prosecution fails. [Test one to be applied.]

If it was dishonest by those standards, then the jury must consider whether the defendant himself must have realised that what he was doing was by those standards dishonest. [Test two to be applied.]

v. With the intention of permanently depriving the other of it

It might be an idea at this stage to take another look at the definition of theft according to section 1 of the Theft Act 1968:

'A person is guilty of theft if he dishonestly appropriates property belonging to another with the intention of permanently depriving the other of it.'

If the definition did not contain this last phrase, 'with the intention of permanently depriving the other of it', then according to what we know already from this chapter, it would be theft if someone dishonestly borrowed a book from the library by intending to keep it longer than the date of return, although intending to return it at some time in the future. It would not be relevant that the librarian concerned had consented to the taking. However, because the definition does contain this last phrase then the borrower above would be just that, a borrower, who would not be guilty of theft because he did not intend to permanently deprive the library of the book. This example goes to the heart of the problem with the notion of permanent deprivation in theft. It does not seem 'fair' that a person can be considered not guilty of theft just because he only appropriated the property belonging to someone else for a length of time shorter than 'permanently'. Arguably, this part of the law does avoid the courts being overburdened with many trivial cases. Another key issue seems to be whether or not the victim has suffered total loss. If an item of property is taken from the victim but is returned to the victim at some later stage, then the victim has not suffered total loss. Of course, the victim may have suffered some loss, if only the loss of possession of the item for the length of time it was in the possession of the thief.

4

The courts have struggled with the notion of permanent deprivation in theft since the Theft Act 1968 and, in particular, in deciding what effect section 6 has upon the notion. Let us take a closer look at section 6(1):

> *A person appropriating property belonging to another* without *meaning the other permanently to lose the thing itself is nevertheless* to be regarded *as having the intention of permanently depriving the other of it if his intention is to* treat the thing as his own to dispose of regardless of the other's rights; *and* a borrowing or lending of it *may amount to so treating it if, but only if, the borrowing or lending is for* a period and in circumstances *making it the* equivalent to an outright taking or disposal.

The problem with this section is that the courts have taken opposing stances as to whether or not it allows them to extend the notion of what is meant by permanent deprivation in theft. Those cases in which the court decides that the section allows them to extend what is meant by 'permanently deprive', do, in effect, have a wider net available to them and so are more likely to find an accused guilty of theft.

It would appear from case law that most judges are now more likely to allow an extension of what is meant by 'permanently deprive'.

The leading case which supports a more restrictive view of 'permanently deprive' so that the net is *not* widened to catch more theives, is *R* v. *Lloyd* (1985) which is examined below. Cases which support a more literal and wider interpretation of the key words in section 6(1), as shown in italics above, are *R* v. *Downes* (1983), *R* v. *Bagshaw* (1988), *DPP* v. *Lavender* (1994) and *R* v. *Marshall and others* (1998).

4

R v. Lloyd (1985)

In this case Lloyd and two others had been convicted of conspiracy to steal. They had been caught red handed while copying a film taken from the cinema where Lloyd worked. They had done this many times before and each time they only 'borrowed' the film for about three hours, returning it to the cinema in time for the next showing of it. Their appeal against conviction was based on their claim that the trial judge had misdirected the jury in that he had:

i left it up to them to decide whether or not the removal of the film in these circumstances could amount to theft;

ii allowed them to consider the relevance of section 6(1) of the Theft Act 1968.

The following comments are taken from the judgment of Lord Lane C.J. who delivered the judgment of the Court of Appeal:

... the intention of the appellants could more accurately be described as an intention temporarily to deprive the owner of the film and was indeed the opposite of an intention to permanently deprive.

What then was the basis of the prosecution case and the basis of the judge's direction to the jury? It is said that section 6(1) of the Theft Act 1968 brings such actions as the appellants performed here within the provisions of section 1 ...

That section has been described by J.R. Spencer in his article as a section which 'sprouts obscurities at every phrase', and we are inclined to agree with him ... It seems to us that in this case we are concerned with the second part of section 6(1), namely, the words after the semi-colon:

'and a borrowing or lending of it may amount to so treating it if, but only if, the borrowing or lending is for a period and in circumstances making it equivalent to an outright taking or disposal.'

These films, it could be said, were borrowed by Lloyd from his employers in order to enable him and the others to carry out their 'piracy' exercise. Borrowing is ex hypothesi not something which is done with an intention permanently to deprive. This half of the subsection, we believe, is intended to make it clear that a mere borrowing is never enough to constitute the necessary guilty mind unless the intention is to return the 'thing' in such a changed

state that it can truly be said that all its goodness or virtue had gone: for example R v. Beecham *(1851) ... where the defendant stole railway tickets intending that they should be returned to the railway company in the usual way only after the journeys had been completed. He was convicted of larceny. The judge in the present case gave another example, namely, the taking of a torch battery with the intention of returning it only when its power is exhausted. That being the case, we turn to inquire whether the feature films in this case can fall within that category. Our view is that they cannot. The goodness, the virtue, the practical value of the films to the owners has not gone out of the article. The film could still be projected to paying audiences ...*

That borrowing, it seems to us, was not for a period, or in circumstances, as made it equivalent to an outright taking or disposal.

... accordingly this conviction of conspiracy to steal must be quashed.

R v. Downes (1983)

In this case the appellant had vouchers made out to him from the Inland Revenue. He sold these vouchers to other people in full knowlege that they would return them to the Inland Revenue in order to get tax advantages. (Thus it could be argued that the Inland Revenue was not permanently deprived of the vouchers.) His conviction for theft was upheld in the Court of Appeal because the things returned to the Inland Revenue were, in effect, different things and because section 6(1) was to be given a wide interpretation. On such an interpretation the appellant was guilty of theft as he intended to treat the vouchers as his own to dispose of regardless of the other's (Inland Revenue's) rights.

R v. Bagshaw (1988)

In this case the accused, having *borrowed* some gas cylinders and having returned them before *all* of the gas had been used up, was found guilty of theft. This appears to be an extension to what can amount to 'an outright taking'. In *R* v. *Lloyd* (1985) Lord Lane C.J. said that a borrowing was only equivalent to 'an outright taking' if *all* of the goodness in the thing was used up. Arguably, *most* of the goodness in the thing must have been used up before the borrowing can amount to 'an outright taking', so that using someone else's football season ticket once and then returning it while the rest of the season was still to come might not be the equivalent to 'an outright taking', whereas using the ticket for most of the matches and returning it when there were only two matches left to watch might amount to 'an outright taking'.

DPP v. Lavender (1994)

In this case the accused was found guilty of theft when he removed two doors from one council property and put them on the council property being rented by his girlfriend. It could be argued that the council was not permanently deprived of the two doors because they were put on another house which they owned. Nevertheless, the court held that the accused did intend to permanently deprive the council of the doors because he had *treated the doors as his own to dispose of regardless of the rights of the council*. It must be noted here that while the accused treated the doors as his own he did not dispose of the doors in the sense of destroying the doors; he merely moved them from one council property to another.

R v. Marshall and others (1998)

In this case the three appellants, Marshall, Coombes and Eren, had been caught on video camera obtaining underground tickets and travelcards from travellers who had finished with them. They then sold the tickets on to other potential travellers and were convicted of theft at Southwark Crown Court. They appealed against the convictions, arguing that there was no evidence of an intention permanently to deprive London Underground of the tickets. The Court of Appeal upheld their convictions for theft. They had dealt with the tickets as if they were their own to dispose of, regardless of the rights of London Underground. The fact that the tickets might return to London Underground, with their value exhausted, was irrelevant and section 6(1) prevailed. This case is significant as it has implications for motorists who pass on unexpired parking tickets to other motorists as they leave car parks. However, it is unlikely that people would be charged with theft for passing on a ticket unless they had been warned that the tickets were not transferable. Once so warned, a motorist would be acting dishonestly if he passed on an unexpired ticket.

In *'Temporary Appropriation Should be Theft'* (1981) CLR 129. Glanville Williams suggests that the word 'permanently' should be removed from section 1(1) of the Theft Act 1968. The definition of theft would then be: a person is guilty of theft if he dishonestly appropriates property belonging to another with the intention of depriving the other of it. In this way, temporary appropriation of someone else's property could amount to theft and the courts would be spared the need to elaborate on whether the accused's behaviour fell within the parameters (which are not clearly established) of section 6(1).

Figure 4.5 should be of help when approaching examination questions on this topic.

Figure 4.5 Intention to permanently deprive

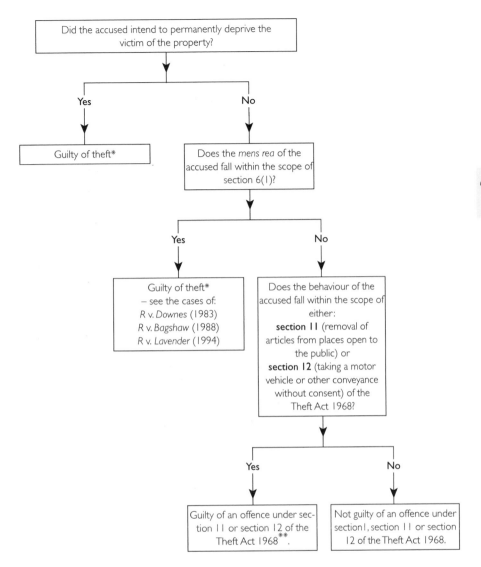

Did the accused intend to permanently deprive the victim of the property?

Yes → Guilty of theft*

No → Does the *mens rea* of the accused fall within the scope of section 6(1)?

Yes → Guilty of theft*
– see the cases of:
R v. *Downes* (1983)
R v. *Bagshaw* (1988)
R v. *Lavender* (1994)

No → Does the behaviour of the accused fall within the scope of either:
section 11 (removal of articles from places open to the public) or
section 12 (taking a motor vehicle or other conveyance without consent) of the Theft Act 1968?

Yes → Guilty of an offence under section 11 or section 12 of the Theft Act 1968**.

No → Not guilty of an offence under section1, section 11 or section 12 of the Theft Act 1968.

*So long as all the other ingredients of theft are proven.

**Section 11 and section 12 are sections within the Theft Act 1968 which do make it an offence to *borrow* something, either a conveyence or, for instance, a painting or statue from an art gallery. For section 12, see the statutory provisions section (page 82) and the key points section (page 91); for section 11, see the statutory provisions section.

Applying principles to examination questions

If you have worked through this chapter carefully you should have a good understanding of theft and some of its related offences. What you need to practise now is the application of the principles of theft to examination questions. Quite often questions on theft are posed in a problem format; you are given a scenario in which one or more thefts may or may not have occurred and it is your task to isolate the key aspects of the *mens rea* or *actus reus* of theft which merit most discussion and analysis. However, questions on theft also appear in straight essay format, requiring you to discuss, for example, the notion of dishonesty or appropriation within the law of theft. In many ways, as long as you know the subject matter, this latter type of question is the easier of the two. For this reason I have devised a problem-solving question for you to consider. As you read through the question you should highlight what you regard as key points which need addressing and then look back over the chapter to see if you are on the right lines, pick out the key cases and make sure that you have not missed anything. The question only involves issues relating to the topics within this chapter; theft will be integrated into questions covering other topics later. My annotated version of the question should only be consulted after you have attempted the task for yourself.

Brian is leaving a football match having watched his favourite team win the local derby. He notices a season ticket lying on the floor and picks it up, telling his friend Alan that he will hand it in to the club secretary the next day. He then remembers that he will be too busy revising to go to the club. Alan tells Brian that he will hand the ticket in to the club secretary for him and so Brian gives the ticket to Alan.

There are three weeks left in the season and Alan decides to keep the ticket for himself. He does not believe that he is being dishonest as he thinks that any other football fan in his position would do the same thing.

Nevertheless, Alan decides to hand the ticket in to the club secretary when there is one match still to play.

Consider whether or not Alan and/or Brian could be guilty of theft.

Tips on how to approach such a question

as the ticket
andoned?
likely, so was
ere an
ppropriation?
t is Brian acting
shonestly?

Alan is charged
ith theft could
e argue that
 here was no
ppropriation
ecause Brian
onsented to him
king the ticket?
ee R v. Gomez
993), Lawrence
ase (1972) and
v. Morris (1984).
it relevant that
lan deceived
rian? See
v. Gomez (1993)

hould the
uestion of
ishonesty be
ecided by
eference to the
vo tests in
v. Ghosh (1982)?

as Alan
ermanently
eprived the
wner of the
icket? How much
alue is left in the
icket? See
v. Lloyd (1985),
v. Bagshaw
988) and DPP v.
avender (1994)

Brian is leaving a football match having watched his favourite team win the local derby. He notices a season ticket lying on the floor and picks it up, telling his friend Alan that he will hand it in to the club secretary the next day. He then remembers that he will be too busy revising to go to the club. Alan tells Brian that he will hand the ticket in to the club secretary for him and so Brian gives the ticket to Alan.

Does Brian intend to permanently deprive the owner of the ticket?

Was it possible for Alan to steal the ticket from Brian? *See section 5* – Brian has possession and control of the ticket so does it belong to him in this context?

There are three weeks left in the season and Alan decides to keep the ticket for himself. He does not believe that he is being dishonest as he thinks that any other football fan in his position would do the same thing.

Is Alan not dishonest according to section 2(1)? Could the owner of the ticket have been found by taking reasonable steps?

Nevertheless, Alan decides to hand the ticket in to the club secretary when there is one match still to play.

Brian is not guilty of theft – he was not dishonest and did not intend to permanently deprive the owner of the ticket. Alan is probably guilty of theft.

Consider whether or not Alan and/or Brian could be guilty of theft.

Explain that the relevant Act is the *Theft Act 1968* – that theft is defined in section 1(1) and that to be guilty of theft the five parts of the *mens rea* and *actus reus* must be proved.

Proposals for reform

As society progresses and becomes more advanced it becomes possible to commit theft by methods and in situations not anticipated and therefore not provided for in existing legislation. A lot of time can be taken up in court trying to find out whether new types of human activity are actually within the scope of the legislation. The Larceny Acts of 1861 and 1916 were introduced merely to re-state the law of theft as it existed in either common law cases or in various statutory provisions. However, the Theft Acts of 1968 and 1978 were introduced to provide a new starting point for theft – a code which could be referred to in order to find out what the law was on theft. As has been seen in the course of this chapter, these Acts are not perfect and there is considerable debate as regards some aspects of them, for instance, as regards dishonesty, consent and appropriation in theft itself. Thus, the Law Commission is currently undertaking a comprehensive review of the law of dishonesty.

The following extracts are from the Law Commission's 29th Annual Report 1994 (Law Com. No. 232):

Paragraph 2.39   *And finally, by the time we prepared our report, we had already decided to embark on a comprehensive review of offences of dishonesty ... The comprehensive nature and size of our dishonesty project means that a long time is bound to elapse before it is finally completed ...*

Paragraph 2.43   *As we have already said, we have now embarked on a comprehensive review of offences of dishonesty, including those created by the Theft Acts 1968 and 1978. We are doing this for a number of reasons. The first reason for this review is that there was cogent judicial criticism during 1994 that 'the law of theft is in urgent need of simplification and modernisation'. Secondly, in the period since the enactment of the Theft Act 1968 and the Forgery and Counterfeiting Act 1981, there have been radical and multifarious technological advances. In consequence, it is likely that some acts of dishonesty are not effectively covered by present legislation because Parliament could not possibly have envisaged all the technical advances which are now creating such problems for the courts.*

In Chapter 5, on deception offences, you will discover that section 15(1) of the Theft Act 1968 is closely linked with section 1(1) of the same Act and you should look to this chapter for details of the Theft (Amendment) Act 1996 and a discussion of the case of *Preddy* (1996).

CHAPTER Summary

4

THEFT ACT 1968

1(1)	12	13	22	25
Theft	Taking a conveyance without authority	Abstracting electricity	Handling stolen goods	Going equipped for stealing
Dishonestly	Takes a conveyance	Dishonestly uses	Otherwise than during the theft	When not at place of abode
appropriate	or rides knowingly	or causes to be wasted or diverted	handles if	has with him
property	or drives knowingly		receives retains	any article
belonging to another	without the consent of the owner	electricity	removes disposes of or	to use in connection with or during
with intention of permanently depriving the other of it	or without lawful authority		realises	any burglary
			stolen goods dishonestly	theft or
			for someone else	cheat

R v. *Gomez (1993)*
R v. *Ngan (1997)*
Oxford v. *Moss (1978)*
R v. *Hall (1973)*
Lewis v. *Lethbridge (1987)*
R v. *Ghosh (1982)*
R v. *Lloyd (1985)*
DPP v *Lavender (1994)*
R v. *Kelly and Lindsay (1998)*
R v. *Marshall and others (1998)*

R v. *Ellames (1974)*
R v. *Goodwin (1996)*
R v. *Lester & Byast (1955)*

This summary will help you when you are preparing for examinations.

I have given only a selection of cases which should suffice for most purposes. It is a good idea to make a cardex system for the key cases so that you can carry these around with you to read at any time. It should be sufficient for sections 12, 13, and 22 that you can quote them and apply them without remembering any cases.

5 Deception offences

OVERVIEW

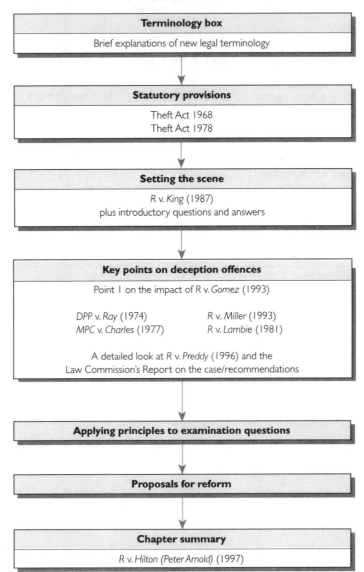

Terminology box
Brief explanations of new legal terminology

Statutory provisions
Theft Act 1968 Theft Act 1978

Setting the scene
R v. *King* (1987) plus introductory questions and answers

Key points on deception offences
Point 1 on the impact of *R* v. *Gomez* (1993) *DPP* v. *Ray* (1974)   *R* v. *Miller* (1993) *MPC* v. *Charles* (1977)   *R* v. *Lambie* (1981) A detailed look at *R* v. *Preddy* (1996) and the Law Commission's Report on the case/recommendations

Applying principles to examination questions

Proposals for reform

Chapter summary
R v. *Hilton (Peter Arnold)* (1997)

In this chapter you will discover how the criminal law has acknowledged the difference between those situations where property is stolen and those where property is obtained from the victim by deception. Originally the law treated the latter offence more leniently than the former, which seems strange as it could be argued that the offender who tells lies in order to obtain property is more blameworthy than the 'ordinary' thief. The law then made the two offences equally blameworthy (each had a punishment of a maximum term of 10 years' imprisonment) but since the Criminal Justice Act 1991(by section 26) theft is regarded as less blameworthy than the offence of obtaining property by deception as theft now has a punishment of a maximum term of seven years' imprisonment. You will see how this distinction has had little application since *R* v. *Gomez* (1993).

5

While theft is concerned solely with property, deception offences (as defined in the statutory provisions section) are concerned with property, money transfers, pecuniary advantage, services and evasion of liability. The origins of the Theft Act 1978 were noted in the introduction to Chapter 4, on theft. In this chapter the emphasis is placed on two important cases and their impact on theft and deception offences. The two cases are:

i   *R* v. *Gomez* (1993) – as a result of this case it is now probably true to say that section 15 of the Theft Act 1968 has been 'swallowed up' by section 1 of the Theft Act 1968;

ii *R* v. *Preddy* (1996) – as a result of this case sections 15A and 24A were inserted into the Theft Act 1968 by the Theft (Amendment) Act 1996.

To clarify any misconceptions in terminology some key words have been included in the box overleaf. Read these brief explanations before you progress further in the chapter.

TERMINOLOGY: Deception offences

Property
Property essentially refers to some *thing* which can be owned. It is possible to own tangible property which can be physically touched and it is also possible to own intangible property which cannot be physically touched, such as a credit balance in a bank. A detailed consideration of the meaning of property for the purposes of the Theft Act 1968 is given in Chapter 4, on theft.

Services
A service is not some *thing* which can be touched; rather, it involves the utilisation of the skills and time of another person for your benefit, such as when you take a taxi ride, have your hair done at the hairdressers, have singing lessons, and so forth.

Deception
This basically involves someone telling a lie (making an untrue statement) in order to achieve a certain result.

Fraud
This is where someone uses deception in order to obtain property/services and so forth from someone else. Thus, the word fraud is commonly used to describe deception offences.

Statutory provisions

The statutory provisions for the *deception offences* to be considered in this chapter are to be found in the Theft Acts 1968 and 1978. They are as follows:

Theft Act 1968	section 15	Obtaining property by deception
	section 15A	Obtaining a money transfer by deception
	section 16	Obtaining a pecuniary advantage by deception
Theft Act 1978	section 1	Obtaining services by deception
	section 2	Evasion of liability by deception

Three other offences, which do not involve deception, will also be mentioned briefly in this chapter:
dishonestly retaining a wrongful credit,
blackmail;
making off without payment.

Theft Act 1968

Deception Offences

Obtaining property by deception

15   (1) A person who by any deception dishonestly obtains property belonging to another, with the intention of permanently depriving the other of it, shall on conviction on indictment be liable to imprisonment for a term not exceeding ten years.

        (2) For purposes of this section a person is to be treated as obtaining property if he obtains ownership, possession or control of it, and 'obtain' includes obtaining for another or enabling another to obtain or retain.

        (3) Section 6 above shall apply for purposes of this section, with the necessary adaptation of the reference to appropriating, as it applies for purposes of section 1.

        (4) For purposes of this section 'deception' means any deception (whether deliberate or reckless) by words or conduct as to fact or as to law, including a deception as to the present intentions of the person using the deception or any other person.

Obtaining a money transfer by deception

15(A) (1) A person is guilty of an offence if by any deception he dishonestly obtains a money transfer for himself or another.

        (2) A money transfer occurs when –

            (a) a debit is made to one account;

            (b) a credit is made to another; and

            (c) the credit results from the debit or the debit results from the credit.

        (3) References to a credit and to a debit are to a credit of an amount of money and to a debit of an amount of money.

        (4) It is immaterial (in particular) –

            (a) whether the amount credited is the same as the amount debited;

            (b) whether the money transfer is effected on presentment of a cheque or by another method;

            (c) whether any delay occurs in the process by which the money transfer is effected;

            (d) whether any intermediate credits or debits are made in the course of the money transfer;

            (e) whether either of the accounts is overdrawn before or after the money transfer is effected.

        (5) A person guilty of an offence under this section shall be liable on conviction on indictment to imprisonment for a term not exceeding ten years.

Obtaining a pecuniary advantage by deception

16   (1) A person who by any deception dishonestly obtains for himself or another

5

any pecuniary advantage shall on conviction on indictment be liable to imprisonment for a term not exceeding five years.

(2) The cases in which a pecuniary advantage within the meaning of this section is to be regarded as obtained for a person are cases where –

(b) he is allowed to borrow by way of overdraft, or to take out any policy of insurance or annuity contract, or obtains an improvement of the terms on which he is allowed to do so; or

(c) he is given the opportunity to earn remuneration or greater remuneration in an office or employment, or to win money by betting.

(3) For purposes of this section 'deception' has the same meaning as in section 15 of this Act.

Theft Act 1978

Obtaining services by deception

1 (1) A person who by any deception dishonestly obtains services from another shall be guilty of an offence.

(2) It is an obtaining of services where the other is induced to confer a benefit by doing some act, or causing or permitting some act to be done, on the understanding that the benefit has been or will be paid for.

Evasion of liability by deception

2 (1) Subject to subsection (2) below, where a person by any deception –

(a) dishonestly secures the remission of the whole or part of any existing liability to make a payment, whether his own liability or another's; . . .

he shall be guilty of an offence.

Other offences

Theft Act 1968

Blackmail

21 (1) A person is guilty of blackmail if, with a view to gain for himself or another or with intent to cause loss to another, he makes any unwarranted demand with menaces; and for this purpose a demand with menaces is unwarranted unless the person making it does so in the belief –

(a) that he has reasonable grounds for making the demand; and

(b) that the use of the menaces is a proper means of reinforcing the demand.

(2) The nature of the act or omission demanded is immaterial, and it is also immaterial whether the menaces relate to action to be taken by the person making the demand.

(3) A person guilty of blackmail shall on conviction on indictment by liable to imprisonment for a term not exceeding fourteen years.

Dishonestly retaining a wrongful credit

24A (1) A person is guilty of an offence if –

    (a) a wrongful credit has been made to an account kept by him or in respect of which he has any right or interest;

    (b) he knows or believes that the credit is wrongful; and

    (c) he dishonestly fails to take such steps as are reasonable in the circumstances to secure that the credit is cancelled.

(2) References to a credit are to a credit of an amount of money.

(3) A credit to an account is wrongful if it is the credit side of a money transfer obtained contrary to section 15A of this Act.

(4) A credit to an account is also wrongful to the extent that it derives from –

    (a) theft;

    (b) an offence under section 15A of this Act;

    (c) blackmail; or

    (d) stolen goods.

(5) In determining whether a credit to an account is wrongful, it is immaterial (in particular) whether the account is overdrawn before or after the credit is made.

(6) A person guilty of an offence under this section shall be liable on conviction on indictment to imprisonment for a term not exceeding ten years.

Theft Act 1978

Making off without payment

3 (1) Subject to subsection (3) below, a person who, knowing that payment on the spot for any goods supplied or service done is required or expected from him, dishonestly makes off without having paid as required or expected and with intent to avoid payment of the amount due shall by guilty of an offence.

(2) For purposes of this section 'payment on the spot' includes payment at the time of collecting goods on which work has been done or in respect of which service has been provided . . .

(4) Any person may arrest without warrant anyone who is, or whom he, with reasonable cause, suspects to be, committing or attempting to commit an offence under this section.

4 (1) Offences under this Act shall be punishable either on conviction on indictment or on summary conviction.

(2) A person convicted on indictment shall be liable –

    (a) for an offence under section 1 or section 2 of this Act, to imprisonment for a term not exceeding five years; and

    (b) for an offence under section 3 of this Act, to imprisonment for a term not exceeding two years.

5 (1) For purposes of section 1 and 2 above 'deception' has the same meaning as in section 15 of the Theft Act 1968 . . .

Setting the scene

Read through the case below and then answer the questions.

R v. King (1987) *Court of Appeal*

In this case the appellants, David King and Jimmy Stockwell, told an elderly householder, Nora Mitchell, that they were from J.F. Street, Tree Specialists, and that it was necessary to remove several trees from her property in order to prevent damage to the gas supply and the foundations of the house. They said that the necessary work would cost £470 and she agreed to the work being carried out. Before they started any work they were arrested by the police and charged with dishonestly attempting to obtain £470 in money with the intention of permanently depriving Nora Mitchell of it by deception. The deception lay in their false representations that they were from J.F. Street and that the work was necessary to prevent damage. They were convicted and appealed.

NEILL L.J. gave the judgment of the court:

In support of the appeal against conviction counsel for the appellants argued that the judge erred in rejecting the motion to quash the indictment, or alternatively the submission that there was no case to answer . . .

In our view, the question in each case is: was the deception an operative cause of the obtaining of the property? This question falls to be answered as a question of fact by the jury applying their common sense . . .

In the present case there was, in our judgment, ample evidence on which the jury could come to the conclusion that had the attempt succeeded the money would have been paid over by the victim as a result of the lies told to her by the appellants. We consider that the judge was correct to reject both the motion to quash the indictment and the submission that there was no case to answer. For the reasons which we have set out, we consider that the appellants were rightly convicted in this case, and the appeals must therefore be dismissed.

Questions

You will need to look back to the statutory provisions on pages 119–21 to answer some of these questions.

1   Which section of which Act would the two defendants have been charged under?

2   What is the maximum term of imprisonment for this offence?

3   Would it have made any difference to the outcome of the case if the defendants had said that the money was not for them but was for someone else?

4   If the defendants had not said that they were from J.F. Street but had been wearing a distinctive uniform which all empoyees of that firm had to wear, could they still have been charged as they were?

5 What is meant by 'counsel for the appellants'?

6 Was the original trial heard in the Magistrates' Court or the Crown Court? Explain.

7 What does it mean if there is 'no case to answer'?

8 What is meant by the question: 'was the deception an operative cause?'

9 Why could the defendants not have been charged under section 16(2)(c) of the Theft Act 1968?

Answers

1 If you look back to the overview for Section Three, offences against property (page 78), you will be reminded that there are two Theft Acts and that the Theft Act 1978 has far fewer sections than the Theft Act 1968. The reasons for this are given in the introductory paragraphs in Chapter 4, on theft and it would be a good idea to read this again. In a situation such as this you have to ask yourself whether or not this was a 'straightforward' attempted theft or whether there were additional factors. In this case not only would Nora Mitchell have been deprived of property (the money) permanently, she would also have been deceived into handing it over to the appellants. Thus, the crime concerned is not theft but obtaining property by deception. In the overview to Section Three you can see that the deception offences dealt with in this book are provided for in sections 15, 15A and 16 of the Theft Act 1968 and in sections 1 and 2 of the Theft Act 1978. When you read the definitions of these offences in the statutory provisions on page 119–21, you should determine that the deception offence involved in this case is provided for by section 15(1) of the Theft Act 1968.

2 In section 15(1) you are told that when a person is convicted of this offence on indictment he shall be liable to imprisonment for a term not exceeding 10 years. The conviction would have to be on indictment for any term of imprisonment over six months as the magistrates in the Magistrates' Court can only impose a maximum term of imprisonment of six months for one offence. Note how the Act refers to maximum terms of imprisonment as opposed to minimum terms of imprisonment. This is because it is the job of the judiciary (judges or magistrates) to determine a sentence in any one case up to the maximum set in the Act which has been enacted by the legislature (Parliament). See Chapter 14, on sentencing, to see how inroads have been made on the idea of maximum sentences.

3 When parliamentary counsel draft Bills (which may become Acts of Parliament), they use words which they hope will be clear and unambiguous. At the same time they have to encompass the full range of activity which the Act is hoping to provide for. Thus, in section 15(2) of the Theft Act 1968 the meaning of the word 'obtains' is elaborated on and we are told that it includes those situations where the defendant obtains for another. Thus, it would not have made any difference to the outcome of this case if the appellants had said that they were obtaining the money for someone else.

4 In this case the appellants had told Nora Mitchell a lie, that they were from J.F. Street, tree specialist. This is the most obvious form of deception. Is it possible to deceive someone other than by telling a lie? Can deception be inferred from conduct? It is possible because in section 15(4) it states that deception means 'any' deception whether by words or *conduct*. Thus, if the appellants had conducted themselves in such a way as to imply that they worked for J.F. Street, this might be enough to amount to a deception.

5 After a person has committed a crime or is alleged to have committed a crime, he is referred to in different ways depending on where the case is in the criminal justice process. On arrest, the person is the suspect. After being charged with a crime, he is the accused, and at trial in the Magistrates' Court or Crown Court, he is the defendant. If the person appeals from the decision at trial, they become the appellant and if the prosecution appeal from the trial, the person becomes the respondent. In this case we can refer to the two men as the appellants as they have appealed from the court where they were tried; they are appealing against their convictions. The barristers acting on behalf of the appellants are known as counsel.

6 The case would have been heard in the Crown Court and there are several clues in the extract to help you come to this conclusion. The appellants had argued that the 'judge' had erred (it would have been a magistrate if in the Magistrates' Court) in rejecting the motion to quash the 'indictment' (which means that the offence is indictable and so only triable in the Crown Court – Magistrates' Courts can only try summary offences) and there are references to the jury (which does not sit in the Magistrates' Court).

7 The phrase 'no case to answer' means that there is not enough *prima facie* evidence to support the charged offence and so the case should not proceed. At the start of the trial the prosecution barristers would have outlined their case to the court and if the judge had felt that there was not enough evidence to support the prosecution the case could have been dismissed then.

8   In section 15(1) it states that, '*A person who by deception ...*' – the key word being shown in bold. Thus, the prosecution have to prove that the deception actually affected the victim and made the victim act as he did. Thus, the deception, the lie, has to be the 'operative cause' of the victim's behaviour. In this case Nora Mitchell only agreed to the work because she believed that the two men were *bona fide* that is, genuine, employees of a reputable firm of tree surgeons.

9   A pecuniary advantage is defined in section 16(2)(b) and section 16(2)(c) and you might have thought that it was possible for these two defendants to fall within the scope of section 16(2)(c) in that they were given the opportunity to earn remuneration (pay). However, to be caught in this way they would have needed to be 'in an office or employment' which they were not.

5

Key points on deception offences

►   Why is there an overlap between theft (section 1 Theft Act 1968) and the offence of obtaining property by deception (section 15 Theft Act 1968) ? Let us first take a look at the definitions of these two offences.

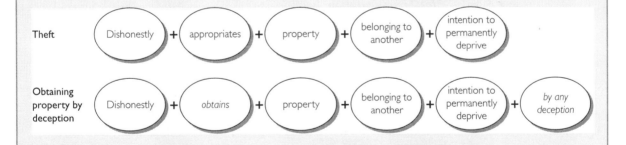

Figure 5.1

Thus, it can be seen that the definitions are nearly the same except that for the section 15 offence the word *obtains* is used instead of *appropriates* and there is the addition of the phrase *by any deception*. It follows logically that if property was obtained by deception, the correct offence to charge the suspect with would be an offence under section 15. This offence would be harder to prove than theft because the prosecution would have to prove the deception aspect of the offence. This may help to explain why, in many cases where deception is involved, the accused is charged with theft rather than obtaining by deception, such as happened in the *Lawrence* case and in the *Gomez* case (see Chapter 4, on theft, for details).

However, since the *Gomez* case if property is obtained by deception, the practice of charging the suspect with theft has been given the seal of approval.

Let us quickly recap on the facts of that case:

The assistant manager of an electrical goods shop, by deception, got the consent of the manager of the shop to release certain expensive items to another person who was the accomplice of the assistant manager. The assistant manager deceived the manager because he told him that the cheques which were to be used to pay for the goods were valid building society cheques when he knew all along that the cheques were stolen. Thus, the goods were obtained by deception. Despite this, the assistant manager was charged with theft under section 1 of the Theft Act 1968. The issue of whether or not there could be an *appropriation* for theft when the manager had *consented* to the removal of the goods received much consideration as described in Chapter 4. However, what is significant is the certificated question which asked:

> *When theft is alleged and that which is alleged to be stolen passes to the defendant with the consent of the owner, but that has been obtained by a false representation, has*
>
> *(a) an appropriation within the meaning of section 1(1) of the Theft Act 1968 taken place ... ?*

This was answered in the affirmative. The key phrase in this question is *that has been obtained by a false representation*. The result of this is that whenever property is obtained from someone with their consent which was only given because of some deception, then this can amount to an appropriation for the purposes of theft. This actually means that there is no need to bring any more charges under section 15 as offences which, before *R* v. *Gomez* (1993), could only be brought under section 15, can now be brought under section 1. As already stated, it is easier to secure a conviction under section 1 as, under this section, there is no need to prove *by any deception*. In the *Lawrence* case and the *Gomez* case if the accused had been charged with *obtaining property by deception* rather than theft then, arguably, it would not have been necessary to extend the law of theft to cover their wrongful actions. It is worth reminding ourselves at this point that the maximum term of imprisonment for a theft conviction is now seven years while it is 10 years for a conviction of obtaining property by deception. How is this to be reconciled?

▶ In section 34 of the Theft Act 1968 it is stated that sections 4(1) and 5(1) of the Act shall apply generally for the Act. This means that, for the deception offences, *'property'* includes money and all other property, real or personal, including things in action and other intangible property. (Note that, unlike theft, deception offences can therefore be committed in respect of land, wild plants and wild animals.) It also means that the phrase *'belonging to another'* can include any person having possession or control of the property. Refer to Chapter 4 for a discussion of these topics and also see below for details on the problems caused by the phrase *belonging to another* and its application to a *chose in action* as raised in the case of *R* v. *Preddy* (1996).

▶ The deception offences which are to be considered in this chapter (sections 15,15A and 16 of the Theft Act 1968 and sections 1 and 2 of the Theft Act 1978) have some common elements. Their definitions all contain the phrase *by any deception* and, apart from section 2 of the 1978 Theft Act, they all contain the phrase *dishonestly obtains*. The phrase used in section 2 is *dishonestly secures* and this is generally taken to mean the same as dishonestly obtains. 'Obtaining' now means much the same as 'appropriating' in theft. These common elements will be considered by way of the 'You Decide' cases which follow.

5

YOU DECIDE

Look back to the statutory provisions section on page 118 and try to apply them to the cases shown below. Case 1 was decided before section 16(2)(a) Theft Act 1968 was replaced by sections 1 and 2 of Theft Act 1978 and it is suggested that you approach the case in terms of the latter Act by concentrating on the issue of whether or not the obtaining was by deception.

1 DPP v. Ray (1974)

In this case two men went into a restaurant and ordered a meal. They fully intended to pay for the meal at this stage. After they had eaten the meal, the men decided not to pay for it. They decided to wait until the waiter was out of the dining room and then run out of the restaurant, which they did. Could the men be said to have obtained services by deception? Did they deceive the waiter?

You decide.

2 R v. Miller (1993)

In this case the victim got into a car beleiving it was a taxi. However, as the journey progressed the victim suspected that the vehicle was not a properly licensed taxi. Nevertheless, at the end of the journey the victim, being fearful of the driver, paid the amount asked for as the fare. Could the driver of the vehicle be convicted of obtaining property by deception? Was the passenger deceived?

You decide.

3 Metropolitan Police Commissioner v. Charles (1977)

In this case the defendant obtained gaming chips by presentation of a cheque backed by a cheque card. He knew that his account was overdrawn and that he should not be making any demands on the account. He was charged with obtaining a pecuniary advantage by deception (increased borrowing by way of overdraft). The manager of the gaming club said that if a cheque is backed by a cheque card and all the details are correct, then the club does not worry about the state of the person's account in the bank. Could the defendant be said to have induced the manager to give him the chips by deception?

You decide.

4 R v. Lambie (1981)

In this case a woman used her Barclaycard to buy goods in a shop when she had gone over her limit of £200. She was charged with obtaining a pecuniary advantage by deception. The shop keeper concerned said that the shop regarded credit cards as the same as cash knowing that the amount concerned will always be forthcoming from the bank. Thus, the shop keeper was totally unconcerned about the state of the woman's account with Barclaycard. Could the woman be convicted under section 16(1) of the Theft Act 1968?

You decide.

Answers

1 This case went to the House of Lords. It was held (by 3:2) that the two men had obtained services by deception [at this time section 16(2)(a) still applied and so they were actually convicted of obtaining a pecuniary advantage by deception] – they had deceived the waiter. Lord Pearson said: *'The essential feature of this case . . . is that there was a **continuing representation** to be **implied from the conduct** of the respondent and his companions.'* While the men still intended to pay for their meal, their representation to the waiter, that they would pay, was a true representation. However, once they had decided not to pay for the meal, their continuing representation by conduct that they would still pay for the meal was a false representation and this is what deceived the waiter.

2 It could be argued that the driver had not obtained *by deception* because the passenger had realised that the car was not a proper taxi. However, the driver was convicted of obtaining by deception – it mattered not that at the time of handing over the money the passenger had realised that it was not a real taxi.

3 This case went to the House of Lords – the position with regards to cheques backed by cheque cards or credit cards is that, provided all the conditions on the cards are correct, i.e. still in date and correct signature, then the bank promises to pay the businessman who accepts the card, regardless of the state of the account in question – where it was held that the defendant had impliedly represented that he had authority to use his cheque card and so had deceived the manager.

4 The case went to the House of Lords – the woman's conviction under section 16(1) was restored. NB: the point with this case and the case in number 3 is that it is difficult to see how the businesspeople concerned can truly be said to have been 'deceived' when they did not care about the state of the accused's funds. Surely they could only be deceived if they thought there were sufficient funds in the account but in fact there was not?

A detailed look at the case of *R* v. *Preddy* (1996)

The case of *R* v. *Preddy* (1996) and a similar case of *R* v. *Dhillon* (1996) involved mortgage frauds which basically involved the defendants obtaining mortgage advances on properties by making fraudulent statements (they received transfers of money from building societies by telling lies). From what you have learnt so far you should be thinking that these cases are obvious candidates for prosecution under section 15(1) of the Theft Act 1968 – obtaining property (money) by deception – and, indeed, this is what they were charged with. At trial they were convicted and, on appeal to the Court of Appeal, the convictions were upheld. However, on appeal to the House of Lords their convictions were quashed. This came about due to close scrutiny and interpretation of section 15(1) as it applied to the money transfers. The appeal was decided on the basis that the *chose in action*, the credit balance which was created in the accounts of the appellants, was *not property belonging to another* and, as such, how could it fall within the scope of section 15(1) or indeed section 1 of the Theft Act 1968? The result of this decision was that it could have opened the door to fraudsters to secure transfers of money by deception without fear of committing a criminal offence! Needless to say this situation could not be allowed to continue for long and so, while the Law Commission was already undertaking a review of dishonesty offences, it decided to address this problem immediately.

To help your understanding of this case I have included extracts from the Law Commission's report on the problem created by the House of Lords decision in the *Preddy* case. Read the extracts and then consider the questions which follow.

Law Commission (Law Com. No. 243)
'Offences of Dishonesty : Money Transfers'
Ordered by The House of Commons to be printed 14 October 1996

Part I: Introduction

1.1 *In this report, we are looking at the problem of prosecuting those who commit mortgage fraud or otherwise obtain a transfer of funds dishonestly and by deception. As we shall show, the very recent decision of the House of Lords in Preddy has radically changed the law, creating important lacunae in the law ...*

1.4 *On 10 July 1996, the House of Lords unanimously allowed the appeals of Preddy and others. They were alleged to have committed mortgage fraud and had been charged under section 15(1) of the Theft Act 1968. The basis of the House of Lord's decision was that the borrowers, the alleged mortgage fraudsters, had not obtained 'property belonging to another' as required by section 15.*

1.5 *Essentially, the House of Lords did not accept that when the bank accounts of the appellants or their solicitors were credited they had obtained any property belonging to the lending institution. According to the House of Lords, the proper analysis was that the lending institution's credit balance was a chose in action (the debt owed to the institution by the bank) which was extinguished* and subsequently the defendant obtained something different, namely the chose in action constituted by the debt owed to him by his bank as represented by a credit in his own bank account. This asset was created for him and had therefore **never** belonged to anybody else. Thus the prosecution could not show that the borrower defendant had obtained property 'belonging to another' ...

1.7   As a result of the decision in Preddy it is now difficult to prosecute an individual who obtains by deception any form of payment by any form of banking transfer. Banking and other institutions were justifiably deeply concerned about this ...

1.11   As is widely known, the Commission invariably carries out some form of preliminary consultation in order to decide the full extent of the problem; thereafter it issues a consultation paper giving a lengthy consultation period and decides on its policy in the light of the responses to this. Such procedures require a great deal of time. We were very conscious from the initial responses to the decision in Preddy that there was a unanimous demand for urgent legislation to ensure that it would be possible to prosecute in cases of fraud involving the transfer of funds between accounts (whether electronically or by way of cheque). We therefore decided to endeavour to produce proposals for such an offence without a consultation paper and relying instead on informal consultation carried out over a period of only one month ...

1.15   As we have said, we were very conscious that we should produce a simple but comprehensive offence that can be easily understood and applied. We soon came to the conclusion that it would be desirable to create a new offence and this is what we have done ...

Part II : The lacuna in the law of deception exposed by Preddy

2.3   Lord Goff of Chieveley, in his speech in Preddy, set out the facts of the case.

       [Preddy and Slade] applied to building societies or other lending institutions for advances which were to be secured by mortgages on properties to be purchased by the applicant. In relation to each count, the mortgage application or accompanying documents contained one or more false statements, the applicant knowing the statements to be false. The statements referred to, for example, the name of the applicant; his employment and/or income; the intended use of the property; or the purchase price ...

       In [Dhillon's] case, the misrepresentations related to the intended occupancy of the properties in question ...; failure to declare the existence of other commitments; or particulars of employment ...

5

2.4   The mortgage advances were paid by the lenders to the appellants in various ways: by cheque, by telegraphic transfer and by the Clearing House Automated Payment System ('CHAPS').

2.5   Having dismissed the appeals in Preddy and Slade and Dhillon, the Court of Appeal (Criminal Division) certified the following questions as points of law of general public importance:
        (1) Whether the debiting of a bank account and the corresponding credit of another's bank account brought about by dishonest misrepresentation amounts to the obtaining of property within section 15 of the Theft Act 1968?

2.9   Lord Goff describes the difficulty in applying section 15 of the Theft Act 1968 in these circumstances and, in particular, in satisfying the requirement that the property should have **belonged to another:**
        ... In truth the property which the defendant has obtained is the new chose in action constituted by the debt now owed to him by his bank, and represented by the credit entry in his own bank account. This did not come into existence until the debt so created was owed to him by his bank, and so **never belonged to anyone else.**

2.10   On that vital reasoning, the House of Lords answered the first question in the negative ...

Part III: The difficulty in filling the lacuna under the present law

3.2   In this part we consider whether the lacuna in the law of criminal deception exposed by Preddy can be filled under the present law. We review the options available under section 15, other offences under the Theft Acts of 1968 and 1978 and the common law offence of conspiracy to defraud.

3.3   We conclude that, although some of the offences considered provide partial assistance, none of them provides an alternative that is sufficiently comprehensive or sufficiently reflects the gravamen of the defendant's dishonest conduct ...

Part IV: Filling the lacuna by extending the existing offences

4.11   **We recommend the insertion into the Theft Act 1968 of a new section 15A, creating an offence of dishonestly obtaining a money transfer by deception ...**

Part V: The new offence of obtaining a money transfer by deception

5.1   In the previous part we explained our reasons for concluding that the lacuna exposed by Preddy in the law of deception should be filled by the creation of a new offence. In this Part we consider the form that that offence should take.

5.2 *All the existing deception offences require that the defendant should dishonestly procure a specified result by deception, and the new offence should clearly take the same form: the main issue to be resolved is what the specified result should be. The draft Bill describes that result as the obtaining by the defendant, for himself or another, of a 'money transfer' – a phrase which seems to us to convey in simple terms the essence of the offence – and defines the circumstances in which a money transfer occurs ...*

Part VI: Preddy and the law of handling stolen goods

6.3 *... Before Preddy it had been held by the Court of Appeal ... that a person who dishonestly accepts a transfer of stolen funds from another's account into his or her own account is 'receiving' stolen goods within the meaning of section 22(1). But it is hard to see how this reasoning can survive Preddy. It assumes that the funds received by the transferee are the **same** funds as those that, before the transfer, were in the transferor's account; and according to Preddy this is not so ...*

6.8 *In order to ensure that the transferee of stolen funds (including funds obtained by deception) can be charged with handling them, additional provisions appear to be needed ...*

6.18 *We recommend the insertion into the Theft Act 1968 of a new section 24A, creating an offence of retaining a credit from a dishonest source, ...*

At the back of the report the Law Commission provided a draft Bill to amend the Theft Act 1968 and the Theft Act 1978, and for connected purposes. The Bill went through both Houses of Parliament in one day and became the Theft (Amendment) Act 1996 by which section 15A and section 24A were inserted into the Theft Act 1968.

Questions

1 What is meant by the phrase 'creating important lacunae in the law'? (1.1)

2 Did the House of Lords think that it made any difference to their deliberations that the money was transferred into the account of the appellant's solicitors? (1.5)

3 Explain what is meant by a chose in action. (1.5)

4 Why can a chose in action be described as a 'debt' owed by a bank? (1.5)

5 Why was it important that the lending institution's chose in action was *extinguished* when the money was transferred? (1.5)

6 Why did the Law Commission forego its usual practice of consultation in this case ? (1.11)

7 Why did the Law Commission wish to produce a simple but comprehensive offence? (1.15)

8 What did Lord Goff say was the most difficult aspect of section 15 in this situation? (2.9)

9 Why did the Law Commission not deal with the problem of money transfers under an existing section of the Theft Act 1968? (3.2, 3.3)

10 What did the Law Commission say were the common elements in existing deception offences? (5.2)

11 List the *result*s of all the deception offences, including the new one. (5.2)

12 How did the Law Commission solve the problem raised in paragraph 6.3?

Answers

1 Lacunae is the plural of lacuna which means a gap. Thus the phrase 'creating important lacunae in the law' means that important gaps in the law have been created and they have been created by the *Preddy* case.

2 In paragraph 1.5 we are told that the House of Lords did not accept that when the bank accounts of the appellants or their solicitors were credited they had obtained any property belonging to the lending institution. The solicitors' accounts were only credited on behalf of the appellants.

3 A chose in action is a form of personal property which is intangible, that is, it cannot be touched. As it is not possible to physically possess a chose in action the only way in which it can be protected is by bringing a legal action in court, such as suing someone for a debt owed to you. In the *Preddy* case the chose in action is the credit balance in the bank or building society.

4 A chose in action gives the person whose account is in credit the ability to demand (by legal action if necessary) money up to the value of the credit from the bank where it is deposited. Remember (from Chapter 4) that the bank owns the money while the person with the account in credit owns the chose in action, the right to enforce their right to an amount of money up to the value of their credit balance (or agreed overdraft limit). In this way it can be seen that, because it can be called upon to pay money to people with accounts in credit, the bank is in debt to such people.

5

Figure 5.2

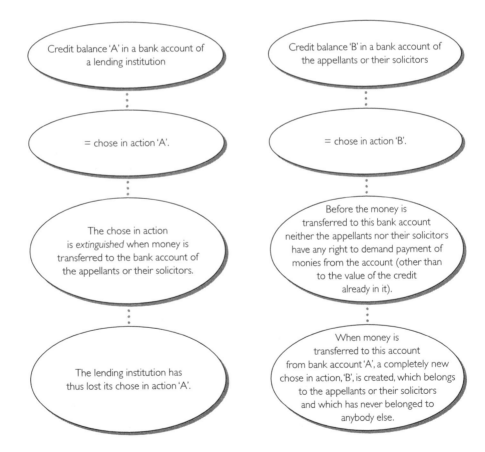

Credit balance 'A' in a bank account of a lending institution

= chose in action 'A'.

The chose in action is *extinguished* when money is transferred to the bank account of the appellants or their solicitors.

The lending institution has thus lost its chose in action 'A'.

Credit balance 'B' in a bank account of the appellants or their solicitors

= chose in action 'B'.

Before the money is transferred to this bank account neither the appellants nor their solicitors have any right to demand payment of monies from the account (other than to the value of the credit already in it).

When money is transferred to this account from bank account 'A', a completely new chose in action, 'B', is created, which belongs to the appellants or their solicitors and which has never belonged to anybody else.

5 It may help you to understand why it was important that the lending instituton's chose in action was extinguished when the money was transferred by studying Figure 5.2. If the lending institution's chose in action had not been extinguished on transfer of the money then the appellants would, indeed, have obtained property belonging to another as the lending institution would still own it.

Thus, because the chose in action 'A' was extinguished, and a new chose in action 'B' was created, how could it be said that the appellants had obtained property belonging to somebody else? What they now own is chose in action 'B' which has only ever belonged to them.

6 The Law Commission decided to forego its usual practice of consultation in this case because it acknowledged the fact that such consultations take a lot of time. In this instance they decided that they had to act very quickly otherwise it could have proved very difficult to prosecute future fraudulent money transfers.

7 The Law Commission wished to produce a simple but comprehensive offence which could be easily understood. This whole area of law on money transfers can be difficult to grasp and so there would be no point in making it even more difficult by virtue of a badly drafted piece of legislation. You must also remember that the Law Commission has embarked on a whole review of offences of dishonesty generally, the whole idea being to simplify such law.

8 Lord Goff said that the most difficult aspect of this case arose in relation to that part of section 15 which demands that the prosecution show that the property concerned *belonged to another*. As has been shown in the answer to question 5, the chose in action which was created for the appellants or their solicitors had never belonged to anybody else.

9 The Law Commisson felt that none of the existing deception offences provided a sufficiently comprehensive coverage of this type of deception (money transfers) and that none of the existing offences sufficiently matched the gravamen (worst part) of the defendant's conduct.

10 The common elements in the existing deception offences were stated as:

  i dishonestly;
  ii procure;
  iii a specified result;
  iv by deception.

11 The specified *results* of the deception offences are as shown below:

Theft Act 1968
 i section 15   obtains property;
 ii section 15A   obtains a money transfer;
 iii section 16   obtains a pecuniary advantage;

Theft Act 1978
 iv section 1   obtains services;
 v section 2   evades liability;

The Law Commission felt that the new offence to be created should take the same form as existing deception offences by requiring that the defendant should dishonestly procure a specified result by deception and they decided that the appropriate result for the new offence would be '*to obtain a money transfer*', which phrase, in simple terms, conveys the essence of the offence.

12 In paragraph 6.3 the Law Commission raises the point that if a money transfer creates a new chose in action then if A, by deception, dishonestly secures a transfer of money from B's account and then transfers the money into C's account, how can C be charged with receiving stolen goods? The goods are not stolen, as explained in the answer to question 5. Thus, in order to make sure this loophole was closed, they recommended the insertion into the Theft Act 1968 of a new section 24A, which created an offence of retaining a credit from a dishonest source.

5

Applying principles to examination questions

The following question concentrates on those aspects of this chapter which have not already received comprehensive coverage. In order to isolate which offences have possibly been committed you will have to look back over the statutory provisions on page 124. Highlight key areas and note the relevant sections of the Theft Acts 1968 and 1978. My suggested points for this question are shown opposite but you should only look at them when you have attempted the question for yourself.

John drove his car into a car wash and inserted a piece of metal shaped like the token which should have been purchased from the garage to work the car wash. The car wash machine washed John's car and he drove home.

On the way home John stopped at another garage to fill up with petrol. When he reached into the car to get his wallet, his mobile phone rang. He answered it to discover that his house had been burgled. He jumped into his car and drove off without paying for the petrol.

Later in the day the garage owner, Alan, sees John in the town and realises that he is the person who, earlier, had made off from his garage without paying for petrol. Alan approaches John and tells him that unless he pays him what he owes him for the petrol he will sue him in the civil courts.

The next day John attends an interview at work. If John manages to get the job he knows that he will move up the management spine and receive a higher salary. He dishonestly tells the interview panel that he has recently obtained an Open University degree. John gets the job.

Consider the criminal liability of John and Alan under the Theft Acts 1968 and 1978.

Tips on how to approach such a question

What has John obtained? A 'service'. Could he be charged with a 'deception' offence? No – a machine does not have a human mind and so cannot be deceived.

John drove his car into a car wash and inserted a piece of metal shaped like the token which should have been purchased from the garage to work the car wash. The car wash machine washed John's car and he drove home.

So what could he be charged with? Possibly making off without payment [*section 3(1) Theft Act 1978*] which does not require any deception and possibly the abstraction of electricity under *section 13 Theft Act 1968* – see Chapter 4, on theft.

Was John dishonest when he started to fill up with petrol? The implication is that he was not as he reached for his wallet. Is payment on the spot required here? Yes. Thus he could be charged under *section 3(1) Theft Act 1978* if the garage can trace him.

On the way home John stopped at another garage to fill up with petrol. When he reached into the car to get his wallet, his mobile phone rang. He answered it to discover that his house had been burgled. He jumped into his car and drove off without paying for the petrol.

The petrol in John's tank represents goods supplied under *section 3(1) Theft Act 1978.*

But was John 'dishonest'? This is for the jury to determine on the facts using the principles laid down in the case of *R* v. *Ghosh (1982)* if John claims that he was not dishonest – see Chapter 4, on theft.

Could Alan be charged with blackmail under *section 21 Theft Act 1968*? Was his demand unwarranted? Does Alan believe that he has reasonable grounds for making the demand? Probably he does – see *section 21(1)(a) and (b)*.

Later in the day the garage owner, Alan, sees John in the town and realises that he is the person who, earlier, had made off from his garage without paying for petrol. Alan approaches John and tells him that unless he pays him what he owes him for the petrol he will sue him in the civil courts.

Would it be blackmail if Alan had told John that unless he paid him for the petrol he would get his brother to 'teach him a lesson'? Probably, yes See *section 21(2) Theft Act 1968*.

Has John obtained a pecuniary advantage under *section 16(1) of the Theft Act 1968*? Probably, yes. See *section 16(2)(c)* – by deception he is being given the opportunity to earn greater remuneration (pay) in his employment.

The next day John attends an interview at work. If John manages to get the job he knows that he will move up the management spine and receive a higher salary. He dishonestly tells the interview panel that he has recently obtained an Open University degree. John gets the job.

You are not told that the scenario is mainly concerned with deception offences and as such you have to be alert to other provisions in the Theft Acts such as *section 13 Theft Act 1968*.

Consider the criminal liability of John and Alan under the Theft Acts 1968 and 1978.

Proposals for reform

It has been shown in this chapter that there is overlap between various sections in the Theft Acts 1968 and 1978. For example, there is an overlap between sections 1 and 15 of the 1968 Act (theft and obtaining property by deception) which has been made even more of an overlap since the case of *R* v. *Gomez* (1993). There is also a potential overlap between section 15 of the 1968 Act and sections 2 and 3 of the 1978 Act, depending on the facts.

It has also been shown how reform has already taken place by virtue of the Theft (Amendment) Act 1996 which inserted sections 15A and 24A into the 1968 Act. The Law Commission is currently undertaking a review of the offences involving dishonesty and this review obviously encompasses the deception offences. Given all the problems of interpretation and overlap of offences it would be a good idea to provide an up-to-date 'code' of all offences involving dishonesty.

CHAPTER Summary

In this chapter we have looked at the deception offences contained in the Theft Acts of 1968 and 1978 and noted how they have, in one sense, been narrowed down by the case of *R* v. *Gomez* (1993), while, in another sense, they have, been extended since the case of *R* v. *Preddy* (1996). The Law Commission's Report (Law Com. No. 243) has been considered in detail. Offences not covered in detail have been the subject of 'You Decide' cases and the application of principles to examination questions. In order to gain a comprehensive knowledge of deception and related offences it is necessary for you to study the whole of this chapter. The in-depth coverage of the cases of *R* v. *Gomez* (1993) and *R* v. *Preddy* (1996) should help you to understand potentially difficult topics (especially as regards choses in action) and at the same time prepare you for examination questions which focus on one or more aspects of an offence and require essay answers. Thus, after completion of this chapter, you should be prepared to face both problem and essay questions in an examination.

To round off the chapter I have included the report of a case, *R* v. *Hilton* (*Peter Arnold*), which appeared in *The Times* on 18 April 1997. Under which section of the Theft Act 1968 do you think the defendant was charged? You may wish to compare this case with the case of *R* v. *Ngan* (1997) where the defendant did not obtain money transfers to her account by deception; the money was transferred into her account by mistake. Why would Sui Ngan not be liable under the new section 24A of the Theft Act 1968?

Theft of credit

***Regina* v. *Hilton* (*Peter Arnold*)**

Where a person was charged with theft of property consisting of a credit balance, that person appropriated it by assuming the rights of the owner of the balance so causing a transfer to be made.

The Court of Appeal. Criminal Division (Lord Justice Evans. Mr Justice Clarke, and Judge Brian Walsh, QC, Recorder of Leeds) so held in a reserved judgment on March 7, dismissing the appeal of Peter Arnold Hilton against conviction on July 23, 1996 at Bolton Crown Court (Judge Lakin and a jury) for theft for which he was sentenced to two years imprisonment.

LORD JUSTICE EVANS said that the appellant was chairman of a charitable organisation who on two counts had caused its bank to transfer sums of money by way of faxed instructions, and on a third count by way of cheque.

The appellant's instructions, whether by cheque or otherwise, were the key which set the relevant inter-bank, or inter-account machinery in motion. The fact a transfer was made was enough to complete the offence, even if there remained an obligation on the bank, as debtor to its customer, to replenish the account.

6 Burglary, Robbery and Criminal Damage

OVERVIEW

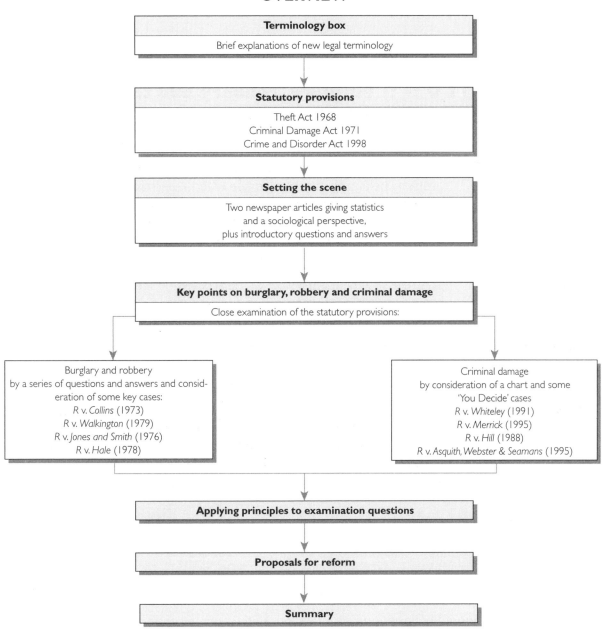

Terminology box

Brief explanations of new legal terminology

Statutory provisions

Theft Act 1968
Criminal Damage Act 1971
Crime and Disorder Act 1998

Setting the scene

Two newspaper articles giving statistics
and a sociological perspective,
plus introductory questions and answers

Key points on burglary, robbery and criminal damage

Close examination of the statutory provisions:

Burglary and robbery
by a series of questions and answers and consideration of some key cases:
R v. Collins (1973)
R v. Walkington (1979)
R v. Jones and Smith (1976)
R v. Hale (1978)

Criminal damage
by consideration of a chart and some
'You Decide' cases
R v. Whiteley (1991)
R v. Merrick (1995)
R v. Hill (1988)
R v. Asquith, Webster & Seamans (1995)

Applying principles to examination questions

Proposals for reform

Summary

In this chapter we will consider three more property offences. Burglary involves trespassing coupled with committing/attempting to commit/intending to commit one of several offences, such as theft. Robbery is essentially theft with violence, as when someone is mugged, and criminal damage occurs when property is damaged or destroyed. In order to help you get a feel for these offences I have taken a more sociological approach to the offences in the setting the scene section.

TERMINOLOGY: Burglary, robbery and criminal damage

Trespasser	The word 'trespasser' appears in the statutory definition of burglary. In ordinary usage it means that a person has gone onto or entered property belonging to someone else without permission. As far as the law is concerned, trespassing features in both the civil law (where it is a tort or wrong) and in the criminal law, as in burglary. You will find that, as far as burglary is concerned, whether or not someone is to be regarded as a trespasser is determined by the jury.
Intention	This refers to the mental state of the accused, his *mens rea*. As you will know from earlier chapters, when a person *intends* to commit a crime he has the most blameworthy state of mind.
Recklessness	This also refers to the mental state of the accused. In this instance the accused is regarded as less blameworthy because, in essence, what he did was take a risk.
Lawful excuse	If the actions/omissions of the accused amount to a crime, he may, nevertheless, be able to avoid conviction for the offence if he can prove that he had a lawful excuse for his behaviour. Sometimes the lawful excuse is included in a statute but not always.

Statutory provisions

The statutory provision for burglary and robbery is in the Theft Act 1968.

The statutory provision for criminal damage is in the Criminal Damage Act 1971 and in the Crime and Disorder Act 1998.

Theft Act 1968

Burglary

9 (1) A person is guilty of burglary if –
  (a) he enters any building or part of a building as a trespasser and with intent to commit any such offence as is mentioned in subsection (2) below; or
  (b) having entered into any building or part of a building as a trespasser he steals or attempts to steal anything in the building or that part of it or inflicts or attempts to inflict on any person therein any grievous bodily harm.

(2) The offences referred to in subsection (1)(a) above are offences of stealing anything in the building or part of a building in question, of inflicting on any person therein any grievous bodily harm or raping any person therein, and of doing unlawful damage to the building or anything therein.

(3) A person guilty of burglary shall on conviction on indictment be liable to imprisonment for a term not exceeding –
  (a) where the offence was committed in respect of a building or part of a building which is a dwelling, fourteen years;
  (b) in any other case, ten years.

(4) Reference in subsection (1) and (2) above to a building, and the reference in subsection (3) above to a building which is a dwelling, shall apply also to an inhabited vehicle or vessel, and shall apply to any such vehicle or vessel at times when the person having a habitation in it is not there as well as at times when he is.

Aggravated burglary

10 (1) A person is guilty of aggravated burglary if he commits any burglary and at the time has with him any firearm or imitation firearm, any weapon of offence, or any explosive; and for this purpose –
  (a) 'firearm' includes an airgun or air pistol, and 'imitation firearm' means anything which has the appearance of being a firearm, whether capable of being discharged or not; and
  (b) 'weapon of offence' means any article made or adapted for use for causing injury to or incapacitating a person, or intended by the person having it with him for such use; and

(c) 'explosive' means any article manufactured for the purpose of producing a practical effect by explosion, or intended by the person having it with him for that purpose.

(2) A person guilty of aggravated burglary shall on conviction on indictment be liable to imprisonment for life.

Robbery

8 (1) A person is guilty of robbery if he steals, and immediately before or at the time of doing so, and in order to do so, he uses force on any person or puts or seeks to put any person in fear of being then and there subjected to force.

(2) A person guilty of robbery, or of an assault with intent to rob, shall on indictment be liable to imprisonment for life.

Criminal Damage Act 1971

Criminal Damage

1 (1) A person who without lawful excuse destroys or damages any property belonging to another intending to destroy or damage any such property or being reckless as to whether any such property would be destroyed or damaged shall be guilty of an offence.

(2) A person who without lawful excuse destroys or damages any property, whether belonging to himself or another –

(a) intending to destroy or damage any property or being reckless as to whether any property would be destroyed or damaged; and

(b) intending by the destruction or damage to endanger the life of another or being reckless as to whether the life of another would be thereby endangered; shall be guilty of an offence.

(3) An offence committed under this section by destroying or damaging property by fire shall be charged as arson.

4 (1) A person guilty of arson under section 1 above or of an offence under section 1(2) above (whether arson or not) shall on conviction on indictment be liable to imprisonment for life.

(2) A person guilty of any other offence under this Act shall on conviction on indictment be liable to imprisonment for a term not exceeding ten years.

[NB: In this Act 'property' means property of a 'tangible' nature (which is capable of being *physically* destroyed or damaged) and includes real and personal property as described in section 4 of the Theft Act 1968.]

5 (1) This section applies to any offence under section 1(1) above . . .

(2) A person charged with an offence to which this section applies . . . be treated for those purposes as having a lawful excuse –

(a) if at the time of the act or acts alleged to constitute the offence he believed that the person or persons whom he believed to be entitled to

> consent to the destruction of or damage to the property in question had so consented, or would have so consented to it if he or they had known of the destruction or damage and its circumstances; or
>
> (b) if he destroyed or damaged or threatened to destroy or damage the property in question ... and at the time of the act or acts alleged to constitute the offence he believed –
>
>   (i) that the property, right or interest was in immediate need of protection; and
>
>   (ii) that the means of protection adopted or proposed to be adopted were or would be reasonable having regard to all the circumstances.
>
> **9** (3) For the purposes of this section it is immaterial whether a belief is justified or not if it is honestly held.
>
> ### Crime and Disorder Act 1998
>
> **30** (1) A person is guilty of an offence under this section if he commits an offence under section 1(1) of the Criminal Damage Act 1971 ... which is racially aggravated ...

6

Setting the scene

Read the following extracts from *The Times* and answer the questions which follow. These articles are not concerned with details on the substantive offences of burglary, robbery and criminal damage; rather, they help to put such offences into their sociological setting. Such information is often required in order to answer essay questions in examinations which are increasingly taking a broader look at criminality and often incorporate statistical data.

Article I

The following extract is taken from an article in *The Times* dated 15 October 1997, by Stewart Tendler, the crime correspondent.

Rising violence defies general fall in crime

BY STEWART TENDLER, CRIME CORRESPONDENT

Burglaries and car crime are falling but violence is on the increase, according to the latest figures for serious recorded crime in England and Wales issued yesterday by the Home Office.

Overall the figures reveal a fall of 5.5 per cent to 4.8 million crimes for offences committed between June 1996 and June this year. This is the first time the total has fallen below five million since 1989. Only five forces (the Metropolitan Police, Sussex, Gwent, North Wales and Norfolk) recorded any increases.

According to the figures, property crime was down 6 per cent to 4.4 million offences. Burglaries on homes dropped 10 per cent to 568,000 and car crime fell by 9 per cent to 1.2 million. All but four of the 43 police forces showed a fall in burglaries and 36 reported less car crime.

But the figures also show a 5.2 per cent rise in violent crime to 348,000 offences ... The only category of violent crime that fell in the 12 months was robbery, which mainly covers muggings. These dropped by 2.5 per cent to 70,500. In the previous 12 months they had risen by 14.8 per cent ...

Commenting on the figures, Chris Nuttall, director of research and statistics at the Home Office, said that the changes in property and violent crime could be linked to increased consumption of alcohol, spurred by economic recovery.

More money meant more drinking and this led to more violence. He said drug-related crime was more likely to be linked to theft and burglary. Burglaries generally fell in times of economic recovery. He said violent crimes had been rising since the Second World War and had rarely fallen. On average, there had been an annual rise of about 6.5 per cent in violent crime over the last 50 years.

Mr Nuttall admitted that the figures did not give a full picture of crime in Britain and said that there could be as many as 60 million crimes each year. He said that the latest British Crime Survey in 1996 showed about 19 million crimes each year against households and the figures did not include the total crime against businesses. Many crimes were not reported and the Home Office statistics ignored others.

Next year the Home Office is launching a new accounting system which will increase the number of reported crimes by up to one million. For the first time the figures will include common assault, assault on a constable, dangerous driving, possession of drugs and tampering with vehicles.

Some groups of crimes will be divided into separate offences in an attempt by ministers to make the figures representative of victims. Alun Michael, the Home Office minister responsible for the police, said that, when someone broke into 20 cars in a car park, this would no longer be registered as a single offence.

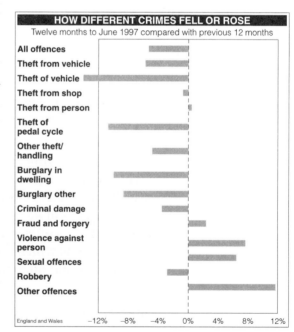

HOW DIFFERENT CRIMES FELL OR ROSE
Twelve months to June 1997 compared with previous 12 months

All offences
Theft from vehicle
Theft of vehicle
Theft from shop
Theft from person
Theft of pedal cycle
Other theft/handling
Burglary in dwelling
Burglary other
Criminal damage
Fraud and forgery
Violence against person
Sexual offences
Robbery
Other offences

England and Wales   −12%   −8%   −4%   0%   4%   8%   12%

Figure 6.1

Article II

The following extract is from an article in *The Times* dated 10 October 1997, by Polly Newton, political reporter.

Straw is accused of being soft on burglars

BY POLLY NEWTON,
POLITICAL REPORTER

The Shadow Home Secretary, Sir Brian Mawhinney, accused the Government yesterday of turning its back on burglary victims. He said that Labour's failure to bring in mandatory minimum sentences for repeat house-breakers proved that the party was on the side of the burglar, not the victim.

In a debate on law and order at the party conference, Sir Brian said that the previous Government had promised to implement minimum sentences for 'career' burglars by 1999. He challenged Jack Straw, the Home Secretary, to do the same ...

Sir Brian said: 'Burglary may be driven by drug addiction, so we will help the Government build on our approach to reduce the amount, the effect and the consequences of drugs in our society.' ...

Among the speakers in yesterday's debate was Jemma Nicholls, 15, who won loud applause when she condemned pop stars who took drugs. In an apparent reference to the appearance of Noel Gallagher, from Oasis, at a party given by Tony Blair this summer, she said that the fight against drugs was not helped 'when one of them is entertained by the Prime Minister at No.10'.

6

Questions

These questions represent a mix of data-response questions and stimulus-response questions. This means that some of the answers will not be found in the text and will have to be researched.

Article I

1 What is the approximate total population of the UK?

2 How many crimes were committed between June 1995 and June 1996? (Use the percentage fall of 5.5% to work this out.)

3 Find a map which shows the 43 police forces in England and Wales; is there any geographical pattern to be seen with regard to the five police forces which have recorded increases in recorded serious crime?

4 How many burglaries on homes were there between June 1995 and June 1996? (Use the percentage fall of 10% to work this out.)

5 Do you know why robbery, which mainly covers muggings, is regarded as a violent crime?

6 As far as the criminal law is concerned, what is the downside of an economic recovery?

7 In the article are we given any indication as to whether the people committing violent crimes are likely to be the same people who commit burglaries and theft?

8 Apart from the Home Office statistics on crime, name another source of crime statistics?

9 Why do you think crimes such as common assault, assault on a constable and the like have hitherto been left out of the Home Office statistics?

10 Why would the proposed new accounting system for crimes be more representative of the victims of crime than it is at present?

Article 2

11 What is meant by the phrase, 'the Shadow Home Secretary'?

12 Who is being referred to by the expression 'the Government'?

13 What is the Home Secretary responsible for?

14 What did Sir Brian Mawhinney mean when he said that, 'the previous Government had promised to implement minimum sentences for "career" burglars by 1999'?

15 What is a knock-on benefit for the criminal law of the Government getting tough on drug addiction?

16 Do you think legalisation of the taking of cannabis would affect the statistics for burglary and theft? Explain your answer.

Answers

1 The approximate total population of the UK is 57,000,000 (57 million).

2 It may help to approach this question as follows:
4.8 million represents 94.5% of the crimes committed between 1995–96.

Thus, in 1995–96, $\dfrac{4.8\text{ million}}{94.5} \times 100 = 100\%$ of crimes committed
which comes to 5,079,365 on a calculator, which can be rounded up to the nearest hundred thousand to 5.1 million.

3   From the map showing police forces you should have discovered that the police forces do not correspond to county boundaries; there are far more counties than there are police forces. Police force 29 (North Wales) and 40 (West Mercia) run into one another and form a band running along the northern edge of Wales (taking in five Welsh counties) and the western edge of England (taking in the counties of Shropshire and Hereford & Worcestershire). Police force 26 (Norfolk) encompasses the northern edge of East Anglia. Police force 25 (Metropolitan) occupies the northern side of the River Thames in London, and police force 37 (Sussex) encompasses West Sussex and East Sussex on the south coast below London.

To help you analyse these findings it would be a good idea to look in a modern school atlas which shows the following types of statistics for the UK:

   population density;
   urbanisation;
   income;
   education;
   unemployment;
   density of young/old people.

It would also be a good idea to look at the publication *Key Data* which is published by the Central Statistical Office every year. This publication provides useful statistics on a range of topics including population statistics and statistics relating to law and order. This publication is aimed at students so its style is particularly user friendly; there should be a copy in your school/college library.

4   It may help to approach this question as follows:

568,000 represents 90% of the crimes committed between 1995–96. Thus, $\dfrac{568,000}{90} \times 100 = 100\%$ of crimes committed 1995–96, which comes to 631,111 on a calculator which can be rounded down to the nearest thousand to 631,000.

5   Robbery is regarded as a violent crime because it is essentially theft with violence.

6   The downside of an economic recovery is that more money in society tends to lead to more drinking and this, in turn, tends to lead to more violence. You should ask yourself 'who' is drinking more and so being more violent? If you look up commentary on such statistics you may find that it is young people who are drinking more during an economic recovery and that it is mainly young males who get involved in violence. The upside of an economic recovery is that burglaries tend to decrease.

7   Not as such but the implication seems to be that we are looking at two different groups of people here. Drug takers may steal or burgle in order to finance their drug habit when the economy is flat or on a downwards cycle (when there is likely to be more unemployment as jobs are cut by businesses which are struggling to stay viable). However, during an economic recovery these same people are probably prepared to finance their drug habit from their earnings. The other implication is that during an economic recovery, when more people are in employment, more money is spent on alcohol which, in turn, tends to lead to more drunken people and more violence by these people. You may have noticed the difference between the timing of the occurrence of violent crimes and theft-related crimes:

Violent crimes ▶ economic recovery ▶ more drinking ▶ *more violent crimes*

theft/burglary ▶ flat/falling economy ▶ *more theft/burglary* ▶ drug taking

With violent crimes the crimes themselves seem to *follow* the increased drinking; with theft/burglary the crimes come *before* the drug taking. The implication here is that drug takers do not offend after taking drugs but in order to secure the drugs, whereas after getting drunk some people tend to commit violent crimes. It is worth thinking about this. How does this information impact on the debate to legalise the use of drugs such as cannabis? Maybe the Government should be taking a tougher line on the consumption of alcohol? Does the timing of the crimes matter? Is the crucial point that both alcohol and drugs have a tendency to increase the incidence of crime?

8   Another source of crime statistics is the British Crime Survey (BCS) which includes more categories of offences in its statistical data. The BCS statistics indicate that more crimes are being committed than the Home Office statistics would have us believe.

9   Presumably because they have been regarded as not serious enough (consider the actual *harm* to others caused by these offences), too numerous to record, or a combination of both these factors.

10   The proposed new accounting system for crimes would be more representative of the victims of the crime than at present because, at present, if a burglar, for instance, enters a hotel and steals from several rooms this spree of criminal activity is likely to be reported as one crime, when in fact there have been several crimes against several victims. What is the point of gearing the statistics towards recording the number of victims? It is interesting to note that the victim is getting more and more attention in the criminal justice system at present than ever before. In the pre-trial stages, during the trial and after the trial of the accused, the victim is gaining a higher profile. In the example given above, the burglar has embarked on a criminal spree and during this one criminal spree he affects several people, who thereby become victims. Surely, as far as criminality is concerned, what we are looking at here is one incidence of criminality? What is to be gained from recording this spree as several crimes? It could make the police look busier and, by implication, also the courts. It could help to justify spending the amounts of money that are spent in these areas and could even lead to more money being spent in these areas. You should follow up this line of thinking with your tutor.

11   The Shadow Home Secretary is the Home Secretary for the main opposition party which is not in power. As the Labour Party is in power at the time of writing, with Tony Blair as Prime Minister, the main opposition party is the Conservative Party. Thus, Sir Norman Fowler is the Shadow Home Secretary for the Conservative Party.

6

12   The Government represents the political party in power, which at present is the Labour Party.

13   The Home Secretary is Jack Straw. He is responsible for law and order in the UK.

14   The previous government was a Conservative Government led by John Major. Their last Home Secretary was Michael Howard who issued a White Paper entitled, 'Protecting the Public' in which, among other things, he proposed that minimum sentences should be brought in to deal with those criminals convicted of burglary for the third time. The idea of a *minimum* sentence is new as, currently, apart from the mandatory life sentence for murderers, statutes only provide maximum sentences for crimes. For more details on this you should look at Chapter 14, on sentencing. In this respect it could be argued that Sir Brian Mawhinney is trying to make 'political capital' out of the issue of burglary and criminal statistics. Jack Straw has said that he intends to take the politics out of such statistics by issuing them twice a year instead of four times a year and by publishing them on fixed dates so that the government cannot be accused of manipulating the publication dates for political ends. In this way it could be said that the statistics will be presented more objectively and possibly more accurately and will therefore reflect the true crime picture.

15 The knock-on benefit for the criminal law of the government getting tough on drug addiction is that if fewer people take drugs, fewer people are likely to commit theft and/or burglary in order to finance their drug habit in times of ecomonic hardship.

16 The legalisation of the taking of cannabis would probably not affect the statistics for burglary and theft. All legalisation would do is to bring takers of cannabis out into the open and to reduce the criminal statistics for drug taking – people who take cannabis would no longer be committing a criminal offence. However, this does not necessarily mean that fewer thefts or burglaries would be committed by drug takers who will still have to pay for the cannabis.

Key points on burglary, robbery and criminal damage

When studying the offences of burglary, robbery and criminal damage it is essential to have a good working knowledge of the statutory provisions. This is because the provisions appear to have been framed in order to provide 'catch all' provision, and in this case one wonders whether the offences have been over-defined. In order to develop such a working knowledge, we will examine the key points on burglary and robbery by a series of questions which will entail scrutiny of the statutory provisions. Relevant cases will be mentioned in the answers to these questions. We will consider criminal damage by a selection of 'You Decide' cases.

Look back over the statutory provisions for an initial overview and impression of the offences and then attempt to answer the questions which follow by constant referral to the provisions. At this stage we will deal with each offence separately.

Questions on burglary

1   For what sort of building is burglary applicable?

2   What do you think is meant by the phrase 'as a trespasser' for the purposes of burglary?

3   In order to 'enter' a building, how much of the accused's body must be in the building? Does all of his body have to be in the building or is it sufficient that his foot or arm entered the building?

4   In section 9(1)(a) burglary, the burglar enters any building or part of a building as a trespasser *'and with intent to commit any such offence ...'.* This means that when the trespasser enters the building/part of the building he already has an intent to commit a crime. How is burglary under section 9(1)(b) different to this?

5   If a person entered a building as a trespasser and, once in the building, then decided to rape someone, should the charge be one of burglary or rape?

6   If a person enters a building as a trespasser and, once in the building, then decides to steal something, but is caught before the something is actually stolen, could the person be charged with burglary?

7   What is the maximum sentence a convicted burglar of a warehouse could receive?

8   If a burglar went equipped with a long stave of wood into the end of which he had hammered several long nails, could he be charged with aggravated burglary contrary to section 10(1)?

9   Would it make any difference to your answer to question 8 above if the burglar left his stave of wood outside the building and then entered as a trespasser to burgle?

10   If found guilty and convicted of aggravated burglary contrary to section 10(1), what effect could this have on the sentence?

11   Divide section 9(1)(a) burglary into *mens rea* and *actus reus*.

Questions on robbery

12   Which crime has to be proved before there can be a conviction for robbery?

13   In order to find someone guilty of robbery, when must the robber have used force?

6

14 If someone comes up to you in the street and hits you for no apparent reason, and you drop your wallet in alarm, and the person then steals your wallet, could this person be charged with robbery? Explain.

15 Does the robber have to use force on the person he is actually robbing?

16 Does the robber actually have to use force on anyone?

17 How much force has to be used for someone to be found guilty of robbery?

18 How *immediately before* the stealing does the force have to be?

Answers

1 In section 9(1)(a) and section 9(1)(b) it states that burglary can apply to 'any building' or 'part of a building' and in section 9(4) it states that a building can mean an inhabited vehicle or vessel even when the inhabitant is not there. It must be noted that what constitutes a building, for the purposes of burglary, might be peculiar to burglary as the word might be given a different meaning in a different context. It is generally held that the word 'building' is an ordinary word which should be given its ordinary meaning by the jury. Thus, houses are buildings whatever they are made of, and houses under construction which are substantially finished are probably to be regarded as buildings. A portable structure can also be a building, such as a caravan so long as it is being used to live in (see section 9 [4]), or a boat which is being used to live in. A portable structure can also be a building even if no one is living in it, such as portakabins being used as temporary offices or temporary classrooms. It is generally held that tents are not buildings as they lack permanence.

The phrase, 'or part of a building', seems to cover those situations where someone is lawfully in one part of a building but then goes into a part of the building where he is not allowed to go. While it is generally obvious which parts of a building you may or may not enter (especially if doors are marked, 'Staff only'), the following case shows how the dividing line is not always that clear.

R v. Walkington (1979)

In this case the accused had entered a department store and had stolen money from a till which was surrounded by a movable three-sided enclosure. He was convicted of burglary and appealed. His appeal was dismissed. Geoffrey Lane L.J. said:

Here, it seems to us, there was a physical demarcation. Whether there was sufficient to amount to an area from which the public were plainly excluded was a matter for the jury. It seems to us that there was ample evidence on which they could come to the conclusion:
(a)   that the management had impliedly prohibited customers entering that area; and
(b)   that this particular defendant knew of that prohibition.

At this point it should be noted that the Crown Prosecution Service might be pursuing a case on the basis of burglary rather than solely for theft as the maximum term of imprisonment for burglary is longer than for theft. (See the statutory provisions on page 148.)

2   Consider the following two cases. The key sentences with regards to tresspassing are highlighted.

6

R v. Collins (1973)
Edmund Davies L. J.:

Let me relate the facts. Were they put into a novel or portrayed on the stage, they would be regarded as being so improbable as to be unworthy of serious consideration and verging at times on farce. At about 2 o'clock in the early morning of Saturday, July 24th, 1971, a young lady of 18 went to bed at her mother's home in Colchester. She had spent the evening with her boyfriend. She had taken a certain amount of drink, and it may be that this fact affords some explanation of her inability to answer satisfactorily certain crucial questions put to her at the trial.

She has the habit of sleeping without wearing night apparel in a bed which is very near the lattice-type window of her room . . .

At about 3.30 or 4 o'clock she awoke and she then saw in the moonlight a vague form crouched in the open window. She was unable to remember, and this is important, whether the form was on the outside of the window sill or on that part of the sill which was inside the room, and for reasons which will later become clear, that seemingly narrow point is of crucial importance.

The young lady then realised several things: first of all that the form in the window was that of a male; secondly, that he was a naked male; and thirdly, that he was a naked male with an erect penis. She also
saw in the moonlight that his hair was blond. She thereupon leapt to the conclusion that her boyfriend, with whom for some time she had been on terms of regular and frequent sexual intimacy, was paying her an ardent nocturnal visit. She promptly sat up in bed, and the man descended from the sill and joined her in bed and they had full sexual intercourse. But there was something about him which made her think that things were not as they usually were between her and her boyfriend. The length of his hair, his voice as they exchanged what was described as 'love talk', and other features led her to the conclusion that somehow there was something different. So she turned on the bed-side light, saw that her companion was not her boyfriend and slapped the face of the intruder, who was none other than the defendant. She then went into the bathroom and he promptly vanished.

The complainant said that she would not have agreed to intercourse if she had known that the person entering her room was not her boyfriend . . .

The defendant . . . had taken a lot of drink. . . . He found a step ladder, leaned it against the wall and climbed up and looked into the bedroom. He could see through the wide-open window a girl who was naked and asleep. So he descended the ladder and stripped off all his clothes, with the exception of his socks, because apparently he took the view that if the girl's mother entered the bedroom it would be easier to effect a rapid escape if he had his socks on than if he was in bare feet. This is a matter about which we are not called upon to express any view, and would in any event find ourselves unable to express one.

Having undressed, he then climbed the ladder and pulled himself up on to the window sill. His version of the matter is that he was pulling himself in when she awoke. She then got up and knelt off the bed, put her arms around his neck and body, and she seemed to pull him into the bed. He went on: 'I was rather dazed because I didn't think she would want to know me ...'

Now, one feature of the case which remained at the conclusion of the evidence in great obscurity is where exactly Collins was at the moment when, according to him, the girl manifested that she was welcoming him. Was he kneeling on the sill outside the window or was he already inside the room having climbed through the window frame, and kneeling on the inner sill? It was a crucial matter, for there were certainly three ingredients that it was incumbent on the Crown to establish. Under section 9 of the Theft Act 1968, which renders a person guilty of burglary if he enters any building or part of a building as a trespasser and with intention of committing rape, the entry of the accused into the building must first be proved. Well, there is no doubt about that, for it is common ground that he did enter this girl's bedroom. Secondly, it must be proved that he entered as a trespasser. We will develop that point a little later. Thirdly, it must be proved that he entered as a trespasser with intent at the time of entry to commit rape therein ...

In the judgment of this court there cannot be a conviction for entering premises 'as a trespasser' within the meaning of section 9 of the Theft Act unless the person entering does so knowing that he is a trespasser and nevertheless deliberately enters, or, at the very least, is reckless as to whether or not he is entering the premises of another without the other party's consent ...

We have to say that this appeal must be allowed on the basis that the jury were never invited to consider the vital question whether this young man did enter the premises as a trespasser, that is to say knowing perfectly well that he had no invitation to enter or reckless of whether or not his entry was with permission ...

R v. *Jones and Smith* (1976)

In this case Smith had been given permission by his father to enter the father's house at any time. Smith and his friend Jones entered the house one night and stole two television sets. They were convicted of burglary contrary to section 9(1)(b) of the Theft Act 1968 and appealed.

In the Court of Appeal, James L.J. said:

... it is our view that a person is a trespasser for the purpose of section 9(1)(b) of the Theft Act 1968 if he enters the premises of another knowing that he is entering in excess of the permission that has been given to him to enter, providing the facts are known to the accused which enable him to realise that he is acting in excess of the permission given or that he is acting recklessly as to whether he exceeds that permission, then that is sufficient for the jury to decide that he is in fact a trespasser. ...

Finally, before parting with the matter, we would refer to a passage of the summing up to the jury ... In the course of that the recorder said:

'*I have read out the conversation they had with* Detective Sergeant Tarrant and in essence Smith said, "My father gave me leave to take these sets and Jones was invited along to help". If that account may be true, that is an end of the case, but if you are convinced that that night they went to the house and entered as trespassers and had no leave or licence to go there for that purpose, and they intended to steal these sets and keep them permanently themselves, acting dishonestly, then you will convict them ...'

Then the recorder gave an illustration of the example of a person who is invited to go into a house to make a cup of tea and that person goes in and steals the silver and he went on ...

'*I hope that illustrates the matter sensibly. Therefore you may find it difficult not to say, if they went in there they must have gone in order to steal because they took elaborate precautions, going there at dead of night, you really cannot say that under any circumstances their entry to the house could have been other than trespass.*'

The appeals were dismissed.

It can be seen from these two cases that it can be very difficult to determine whether or not the accused's behaviour amounted to trespass. If his behaviour did not amount to trespass than you must remember that he could still be found guilty of the ulterior offence which could be theft, rape, grievous bodily harm or criminal damage depending on the facts of the case.

3   In the case of *R* v. *Collins* (1973) Edmund Davies L.J. remarked that the entry had to be 'an effective and substantial entry'. However, in the case of *R* v. *Brown* (1985) it was held that the entry need not be substantial, just effective, so it was possible to be guilty of burglary by leaning through a shop window and stealing goods. Since the case of *R* v. *Ryan* (1996) it is probable that the entry need not be effective either, as in this case the defendant had managed to get his head and arm through a window of a house but had then got stuck. Obviously, he could not get away but his head and arm had entered the building and he had intended to steal and his conviction was upheld. It is still the case that whether or not an entry has been made is a matter for the jury to decide on the facts presented to them.

4 Under section 9(1)(b) the trespasser entered the building/part of a building without any intent to steal or inflict grievous bodily harm, but once inside the building/part of a building *then decided* to steal or inflict grievous bodily harm. Thus, if you go into an office marked 'Staff Only' just to be nosy and you are not staff, you will probably be trespassing. If, once inside the office, you notice a lap-top computer and decide to steal it you become a section 9(1)(b) burglar rather than a section 9(1)(a) burglar because when you entered the office you did not, at that time, intend to steal anything.

5 The charge would be rape. If the trespasser had entered the building/part of a building with intent to rape this would come under section 9(1)(a) burglary but in this example the trespasser did not have the intention to rape as he entered the building/part of a building and rape is not included in section 9(1)(b) burglary.

6 Yes. This is because section 9(1)(b) burglary covers attempts to steal as well as stealing and also covers attempts to inflict grievous bodily harm as well as actually committing grievous bodily harm.

7 The maximum sentence for a non-domestic burglary is 10 years – see section 9(3)(b).

8 Yes, the stave of wood plus nails would amount to a 'weapon of offence' – see section 10(1)(b).

9 Yes, it would make a difference because in section 10(1) it states that to be guilty of aggravated burglary the burglar has to have the weapon of offence *with him at the time of the burglary*. If the stave of wood is left outside the building, when the person enters the building as a trespasser he does not have with him a weapon of offence. Read the case of *R* v. *Klass* (1997) shown below which appeared in *The Times* on 17 December 1997. This case reinforces the point that the burglar must have the weapon of offence with him at the time of the burglary to be guilty of aggravated burglary and demonstrates that although all three men present at the scene could be convicted of burglary under the rules for accomplices (see Chapter 7 for more details), even though only one of them entered the caravan, the rules for accomplices would not be taken to extend the liability from ordinary burglary to aggravated burglary, for the reasons stated and highlighted.

Aggravated burglary offence

Regina v. *Klass*

Before Lord Justice Mantell, Mr Justice Hooper and Judge Michael Walker

[Judgment November 27]

To commit an offence of aggravated burglary contrary to section 10 of the Theft Act 1968, a person must have with him a weapon of offence at the time of entry. The offence could not be committed if the weapon was not being carried by one of the people effecting entry to the building.

The Court of Appeal, Criminal Division, so held in allowing an appeal by Kennedy Francis Klass against his conviction in January 1997 at Chelmsford Crown Court (Mr Recorder Parkins, QC) of aggravated burglary for which he was sentenced to three years detention in a young offender institute.

Section 9 of the Theft Act 1968 provides: "(1) A person is guilty of burglary if – (a) he enters any building … as a trespasser and with intent to commit any … offence ….[such as] stealing anything in the building."

Section 10 provides: '(1)A person is guilty of aggravated burglary if he commits any burglary and at the time has with him … any weapon of offence… and for this purpose – … (b) 'weapon of offence' means any article made or adapted for use for causing injury to or incapacitating a person…"

Mr John C. Barker, assigned by the Registrar of Criminal Appeals, for the appellant; Miss Susannah Farr for the Crown.

MR JUSTICE HOOPER, giving the judgment of the court, said that the appellant and the two other men, one of whom had a piece of pole in his hand, wrenched open the door of a caravan and demanded money of the occupant who told them he did not have any. The man with the pole than hit the occupant of the caravan over the head and pursued him as he ran away, hitting him repeatedly. When the appellant was subsequently arrested he admitted being outside the caravan but denied entering it although his fingerprints were found on a worktop inside. He said that when he saw the victim being hit he and the third man ran away.

On appeal, the question of law raised was whether the offence of aggravated burglary could be committed if the weapon was not being carried by the burglar or one of the burglars who entered the building.

Assuming there was only one weapon and that weapon was with the person on the outside, that person committed burglary if he was aiding and abetting the burglary being committed by the person effecting entry.

A strict interpretation of section 10 would therefore lead to the conclusion that both could be convicted of aggravated burglary. However, the gravamen of the offence was entry with a weapon.

The purpose of section 10 was to deter people from taking weapons into buildings and other people's houses while committing burglary. The fact that a getaway driver had a weapon with him in the car would not, in their Lordship's judgment, be sufficient to turn an offence of burglary into one of aggravated burglary. Although there were certain academic attractions in the strict interpretation, the purposive approach was to be preferred.

In the circumstances, the conviction of aggravated burglary had to be quashed. Relying on section 3 of the Criminal Appeal Act 1968, a conviction for burglary would be substituted and the sentence would be reduced to two years detention. Solicitors: Crown Prosecution Service, Chelmsford.

Source: *The Times*, 17 December 1997

6

10 The effect on the sentence is enormous as a person convicted of aggravated burglary could be sentenced to imprisonment for life which is an indeterminate sentence. Ordinary burglary has maximum determinate sentences of 14 years (for a dwelling) and 10 years in all other cases.

11 *Mens rea –*

 i intention to enter as a trespasser or reckless as to whether entry was as a trespasser (as stated in *R v. Collins* [1973] above);

 ii with intent to commit an *ulterior offence,* as listed in section 9(2):

   a) theft;

   b) inflicting grievous bodily harm;

   c) rape;

   d) criminal damage.

Actus reus –

 i entering;

 ii a building or part of a building;

 iii as a trespasser.

12 Before there can be a conviction for robbery, it is necessary to prove theft.

13 In order to prove robbery the robber must have used force either:

 i immediately before the stealing; or

 ii at the time of stealing.

R v. Hale (1978)

In this case the accused and an accomplice went into a house wearing stocking masks. The accomplice went upstairs to look around while the accused put his hand over the mouth of the woman who lived in the house. The accomplice came downstairs with a jewellery box. At this point they tied the woman up, threatening to harm her child if she got in touch with the police within five minutes of them leaving the house. The accused was convicted of robbery and appealed.

In the Court of Appeal, Eveleigh L.J. remarked:

 ... There remains the question whether there was a robbery. Quite clearly the jury were at liberty to find the appellant guilty of robbery relying upon the force used when he put his hand over Mrs Carrett's mouth to restrain her from calling for help. We also think that they were also entitled to rely upon the act of tying her up provided they were satisfied (and it is difficult to see how they could not be satisfied) that the force so used was to enable them to steal. If they were still engaged in the act of stealing the force was clearly used to enable them to continue to assume the rights of the owner and permanently to deprive Mrs Carrett of her box, which is what they began to do when they first seized it ...

Thus, it will be noted that it is possible to regard theft as an ongoing event and so long as force is used while the theft is still ongoing, then such actions can amount to robbery. In the case above the stealing of the jewellery box was held to continue during the tying up despite the fact that the *appropriation* (the touching of the jewellery box) first took place upstairs.

14 There has been a theft and force has been used. Was the force used immediately before or at the time of the theft? Yes, but was the force used *in order to steal*? It is hard to say in this example but on the face of it the use of force was not used in order to steal; the use of force had been 'for the hell of it' and the theft came afterwards without any reliance on the use of force.

15 The robber does not have to use force on the person he is actually robbing. The force can be used on *any* person – see section 8(1). Thus, it could be robbery if your wallet was stolen and in order to steal it and at the time of stealing it the thief pushed your sister out of the way.

16 No. It is sufficient that any person was put in fear of there and then being subjected to force or that the robber sought to put any person in fear of there and then being subjected to force.

17 The degree of force necessary to constitute a robbery is a matter of fact which has to be left to the jury to decide. Thus, the amount of force may be very slight and may be as little as a common law battery. In the case of *R* v. *Dawson* (1976) it was held by the jury that merely jostling a sailor in the street in order to steal his wallet was enough force for the purposes of robbery.

18 It is difficult to say whether we are looking at seconds, minutes or hours here. J.C. Smith in *Criminal Law*, 8th edition, states that if a gang decided to steal from a factory and had to overpower the nightwatchman at the main gate first, then such use of force could amount to force used immediately before the stealing even though it might take the gang several minutes to get from the main gate to the inside of the factory. He further suggests that it would also be robbery if some gang members detained the nightwatchman at home while other members of the gang stole from the factory. Thus, in this latter example, we have a time lapse and a combination of geographical locations.

Criminal damage

We will look at the offence of criminal damage by reference to Figure 6.2 and by application of the statutory provisions to the 'You Decide' cases which follow.

6

Figure 6.2

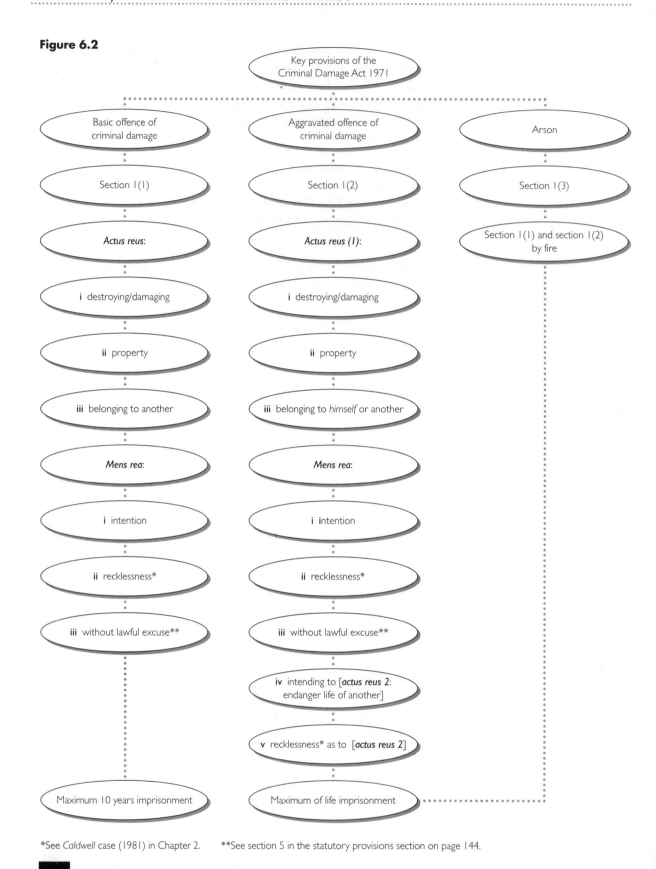

*See *Caldwell* case (1981) in Chapter 2.   **See section 5 in the statutory provisions section on page 144.

YOU DECIDE

The following cases are concerned with criminal damage. Students should refer to Figure 6.2 and to the relevant statutory provisions.

1 R v. Whiteley (1991)

In this case the defendant was convicted of criminal damage after he altered data contained on computer disks. He had not physically damaged the disks though and so appealed.

You decide the appeal.

2 R v. Merrick (1995)

In this case the defendant was convicted of criminal damage under section 1(2) when he left a mains cable exposed for about six seconds during which time there was a risk that life could be endangered. He had the consent of the owner of the cable to cut it and, within the six seconds, had buried it and cemented over it. He appealed.

You decide the appeal.

3 R v. Hill (1988)

In this case Mrs Hill was convicted under section 3 of the Criminal Damage Act 1971 for having with her a hacksaw blade without lawful excuse which she intended to use to cut the perimeter fence of a US naval base in Wales. She had claimed that she had a lawful excuse as, fearing that the base might come under attack by Soviet missiles, she wanted to protect her property and she hoped that by cutting the fence she would hasten the closure of the base. She appealed claiming lawful excuse under section 5(2).

You decide the appeal.

4 R v. Asquith, Webster and Seamans (1995)

In this case the defendants had pushed a large stone from a railway bridge onto a passenger train going under the bridge. While the stone did not actually enter the passenger carriage and while no one was actually injured, they were convicted of criminal damage contrary to section 1(2) and appealed.

You decide the appeal.

6

Answers

1 The appeal was dismissed. It was held that while physical damage may obviously amount to criminal damage, though not necessarily, it was also possible for there to be damage of an intangible nature. Thus, interference with the disks which amounted to *an impairment of the value or usefulness of them* to the owner, could amount to criminal damage. Nowadays, the defendant would be liable under The Computer Misuse Act 1990 which, by section 1, aims to catch computer 'hackers' who access data on computers of others without their knowledge or authority..

2 The appeal was dismissed according to a straight application of the test for recklessness in *Caldwell* (1982) – see earlier chapter for details. Thus, here, the appellant had realised that he would be creating a risk by exposing the cable but, nevertheless, went ahead with his actions and created the risk. It matters not that he immediately took steps to get rid of the risk.

3 The appeal was dismissed. The danger percieved was *too remote* and so there was no need for her to take *immediate action* to cut the perimeter fence of the base.

4 The jury had convicted them of intending to endanger life by the *stone itself* which is not covered by section 1(2) – for section 1(2) to apply they need to have intended/been reckless as to whether the stone would cause criminal damage and have intended/been reckless as to whether such *resultant damage* would endanger life. [See section.1 (2)(b).] The Court of Appeal substituted a conviction on this basis.

Applying principles to examination questions

When you have worked through this chapter you should be ready to attempt to answer the question below which is only concerned with the offences of burglary, robbery and criminal damage. More demanding questions, which incorporate defences and other factors, will be considered later. Note key points and refer back through the chapter to ensure that you have covered all the main points and cited appropriate cases and/or statutory provisions. My own approach to the question is shown below and should be referred to only after you have attempted the question for yourself.

6

A new bypass is being constructed to divert traffic out of Little-Snoring-on-the-Marsh. Several protesters have camped nearby. Sue and Rachel are two of the protesters. One night Sue approaches the compound where heavy machinery and vehicles are kept and cuts the security fence with wire cutters.

She is not worried about the security guard because she has already knocked him unconscious.

Once inside the compound she enters a vehicle storage shed, cuts the hydraulic cables on a large tractor and then decides to break into one of the portakabins.

She is half-way through a window and has got hold of some keys and maps when she becomes stuck and is apprehended.

While Sue is away from the campsite, Rachel enters Sue's tent and steals her handbag.

The next day the driver of the tractor narrowly escapes serious injury when the brakes fail.

Ignoring any offences against the person as such, consider the possible criminal liability of Sue and Rachel in terms of burglary, robbery and criminal damage.

Tips on how to approach such a question

Criminal damage contrary to *section 1(1) CDA 1971*.

Is she a trespasser?

Is this a building for the purposes of *section 9(1) TA 1968*?

Is a portakabin a building for the purposes of section 9(1) TA 1968? 'Building' is an ordinary word for the consideration of the jury.

(Touching can amount to an appropriation for theft). Has she entered the building for the purposes of *section 9 TA 1968*? See *R v. Collins* (1973) *R v. Jones and Smith* (1976) *and R v Ryan* (1996)

Is a tent a building for the purposes of *section 9(1) TA 1968*?

Would this make Sue liable to be charged with criminal damage contrary to *section 1(2) CDA 1971*? Was she *reckless* as to whether the life of anyone would be endangered *by the damage* she had done? Could she have been so charged as soon as she had cut the cable? Probably, yes.

A new bypass is being constructed to divert traffic out of Little-Snoring-on-the-Marsh. Several protesters have camped nearby. Sue and Rachel are two of the protesters. One night Sue approaches the compound where heavy machinery and vehicles are kept and cuts the security fence with wire cutters.

She is not worried about the security guard because she has already knocked him unconscious.

Once inside the compound she enters a vehicle storage shed, cuts the hydraulic cables on a large tractor and then decides to break into one of the portakabins.

She is half-way through a window and has got hold of some keys and maps when she becomes stuck and is apprehended.

While Sue is away from the campsite, Rachel enters Sue's tent and steals her handbag.

The next day the tractor driver narrowly escapes serious injury when the brakes fail.

Ignoring any offences against the person as such, consider the possible criminal liability of Sue and Rachel in terms of burglary, robbery and criminal damage.

Abbreviations:
TA 1968 – Theft Act 1968
CDA 1971 – Criminal damage Act 1971

Could the wire cutters be classed as a weapon of offence for *section 10 TA 1968*? Did she use them to knock the security guard unconscious and/or did she carry them with her throughout just in case she needed to hit anyone else?

Motive is irreleva[n]

Sue *intends* to damage this property, the fenc[e]

We are told not t[o] consider any 'offence against the person' – if you do you are wasting time and effort.

Criminal damage contrary to *section 1(1) CDA 1971*.

When did she form the intent to damage the property? Argue this point because criminal damage is only listed as a[n] offence for *section 9(1)(a)* burglary.

Could she be guilty of robber[y] contrary to *section 8 TA 1968*? Did sh[e] use force on the security guard immediately before stealing and in order to steal? See *R v. Hale* (1978).

For *section 9(1)(a)* burglary is mere intent to steal sufficient?

See *R v. Asquith, Webster & Seamans* (1995).

You need only consider the assault on the security guard as regards robbery.

Proposals for reform

There has been some parallel development with regard to *stealing* property and *damaging* property:

▶ Larceny Act 1861 ⟶ replaced by ⟶ Theft Act 1968
Larceny Act 1916

▶ Malicious Damage ⟶ replaced by ⟶ Criminal
Act 1861 Damage Act
1971

Both of these modern Acts developed a new *code* for their respective types of offences against property and in both of them the definition of property is similar.

Burglary, robbery and criminal damage are not regarded as being in need of urgent reform, probably because of the fact that the law as regards these property offences has already been codified in the 1960s and 1970s. This contrasts with the law concerning offences against the person which is regarded as in need of urgent reform, probably due to the fact that the main statutory provision is the Offences Against the Person Act 1861.

6

CHAPTER Summary

Burglary

In this chapter we have looked at burglary from a sociological point of view and in terms of the substantive law – the statutory provisions and the case law.

What is of concern to most people in society is domestic burglary. People do not like the fact that the privacy of their home can be violated and items removed from it. Unfortunately, the police forces in England and Wales find it difficult to detect many burglars who are often involved in such criminal activity solely to finance their drug habit. Burglary is therefore a crime which leaves many victims feeling aggrieved that the villain has not been brought to justice. The knock-on effect of burglaries is that home insurance policies are likely to become more expensive; people make sure that they have a comprehensive policy against which they can claim if they are burgled and when insurance companies have to pay out after burglaries the costs to the company will obviously be passed on to the customers.

Robbery

Most people think of muggings or armed (bank) robberies when robbery is mentioned. This is probably due to the fact that these types of robbery often receive media coverage. Muggings of vulnerable people in society, such as old age pensioners, children or disabled people, are particularly unpleasant. In these instances the victim is directly affected, not only as a victim of a property offence (stealing) but also as a victim of an offence against the person (force).

Criminal damage

When physical property (a car, a window, a door, a television, etc.) is damaged or destroyed it is not difficult to see how a charge of criminal damage can be brought. However, we have seen in this chapter that it might be possible to damage property in a less obvious physical sense as regards the information contained on computer disks (and cassette tapes and video tapes) if such information is impaired in value or usefulness to the owner. The *mens rea* of criminal damage in terms of recklessness has not been fully explored in this chapter as it has already been considered in an earlier chapter; see the case of *Metropolitan Police Commissioner* v. *Caldwell* (1982).

By section 30 of the Crime and Disorder Act 1998 a new offence of 'Racially aggravated criminal damage' has been created. See the statutory provisions section of this chapter.

SECTION FOUR:
General principles

The following topics are covered in this section:

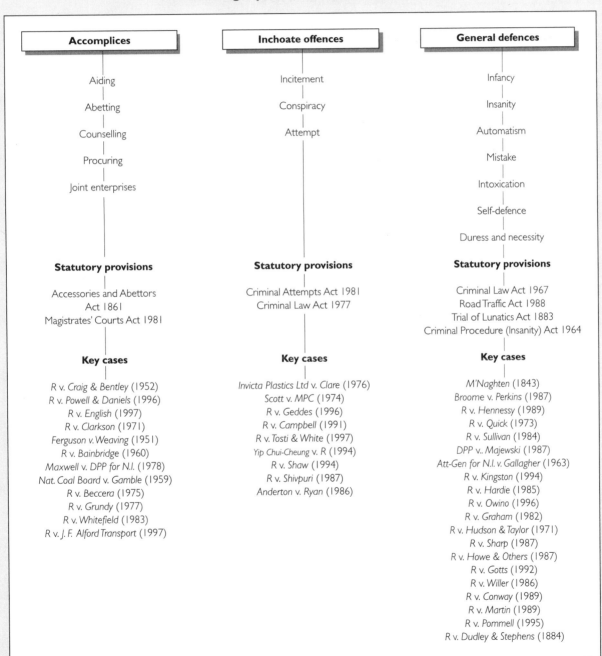

Accomplices	**Inchoate offences**	**General defences**
Aiding	Incitement	Infancy
Abetting	Conspiracy	Insanity
Counselling	Attempt	Automatism
Procuring		Mistake
Joint enterprises		Intoxication
		Self-defence
		Duress and necessity

Statutory provisions	**Statutory provisions**	**Statutory provisions**
Accessories and Abettors Act 1861	Criminal Attempts Act 1981	Criminal Law Act 1967
Magistrates' Courts Act 1981	Criminal Law Act 1977	Road Traffic Act 1988
		Trial of Lunatics Act 1883
		Criminal Procedure (Insanity) Act 1964

Key cases	**Key cases**	**Key cases**
R v. Craig & Bentley (1952)	Invicta Plastics Ltd v. Clare (1976)	M'Naghten (1843)
R v. Powell & Daniels (1996)	Scott v. MPC (1974)	Broome v. Perkins (1987)
R v. English (1997)	R v. Geddes (1996)	R v. Hennessy (1989)
R v. Clarkson (1971)	R v. Campbell (1991)	R v. Quick (1973)
Ferguson v. Weaving (1951)	R v. Tosti & White (1997)	R v. Sullivan (1984)
R v. Bainbridge (1960)	Yip Chui-Cheung v. R (1994)	DPP v.. Majewski (1987)
Maxwell v. DPP for N.I. (1978)	R v. Shaw (1994)	Att-Gen for N.I. v. Gallagher (1963)
Nat. Coal Board v. Gamble (1959)	R v. Shivpuri (1987)	R v. Kingston (1994)
R v. Beccera (1975)	Anderton v. Ryan (1986)	R v. Hardie (1985)
R v. Grundy (1977)		R v. Owino (1996)
R v. Whitefield (1983)		R v. Graham (1982)
R v. J. F. Alford Transport (1997)		R v. Hudson & Taylor (1971)
		R v. Sharp (1987)
		R v. Howe & Others (1987)
		R v. Gotts (1992)
		R v. Willer (1986)
		R v. Conway (1989)
		R v. Martin (1989)
		R v. Pommell (1995)
		R v. Dudley & Stephens (1884)

7 Accomplices

OVERVIEW

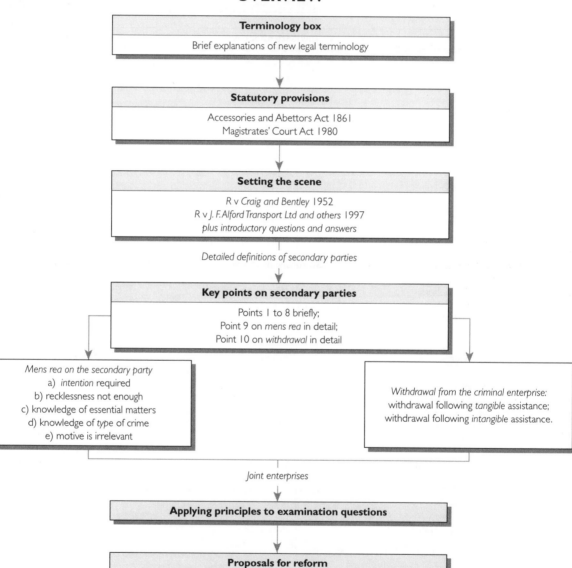

Terminology box

Brief explanations of new legal terminology

Statutory provisions

Accessories and Abettors Act 1861
Magistrates' Court Act 1980

Setting the scene

R v *Craig and Bentley* 1952
R v *J. F. Alford Transport Ltd and others* 1997
plus introductory questions and answers

Detailed definitions of secondary parties

Key points on secondary parties

Points 1 to 8 briefly;
Point 9 on *mens rea* in detail;
Point 10 on *withdrawal* in detail

Mens rea on the secondary party
a) *intention* required
b) recklessness not enough
c) knowledge of essential matters
d) knowledge of *type* of crime
e) motive is irrelevant

Withdrawal from the criminal enterprise:
withdrawal following *tangible* assistance;
withdrawal following *intangible* assistance.

Joint enterprises

Applying principles to examination questions

Proposals for reform

Law Commission's Consultation Paper No. 131 1993
Case of Philip English

Chapter summary

Having considered theft, burglary, robbery, criminal damage and other property offences as separate topics, involving the commission of any one offence by only one person, you should now be ready to consider those situations where more than one person is involved in the commission of an offence. Such persons can be termed accomplices. You will discover that it is not just the actual perpetrator of a crime who may be liable to be charged and tried for the crime. In this chapter we will consider the topics of secondary parties and joint enterprises.

While studying these new topics we will inevitably use new terminology as outlined below. It might be an idea to cover up the explanations given on the right-hand side of the box to see what you already know. You can use the box later as part of your revision prior to examinations.

7

T E R M I N O L O G Y: Accomplices

Principal offender	The person (with appropriate *mens rea*) whose actions are the most direct cause of the *actus reus* of the crime.
Accomplice	Someone who participates in the commission of a criminal offence; they may be classed as a principal offender themselves if they are involved in a joint enterprise, or they may be classed as a secondary party.
Joint enterprise	Where two or more persons carry out actions which constitute *the actus reus* of the crime; they are all classed as principal offenders.
Secondary parties	Persons whose actions do not constitute part of the *actus reus* of the offence committed by the principal offender, but whose actions constitute aiding, abetting counselling or procuring the commission of the offence by the principal offender.
Aiding	Giving some *practical* assistance to the principal offender either before or at the time of the crime.
Abetting	Inciting or encouraging the commission of the offence by the principal offender *at the time* it is happening.
Counselling	Inciting or encouraging the commission of the offence by the principal offender *before* it takes place.
Procuring	Doing some acts which bring about or cause the crime to be committed.

Statutory provisions

Lawyers are given statutory guidance to help them decide whether or not an offence by a principal offender involves criminality on the part of a secondary party. As will become apparent as we study the topic, this statutory guidance is not very comprehensive. Most of the law on accomplices is to be found in case law which has developed over the years in a haphazard fashion and lacks clarity. It is for this reason that the Law Commission has suggested reforming this area of law.

The statutory provision is to be found in two Acts of Parliament as shown below.

Indictable offences:

Accessories and Abettors Act 1861

8   Whosoever shall aid, abet, counsel, or procure the commission of any *indictable* offence, whether the same be an offence at common law or by virtue of any Act passed or to be passed, shall be liable to be tried, indicted, and punished as a *principal* offender.

Summary offences and offences triable either way:

Magistrates' Courts Act 1980

44

(1) A person who aids, abets, counsels or procures the commission by another person of a *summary* offence *shall be guilty of the like offence* and may be tried (whether or not he is charged as a principal) either by a court having jurisdiction to try that other person or by a court having by virtue of his own offence jurisdiction to try him.

(2) Any offence consisting in aiding, abetting, counselling or procuring the commission of an offence *triable either way* (other than an offence listed in Schedule 1 to this Act) shall by virtue of this subsection *be triable either way.*

Setting the scene

Read the cases below and consider the questions which follow.

Case 1

> *R v Craig & Bentley* (1952)
>
> In this case Christopher Craig (aged 16 years) and Derek Bentley (aged 19 years) were attempting to burgle a warehouse in South London when they were interrupted by the police. Bentley was arrested by a police officer and was alleged to have shouted to Craig, *'Let him have it, Chris.'* Bentley knew that Craig was carrying a gun which was actually loaded. Craig shot and wounded one police officer and in the exchange of shots which ensued, another police officer was shot and killed by Craig. Both Craig and Bentley were charged with murder and convicted of murder. Because Bentley was an adult he was sentenced to be hanged and was hanged for this murder in 1953. Craig could not be sentenced to be hanged because he was not an adult.

7

Questions

1 Who actually fired the shot which killed the police officer?

2 Who had the intention to kill or cause serious bodily harm when the fatal shot was fired?

3 Who, on the face of the evidence provided, was the person who could obviously have been charged and tried for the murder of the police officer?

4 At the time of the killing, where was Bentley?

5 Did Bentley agree that he had shouted, 'Let him have it, Chris'?

6 Even if Bentley had shouted, 'Let him have it, Chris', what two possible meanings could be attributed to this instruction?

7 Which criminal enterprise can we say for certain that the two had set out on together?

8 On what legal basis could Bentley have been convicted of the murder of the police officer?

9 Do you think that it is *'fair'* in such instances to attach criminal liability to the person who has not *'actually'* carried out the *actus reus* of the crime?

Answers

1 Christopher Craig.

2 Christopher Craig.

3 Christopher Craig.

4 He was under arrest.

5 No; this was *alleged*.

6 The instruction could have meant that Craig was to shoot the police officer or it could have meant that Craig was to hand over his gun to the police officer.

7 Burglary.

8 It was probably the fact that the two had set off on a *joint enterprise* to burgle the warehouse and, in doing so, Bentley had *known* that Craig had a *loaded* gun; the implication being that Bentley was prepared to take the *risk* that his partner in crime might actually shoot and kill someone during the course of the burglary.

9 In one way such legal reasoning seems to be fair; how else can the law deter criminals who are prepared to take part in joint criminal activities which involve a risk of physical violence or killing? In another way such legal reasoning seems to go against the whole way in which criminal liability attaches to people; to be guilty of most criminal offences the accused has to be proven to have committed the *actus reus* of the crime in question and to have had the appropriate *mens rea* for the crime.

Case 2

Read the case overleaf which was reported in *The Times* on 31 March 1997, and then consider the questions which follow.

Passive acquiescence is not aiding and abetting

Regina v. J. F. Alford Transport Ltd
Regina v. Alford
Regina v. Payne
Before Lord Justice Kennedy, Mr Justice Blofeld and Judge Brian Walsh, QC
[Reasons March 7]

[a] Knowledge of and passive acquiescence in a principal's offence was insufficient to amount to aiding and abetting the commission of an indictable offence but [b] knowledge of the principal offence and the ability to control the action of an offender coupled with a deliberate decision to refrain from doing so could be sufficient.

The Court of Appeal, Criminal Division, so held in giving reasons for allowing appeals on February 27 by J. F. Alford Transport Ltd, James Alford and Alex Peter Payne against their convictions in June 1996 at Southampton Crown Court (Judge McLean and a jury) of eight specimen counts of aiding and abetting the making of a false entry on a record sheet contrary to section 99(5) of the Transport Act 1968.

The company was fined £10,000 to be paid within 30 days and was ordered to pay £22,000 towards the costs of the prosecution; James

Alford was fined £5,000 to be paid within 30 days with three months imprisonment in default and Alex Peter Payne was fined £1,000 to be paid within 30 days with 28 days imprisonment in default.

Mr Simon Hawkesworth, QC and Mr Christopher Hough for the appellants; Mr Robin Belben for the Crown.

LORD JUSTICE KENNEDY said that the appellant company was a transport company with a fleet of lorries, Mr Alford was the managing director and Mr Payne the transport manager. The company's drivers' tachograph records were compared on police investigation with daily and weekly timesheets and showed widespread discrepancies.

The drivers concerned pleaded guilty to specimen offences of making a false entry on a record sheet, that is, a tachograph record, contrary to section 99(5) of the Transport Act 1968.

The prosecution case against the individual appellants was that as managers of the company they must have known and accepted, if not actively encouraged, what the drivers did and, as the "brains" of the company if they or either of them were criminally liable the company

was liable too. On appeal, Mr Hawkesworth submitted that the trial judge in summing up wrongly indicated to the jury that passive acquiescence would suffice to amount to aiding and abetting.

Their Lordships accepted that in the context of the present case it would have had to be proved that the defendant under consideration intended to do the acts which he knew to be capable of assisting or encouraging the commission of the crime, but he need not have intended that the crime be committed.

Thus if the management's reason for turning a blind eye was to keep the drivers happy rather than to encourage the production of false tachograph records that would afford no defence.

If knowledge could be shown on the part of one of the individual appellants in relation to any given count it would have been open to the jury to find that he positively encouraged the commission of the offence.

However, there being no sufficient evidence of knowledge in this case the appeal succeeded.

Solicitors: Wedlake Saint, London; Crown Prosecution Service, Eastleigh.

7

Questions

1 What is meant by 'passive acquiescence'?

2 The part sentence marked (a) reflects which premise of the criminal law?

3 The part sentence marked (b) reflects which *caveat* to the premise mentioned in question 2?

4 Who were the *principal* offenders in this scenario?

5 Where and when was the case first heard, before which judge and what was the verdict?

6 With what criminal offence were the defendants charged?

7 List the three defendants and their respective sentences.

8 Which counsel represented the appellants, and was their appeal against conviction successful?

9 What is meant by corporate liability and vicarious liability?

10 On what basis was J.F. Alford Transport Ltd said to be corporately liable as an aider and abettor to the crime in question?

11 What would have to be proved to make the managers liable as aiders and abettors?

12 Was the motive of the managers relevant?

13 If there had been sufficient evidence that one of the managers knew that his actions were capable of assisting the commission of the crime, who bore the responsibility of finding him liable as an aider and abettor?

14 Why was the appeal successful?

Answers

1 It means inactive consent or agreement.

2 That to be criminally liable the accused must have the necessary *mens rea* for the *actus reus* of the crime and that, generally, *omissions* do not constitute the *actus reus*.

3 That an omission can amount to the *actus reus* of a crime in certain circumstances, such as when the accused has a duty to act or has a degree of control over the action of the principal offender.

4 The lorry drivers who had pleaded guilty.

5 The case was first heard in Southampton Crown Court in June 1996 before Judge McLean where the defendants were found guilty.

6 They were charged with *aiding and abetting* the making of a false entry on a record sheet contrary to section 99(5) of the Transport Act 1968.

7 The defendants were J.F. Alford Transport Ltd (fined £10,000), Mr Alford the managing director (fined £5,000) and Mr Payne the transport manager (fined £1,000).

8 The appellants were represented by Mr Simon Hawkesworth QC and Mr Christopher Hough, and their appeal was successful.

9 Usually criminal liability is attributable to individual citizens who are above the age of criminal liablility (aged 10 years or more). Thus, criminal liability usually attaches itself to 'real' people. However, it is possible to attribute criminal liablility to a non-real person, to an entity such as a company, which is said to have 'juristic personality'. Thus, for example, a company can be charged with the commission of criminal offences under the Health and Safety at Work Act 1974. This is known as corporate liability. By the same logic it is, therefore, possible to charge a company with aiding and abetting a criminal offence. Because the company is not a real person you may be wondering how it can have a guilty mind or *mens rea*. The answer is that certain people within the company, usually at least at managerial level, are regarded as the 'agents' of the company and it is their acts and *mens rea* which are deemed to be the acts and *mens rea* of the company.

If an individual commits a criminal offence he is usually the principal offender (unless he is an innocent agent) and will be held criminally liable for his actions. However, it is also possible that if the individual committed the criminal offence while in the course of his employment then his employers might also be held criminally liable as principal offenders under the principle of vicarious liability. In the present case the defendants have not been charged as principal offenders under the doctrine of vicarious liablility; they have been charged with aiding and abetting the commission of the offence committed by the drivers as principal offenders.

10 On the basis that if the *managers* were criminally liable then the *company* was also liable because the managers represented the 'brains' of the company.

11 It would have to be proved that they *intended* to do the acts which they knew to be capable of assisting or encouraging the commission of the crime. (Note that it is not necessary to prove that they intended that the crime be committed.)

12 No.

13 The jury.

14 The appeal was successful because there was not sufficient evidence of knowledge that their acts were capable of assisting or encouraging the crime.

7

Detailed definitions of secondary parties

To qualify as a secondary party a person has to be classed as an aider, an abettor, a counsellor or a procurer of the crime committed by the principal. What is the difference between these types of secondary party? They are listed in section 8 of the Accessories and Abettors Act 1861 and in section 44 of the Magistrates' Courts Act 1980 but the Acts do not give much help in defining these words and so their meanings have to be found in case law. There has been much discussion about what the words actually mean and in 'Attorney-General's Reference (No. 1 of 1975)' 1975 it was stated that the words should have different meanings but one wonders why this is so important when a defendant is usually charged with the all-encompassing 'aiding, abetting, counselling and procuring' of the offence in question. The difference between the words was more important prior to the Criminal Law Act 1967 which abolished the division of participatory offences into those occurring before the actual crime, those occurring at the scene of the crime and those occurring after the crime. Secondary parties are those people who participate in the commission of a crime either before the crime is committed or at the scene of the crime. People who help after the crime has been committed are not regarded as secondary parties; they may be charged under the Criminal Law Act 1967 with 'assisting offenders' (section 4) or with 'concealing an arrestable offence' (section 5).

We will now look at some suggested meanings of those actions (usually not omissions) which comprise the *actus reus* of the secondary party.

Aiding

Giving some practical assistance to the principal offender either before or at the scene of the crime, such as holding a victim of an assault, driving the principal offender to the scene of the crime, acting as a look-out or supplying the principal offender with the tools with which the latter can carry out the crime. Thus, an aider need not be present at the scene of the crime. Also, the principal offender need not be aware that he is being aided; there is a link between him and the aider by virtue of the practical assistance.

Abetting

Inciting or encouraging the commission of the offence at the time it is happening. Thus the abettor takes no practical part in the commission of the offence and it is generally thought that the principal offender must be aware of the encouragement, presumably for there to be some link between the principal offender and the abettor.

Counselling

Inciting or encouraging the commission of the offence before it takes place. As with abetting, the principal offender has to be aware of the counselling so that there is a link between him and the counsellor.

Procuring

This means that the secondary party does some acts which bring about or *cause* the crime to be committed. The principal offender need not be aware that he is being helped to break the law. It is crucial for the prosecution to prove the *causal link* between the actions of the secondary party and the offence committed by the principal offender. An obvious example is where the secondary party laces the drinks of the principal offender who then unwittingly drives with excess alcohol in his blood.

Key points on secondary parties

I will now outline the key points on secondary parties, some of which are explained in further detail later on.

▶ The person who is directly responsible for the *actus reus* of a crime and who has the appropriate *mens rea* for the crime is referred to as the principal offender.

▶ If other people are indirectly involved in the crime by aiding, abetting, counselling or procuring the crime, they are referred to as secondary offenders and may be dealt with as though they were principal offenders.

▶ The criminal liability of the principal offender will be determined by his own *mens rea* for the *actus reus* and the criminal liability of the secondary party will be determined by his own *mens rea* for the *actus reus*. Thus, it is possible for the principal and secondary party to be charged and tried for different offences and it is possible for the secondary party to be charged and tried for a more serious offence than the principal if the secondary party had a more blameworthy type of *mens rea* for the *actus reus* (*Howe* [1987]). For example, if the principal offender attacked a victim who died and the principal did not intend to cause serious bodily harm, he is unlikely to be charged with the murder of the victim. If the secondary party involved in the attack did intend the victim

7

to suffer serious bodily harm, then he might be charged with the murder of the victim.

▶ To be charged as a secondary party the principal offender has to have brought about the *actus reus* of the crime, that is, a crime must have been committed. So long as a crime has been committed then a person can be charged as a secondary party even if the principal has a defence to the crime, such as lack of *mens rea* (*R* v. *Cogan and Leak* [1975]) or duress (*R* v. *Bourne* [1952]). It is also possible to be a secondary party to an attempted crime, to incitement and to conspiracy. It is because the criminal liability of the secondary party is dependent on what the principal offender does that the liability of the secondary party is often described as *derivative* liability.

▶ It is possible to be a secondary party to any criminal offence unless an Act of Parliament says to the contrary (*Jefferson* [1994]).

▶ There are instances when a person is incapable of being the principal offender but can be a secondary party. For instance, a woman cannot be the principal offender in a rape charge but she can be a secondary party (*Ram & Ram* [1893]).

▶ If the actual perpetrator of a crime is an innocent agent, then the person who made use of the innocent agent is regarded as the principal for the offence. An innocent agent is someone who, for instance, lacks *mens rea*, is below the age of criminal responsibility (*Micheal* [1840]), is acting under duress (*R* v. *Manley* [1844]) or is insane (*Tyler* v. *Price* [1838]).

▶ A person is not necessarily liable as a secondary party just because they are present at the scene of the crime but do nothing to stop it (see *R* v. *Clarkson* [1971] below). This is in accord with the general principles of criminal liability that no criminal liability attaches itself for omissions; usually the accused has to have done some positive act (*actus reus*) to be criminally liable. However, you may recall that it is possible to be held criminally liable for omissions, for instance, where the accused has a 'duty to act' and does not (see *R* v. *Pittwood* [1902], *R* v. *Stone and Dobinson* [1977] and *R* v. *Gibbins and Proctor* [1918]. The same approach is taken with regard to secondary parties. Thus, if a husband sees his wife drowning their children and he does not intervene to try to stop her, he is guilty of aiding and abetting the homicide because parents have a duty to look after the well-being of their children. In *Tuck* v. *Robson (1970)* a landlord was liable as a secondary party for not stopping his customers drinking after hours; it was no defence that he had called 'Time, glasses please'. The landlord is under a duty not to sell alcohol after hours. (Note how this case is different to *Ferguson* v. *Weaving* (1951) where the duty was on the customers not the landlord and where the landlord had no knowledge of the after-hours drinking.)

▶ The *mens rea* (guilty mind) of the secondary party requires a lot of discussion (see below).

▶ Once someone has started to act as a secondary party is it possible for them to withdraw themselves from it? This is another area which requires a lot of discussion (see below).

Figure 7.1

The following newspaper cutting was taken from *The Times*, 26 September 1997.

Discuss this with your tutor and/or fellow students in terms of who is the principal/secondary offender and what offences they have been charged with. What do you think about the custodial sentence which was awarded?

Girl 'punished' by having her baby taken away

By Joanna Bale and Richard Ford

A JUDGE who condemned a pregnant girl to a prison without childcare facilities told her yesterday that the removal of her baby at birth was a "real punishment".

Judge Hutton drew immediate criticism from penal reformers after refusing an appeal from the 17-year-old shoplifter for her five-month sentence to be reduced by two weeks so that she would be out of prison in time for the birth. Rejecting her appeal, Judge Hutton said: "We accept that the immediate loss of your child after the birth will be a real punishment.

"But you deserve a real punishment to try to break once and for all this habit of stealing other people's property. We are quite satisfied that only a custodial sentence can be justified."

The girl, who cannot be named for legal reasons, received her ninth conviction for shoplifting after acting as a lookout while an accomplice stole four shirts.

The court was told that the teenager was too young to be transferred to Holloway women's prison in north London where there are facilities for new mothers to care for their children. As a result, she would give birth in a Bristol hospital and the child would then go into temporary care while she completed her sentence.

Judge Hutton said it was "very unfortunate" that a recent change to prison rules mean that, because of her age, she could not be sent to Holloway.

The decision not to allow the appeal was last night condemned by Frances Crook, director of the Howard League for Penal Reform. She said: "The forcible separation of mother and baby at birth has a catastrophic effect, not only on the mother but also on the child which can cause longlasting damage.

"This is as much a punishment for the baby who has done nothing as it is a punishment of the mother and is a wholly disproportionate response to this particular offence.

"It is not up to the judge to say when a mother is separated from her baby. That is a matter for others, usually the prison service and social services." The decision was also criticised by the National Association for the Care and Resettlement of Offenders. Its principal officer, Paul Cavadino, said: "The judge's comments ignore the fact that the offender is not the only one being punished."

The court was told that the girl was given the five-month youth detention sentence by youth court justices in Cheltenham last week when she admitted stealing four shirts worth £60 from the town's Marks & Spencer store.

Christopher Jervis, for the prosecution, said her role was to act as a lookout while a 20-year-old woman stole the shirts. The accomplice had no previous convictions and escaped with a caution.

The girl had been shoplifting since she was 14, he said, and had breached numerous non-custodial penalties including supervision orders, a conditional discharge and community service.

Carolyn Poots, for the defence, said the penalty was too harsh in view of her lesser role in the theft and the fact that her accomplice had not been prosecuted. "I ask that she be given one last chance."

Her mother also has a criminal record and would not be available to care for the child. Her boyfriend, the child's father, was serving a custodial sentence himself.

The Prison Service said last night that the decision on whether the baby was removed from the girl was not for the judge. A panel including representatives from social services, the probation and the prison services would make the decision.

Mens rea of the secondary party

a) Intention

The *actus reus* of the secondary party consists of the aiding, abetting, counselling or procuring of an offence by the principal offender. What *mens rea* does the secondary party need to have to incur criminal liability?

It appears from case law that the secondary party needs to have *intended* to aid, abet, counsel or procure. In other words, the secondary party knew exactly what he was doing; that his actions were in some degree a contributory factor to the commission of a criminal offence by the principal offender.

It is important to remember that this intention attaches itself to the aiding, abetting, counselling or procuring and not to the actual offence committed by the principal offender. Thus, if a secondary party intends to aid the commission of a criminal offence by the principal offender by supplying him with a weapon but is totally horrified at the planned offence, the secondary party can still be liable as an abettor; he supplied the weapon (the *actus reus*) and intended to aid the commission of the offence (*mens rea*).

See *Lynch* v. *Director of Public Prosecutions for Northern Ireland* (1975) where the secondary party intentionally drove the principal offender to a place where he knew that he was going to murder a police officer. The secondary party did not like the plan to murder the police officer but, because he intentionally drove the car to the scene, he was aiding the principal offence.

See also *R* v. *Clarkson* (1971) where two defendants, Clarkson and Carroll, who were drunk, heard a disturbance in a room and went to see what it was. They discovered that a woman was being raped and stood and watched without verbally or physically assisting the crime. At trial they were convicted as secondary parties to the crime of rape and they appealed. Their appeal was allowed and their convictions were quashed.

Megaw L.J. said:

> *It is not enough, then, that the presence of the accused has, in fact, given encouragement. It must be proved that the accused intended to give encouragement; that he wilfully encouraged. In a case such as the present, more than in many other cases where aiding and abetting is alleged, it was essential that that element should be stressed; for there was here at least the possibility that a drunken man with his self-discipline loosened by drink, being aware that a woman was being raped, might be attracted to the scene and might stay on the scene in the capacity of what is known as a voyeur; and, while his presence and the presence of others might in fact encourage the rapers or discourage the victim, he, himself, enjoying the scene or at least standing by assenting, might not intend that his presence should offer some encouragement to rapers and would-be rapers or discouragement to the victim; he might not realise that he was giving encouragement; so that, while*

7

encouragement there might be, it would not be a case in which, to use the words of Hawkins J., the accused person 'wilfully encouraged'.

b) Recklessness

Recklessness is probably not a sufficiently blameworthy state of mind, and so neither is negligence, on which to base liablility as a secondary party.

Thus, if a person drove someone to a deserted place at night being reckless as to whether or not that person was going to commit a particular crime, such *mens rea* is probably insufficient to make the person liable as a secondary party should that offence be committed.

c) Knowledge of essential matters

In *Johnson* v. *Youden* (1950) Lord Goddard C.J. said, *'Before a person can be convicted of aiding and abetting the commission of an offence he must at least know the essential matters which constitute that offence.'*

> This basically means that someone should not be held liable as a secondary party to an offence they did not know was being committed.

The leading case is *Ferguson* v. *Weaving* (1951). In this case the licensee, a woman, was charged with counselling and procuring the drinking of alcoholic drinks on licensed premises outside of normal opening times. The relevant statute is the Licensing Act 1921 section 4 which made it an offence for any person, except during the permitted hours, to consume on licensed premises any intoxication liquor. Thus, the primary offenders would be the people actually drinking the alcohol. In this case the licensee had not supplied the drinks to the customers out of hours, rather, her waiters had. There was no evidence to show that she knew of the fact that the out of hours drinking was taking place. Thus, when the case went to appeal, Lord Goddard C.J. said,

The substantive offence is committed only by the customers. She can aid and abet the customers if she knows that the customers are committing the offence, but we are not prepared to hold that knowledge can be imputed to her so as to make her not a principal offender, but an aider and abettor ... As no duty is imposed on her by the section to prevent the consumption of liquor after hours there was no duty in this respect that she could delegate to her employees. While it may be that the waiters could have been prosecuted for aiding and abetting the consumers, as to which we need express no opinion, we are clearly of opinion that the licensee could not be.

d) Does the secondary party need to know the exact offence which the principal intends to commit or is it sufficient that the secondary party merely anticipates some illegality on the part of the principal offender?

In many ways this is the most complicted aspect of the law on secondary parties. Two leading cases are *R* v. *Bainbridge* (1960) and *Maxwell* v. *Director of Public Prosecutions for Northern Ireland* (1978). This latter case went to the House of Lords on appeal against conviction but was dismissed.

In the *Bainbridge* case the defendant had purchased some oxygen-cutting equipment for the principal offender who used it six weeks later to break into a bank at Stoke Newington. The defendant said that he had suspected that the equipment would be used for some illegal purpose but that he had not anticipated that it would be used to break into a bank.

> It was held that for the defendant to be found liable as a secondary party it was not sufficient that he anticipated *some kind* of illegal activity; rather, he had to anticipate the *type of crime* that was going to be committed.

If the defendant had suspected that the equipment was going to be used for a break in, that would have been sufficient. It was not necessary to show that he knew exactly which bank or premises would, in fact, be broken into.

In the *Maxwell* case the applicant had driven the car containing other terrorists who had thrown a pipe bomb into the hallway of the Crosskeys Inn public house. Among other things, he had been charged as a secondary party. Lord Scarman said,

> *In R v. Bainbridge the Court of Criminal Appeal (for England and Wales) held that it was not necessary that the accused should know the particular crime intended or committed by those whom he assisted, and upheld a direction in which the judge had made it clear that it was enough if the accused knew the type of crime intended . . . I think R v. Bainbridge was correctly decided. But I agree with counsel for the appellent that in the instant case the Court of Appeal in Northern Ireland has gone further than the Court of Appeal for England and Wales found it necessary to go in R v. Bainbridge . . . The Court . . .*

7

refused to limit criminal responsibility by reference to knowledge by the accused of the type of crime intended by those whom he assisted. Instead the Court has formulated a principle which avoids the uncertainties and ambiguities of classification. The guilt of an accessory springs, according to the Court's formulation, 'from the fact that he comtemplates the commission of one (or more) of a number of crimes by the principal and he intentionally lends his assistance in order that such a crime will be committed' per Sir Robert Lowry C.J. 'The relevant crime,' the Lord Chief Justice continues, 'must be within the contemplation of the accomplice, and only exceptionally would evidence to found to support the allegation that the accomplice had given the principal a completely blank cheque.' ... The principle thus formulated has great merit ... I accept it as good judge-made law in a field where there is no statute to offer guidance.

Thus, both cases consider it unlikely for the secondary party to be liable if all he suspected was *some kind* of criminal activity (a blank cheque), and the *Maxwell* case states that he will only be liable if the crime committed was one of a number of crimes *contemplated* by him.

In this case, the applicant had contemplated that the other terrorists in the car might plant a bomb at the public house or might shoot someone. As such, the crime committed was within his contemplation and he could be liable as a secondary party. The problem presented for the courts is deciding which offences are to be considered as belonging to the type of offence contemplated by the accused. This problem is addressed by Sir John Smith in the 8th edition of *Smith & Hogan Criminal Law* where he writes,

Bainbridge and Maxwell leave some unsolved problems. Whether a crime is of the same type as another may not always be easy to discover. If D lends a jemmy to E, contemplating that E intends to enter a house in order to steal, is D guilty of any offence if E enters a house intending to rape? Clearly D cannot be convicted of rape, because that is an offence of a different type; but he is probably guilty of burglary, because burglary was the crime he had in view – though this particular variety of burglary may be abhorrent to him.

e) Is the motive of the secondary party relevant?

If a secondary party intended to aid, abet, counsel or procure an offence by the principal offender, then it matters not what motive the secondary party had.

The leading case is *National Coal Board* v. *Gamble* (1959). In this case the National Coal Board (NCB) had a contract to supply coal to carriers sent by the Central Electricity Authority. The lorries sent were loaded at the colliery and, once weighed, the loaded coal became the property of the purchaser. One driver got his lorry loaded and went to the weighbridge to discover that he had too much coal as the weight of the lorry and coal exceeded the maximum permitted weight for it to be driven on a road. Despite the fact that the driver could have offloaded the excess coal, he told the weighbridge operator that he was prepared to risk it and so the operator issued him with a weighbridge ticket. The driver then drove the lorry onto the public roads thereby committing an offence against the Motor Vehicles (Construction and Use) Regulations 1955. The NCB were charged and convicted of aiding, abetting, counselling and procuring the commission of this offence by the carrier concerned. The NCB appealed against this decision, arguing, among other things, that it was necessary to show not only intent on their part but also a motive to encourage the crime. Their appeal was dismissed. Devlin J. said,

> ... an indifference to the result of the crime does not of itself negative abetting. If one man deliberately sells to another a gun to be used for murdering a third, he may be indifferent about whether the third man lives or dies and interested only in the cash profit to be made out of the sale, but he can still be an aider and abettor. To hold otherwise would be to negative the rule that **mens rea** is a matter of intent only and does not depend on desire or motive.

Thus, the general rule is that any motive, whether good or bad, is irrelevant to the issue of *mens rea*.

An interesting case is *Gillick* v. *West Norfolk & Wisbech AHA* (1986), which was a civil case in which the House of Lords held that in certain circumstances a doctor may lawfully give contraceptive advice to girls under the age of 16 years without their parents' consent. It is unlawful to have sexual intercourse while under the age of 16 and so it is possible to argue that by issuing contraceptives to under-age girls the doctor concerned might be a secondary party to unlawful sexual intercourse by a man. Following the NCB case it should be irrelevant that the motive of the doctor was a good one, to stop unwanted pregnancies. The decision that a doctor does not act unlawfully in such instances was not fully explained but it might be explained by saying that the doctor did not intend to aid or abet the crime or that he had a defence of necessity.

7

What if an accomplice decides that he no longer wishes to be part of the criminal venture? Can he 'withdraw' from it?

We can approach this topic by asking whether the involvement of the secondary party was *tangible* or *intangible*. *Tangible* involvement could be said to cover situations where the secondary party gives physical assistance to the principal offender as when the secondary party supplies a weapon, holds down the victim of an assault or drives a vehicle involved in the crime. *Intangible* involvement could be said to cover situations where the secondary party gives non-physical assistance to the principal offender as when the secondary party supplies information or encourages commission of the offence. From case law it would seem that it is easier for a secondary party to withdraw from the criminal activity after supplying *intangible* assistance to the principal.

However, the issue of whether a secondary party has effectively withdrawn from the criminal enterprise is one which has to be left for the jury to determine on the facts. It must also be pointed out that if a secondary party is found to have withdrawn from the enterprise, he may still be criminally liable for conspiracy to commit the crime or for incitement (see Chapter 8, on inchoate offences).

Withdrawal following tangible assistance

R v. *Becerra* (1975)

In this case, Becerra and two others broke into a house intending to steal from it. Becerra gave a knife to one of the other men, Cooper, for him to use if anyone interrupted them. Someone upstairs heard a noise downstairs and came down to investigate, at which point Becerra said, ' There's a bloke coming. Let's go'. He then jumped out of a window and ran away. Cooper then stabbed the man with the knife and the man died. Becerra argued that he had effectively withdrawn from the enterprise by shouting, 'There's a bloke coming. Let's go', and because he ran away before the stabbing took place. This argument was rejected. It was held that what Becerra did was insufficient to absolve himself as a secondary party. The Court of Appeal did not say exactly what he would have had to do to absolve himself, but the implication is that in such a situation the secondary party would have to 'physically' intervene to prevent the stabbing.

Withdrawal following intangible assistance

R v. *Grundy* (1977)

In this case the the informant supplied burglars with useful information concerning the movements of the owners of some premises, such that it would be easier for them to burgle the premises. However, for two weeks before the burglary took place the informant had been trying to stop them breaking into the premises. It was held that this behaviour could amount to effective withdrawal from the criminal enterprise and the jury should have been left to decide on the issue.

R v. *Whitefield* (1983)

In this case, Whitefield told the principal offender when the occupants of the flat next to his would be away, with a view to breaking into the flat using Whitefield's balcony to effect entry. However, Whitefield changed his mind and told the principal offender in unequivocal terms that he no longer wished to proceed with the burglary. When the principal offender did break into the neighbouring flat, Whitefield heard him but did nothing about it. It was held that *if* the jury believed the evidence then it would be a defence. It was held that Whitefield did not have to inform the police of what had been planned to absolve himself from liability as a secondary party; the fact that he had unequivocally told the principal offender that he no longer wished to be part of the venture was enough in itself.

What appears to be relevant for the jury in deciding whether or not a secondary party has absolved himself from liability is not only the tangible or intangible nature of the assistance given, but also the timing of the communication of intention to withdraw from the venture. In *R* v. *Becerra* (1975) the crime was actually in the process of being committed, whereas in *R* v. *Grundy* (1977) and *R* v. *Whitefield* (1983) the criminal enterprise had not actually started when the secondary party communicated their intention to withdraw from it.

Joint enterprises

We have already stated that if someone aids, abets, counsels or procures the commission of a criminal offence, then that someone may become criminally liable as a secondary party, in which case they can be dealt with *as though they had themselves* committed the *actus reus* of the crime.

It is of course possible that more than one person may, *in reality*, actually carry out the *actus reus* of a crime, for instance, two people might attack someone and both of the attackers might intend to cause that person serious bodily harm. In which case, if the victim dies, both attackers could be charged and tried as principal offenders for the murder of the victim. The *actus reus* is the attack and the *mens rea* is the intention to cause serious bodily harm.

Sometimes it is difficult to determine whether or not a person is a joint principal (as described above) or a secondary party. However, this should not cause too much concern as a secondary party is dealt with as though he is the principal offender and so the distinction is quite often unnecessary. The main test is to determine whether or not the person in question in any way brought about the *actus reus* of the crime himself, by his own acts. If he did, then he is a joint principal. If he did not bring about the *actus reus* of the crime directly, but aided, abetted, counselled or procured the commission of the *actus reus*, he is liable as a secondary party.

A problem area for joint enterprise liability is to determine to what extent a person can be held liable for *other* crimes committed during the joint venture. We can consider this as follows.

Where A and B set out on a joint enterprise to burgle a house and, during the course of the burglary, A kills the occupant of the house, to what extent can B also be held responsible for the killing?

1   If B knew that A *would kill* someone during the burglary *if it became necessary* to do so (to prevent identification or to prevent the police being summoned or for whatever reason) then B is also responsible for the killing as it can be regarded as part of the original common design (see *Betts & Ridley* [1930]).

2   If B thought that A *might kill* someone during the burglary *if it became necessary* to do so then B is also responsible for the killing. In such cases *B has taken a risk* that A might kill. In the case of *R* v. *Powell & Daniels* (1996) a drug dealer was shot dead when he answered his door. It was held that the two accomplices who had gone with the principal offender were also liable for the murder of the drug dealer because there was a tacit agreement between them that the principal offender *might kill* or seriously injure in pursuit of the common design. The case went to the House of Lords in August 1997 and the Law Lords upheld the murder convictions of the accomplices. This case was consistent with the cases of *Chan Wing-sui* v. *R* (1985) and *R* v. *Slack* (1989). In the latter case Slack and Buick burgled the flat of an old lady and during the course of the burglary Slack gave Buick a knife so that he could use it to *threaten* the old lady if need be. While Slack was in another room, Buick murdered the old lady with the knife and both of them were charged with her murder. Slack was convicted of the murder and appealed but his appeal was dismissed. He was guilty of murder because he had tacitly agreed that if necessary serious harm should be done to the old lady. See *R* v. *Craig & Bentley* (1952) which appears at the beginning of this chapter and the commentary on the joint appeal to the House of Lords of *R* v. *Powells and Daniels* and *R* v. *English* (1997) on pages 199–200.

3   If B knew that A had a gun but thought that it was unloaded and was being taken along just to frighten the occupants, or that A had a knife but did not contemplate that A would use it to cause death or serious injury, then it is unlikely that B would be convicted of murder. This is because A has gone beyond the scope of the original joint design. In the case of *Mahmood* (1995) a car was taken without the consent of the owners and abandoned while still in gear and with the engine running. The car ran on down the pavement and killed a baby in a pram. The driver of the car was convicted of manslaughter and so was his accomplice. However, on appeal, the accomplice's conviction was quashed because manslaughter went beyond his comtemplation of the common design which was 'joyriding'. In the case of *Perman* (1996) a shop assistant was shot and killed during an armed robbery. The principal offender was convicted of murder and robbery and the accomplice was convicted of manslaughter and robbery. The accomplice appealed arguing that he could not be held guilty of manslaughter as he believed that the gun used was unloaded and had been taken along just to frighten people. His conviction for manslaughter was quashed; in order to be guilty of manslaughter he would have had to have known that the gun was real and was loaded.

7

Applying principles to examination questions

If you have worked through this chapter methodically you should now be ready to apply the principles learnt to a simple examination-style question. In the question below I have integrated several key aspects of the law on accomplices. In order to answer it proficiently you will have to look back over the chapter and this, in itself, is a form of revision. At this stage I am not asking you to identify other substantive criminal offences; we will assume that the principal offender has committed the offence in question so that the answer concentrates on accomplices. Make notes on what you regard as important points; you can then refer to these when looking back through the chapter to discover the relevant cases and so forth.

Adrian and Brian decide to burgle a house because their friend has left home and has no money; they intend to sell the proceeds of their criminal activity to raise some funds. Brian asks Clive if he can borrow his tool bag. When Clive asks Brian what he wants if for, Brian tells him about the burglary. Clive doesn't like the idea of the burglary but lets Brian borrow the tool bag anyway.

Adrian asks his friend Dave if he will take himself and Brian for a drive on Monday night. Dave agrees. Adrian asks Dave to pick them up at 8 pm. Dave thinks that they are going out for a drink so is surprised when Adrian asks him to drop them off in the middle of a residential area and then asks him to wait there for them for about half an hour. Adrian and Brian put black balaclavas on their heads and take the tool bag with them as they leave the car. When they return to the car the tool bag is full and they are in a big hurry to drive off.

During the course of the burglary the owner of the house heard a noise and came downstairs to investigate. He found Adrian in his lounge holding some silverware. Brian shouted, 'Let him have it, Adrian', and jumped out of an open window. Adrian then hit the owner over the head with a silver candlestick, killing him.

Analyse the criminal liability of Adrian, Brian, Clive and Dave. Assume that Adrian and Brian have committed burglary and that Adrian has committed murder.

Tips on how to approach such a question

Left margin boxes:

onspiracy

otive is relevant. *National al Board* v. *amble* (1959)

nowledge of ssential matters *rguson* v. *eaving* (1951)

nticipation of pe of crime to be ommitted? v. *Bainbridge* 960) *Maxwell* v. *PP for N. Ireland* 978)

oint enterprise ut are Adrian's ctions beyond he common esign? *Craig and entley* (1952) *R* v. *owell & Daniels* 996) *R* v. *Perman* 996)

nalyse their ability as ccomplices – *ccessories & bettors Act 1861 Magistrates' Courts Act 1980* and *ttorney-General's Reference (No. 1 of 975)* (1975)

Central scenario:

Adrian and Brian decide to burgle a house because their friend has left home and has no money; they intend to sell the proceeds of their criminal activity to raise some funds. Brian asks Clive if he can borrow his tool bag. When Clive asks Brian what he wants if for, Brian tells him about the burglary. Clive doesn't like the idea of the burglary but lets Brian borrow the tool bag anyway.

Adrian asks his friend Dave if he will take himself and Brian for a drive on Monday night. Dave agrees. Adrian asks Dave to pick them up at 8 pm. Dave thinks that they are going out for a drink so is surprised when Adrian asks him to drop them off in the middle of a residential area and then asks him to wait there for them for about half an hour. Adrian and Brian put black balaclavas on their heads and take the tool bag with them as they leave the car. When they return to the car the tool bag is full and they are in a big hurry to drive off.

During the course of the burglary the owner of the house heard a noise and came downstairs to investigate. He found Adrian in his lounge holding some silverware. Brian shouted, 'Let him have it, Adrian', and jumped out of an open window. Adrian then hit the owner over the head with a silver candlestick, killing him.

Analyse the criminal liability of Adrian, Brian, Clive and Dave. Assume that Adrian and Brian have committed burglary and that Adrian has committed murder.

Right margin boxes:

'Intention' to act as an accomplice? *Lynch* v. *DPP for N. Ireland* (1975)

Liability for omissions? *R* v. *Clarkson* (1971)

'Recklessness' as regards being an accomplice?

Liability under section 4 or section 5 Criminal Law Act 1967?

Has Brian 'withdrawn' from the enterprise by jumping out of the window? *R* v. *Becerra* (1975)

This means that you are not expected to discuss the *actus reus* and *mens rea* of the principal offences.

7

What you have to do is to work through the highlighted points and discuss them critically, quoting cases and Acts of Parliament where appropriate. Be as discursive as possible. As the law on accomplices is so haphazard, it is important that you show a sound knowledge of case law and can highlight deficiences in the law. It would be difficult to say what the 'correct' answer to such a question would be; you can only offer suggestions. Once you have highlighted points as I have done above, it would be a good idea to work through the scenario using the flow chart provided in Figure 7.1.

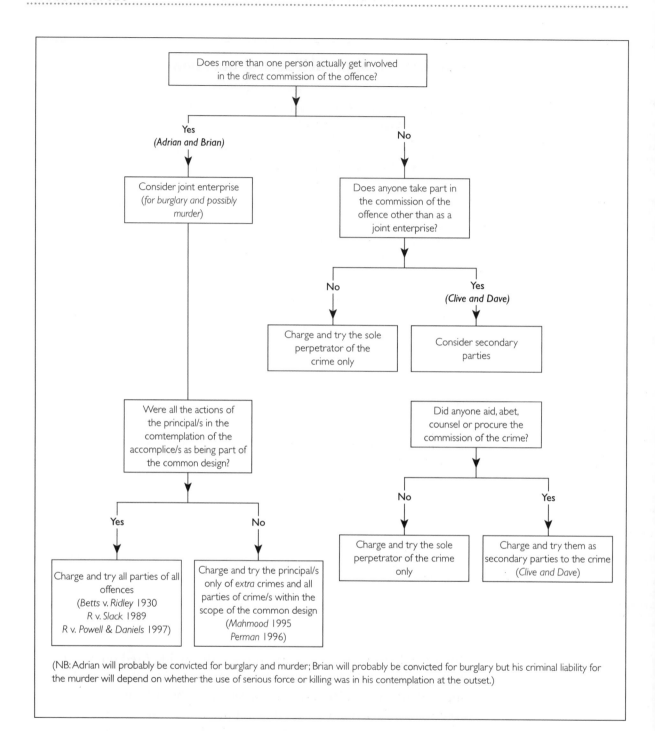

Does more than one person actually get involved in the *direct* commission of the offence?

Yes
(Adrian and Brian)

Consider joint enterprise
(for burglary and possibly murder)

No

Does anyone take part in the commission of the offence other than as a joint enterprise?

No

Charge and try the sole perpetrator of the crime only

Yes
(Clive and Dave)

Consider secondary parties

Were all the actions of the principal/s in the comtemplation of the accomplice/s as being part of the common design?

Yes

Charge and try all parties of all offences
*(Betts v. Ridley 1930
R v. Slack 1989
R v. Powell & Daniels 1997)*

No

Charge and try the principal/s only of *extra* crimes and all parties of crime/s within the scope of the common design
*(Mahmood 1995
Perman 1996)*

Did anyone aid, abet, counsel or procure the commission of the crime?

No

Charge and try the sole perpetrator of the crime only

Yes

Charge and try them as secondary parties to the crime
(Clive and Dave)

(NB: Adrian will probably be convicted for burglary and murder; Brian will probably be convicted for burglary but his criminal liability for the murder will depend on whether the use of serious force or killing was in his contemplation at the outset.)

Proposals for reform

After working through this chapter, it should be apparent that the law on accomplices is haphazard, sometimes confusing and in need of reform. Cases such as *R* v. *Craig and Bentley* (1952) highlight the fact that this area of law sometimes appears too harsh on a defendant who, because he is in a joint enterprise, may be held criminally liable for acts committed by his partner in crime. In *Craig and Bentley*, Bentley was under arrest when Craig fired the shot which killed a police officer, yet Bentley was held liable for the murder of the police officer. This seems very harsh indeed because it could be argued that once someone is under arrest, how can they then commit further offences? This case was particularly harrowing as Bentley was hanged for the murder while Craig, who actually fired the fatal shot, was detained at Her Majesty's pleasure as he was too young to be awarded the death penalty.

7

In 1993 proposals for reform were made by the Law Commission in their Consultation Paper No. 131, 'Assisting and Encouraging Crime'. These are shown on the next page. The crime of *'assisting crime'* is detailed in paragraph 4.99 and this would seem to replace the present crimes of aiding and procuring. The crime of *'encouraging crime'* is detailed in paragraph 4.163 and this would seem to replace the present crimes of abetting, counselling and the inchoate offence of incitement (see Chapter 8).

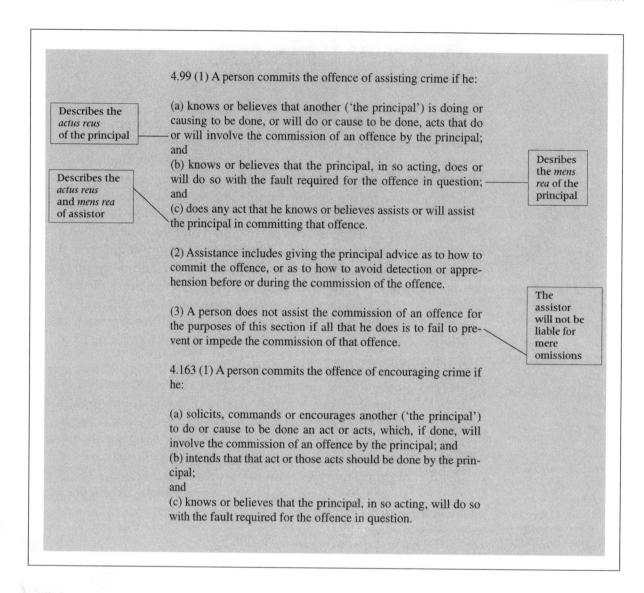

Describes the *actus reus* of the principal —

4.99 (1) A person commits the offence of assisting crime if he:

(a) knows or believes that another ('the principal') is doing or causing to be done, or will do or cause to be done, acts that do or will involve the commission of an offence by the principal; and

(b) knows or believes that the principal, in so acting, does or will do so with the fault required for the offence in question; and

Describes the *mens rea* of the principal

Describes the *actus reus* and *mens rea* of assistor

(c) does any act that he knows or believes assists or will assist the principal in committing that offence.

(2) Assistance includes giving the principal advice as to how to commit the offence, or as to how to avoid detection or apprehension before or during the commission of the offence.

(3) A person does not assist the commission of an offence for the purposes of this section if all that he does is to fail to prevent or impede the commission of that offence.

The assistor will not be liable for mere omissions

4.163 (1) A person commits the offence of encouraging crime if he:

(a) solicits, commands or encourages another ('the principal') to do or cause to be done an act or acts, which, if done, will involve the commission of an offence by the principal; and

(b) intends that that act or those acts should be done by the principal; and

(c) knows or believes that the principal, in so acting, will do so with the fault required for the offence in question.

It must be pointed out that these two new offences would be *inchoate* offences. Thus, it would be possible to be found guilty of them even if the principal offender never committed the crime which was assisted or encouraged. During the course of this chapter we have noted how liability as an accomplice is *derivative*, that is, an accomplice is *only* liable if the principal offender commits the principal offence. Thus, the proposals of the Law Commission would end this notion of derivative liability.

In the Law Commission's *Thirty-First Annual Report* 1996 (Law Com. No. 244) at paragraph 4.21 it says:

> *Assisting and encouraging crime*
> *As we explained in our last annual report, we have been unable*
> *to take this matter forward since analysing the responses to our*
> *consultation paper. An important decision of the House of Lords*
> *is awaited but we are anxious to produce a report as soon as*
> *staffing resources permit and hope that might be possible in the*
> *later part of 1997.*

The decision of the House of Lords which is referred to concerns Philip English. English, aged 15 years old at the time, was involved in a fight with police officers who had been summoned to sort out a disturbance. After English had been arrested, the other man involved in the fight had taken out a knife and had stabbed and killed a police officer. English was convicted of the murder of the police officer along with the other man; he was party to a joint enterprise and had not withdrawn himself from it before the murder took place. The case is extremely similar to the case involving Derek Bentley who was hanged for his part in the crime. However, in this recent case, it is the accomplice rather that the principal who is the young offender. The House of Lords heard the joint appeal concerning the cases of *R* v. *Powell and Daniels* and *R* v. *English* in August 1997 because the appeals used the same argument for appeal that a secondary party could not be convicted of murder unless the secondary party had an intention to kill or an intention to cause grievous bodily harm. In the appeal from *R* v. *English* there was a second argument for appeal, that the secondary party could not be guilty of murder if the principal had with him, and killed with, a weapon the secondary party knew nothing about.

The judgment of the House of Lords is shown on the next page.

7

Foreseeability test in joint enterprise

Regina v Powell and Another
Regina v English

Before Lord Goff of Chieveley, Lord Jauncey of Tullichettle, Lord Mustill, Lord Steyn and Lord Hutton

[Speeches October 30]

It was sufficient of found a conviction for murder for a secondary party to have realised that in the course of a joint enterprise the primary party might kill with intent to do so or to cause grievous bodily harm.

However, if the secondary party did not foresee as a possibility a lethal act by the primary party fundamentally different from any action which they jointly contemplated, he would not be guilty of homicide, unless the weapon whose use he did contemplate was as dangerous as the weapon actually used by the principal.

The House of Lords so held dismissing appeals by Anthony Glassford Powell and Antonio Eval Daniels against the dismissal by the Court of Appeal (*The Times* June 2, 1995) of their appeals against conviction on February 28, 1994 in the Central Criminal Court (Sir Lawrence Verney, Recorder of London and a jury) of murder of David Andrew Edwards, who was shot on May 29, 1993, for which they were sentenced to life imprisonment.

The House allowed an appeal by Philip English against the rejection by the Court of Appeal (Lord Justice Simon Brown Mr Justice French and Mr Justice Cresswell) on July 16, 1996 of his appeal against his conviction on February 17, 1995 at Teesside Crown Court (Mr Justice Owen and a jury) of murder of a police sergeant for which he was sentenced to life imprisonment.

Mr Peter Feinberg, QC and Mr Benjamin Squirrell for Powell and Daniels, Mr Christopher Sallon, QC and Mr Julian B. Knowles for English; Mr Anthony Scrivenor, QC and Mr William Boyce for the Crown.

LORD HUTTON said Powell and Daniels had gone with another main to purchase drugs from a drug dealer. The drug dealer was shot when he came to the door.

The Crown was unable to prove which of the three men had fired the gun, but argued that the appellants were guilty of murder because they knew that the third man was armed with a gun and realised that he might use it to kill or cause really serious injury to the drug dealer.

The question certified in the appeal was: "Is it sufficient to found a conviction for murder for a secondary party to a killing to have realised that the primary party might kill with intent to do so or must the secondary party have held such intent himself?"

English and Weddle had jointly attacked a police officer with wooden posts. In the course of the attack Weddle had used a knife to stab the police officer to death.

In English's case the same question had been certified, together with a second question, namely; "Is it sufficient for murder that the secondary party intends or foresees that the primary party would or may act with intent to cause grievous bodily harm, if the lethal act carried out by the primary party is fundamentally different from the acts foreseen or intended by the secondary party?"

In his Lordship's opinion, the first question gave rise to two issues.

The first was whether the authorities established the principle that where there was a joint enterprise to commit a crime, foresight or contemplation by one party to the enterprise that another party to the enterprise might in the course of it commit another crime was sufficient to impose criminal liability for that crime if committed by the other party even if the first party did not intend that criminal act to be carried out.

The second was whether, if there was such an established principle, it could stand as good law in the light of the decisions of the House that foresight was not sufficent to constitute the mens rea for murder in the case of the person who actually caused the death and that guilt only arose if that person intended to kill or cause really serious injury.

His Lordship referred to *R* v *Smith* (Wesley)([1963] 1 WLR 1200) and *R* v *Anderson* ([1966] 2 QB 110) and concluded that when two parties embarked on a joint criminal enterprise one party would be liable for an act which he contemplated might be carried out by the other party in the course of the enterprise even if he had not tacitly agreed to that act.

Mr Feinberg, relying on *R* v *Moloney* ([1985] AC 905) and *R* v *Hancock* ([1986] AC 455) had submitted that as a matter of principle there was an anomaly in requiring proof against a secondary party of a lesser mens rea than needed to be proved against the principal who committed the actus reus of murder.

If foreseeability of risk was insufficient to found the mens rea of murder for a principal than the same test of liability should apply in the case of a secondary party to the joint enterprise.

His Lordship recognised that as a matter of logic there was force in the argument. But the rules of the common law were not based solely on logic but related to practical concerns and in relation to crimes committed in the course of joint enterprises to the need to give effective protection to the public against criminals operating in gangs.

One practical consideration of weight and importance was that the secondary party had lent himself to the joint enterprise and thereby given assistance and encouragement to the principal in carrying out an enterprise which the secondary party recognised might involve murder.

A further consideration was that unlike the principal, the secondary party would not be placed in the situation in which he suddenly had to decide whether to shoot or stab the third person with intent to cause death or really serious bodily harm.

In his Lordship's opinion, there was an argument of considerable force that the secondary party who took part in a criminal enterprise, for example, the robbery of a bank, with foresight that a deadly weapon might be used, should not escape liability for murder because he, unlike the principal party, was not suddenly confronted by the security officer so that he had to decide whether to use the gun or knife or have the enterprise thwarted and face arrest.

The second certified question in the appeal of English arose because of the judge's direction that if English did not know of the knife the jury had nevertheless to ask whether he knew that there was a substantial risk that Weddle might cause some really serious injury with the wooden post.

Mr Sallon had submitted that where the primary party killed with a deadly weapon, which the secondary party did not know that he had and therefore did not foresee his use of it, the secondary party should not be guilty of murder.

He had submitted that to be guilty the secondary party must foresee an act of the type which the principal party committed, and that in the instant case the use of a knife was fundamentally different to the use of a wooden post.

His Lordship considered that submission was correct. In English's case the judge's direction was defective because he did not quality his direction on foresight of really serious injury by stating that if the jury considered that the use of the knife by Weddle was the use of a weapon and an action on Weddle's part which English did not foresee as a possibility, then English should not be convicted of murder.

As the unforeseen use of the knife would take the killing outside the scope of the joint venture the jury should also have been directed that English should be found not guilty of manslaughter.

The issue raised by the second certified question in the appeal of English was to be resolved by the application of the principle in *R* v *Anderson* ([1966] 2 QB 110, 120):

It was undesirable to seek to formulate a more precise answer for fear of appearing to prescribe too rigid a formula for use by trial judges. However, if the weapon used by the primary party was different to, but equally as dangerous as the weapon which the secondary party contemplated he might use, the secondary party should not escape liability for murder because of the difference in the weapon for example, if he foresaw that the primary party might use a gun to kill and the latter used a knife to kill or vice versa.

Lord Mustill and Lord Steyn delivered concurring judgments and Lord Goff and Lord Jauncey agreed.

Solicitors: Thanki Novy Taube, Bindman & Partners Crown Prosecution Service, Headquarters.

Source: *The Times*,
31 October 1997

7

The House of Lords held that:

1 The appeals in the case of Powells and Daniels would be dismissed, that is, their convictions would stand because it was held that it was sufficient to find a conviction for murder for a secondary party to have realised that in the course of a joint enterprise the primary party *might kill* with intent to do so or to cause grievous bodily harm. Lord Hutton said:

> *In his Lordship's opinion, there was an argument of considerable force that the secondary party who took part in a criminal enterprise, for example, the robbery of a bank, with foresight that a deadly weapon might be used, should not escape liability for murder because he, unlike*

the principal party, was not suddenly confronted by the security officer so that he had to decide whether to use the gun or knife or have the enterprise thwarted and face arrest.

2   The appeal in the English case would be allowed. Although the first argument on appeal was the same as in the case of Powells and Daniels, which by itself would have led to the appeal being dismissed, the second argument in the case of English led to the appeal being allowed. Lord Hutton said:

> *Mr Sallon [counsel for English] had submitted that where the primary party killed with a deadly weapon, which the secondary party did not know that he had and therefore did not foresee his use of it, the secondary party should not be guilty of murder. He had submitted that to be guilty the secondary party must foresee an act of the type which the principal party committed, and that in the instant case the use of a knife was fundamentally different to the use of a wooden post. His Lordship considered that submission was correct.*

It will be interesting to see how the Law Commission interprets this judgment.

CHAPTER Summary

Figure 7.2

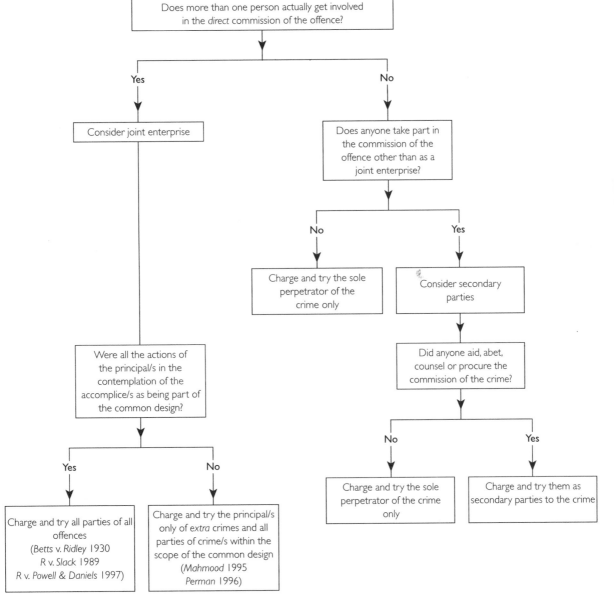

Incitement, conspiracy and attempt – the inchoate offences

OVERVIEW

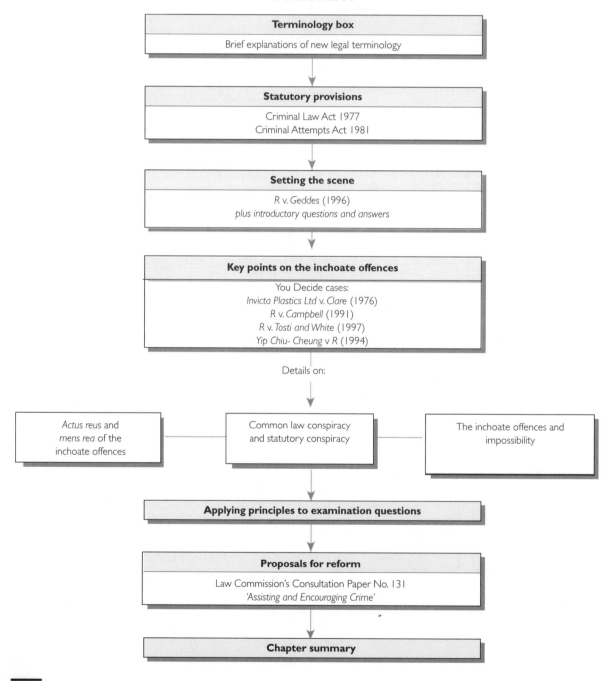

Terminology box

Brief explanations of new legal terminology

Statutory provisions

Criminal Law Act 1977
Criminal Attempts Act 1981

Setting the scene

R v. Geddes (1996)
plus introductory questions and answers

Key points on the inchoate offences

You Decide cases:
Invicta Plastics Ltd v. *Clare* (1976)
R v. *Campbell* (1991)
R v. *Tosti and White* (1997)
Yip Chiu- Cheung v R (1994)

Details on:

Actus reus and *mens rea* of the inchoate offences

Common law conspiracy and statutory conspiracy

The inchoate offences and impossibility

Applying principles to examination questions

Proposals for reform

Law Commission's Consultation Paper No. 131
'Assisting and Encouraging Crime'

Chapter summary

When someone commits a criminal offence, such as theft or robbery, if detected, they may be charged and convicted of the offence in question, the substantive offence. However, what is the position when someone intends to commit a criminal offence, such as theft or robbery, but for some reason the actual offence is not carried out? Is it appropriate that such behaviour could be the subject of the criminal law? For example, if A is intending to rob a post office and is standing outside the post office wearing a black balaclava, should the police, if tipped off to the intended robbery, be able to apprehend A before the robbery takes place or do they have to wait until the robbery is actually in progress? If they take the latter approach then there is the likelihood that an innocent bystander might be harmed. At what point should the police, supported by the criminal law, be able to intervene? It is obvious that a line needs to be drawn somewhere which demarcates criminal thoughts in someone's head and behaviour which goes beyond mere thoughts to overt actions on the way to the implementation of a crime. The criminal law has drawn this line at the point where the inchoate offences come into being.

The inchoate offences are incitement, conspiracy and attempt and they exist to protect society from 'potential' harm. For each of the inchoate offences the line demarcating criminal behaviour is drawn in a different place. First, however, you should consider the box below which gives brief definitions of the inchoate offences and other useful words in this contect.

8

TERMINOLOGY: Inchoate offences

Substantive offence	This is the phrase used to describe a criminal offence which exists in its own right as a complete offence.
Inchoate	This word means 'just begun or undeveloped'.
Inchoate offence	An inchoate offence is one which is *preparatory* in some way to the commission of a substantive offence. Thus, an inchoate offence only exists in relation to a substantive offence. The inchoate offences are incitement, conspiracy and attempt.
Incitement	Incitement refers to words or deeds by the accused which could have encouraged or persuaded any person or persons to commit a criminal offence.

Conspiracy	A conspiracy takes place when two or more people agree to the commission of a substantive offence.
Attempt	An attempt occurs when the accused has taken steps which are more than merely preparatory to the commission of a substantive offence.

Statutory provisions

Criminal Attempts Act 1981

1 (1) If, with intent to commit an offence to which this section applies, a person does an act which is more than merely preparatory to the commission of the offence, he is guilty of attempting to commit the offence.

(2) A person may be guilty of attempting to commit an offence to which this section applies even though the facts are such that the commission of the offence is impossible.

(3) In any case where –
  (a) apart from this subsection a person's intention would not be regarded as having amounted to an intent to commit an offence: but
  (b) if the facts of the case had been as he believed them to be, his intention would be so regarded, then, for the purposes of subsection (1) above, he shall be regarded as having had an intent to commit that offence.

(4) This section applies to any offence which, if it were completed, would be triable in England and Wales as an indictable offence ...

6 (1) The offence of attempt at common law and any offence at common law of procuring materials for crime are hereby abolished ...

Criminal Law Act 1977

1 (1) Subject to the following provisions of this Part of this Act, if a person agrees with any other person or persons that a course of conduct shall be pursued which, if the agreement is carried out in accordance with their intentions, either –
  (a) will necessarily amount to or involve the commission of any offence or offences by one or more parties to the agreement, or
  (b) would do so but for the existence of facts which render the commission of the offence or any offences impossible,

  is guilty of conspiracy to commit the offence or offences in question.

Setting the scene

Consider the case of *R* v. *Geddes* (1996) shown below, which was reported in *The Times* on 16 July 1996, and then answer the questions which follow. This case study should provide you with a good basic understanding of the law of attempts.

Preparatory acts and attempts

Regina v. *Geddes*

Before Lord Bingham of Cornhill, Lord Chief Justice, Mr Justice Ognall and Mr Justice Astill

[Judgment June 25]

No rule of thumb test existed for determining the line of demarcation between acts which were merely preparatory and acts which might amount to an attempt to commit an offence charged. The line was not always obvious or easy to recognise, and there had always to be an exercise of judgment based on the particular facts of the case.

The Court of Appeal, Criminal Division, so stated when allowing an appeal by Garry William Geddes, aged 29, against his conviction at Lewes Crown Court (Judge Gower, QC and a jury) for attempted false imprisonment, contrary to section 1(1) of the Criminal Attempts Act 1981, in that he attempted unlawfully and injuriously to imprison a person unknown, for which he was sentenced to four years imprisonment.

The appellant had entered school grounds and was found in the boys' toilet by a member of staff. He ran away and a rucksack discarded by him was found to contain lengths of string, sealing tape, a knife and other items.

Section 1 of the 1981 Act provides: "(1) If, with intent to commit an offence ... a person does an act which is more than merely preparatory to the commission of the offence, he is guilty of attempting to commit the offence."

Mr John Aspinall, QC and Mr Christopher de Havas for the appellant; Mr John Tanzer for the Crown.

THE LORD CHIEF JUSTICE, delivering the judgment of the court, said that the appeal was concerned not with the correctness of the jury's decision but with the correctness of the judge's ruling of law that there was a case fit for the jury's consideration. Was the evidence sufficient in law to support a finding that the appellant did an act which was more than merely preparatory to the commission of the offence charged?

The cases showed that the line of demarcation between acts which were merely preparatory and acts which might amount to an attempt was not always obvious or easy to recognise. There was no rule of thumb test. There must always be an exercise of judgment based on the particular facts of the case.

An accurate paraphrase of the statutory test under section 1(1) and not an illegitimate gloss on it was to ask whether the available evidence, if accepted, could show that a defendant had done an act which showed that he was actually trying to commit the act in question or whether he had only got ready or put himself in a position or equipped himself to do so.

There was no doubt about the appellant's intention. The evidence, was clearly capable of showing no more than he made preparations, that he equipped himself, got ready and put himself in a position to commit the offence charged.

But was there evidence sufficient in law to support a finding that the appellant had actually tried or attempted to commit the offence of imprisoning someone? Had he moved from the role of intention, preparation and planning into the area of execution or implementation?

He had entered the school but he had never had any contact or communication with any pupil.

The whole story was fraught with the greatest unease. Nevertheless, their Lordships could not escape giving an answer to the fundamental question.

The contents of a rucksack, lengths of string, sealing tape, a knife and other items, might have given a clear indication of what the appellant might well have had in mind but did not throw light on whether he had begun to carry out the commission of the offence.

Their Lordships were bound to conclude that the evidence was not sufficient in law to support a finding that the appellant did an act more than merely preparatory to wrongfully imprisoning a person.

The appeal was allowed and the conviction quashed.

Solicitors: Edward Harte & Co. Brighton; Crown Prosecution Service, Brighton.

Source: *The Times*, 16 July 1996

8

Questions

1 What was the substantive offence in this case?

2 In the Crown Court what are the roles of the judge and the jury?

3 Was this appeal concerned with the correctness of the jury's verdict in Lewes Crown Court or with the judge's ruling of law?

4 The Lord Chief Justice stated that there was 'no rule of thumb' test to determine when a person's acts had gone *beyond* mere preparation to attempt. However, he did suggest a sort of test; what was it?

5 Which part of the evidence demonstrated the *mens rea* of the appellant in relation to the offence of attempted false imprisonment?

6 Why had the appellant not committed the *actus reus* of attempted false imprisonment?

7 Do you think that the test suggested in this case for demarcating the line between mere preparation and attempt is a good one in terms of preventing 'potential' harm to members of the public?

Answers

1 In this case the substantive offence was false imprisonment which is a common law offence. Like common law assault and battery, false imprisonment is also a tort under the civil law and most cases are pursued through the civil courts. However, the definition of the criminal offence of false imprisonment is that the accused has unlawfully and either intentionally or recklessly restrained the freedom of movement of another person from a particular place. In this particular case the accused was convicted of attempted false imprisonment (contrary to section 1(1) of the Criminal Attempts Act 1981) for 'attempting unlawfully and injuriously to imprison a person unknown'. The injurious part of this probably relates to the fact that a knife was found in the rucksack which the accused left behind after he fled the scene.

2 When there is a trial in the Crown Court it is the role of the jury to decide upon the verdict of guilty or not guilty based on the facts brought out in court and in accordance with the judge's direction as to the law. It is the role of the judge to control proceedings in the court, to direct the jury on points of law and to pass any sentence should the accused be found guilty by the jury.

3 In this case the appeal was concerned with the correctness of the judge's ruling of law that there was a case fit for the jury's consideration. In other words, the judge had determined that there was sufficient evidence to support a finding that the accused could be found guilty of attempting the crime of false imprisonment.

4 The Lord Chief Justice stated that there was no rule of thumb test and that there must always be an exercise of judgment based on the particular facts of the case. However, he went on to state that the test for attempt under section 1(1) of the Criminal Attempts Act 1981 could be paraphrased to ask:

> *... whether the available evidence, if accepted, could show that a defendant had done an act which showed that he was **actually trying to commit the act in question** or whether he had only got ready or put himself in a position or equipped himself to do so.*

5 The *mens rea* of the appellant, that he *intended* to falsely imprison someone, that is, he intended to carry out the substantive offence, was demonstrated by the fact that he had made preparations and got himself ready and put himself in a position to commit the offence. He had a rucksack, with him which contained string, tape, a knife and other items, and he had entered the boys' toilet.

6 The appellant, while he had the *mens rea* for the substantive offence of false imprisonment, had not carried out the *actus reus* of attempted false imprisonment as he had not *'actually tried or attempted to commit the offence and had not moved from the role of intention, preparation and planning into the area of execution or implementation'*. He had entered the school but he had never had any contact or communication with any pupil.

7 In this case it is easy to see how a jury would find the accused guilty of attempted false imprisonment as the evidence in the case seems conclusive as to what would have happened if a schoolboy had entered the toilets. However, on appeal it was held that there was not enough evidence to warrant the judge leaving the case to the jury. If a boy had entered the toilets and the accused had done nothing, then the result would have been the same. However, if a boy had entered the toilets and the accused had approached him then such behaviour would probably amount to an act more than merely preparatory as the accused would have moved into the area of execution or implementation. In this case it seems that the criminal law is not protecting society from 'potential' harm as it was no doubt just a coincidence that a school teacher entered the toilets rather than a boy. On the other hand, who is to say that if a boy had entered the toilets the accused might not have changed his mind and left?

8

Key points on the inchoate offences

▶ As with most other offences, the inchoate offences are comprised of the *actus reus* and *mens rea* of the crime. These elements are dealt with in detail below.

▶ Attempt and conspiracy are now defined by statutes, the Criminal Attempts Act 1981 and the Criminal Law Act 1977, respectively. (See the statutory provisions on page 204.) Note, however, that by sections 5(2) and 5(3) of the Criminal Law Act 1977 the *common law* offences of:

  i conspiracy to defraud;
  ii conspiracy to corrupt public morals; and
  iii conspiracy to outrage public decency;

are retained (but see below).

On the whole, incitement is still a common law offence.

▶ An inchoate offence is not an offence in itself. It has to be charged in relation to a substantive offence. Thus, a person cannot be charged with 'incitement' or 'conspiracy'. The charge has to specify the substantive offence which is the subject of the inchoate offence, such as 'incitement to steal' or 'conspiracy to burgle'.

▶ Can a person be convicted of an inchoate offence if it was 'impossible' to carry out the substantive offence? This is considered below in detail in Figure 8.4 and by reference to the case of *R* v. *Shivpuri* (1987).

▶ The sentences for the inchoate offences are shown in Figure 8.1.

Figure 8.1 Sentences for the inchoate offences

Incitement	Common law only	Summary offence	The sentence is the same as for the substantive offence as per section 45(3) of the Magistrates' Court Act 1980
		Indictable offence	There is no maximum sentence – the sentence is left to the discretion of the judge*
Conspiracy	Common law	i Conspiracy to defraud Maximum sentence of 10 years	
		ii Conspiracy to corrupt public morals There is no maximum sentence – the sentence is left to the discretion of the judge	
		iii Conspiracy to outrage public decency Since the case of *R* v. *Gibson* (1990) this should be dealt with as per statutory conspiracy	
	Statutory	The maximum sentence is usually the same as for the substantive offence – section 3 Criminal Law Act 1977	
Attempt	Statutory only	The maximum sentence is usually the same as for the substantive offence – section 4(1) Criminal Attempts Act 1981.	

*This means that, in theory, the sentence for the commission of an inchoate offence (where no harm has been done) could be greater than for the actual commission of the substantive offence, when harm will have been done. Does this make sense?

8

The *actus reus* of the inchoate offences

The amount of evidence required to prove that the *actus reus* of an inchoate offence has been committed is shown below.

Incitement

Words or deeds by the accused, whether express or implied, can be sufficient evidence of incitement of another person to commit a substantive offence.

Attempt

The accused must have taken steps, which are more than merely preparatory, towards the commission of the substantive offence.

Conspiracy

An agreement, verbal, written or even implied, by two or more people to commit an act which would be a crime if committed (statutory conspiracy) or which would satisfy the requirements of common law conspiracy – see below.

Thus, in a scenario where A decides to rob the post office and merely tells B of his plans, there is no inchoate offence, just evil thoughts on the part of A. However, if A actually encourages B to join in (and all B does is listen to A) then A has committed incitement to rob. If B then agrees to join in and they make further plans together, then both A and B are conspiring to rob the post office. If A and B then take steps towards the robbery which are more than merely preparatory, they are both guilty of attempted robbery. If they actually carry out the robbery, then they are guilty of the substantive offence of robbery. We can now look at details of the *actus reus* for each of the inchoate offences.

The *actus reus* of incitement

The *actus reus* of incitement consists of the accused encouraging or persuading another person to commit an act which, *if* committed by the other person, would amount to a criminal offence. Thus, A could incite B to burgle a house. Note the word '*if*'; A is guilty of incitement whether or not B actually commits the offence. This fits in with the notion that the inchoate offences exist to prevent *potential* harm.

The persuasion or encouragement can be by words or deeds and can even amount to threats. The incitement need not be express, such as by words, but can also be implied and it can be to a group of people as well as to one individual. See the 'You Decide' cases which follow.

If A encourages B to commit an act which is not a criminal offence, then A is not guilty of incitement. For instance, if A incites B to throw some stones into a river, A is not guilty of incitement. Similarly, if A, believing B to be 15 years old when in fact B is 17 years old, encourages B to buy some cigarettes from a shop, then A is not guilty of incitement as B can legally buy cigarettes.

Introduction to conspiracy

The law on conspiracy is partly found in the Criminal Law Act 1977 (CLA 1977) and in the common law. This needs clarifaction before the *actus reus* of conspiracy can be dealt with. Consider Figures 8.2 and 8.3 which show the law on conspiracy before and after the CLA 1977.

Conspiracy before the CLA 1977

The law of conspiracy before the CLA 1977 is shown in Figure 8.2.

Note that before the CLA 1977 it was possible to commit the crime of conspiracy in relation to non-criminal behaviour. This was felt to be undersirable by the Law Commission and others (as incitement and attempt relate only to the commission of criminal offences) and so the CLA 1977 was enacted. However, as shown in Figure 8.2, it is still possible to conspire to commit some non-criminal behaviour (however, see footnotes). Certain non-criminal behaviour was left to be covered by the common law of conspiracy because unless these

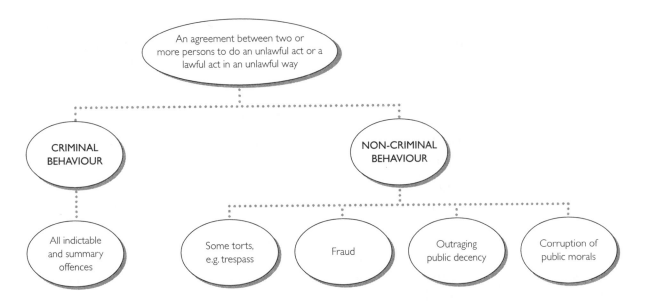

Figure 8.2
Common law
conspiracy before
the CLA 1977

categories of behaviour were left to be covered by conspiracy it became possible for people to escape criminal liability for behaviour which ought to be criminal as a substantive offence in its own right (without the need for a conspiracy charge) but which was not. Thus, the common law conspiracy categories which were retained filled a loop-hole in the substantive criminal law. This can be demonstrated by reference to the case of *Scott* v. *Metropolitan Police Commissioner* (1974). In this case Scott bribed cinema employees to let him borrow films from the cinema without the cinema owners' permission and without permission from the copyright owners, so that he could copy them and rent them out for hire. The films were always returned to the cinema and, as such, Scott had not stolen the films as he did not intend to permenently deprive the cinema owners of the films. Neither had Scott obtained property by deception as the cinema owners were not deceived. Scott's behaviour was obviously criminal in nature but did not fall within the definition of any substantive criminal offence. Thus, in order to make him criminally liable, he was charged with 'conspiracy to defraud' and was convicted. On appeal it was argued that it was necessary to deceive someone in order to defraud them (and the cinema owners were not deceived as they were unaware of events) but this was rejected. The House of Lords did not offer a comprehensive definition of 'defraud' but stated that:

> ... *an agreement by two or more by dishonesty to deprive a person of something which is his or to which he is or would be or might be entitled and an agreement by two or more by dishonesty to injure some proprietory right of his, suffices to constitute the offence of conspiracy to defraud.*

8

In the present case the cinema owners had been deprived of money (economic loss) which they might have received through more people coming to watch the film at the cinema rather than at home on video. Thus, Scott's appeal was dismissed.

Conspiracy after the Criminal Law Act 1977

The law regarding conspiracy after the CLA 1977 is shown in Figure 8.3.

Thus, arguably, the only true common law conspiracy left is conspiracy to corrupt public morals. Should corruption of public morals ever become an offence in itself then it, too, will become a statutory conspiracy and common law conspiracy will be almost defunct. For commentary on whether the law on conspiracy should be retained, students should refer to the proposals for reform on page 224.

Figure 8.3 Conspiracy after the CLA 1977

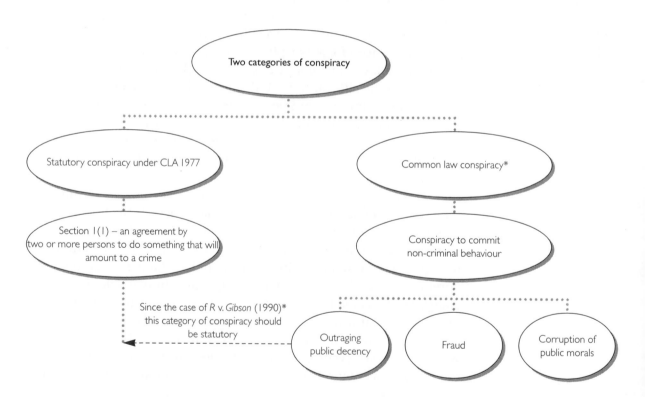

*The essence of post-1977 common law conspiracy was that it covered situations where the conspiracy related to non-criminal behaviour. However, there have been developments since the CLA 1977 which have reduced and changed the nature of common law conspiracy
i Sometimes, in conspiracy to defraud, one or more 'crimes' might be committed and so if it was charged as a common law conspiracy the case might fail as conspiracy to commit crimes had to be charged under the CLA 1977. However, to avoid such problems it is now the case that a conspiracy to defraud can be dealt with as either a statutory conspiracy under the CLA 1977 or as a common law conspiracy.
ii The case of R v. Gibson (1990) has determined that there is now a substantive offence of outraging public decency. Thus, if such behaviour is now regarded as criminal in its own right, conspiracy to outrage public decency should now be a statutory conspiracy under the CLA 1977.

The *actus reus* of conspiracy

The *actus reus* of conspiracy involves two or more people conspiring to:

i commit a criminal offence (statutory conspiracy); or
ii defraud (common law or statutory conspiracy); or
iii corrupt public morals (common law conspiracy); or
iv outrage public decency (included in the CLA 1977 as a common law conspiracy but should be a statutory conspiracy since *R* v. *Gibson* [1990]).

For the full definition of the *actus reus* of statutory conspiracy, refer to the statutory provisions to section 1(1) of the CLA 1977 (page 204). Note also the provisions of section 2 which state that if there are only two conspirators and one of them is the spouse of the other, or under the age of criminal responsibility (under 10 years old) or an intended victim of the conspiracy, then there is no conspiracy under the criminal law.

The *actus reus* of attempt

8

Common law attempt was abolished by the Criminal Attempts Act 1981 (CAA 1981) and replaced with the new statutory offence of attempt as defined in sectioin 1(1) of the Act which only applies to indictable and triable either way offences. It is only possible to be charged with attempting a summary offence if such an offence is specifically created by a statute.

By section 1(1) of the CAA 1981 the *actus reus* of attempt is defined as when a person does an act which is more than merely preparatory to the commission of the offence. In a trial the judge has to determine whether there is sufficient evidence to support the proposition that the accused did acts that were more than merely preparatory to the commission of the offence in question.

If this is so, then the matter can be left to the jury to decide on the evidence. But how does the judge decide whether the evidence supplied supports a possible attempt to commit a crime? The judge is given no help in the CAA 1981. As a result, judges tend to struggle to determine whether the acts (note, not omissions) of the accused have gone past the merely preparatory stage to the commission of the offence according to vague tests. The case of *R* v. *Geddes* (1996) was discussed in setting the scene (page 205) and students should re-read this case, noting the test applied by the Lord Chief Justice. Two interesting and contrasting cases are *R* v. *Tosti and White* (1997) and *R* v. *Campbell* (1991) which are dealt with in the 'You Decide' cases.

YOU DECIDE

Consider the cases shown below concerning inchoate offences and answer the questions which follow. The answers are given on page 215.

1 Invicta Plastics Ltd v. Clare (1976)

In this case the company, Invicta Plastics, advertised a new device called a Radatec in a motoring magazine. The device could detect wireless transmissions such as those used by the police in radar traps to catch speeding motorists. It was very unlikely that the licensing authority would grant motorists licences to use such a device. The company was prosecuted for inciting readers of the magazine to commit the offence of using unlicensed wireless apparatus contrary to the Wireless Telegraphy Act 1949.

Do you think it was significant that:
a) the advertisement warned readers that using the device would be an offence;
b) there was only implied incitement to use the device;
c) the advertisement affected an unknown number of readers?

2 R v. Campbell (1991)

In this case the accused was watched by police (who had been tipped off to the fact that the accused intended to rob a post office) as he loitered outside a post office, having driven to it on his motorbike. He walked up and down outside the post office and acted very suspiciously. Finally, he approached the door to the post office and put his hand in his jacket pocket. He was then arrested by the police and charged with attempted robbery. He was found to have on him an immitation firearm, a pair of sun-glasses and a threatening note for the cashier. He was convicted of attempted robbery and appealed.

Do you think there was sufficient evidence in this case for the trial judge to leave the question of an attempted robbery to the jury? In other words, had the accused done acts which were more than merely preparatory to the commission of the robbery?

3 R v. Tosti and White (1997)

The two accused in this case drove to a barn and hid some oxyacetylene equipment in a hedge. They approached the barn door and examined a padlock on the door. They were convicted of attempted burglary and appealed.

Applying the test as put forward in the Geddes case do you think the two accused were **actually trying to commit the burglary** or that they had only got ready or put themselves in a position and equipped to do a burglary?

4 Yip Chiu-Cheung v. R (1994)

In this case the appellant had agreed with P who, unknown to the appellant, was an undercover drug enforcement officer, to smuggle heroin from Hong Kong to Australia. The smuggling never actually took place and so the appellant was convicted of conspiracy to traffic in heroin. He appealed against his conviction arguing that there was no conspiracy as P did not have mens rea for conspiracy.

You decide the appeal.

Answers

1 The company was convicted of incitement to commit the offence of using unlicensed wireless equipment. It did not matter that the advertisement warned readers that using Radatec would be an offence, that the incitement was not express but implied (readers were not told expressly to use the equipment to avoid the police speed traps but the implication was there) or that the incitement was to a whole group of people rather than to one individual. Note also that the company could be guilty of incitement even if no motorists actually committed the offence.

2 The accused's conviction for attempted robbery was quashed on appeal. It was held that there was not sufficient evidence to show that the accused's acts were more than merely preparatory – he had not even entered the post office and so the case should not have been left to the jury.

3 It was held that the conviction for attempted burglary should remain; that there was sufficient evidence to leave the matter to the jury. How does this compare with the case of *R* v. *Geddes* (1996) and *R* v. *Campbell* (1991)? In those cases it was held that the acts of the accused were merely preparatory and so there was no attempt to commit the crimes in question. It seems that in the present case the two accused moved from mere preparation to commission of the offence because they 'examined' the padlock. This contrast in judgments demonstrates the vagueness of the law in this area.

4 The appeal was dismissed; the conviction for conspiracy was upheld. There are two important points to note here: (i) the fact that P was an undercover drug enforcement officer did not prevent him from intending to commit a crime (although it is unlikely that he would be prosecuted); and (ii) the Privy Council held that the *mens rea* for conspiracy was 'an agreement between two or more persons to commit an unlawful act with the intention of carrying it out. It is the intention to carry out the crime that constitutes the *mens rea* of the offence.' Thus, no reference is made to who actually participates in the commission of the offence.

8

The *mens rea* of the inchoate offences

The *mens rea* for the inchoate offences is that of *specific intention* although there is an exception to this general rule in the case of the *mens rea* of attempts – see below.

The *mens rea* for incitement

The accused has to intend that the offence incited will be committed. The *mens rea* is thus *intention to incite* another to commit acts which, if committed by the other, would amount to a crime. For incitement it is not necessary to show that the accused also had the *mens rea* for the crime incited. However, in the case of *R* v. *Shaw* (1994) the Court of Appeal quashed the conviction of the accused because they held that he did not have the *mens rea* for the offence incited. This decision of the Court of Appeal is generally held to be very dubious. The facts of the case were that the accused, A, encouraged a fellow employee, B, to obtain cheques from the company where they worked as payment for bogus invoices. Thus, A had incited B to obtain property (the cheques) by deception contrary to section 15 of the Theft Act 1968. He was convicted at trial but the conviction was quashed on appeal because the jury had not been invited to consider whether A had the *mens rea* for the section 15 offence. In this case the accused claimed that he had not intended to keep the cheques permanently or to profit from the enterprise other than to reveal to the company their security deficiencies. Is it possible that the Court of Appeal took note of this argument and decided the appeal having regard to the fact that no *harm* was actually done or intended?

Although the inciter, (A), need not have *mens rea* for the offence incited, the person incited, (B), must have *mens rea* for the offence, that is, B must *know* that the acts which he is doing constitute an offence. This is logical because unless B has *mens rea* for the offence incited, B has not committed an offence as most offences require both *actus reus* and *mens rea*. And as was stated earlier, A can only be guilty of incitement if the acts which B does constitute an offence. If B does not have *mens rea* for the offence incited, one of the ingredients of the crime is missing. However, in a situation where B lacks *mens rea*, A can be convicted as principal offender as B can be regarded as an innocent agent.

The *mens rea* for conspiracy

It is submitted that the *mens rea* for all types of conspiracy is that the parties to the conspiracy *intend* that their agreement will be carried out by *one or more of them*; it is not a requirement that the conspirator intends to take part in the commission of the planned crime himself. This proposition was challenged in the case of *R* v. *Anderson* (1985) in which it was held that to be held liable as a conspirator, the accused had to have intended to take part in the commission of the crime himself. This is generally regarded as incorrect as it would mean that gang leaders who organise others to commit criminal offences would escape criminal liability. The case of *Yip Chiu-Cheung* v. *R* (1994), before the Privy Council (thus only persuasive rather than binding on English courts), supported the proposition that it is sufficient *mens rea* for conspiracy if the accused intended that one or more of the conspirators should effect the actual crime (see the 'You Decide' cases).

The *mens rea* for attempt

The general rule

The *mens rea* for attempt is as provided for in section 1(1) of the Criminal Attempts Act 1981 (CAA 1981) which states: 'If, *with intent* to commit an offence to which this section applies ...'.

Thus, the general rule is that a person can only be convicted of attempting a substantive offence if he *intended* to commit the substantive offence in question (that is, he intended the consequences of his act/s). Lower forms of *mens rea*, such as recklessness or negligence, will not suffice for a conviction for attempting an offence. This rule applies even if the substantive offence could be committed with only recklessness or negligence as the *mens rea*.

Thus, while it is possible for the accused to be convicted under section 20 of the Offences Against the Person Act 1861 (OAPA 1861) when *reckless* as to the infliction of harm on another person, it is only possible to be convicted of attempt under section 20 when the accused *intends* to inflict harm on another person. On a murder charge, the *mens rea* to be proved by the prosecution is that the accused either intended to kill the victim or intended to cause the victim grievous bodily harm. However, on a charge of attempted murder, the *mens rea* to be proved is that the accused intended to kill the victim. If the accused intended to cause the victim grievous bodily harm then the appropriate charge would be attempt under either section 20 or section 18 of the OAPA 1861. Why is a more blameworthy state of mind required for attempts? A more blameworthy state of mind is surely appropriate given that the accused has not actually committed the full substantive offence and so, usually, no harm has been done.

8

Exceptions to the general rule

This is relevent when an offence involves *mens rea* as to the *consequences* of the accused's behaviour (discussed above) and, in addition, requires *mens rea* as to the *circumstances* of the offence. It can be demonstrated with reference to the case of *R* v. *Khan* (1990). This case involved, among other things, appeals following convictions for attempted rape. The *mens rea* for the substantive offence of rape involves intention to have sexual intercourse (*mens rea* as regards consequences) plus knowledge of, or recklessness as to, the absence of consent by the victim (*mens rea* as regards circumstances of the offence). The Court of Appeal held that such *mens rea* was also sufficient for attempted rape, that is, it is sufficient *mens rea* for attempted rape if the accused intended to have sexual intercourse and was only reckless as to the absence of consent by the victim.

Conditional intent

What is the position when the accused intends to commit the substantive offence *only if* certain conditions are satisfied, for instance, where A intends to steal from a van only if it contains jewellery? In such a situation A can be convicted of attempted theft so long as the indictment is worded carefully; if the indictment relates to 'attempting to steal from a van' then there is no problem, but if the indictment relates to 'attempting to steal jewellery from a van' then there could be a problem as how can the prosecution prove that A intended to steal jewellery if he did not know there was some in the van? This is demonstrated in the case of *R* v. *Husseyn* (1977). In this case the appellants decided to break into a parked van and steal anything in it which was worth stealing. The van contained valuable sub-aqua equipment and the appellants were convicted of attempting to steal sub-aqua equipment. They appealed against their convictions which were quashed. It is suggested that if they had been charged with attempting to steal from the van then their convictions could have been upheld.

The inchoate offences and impossibility

To what extent can a person be held criminally liable for an inchoate offence if the substantive offence in question was impossible to commit? Remember that the essence of the three inchoate offences is that they relate to the commission of a substantive criminal offence (apart from common law conspiracy). Thus, if the inchoate behaviour relates to behaviour which would not amount to a crime if committed, then there is no liability for an inchoate offence. We have already seen this in relation to incitement by the example of someone inciting another to throw stones into a river – this is not criminal incitement. By the same token, it would not be criminal to conspire to throw stones into a river or to attempt to do so.

When the inchoate behaviour relates to behaviour which *would amount to a crime if committed* (apart from common law conspiracy) then the position regarding impossibility is as shown in Figure 8.4. In these instances the person's *mens rea* is criminal – their intention is to incite another to, conspire with another to, or attempt to do acts which they believe are criminal.

Figure 8.4
Liability for inchoate offences in relation to impossibility

Common law inchoate offences:	
i Incitement ii Conspiracy	Inciting/conspiring the impossible **is** generally a defence. This general rule was provided for in *DPP* v. *Nock* (1978) and *Haughton* v. *Smith* (1975)
	There is one exception to this general rule: where the impossibility is due to the '*inadequacy of the means used*'. For example, if A incites B to break into a warehouse and gives him wirecutters to cut through the perimeter fence, if the wirecutters are not strong enough to cut through the fence, then A may be guilty of incitement to burgle.
Statutory inchoate offences:	
i Attempts	The Criminal Attempts Act 1981 sections 1(2) and (3) provides that it is possible to attempt the impossible, that is, impossibility **is not** a defence.
ii Conspiracy	The Criminal Law Act 1977 section 1(1)(b) provides that it is possible to conspire to do the impossible, that is impossibility **is not** a defence.
Comment: For clarity in the law it would be appropriate if the common law inchoate offences were brought into line with the statutory offences as regards impossibility, which is what was proposed in the Draft Criminal Code, clause 50(1).	

An interesting case to demonstrate impossibility in relation to the inchoate offences is that of *R* v. *Shivpuri* (1987) in which the case of *Anderton* v. *Ryan* (1986) is discussed.

R v. *Shivpuri (1987)*

D was arrested in possession of a suitcase which he believed contained heroin or cannabis. Subsequently the substance in the suitcase was analysed and found to be harmless vegetable matter. D was convicted under section 1(1) of the Criminal Attempts Act 1981 of attempting to be knowingly concerned in dealing with and harbouring prohibited drugs contrary to section 170(1)(b) of the Customs and Excise Management Act 1979. The Court of Appeal dismissed his appeal but

certified the following point of law of general public importance:

*Does a person commit an offence under section 1, Criminal Attempts Act 1981, where, **if the facts were as that person believed them to be**, the full offence would have been committed by him, but where on the true facts the offence which that person set out to commit was in law impossible, e.g. because the substance imported and believed to be heroin was not heroin but a harmless substance?*

To aid clarity and understanding, the judgment of Lord Bridge of Harwich is shown and is broken down into three sections.

Section 1 – talking about the case in hand

LORD BRIDGE OF HARWICH:

The certified question depends on the true construction of the Criminal Attempts Act 1981. The Act marked an important new departure since, by section 6, it abolished the offence of attempt at common law and substituted a new statutory code governing attempts to commit criminal offences. It was considered by your Lordships' House last year in Anderton v. Ryan after the decision in the Court of Appeal which is the subject of the present appeal ...

Applying this language to the facts of the case, the first question to be asked is whether the appellant intended to commit the offences of being knowingly concerned in dealing with and harbouring drugs of class A or class B with intent to evade the prohibition on their importation ...

The answer is plainly Yes, he did. Next, did he, in relation to each offence, do an act which was more than merely preparatory to the commission of the offence? ...

In each case the act was clearly more than preparatory to the commission of the intended offence ...

This very simple, perhaps over-simple, analysis leads me to the provisional conclusion that the appellant was rightly convicted of the two offences of attempt with which he was charged.

Section 2 – discussion of *Anderton* v. *Ryan*

... But can this conclusion stand with Anderton v. Ryan? The appellant in that case was charged with an attempt to handle stolen goods. She bought a video recorder believing it to be stolen. On the facts as they were to be assumed it was not stolen. By a majority the House decided that she was entitled to be acquitted.

[Thus, *Anderton v. Ryan* is in disagreement with Lord Bridge of Harwich's judgment above. Lord Bridge then quoted the following examples taken from the Law Commission's Report, 'Criminal Law: Attempt and Impossibility in Relation to Attempt, Conspiracy and Incitement', (1980)(Law Com. No. 102)]

... An example would be where a person is offered goods at such a low price that he believes that they are stolen, when in fact they are not; if he actually purchases them, upon the principles which we have discussed

he would be liable for an attempt to handle stolen goods. Another case which has been much debated is that raised in argument by Bramwell B in R v. Collins. If A takes his own umbrella, mistaking it for one belonging to B and intending to steal B's umbrella, is he guilty of attempted theft? Again, on the principles which we have discussed he would in theory be guilty, but in neither case would it be realistic to suppose that a complaint would be made or that a prosecution would ensue. [These people are highly unlikely to report themselves!] *... What turns what would otherwise, from the point of view of the criminal law, be an innocent act into a crime is **the intent of the actor to commit an offence** ... A puts his hand into B's pocket. Whether or not there is anything in the pocket capable of being stolen, if A intends to steal his act is a criminal attempt; if he does not so intend his act is innocent ... I am thus led to the conclusion that there is no valid ground on which Anderton v. Ryan can be distinguished ... I am* [thus] *the readier to express that the decision was wrong.*

Section 3 – the problem conflicting decisions from the House of Lords

... What then is to be done? If the case is indistinguishable, the application of the strict doctrine of precedent would require that the present appeal be allowed. Is it permissable to depart from precedent under the 1966 Practice Statement Note notwithstanding the especial need for certainty in the criminal law? The following considerations lead me to answer the question affirmatively. Firstly, I am undeterred by the consideration that the decision in Anderton v. Ryan was so recent. The 1966 Practice Statement is an effective abandonment of our prevention to infallibility. If a serious error embodied in a decision of this House has distorted the law, the sooner it is corrected the better ... I would answer the certified question in the affirmative and dismiss the appeal. [That is, the conviction remains.]

How do we reconcile this case with the example of throwing stones into a river? The key difference is that in *R* v. *Shivpuri* the accused 'intended' to 'commit a criminal offence' (the *mens rea* of attempt), whereas if the accused had only 'intended' to throw stones into a river, the accused did not have a criminal *mens rea*. If you now look back to the statutory provisions on page 204, section 1(3) of the Criminal Attempts Act 1981 might make more sense.

8

Applying principles to examination questions

The inchoate offences frequently appear in examination problem-solving questions. Thus, it is necessary to be able to spot them and to know supporting cases to demonstrate their applicability. In addition, inchoate offences sometimes appear as essay-type questions and in order to answer such questions it is necessary to have studied them in detail. Such questions often focus on the fact that the inchoate offences incur criminal sanctions when no harm has been done (see Chapter 13 for the answer to such a question) or on the difficulty of establishing when acts have gone beyond the merely preparatory stage for attempts. Below is a problem question which highlights some of the key points for inchoate offences. Look back through the chapter to find details on these points, plus supporting cases and statutory provisions, and then consider the suggested approach which follows.

Andrew and Peter decided to rob a warehouse. On the night in question they drove their lorry to the warehouse and parked it next to a high brick wall, topped with broken glass, which surrounded the warehouse. While standing on the roof of the lorry they threw an old carpet over the broken glass and were then apprehended by the police.

Eileen wishes to show her boss that his security systems for cash payments are poor and so, not intending to profit from the venture, she encourages Annie to make payments to her for overtime which she has not worked. Annie does not know of the plan and acts honestly.

Brian agrees with his younger brother Tony, aged nine years, to vandalise their neighbour's new car worth £11,000. Edward also dislikes the neighbour and agrees to join in. Brian does not intend to take part in the act of vandalism himself as he regards himself as the 'brains' of the enterprise.

Consider the criminal liability of Andrew, Peter, Eileen, Annie, Brian, Tony and Edward for any inchoate offences.

Tips on how to approach such a question

Andrew and Peter decided to rob a warehouse. On the night in question they drove their lorry to the warehouse and parked it next to a high brick wall, topped with broken glass, which surrounded the warehouse. While standing on the roof of the lorry they threw an old carpet over the broken glass and were then apprehended by the police.

Eileen wishes to show her boss that his security systems for cash payments are poor and so, not intending to profit from the venture, she encourages Annie to make payments to her for overtime which she has not worked. Annie does not know of the plan and acts honestly.

Brian agrees with his younger brother Tony, aged nine years, to vandalise their neighbour's new car worth £11,000. Edward also dislikes the neighbour and agrees to join in. Brian does not intend to take part in the act of vandalism himself as he regards himself as the 'brains' of the enterprise.

Consider the criminal liability of Andrew, Peter, Eileen, Annie, Brian, Tony and Edward for any inchoate offences.

Left margin notes:

...nspiracy to ...gle – statutory ...spiracy ...erned by *section* ...) CLA 1977

...een does not ...ve the full *mens* ...for theft as she ...es not intend to ...rmanently ...prive the boss of ...e money. Is this ...evant to a ...arge of ...itement to ...al? Discuss the ...se of *R* v. *Shaw* ...994).

...nspiracy to ...mmit criminal ...mage? This ...uld be statutory ...nspiracy ...ntrary to *section* ...) CLA 1977.

...es it matter that ...ian does not ...end to take ...rt himself? ...scuss the cases ...*R* v. *Anderson* ...985) and *Yip* ...ui-Cheung* v. *R* ...994). Brain will ...obably be liable ...r conspiracy to ...mmit criminal ...mage.

Right margin notes:

Have they 'attempted' the burglary? Are their acts more than merely preparatory? Discuss the cases of *R* v. *Campbell* (1991), *R* v. *Geddes* (1996) and *R* v. *Tosti and White* (1997). On the Geddes test they can probably be charged with attempted burglary contrary to *section 1(1) CAA 1981*.

Incitement to steal? Annie is acting honestly and so does not have the *mens rea* for theft. Thus, Eileen has not incited her to commit an offence. However, consider Eileen's possible criminal responsibility for theft as principal offender using Annie as an innocent agent.

Brian cannot conspire with Tony as Tony is under the age of criminal responsibility.

However, when Edward joins in the plan, Brain and Edward can be charged with conspiracy to commit criminal damage contrary to *section 1(1) CLA 1977*.

The question is phrased to direct your attention to inchoate offences. Thus, while you have to recognise the relevant substantive offences of burglary, theft and criminal damage, you are not required to explain them in detail.

223

Proposals for reform

Proposals for reform are discussed in relation to incitement and conspiracy.

Replacement of the common law offence of incitement

In 1993 proposals for reform were made by the Law Commission in their Consultation Paper No. 131, 'Assisting and Encouraging Crime'. The crime of *'assisting crime'* is detailed in paragraph 4.99 and this would seem to replace the present crimes of aiding and procuring. The crime of *'encouraging crime'* is detailed in paragraph 4.163 and this would seem to replace the present crimes of abetting, counselling and the inchoate offence of incitement. (See Chapter 7, on accomplices, for details of paragraph 4.99.) The details of paragraph 4.163 are shown below:

> 4.163 (1) A person commits the offence of encouraging crime if he
>
> > (a) solicits, commands or encourages another ('the principal') to do or cause to be done an act or acts, which, if done, will involve the commission of an offence by the principal; and
> > (b) intends that that act or those acts should be done by the principal; and
> > (c) knows or believes that the principal, in so acting, will do so with the fault required for the offence in question.

The Law Commission has received responses to this consultation paper but, as yet, has not been able to take the matter forward due to staffing difficulties. It is hoped that recommendations might be forthcoming in 1999.

Should the law of conspiracy be retained?

The law on conspiracy is now less of a threat to personal liberty because it is almost entirely based on the CLA 1977 so that a person may generally only be charged with conspiracy for conspiring to commit a *criminal* offence. Thus, it is more in line with the other two inchoate offences of incitement and attempt. The potiential harm from which society is being protected is thus potential criminal harm. In this respect, conspiracy is a useful part of the criminal law as it can be used to make members of criminal gangs criminally liable when they might otherwise escape liability.

However, conspiracy to corrupt public morals and conspiracy to defraud can still be charged as common law conspiracy where no criminal offence as such is being planned. The Law Commission would like to see the former type of conspiracy abolished. However, it is unlikely that conspiracy to defraud will be abolished readily as it is a useful charge for prosecutors not only when there is a situation as in the *Scott* case (see above), but also when it is easier for them to bring a charge of conspiracy to defraud in cases where there has been an offence under the Theft Act 1968 or 1978. Rather than attempt to prove all of the ingredients of the *mens rea* and *actus reus* for such crimes when there might be a problem with the evidence, it is often easier to use a conspiracy to defraud charge for which the rules of evidence are less stringent. Such a charge is particularly favoured by the Serious Fraud Office and was used in the case involving the Maxwell brothers. An obvious argument against this is that more substantive offences should be created so that conspiracy to defraud is not necessary just to 'fill the gaps' in the substantive criminal law. However, it is felt that it is impossible for the legislature to keep pace with the speed at which new ways of defrauding appear. Thus, it is useful to retain conspiracy to defraud to ensure that future instances of fraud do not go unpunished by the criminal law.

CHAPTER Summary

8

In this chapter the inchoate offences of incitement, conspiracy and attempt have been studied and it has been noted that criminal sanctions are incurred by the defendant where no harm has been done so that society is protected from potential harm. We have discovered that the law on inchoate offences is to be found partly in the common law and partly in statutes and that this causes difficulty in accessing and understanding the law. The case of *R* v. *Geddes* (1996) demonstrates the problem of deciding when the defendant's actions have gone beyond the merely preparatory stage for attempt, and the inability of the criminal law to keep pace with new types of fraudulent behaviour is put forward as justification for the retention of common law conspiracy to cover situations where the conspiracy relates to non-criminal behaviour. Whereas in accomplice liability (aiding, abetting, counselling and procuring) the principal offender has to have carried out the principal offence for liability to incur, for inchoate offences it has to be remembered that no substantive offence actually takes place.

General defences

OVERVIEW

Terminology box
Brief explanations of new legal terminology

Statutory provisions
Criminal Law Act 1967 Trial of Lunatics Act 1883 Criminal Procedure (Insanity) Act 1964 Road Traffic Act 1998 Crime and Disorder Act 1998

Setting the scene
Extracts from two newspaper articles, *DPP* v. *H (1997)*, plus introductory questions and answers

Key points on general defences
Infancy, insanity, automatism, mistake, intoxication and self-defence briefly Detail on duress and necessity 'You Decide' cases (Consent is dealt with in Chapter 11 on non-fatal offences against the person)

Applying principles to examination questions

Proposals for reform
Legislating the Criminal Code: Offences Against the Person and General Principles – Law Com. No. 218

Chapter summary

When the accused has been found guilty of an offence he may, nevertheless, try to escape punishment by raising a defence. Defences can be divided into two main categories: general defences which can be used to escape liability for many offences; and specific defences which can only be used to escape liability for prescribed offences. Thus, provocation is a specific defence as it can only be used as a defence to murder. In this chapter we will consider only general defences, leaving specific defences to be dealt with in conjunction with the offences they relate to.

There are several general defences (infancy, insanity, automatism, mistake, intoxication, self-defence, duress, necessity and consent) but not all of them will be discussed in great detail in this chapter. Rather, we will concentrate on those defences which have either come to the fore in recent years and/or been a favourite with examiners. Thus, we will look at the general defences of duress and necessity in detail. The other general defences are covered in the terminology box, in 'You Decide' cases and in applying principles to examination techniques. Consent as a defence is dealt with in detail in Chapter 11 on non-fatal offences against the person, as it is in relation to such offences that the issue of consent is particularly relevant.

Look at the box below in which brief explanations are given for the general defences and other terms. These should help you with the setting the scene articles and associated questions.

9

TERMINOLOGY: General Defences

Doli incapax	This Latin phrase is used to describe the legal proposition that a child aged under 10 years is incapable of committing a criminal offence.
Irrebuttable presumption	This is a presumption which cannot be rebutted or denied. The presumption that a child under 10 years cannot commit a criminal offence is an irrebuttable presumption, so no matter what the child has done, even if they have killed someone, the law applies *doli incapax* and no charges can be brought.
Rebuttable presumption	A rebuttable presumption is a presumption which can be rebutted or denied. Until the Crime and Disorder Act 1998 there was a rebuttable presumption that a child aged 10 years but under 14 years was *doli incapax*. See the key points on general defences for more details.

Insanity	The defendant may raise the defence of insanity at his trial. In doing so the defendant is saying that at the time the offence occurred he did not know what he was doing because he was insane. The definition of insanity in this context is a legal definition, as opposed to a medical one, as set out in the case of *M'Naghten* in 1843. See the key points for more details.
Unfitness to plead	This refers to the fact that the defendant might be unfit to plead at his trial. When this is the case a jury decides whether or not the defendant did the act or omission alleged on the basis of the evidence provided. See Figure 9.1.
Automatism	If the defendant raises the defence of automatism he is saying that at the time the offence was committed he was acting totally involuntarily, like an automaton. For the defence to be successful the automatism must have been caused by external factors, such as a blow to the head.
Mistake	If the defendant makes a mistake as to the facts in a situation then this may be a defence because the *mens rea* will be negated.
Intoxication	A person might become intoxicated either by alcoholic drink, drugs or both. It seems to be that intoxication may be a defence (because *mens rea* is negated) to crimes described as 'specific intent' crimes but not a defence to crimes described as 'basic intent' crimes.
Self-defence	A person may use such force as is reasonable in the circumstances to defend himself or another, or his propery or property of another.
Duress	A person might commit a crime only because he was under duress at the time. This means that the person's will was overborne due to the threat of immediate, serious, physical harm to himself or another.
Necessity	When a person pleads necessity as a defence, he is saying that he only committed the crime out of necessity.

Statutory provisions

Criminal Law Act 1967

3 (1) A person may use such force as is reasonable in the circumstances in the prevention of crime, or in effecting or assisting in the lawful arrest of offenders or suspected offenders or of persons unlawfully at large.

Road Traffic Act 1988

5 (1) If a person –
   (a) drives or attempts to drive a motor vehicle on a road or other public place, or
   (b) is in charge of a motor vehicle on a road or other public place,

   after consuming so much alcohol that the proportion of it in his breath, blood or urine exceeds the prescribed limit he is guilty of an offence.

   (2) It is a defence for a person charged with an offence under subsection (1)(b) above to prove that at the time he is alleged to have committed the offence the circumstances were such that there was no likelihood of his driving the vehicle whilst the proportion of alcohol in his breath, blood or urine remained likely to exceed the prescribed limit.

Trial of Lunatics Act 1883

2 (1) Where in any indictment or information any act or omission is charged against any person as an offence, and it is given in evidence on the trial of such person for that offence that he was insane, so as not to be responsible, according to law, for his actions at the time when the act was done or omission made, then, if it appears to the jury before whom such person is tried that he did the act or made the omission charged, but was insane as aforesaid at the time when he did or made the same, the jury shall return a special verdict that the accused is not guilty by reason of insanity.

Criminal Procedure (Insanity) Act 1964

5 (1) This section applies where –
   (a) a special verdict is returned that the accused is not guilty by reason of insanity; or
   (b) findings are recorded that the accused is under a disability and that he did the act or made the omission charged against him.

9

(2) Subject to subsection (3) below, the court shall either –

    (a) make an order that the accused be admitted, in accordance with the provisions of Schedule 1 to the Criminal Procedure (Insanity and Unfitness to Plead) Act 1991, to such hospital as may be specified by the Secretary of State; or

    (b) where they have the power to do so by virtue of section 5 of that Act, make in respect of the accused such one of the following orders as they think most suitable in all the circumstances of the case, namely

        (i) a guardianship order within the meaning of the Mental Health Act 1983;

        (ii) a supervision and treatment order within the meaning of Schedule 2 to the said Act of 1991; and

        (iii) an order for his absolute discharge.

(3) Paragraph (b) of subsection (2) above shall not apply where the offence to which the special verdict or findings relate is an offence the sentence for which is fixed by law.

Crime and Disorder Act 1998

34 (1) The rebuttable presumption of criminal law that a child aged 10 or over is incapable of committing an offence is hereby abolished.

Setting the scene

Read the three newspaper extracts which follow and answer the questions. You will notice that one of the extracts concerns car thieves in Louisiana in the USA. This should help you to look more critically at the general defences that are available in England and Wales. Also, many syllabuses require a comparitive study of law as practised in other countries and in particular in the USA.

Extract 1

This edited extract is taken from the *The Times* dated 16 July 1996 and was written by a staff reporter.

Man was 'justified' in stabbing burglar

BY A STAFF REPORTER

A man who came home to find a burglar ransacking his flat was fully justified in seizing a kitchen knife and stabbing him, a judge at the Old Bailey said yesterday. The burglar, Brian Firmager, 32, later died from a heart attack on the operating table at Guy's Hospital, where his accomplice, Tony Garrard, had taken him after they fled ...

Firmager had attacked John Campbell with a pepper spray and baseball bat when he returned to his home and disturbed the burglars. 'I have not the slightest doubt that, in my judgment, Mr Campbell was fully justified in what he did in lawful self-defence,' Brian Higgs, QC, the Recorder, said. He jailed Garrard for six years for the aggravated burglary ...

The Crown Prosecution Service had considered prosecuting Mr Campbell but decided not to take action as it was considered to be self-defence.

Source: *The Times*, 16 July 1996

Questions

1 What is the Old Bailey?

2 Who attacked whom first? Do you think that this is significant?

3 If the burglar had not attacked John Campbell or if the burglar had only punched and kicked him, do you think it would still have been self-defence to stab the burglar?

4 Explain what is meant by 'Brian Higgs, QC, the Recorder'.

5 Quote the statutory provision for aggravated burglary and state the maximum prison term which could have been given by the judge.

6 For what crime/s might the Crown Prosecution Service have prosecuted John Campbell?

9

Extract 2

This extract is taken from *The Times* dated 14 August 1997 and was written by Ian Brodie in Washington.

Drivers get the right to kill car thieves

FROM IAN BRODIE IN WASHINGTON

A LAW comes into effect in Louisiana tomorrow giving drivers the right to use deadly force against car thieves. The 'shoot the carjacker' law will mean that courts cannot convict anyone who can show that they killed an assailant, whether armed or not, whom they 'reasonably' believed was trying to take their vehicle by force.

The law was passed overwhelmingly, by 133 votes to one, in the Louisiana state legislature. It makes such killing a justifiable homicide. Under the measure, the person doing the killing will have to be inside the car being stolen and hold a permit for a concealed handgun ...

The Bill was sponsored by Charlie Bruneau, a member of the Louisiana legislature, because 'carjackings' were on the increase in New Orleans ...

George Steimel, a lobbyist for criminal defence lawyers, said: 'Knowing that vehicle owners now have a licence to kill, carjackers won't think twice about pumping a few rounds into a person's head.' He described the proposals as a 'feel-good' law passed without sufficient thought for the consequences.

Critics say the Bill is worded too vaguely and does not specifically define a threat, nor what amounts to a reasonable response. Louisiana already has a law giving householders the right to use deadly force against suspected attackers who have entered their homes. In a tragic case five years ago a 16-year-old Japanese student was shot dead in Louisiana when he knocked on a front door to ask the way and was mistaken for a housebreaker ...

Prosecutors may even extend the law's protection to 'Good Samaritans' who open fire while coming to the aid of potential carjacking vicims ...

Source: *The Times*,
14 August 1997

Questions

7 How many states are there in the USA and will this law apply to all of them?

8 Who would you say carries the burden of proof as far as this defence is concerned? Explain your answer.

9 Why was this law introduced in Louisiana?

10 Why can American citizens carry handguns?

11 Do you think such a law could ever be enacted in the UK? Explain your answer.

12 Look back to the statutory provisions on page 229 and explain how section 3(1) of the Criminal Law Act 1967 is similar, yet different, to the Louisiana law.

Extract 3

This extract is taken from *The Times* dated 2 May 1997.

Insanity defence irrelevant

Director of Public Prosecutions v. *H*

Before Lord Justice McCowan and Mr Justice Popplewell [Judgment April 15] A defence of insanity could only be raised where guilty intent was an essential element of the offence. Therefore, because a charge of driving with excess alcohol was a strict liability offence and no mens rea was required, insanity was not available as a defence.

The Queen's Bench Divisional Court so stated when allowing an appeal brought by the prosecution by way of case stated from a decision of Caistor Justices on October 2, 1996 acquitting the defendant on the ground of insanity in respect of a charge of driving with excess alcohol. The case was remitted to the justices for rehearing with a direction to convict. Mr Nicholas Dean for the prosecution; the defen-

dant did not appear and was not represented.

LORD JUSTICE McCOWAN said that every man was assumed to be sane at the time of an alleged offence so that the burden of establishing insanity was on the accused on a balance of probabilities.

Here it was accepted that the defendant suffered from manic depressive psychosis, an illness which involved symptoms of distorted judgement and impaired sense of time and morals and that he had been behaving particularly irrationally on the day the offence was committed. The justices had had their attention drawn to *R* v. *Horseferry Road Magistrates' Court, Ex parte K* (*The Times* February 22, 1996; [1997]QB 23) which had decided, inter alia, that the common law defence of insanity was available to a defendant in a

summary trial, and the defendant relied on that as authority for the proposition that insanity was a defence to any charge. However, it was clear that insanity could only be a defence to an appropriate charge; that is one in which mens rea was in issue.

The offence of driving with excess alcohol under section 5(1)(a) of the Road Traffic Act 1988 and Schedule 2 to the Road Traffic Offenders Act 1988 was a strict liability offence for which no mens rea was required and therefore the defence of insanity was not available. Accordingly the case would be remitted to the justices for rehearing with a direction to convict.

Mr Justice Popplewell agreed.

Solicitors : CPS, Lincoln.

Source: *The Times*, 2 May 1997

Questions

13 What are the two main ingredients of most crimes?

14 What is meant by a strict liability offence?

15 Briefly explain why there are strict liability offences.

16 Why was this appeal heard in the Queen's Bench Divisional Court and what is meant by the phrase, 'by way of case stated'?

17 What is the usual burden of proof and standard of proof in a criminal case?

18 How are these different when the accused raises insanity as a defence? (Refer to the comments of Lord Justice McCowan.)

19   According to the cited case of *R* v. *Horseferry Road Magistrates' Court, ex parte K* (*The Times*, February 22, 1996; [1997] QB 23) is insanity a general defence or a specific defence?

20   Why was insanity not available as a defence to the offence of driving with excess alcohol under section 5(1)(a) of the Road Traffic Act 1988?

21   Look to the statutory provisions section of this chapter and explain why a person who had been drinking heavily might have a defence to a charge under section 5(1)(b) of the Road Traffic Act 1988.

Answers

Extract 1

1   The Old Bailey is the central criminal court which in London.

2   Firmager, the burglar, attacked John Campbell first. It is extremely significant that the use of force was first used by the burglar otherwise Campbell would have been the aggressor. As Firmager used force first, Campbell was in a postion to assess how much force was necessary to defend himself.

3   Campbell used a knife in response to an attack involving a pepper spray and a baseball bat and this was found to be self-defence. If Campbell had not been attacked and had used a knife against Firmager then Campbell would probably have been prosecuted for an offence against the person; he was not defending himself from an immediate attack. If Firmager had only punched and kicked Campbell, that is, he had not used any kind of weapon, then it is unlikely that it would be regarded as self-defence for Campbell to use a knife.

4   The phrase, 'Brian Higgs, QC, the Recorder', means that Brian Higgs is a Queen's Counsel (a senior barrister) and a part-time judge. Such part-time judges assist circuit judges.

5   Aggravated burglary is defined in section 10 (1) of the Theft Act 1968 (see statutory provisions section of Chapter 4, on theft) and the maximum prison term which could be given is life.

6   Firmager died as a result of the stab wound (the heart attack only occurred due to the surgery made necessary by the stabbing) and so Campbell could have been prosecuted for murder. When he stabbed Firmager (the *actus reus*) he no doubt intended to cause him grievous bodily harm (the *mens rea*).

Extract 2

7 There are 50 states in the USA but this law will only apply in Louisiana.

8 In a criminal court it is usually the case that the prosecution have to prove the guilt of the accused beyond all reasonable doubt, that is, the burden of proof is on the prosecution. For this defence, the burden of proof is initially on the accused as it states in the extract that the courts cannot convict anyone 'who can show' that they killed an assailant etc.

9 This law was introduced into Louisiana because 'car-jackings' were on the increase in New Orleans.

10 American citizens can carry handguns because they are given the right to bear arms in their written constitution.

11 Such a law could not be introduced into the UK at present and not in the foreseeable future. In the UK the trend is to limit the personal possession of firearms and, in particular, handguns. Indeed, after the Dunblane massacre in which several schoolchildren were shot dead, the Government enacted the Firearms (Amendment) Act 1997 which bans the possession of handguns of 0.22 calibre and below.

12 The defence in Louisiana applies to one specific crime, car-jacking, whereas section 3(1) of the Criminal Law Act (CLA) 1967 applies generally to crimes. Under the CLA 1967 the force used has to be 'reasonable in all the circumstances' whereas in the Louisiana law the defence can apply even if the car-jacker was unarmed. In the Louisiana law the driver of the car is the victim of the attempted car-jacking whereas under the CLA 1967 it is not just the victim of the crime who may use reasonable force to prevent a crime. Both laws are concerned with crime prevention and apprehension of the criminal and both set criteria for the use of force.

Extract 3

13 The two main ingredients of most crimes are the *actus reus* and the *mens rea*.

14 Under a strict liability offence the accused can be found guilty of the offence when the prosecution have proved that he was responsible for the act or omission which constituted the *actus reus* of the offence; it is not necessary to prove any *mens rea* as this is not an ingredient of a strict liability offence.

15 Strict liability offences can be found where:

9

     i the crime is a regulatory offence;

     ii the crime is concerned with an issue of social concern;

     iii the penalty for the crime is small;

     iv the words of the relevant statute lead to that conclusion.

For full details on strict liability offences, look back to Chapter 3.

16 Usually only the defendant can appeal from the Magistrates' Court against conviction or against sentence; such an appeal is to the Crown Court. However, it is possible for either the defendant or the prosecution to appeal to the Queen's Bench Divisional Court of the High Court 'by way of case stated'. The grounds for such an appeal are limited (otherwise it would be too easy for the prosecution to appeal when the defendant was acquitted at trial) to instances concerning a 'point of law' and where the magistrates are said to have acted 'beyond their powers'. When the prosecution appeal by way of case stated, as they did in this case on a point of law, the the judges hearing the appeal can remit the case back to the magistrates with a direction to convict the accused. This is what happened in this case.

17 The usual burden of proof is that the prosecution have to prove that the defendant is guilty of the offence concerned. The prosecution have to prove this guilt to a high standard of proof which is *beyond all reasonable doubt*.

18 Lord Justice McCowan said that every man was assumed to be same at the time of an alleged offence so that the burden of establishing insanity was on the accused on a balance of probabilities. Thus, when insanity is raised as a defence by the accused he has to carry the burden of proof of insanity but to a lower standard of proof – *on the balance of probabilities* which is the normal standard of proof in civil cases.

19 Insanity is a general defence which can be raised at summary trial as well as at trial on indictment.

20 Although insanity can be raised as a defence at summary trial (as this trial was) the defence was not available in this instance as the offence concerned was a strict liability offence in which the *mens rea* of the accused is not an ingredient of the crime. Thus, it was only necessary for the prosecution to prove that the accused had committed the *actus reus*; the mental state of the accused was not relevant.

21 A person charged under section 5(1)(b) of the Road Traffic Act 1988 might have a defence as specified in section 5(2) of the Act, for instance, if he had been drinking heavily but only got into the car to sleep, in which case there would be no likelihood of him driving the car.

Key points on general defences

Defences i to vi briefly
i infancy
ii insanity
iii automatism
iv mistake
v intoxication
vi self-defence

Defences vii and viii in more detail
vii duress
viii necessity

(Consent as a defence is dealt with in Chapter 11, on non-fatal offences against the person.)

i Infancy

As mentioned in the terminology box, children aged under 10 years are presumed to be *doli incapax*, which is an irrebuttable presumption. Children aged 14 years and older are dealt with as adults so there is no need to prove more than the *actus reus* and *mens rea* of the offence in question. Until the enacting of the Crime and Disorder Act 1998 there was a rebuttable presumption that children aged 10 years but under 14 years were *doli incapax*. This caused the prosecution many problems. How could the prosecution rebut the presumption of *doli incapax* in children aged 10 years to under 14 years? In addition to proving *mens rea* and *actus reus* for the crime, the prosecution had to show that the child knew what he did was *seriously wrong*. How did the prosecution do this? In recent cases the prosecution tried to rely on the fact that if a child committed a really horrendous crime, then the fact that the crime was committed was in itself enough to rebut the presumption of innocence. However, in *C (a minor)* v. *DPP* (1996) it was held that no matter how horrendous the crime, the fact of the crime itself was not sufficient to negate the presumption of *doli incapax*; the prosecution must introduce some evidence on top of the offence itself to rebut the presumption. Thus, *doli incapax* would not be negated just because the child had tortured and then murdered the victim. How much evidence had to be introduced? If a child ran away from a crime scene this in itself did not demonstrate that the child knew that what was done was

9

seriously wrong. The amount of evidence necessary to negate *doli incapax* varied.

In the case cited above the Divisional Court held that the rebuttable presumption of *doli incapax* in children aged 10 years to under 14 years no longer existed. However, the House of Lords rejected this notion and re-affirmed the existence of the rebuttable presumption. However, in December 1997 the Labour Government published a Crime and Disorder Bill in which they proposed to abolish the rebuttable presumption of *doli incapax* for children aged 10 years to under 14 years. The Bill received Royal Assent on 28 July 1998 and became the Crime and Disorder Act 1998. Under the Act the rebuttable presumption of *doli incapax* is abolished.

ii Insanity

The definition of insanity as a defence is stated in the case of *M'Naghten* in 1843. In this case M'Naghten had intended to kill Robert Peel but killed his secretary by mistake. He was charged with the murder of the secretary and was found not guilty by reason of insanity. The House of Lords put various questions on the defence of insanity to judges and their answers have become the now famous M'Naghten rules, which are as follows:

i every man is to be presumed sane and responsible for his actions until the contrary is proved to the satisfaction of the jury;

ii to establish a defence of insanity it must be proved that, *at the time of committing the crime*, the accused was suffering from *a defect of reason* caused by a *disease of the mind*; which

iii meant that the accused did not know the nature and quality of the act he was doing; or

iv if he did know it, he did not know he was doing what was wrong.

Remember (refer back to extract 3 on page 233) that the accused has only to prove insanity on a balance of probabilities. However, it must be noted that the defence of insanity is very rarely used nowadays, maybe only once or twice a year. This is due in large part to the availability of the defence of diminished responsibility in murder cases. Consider Figure 9.1 which should help you to put insanity and unfitness to plead into perspective. Consider also the 'You Decide' cases.

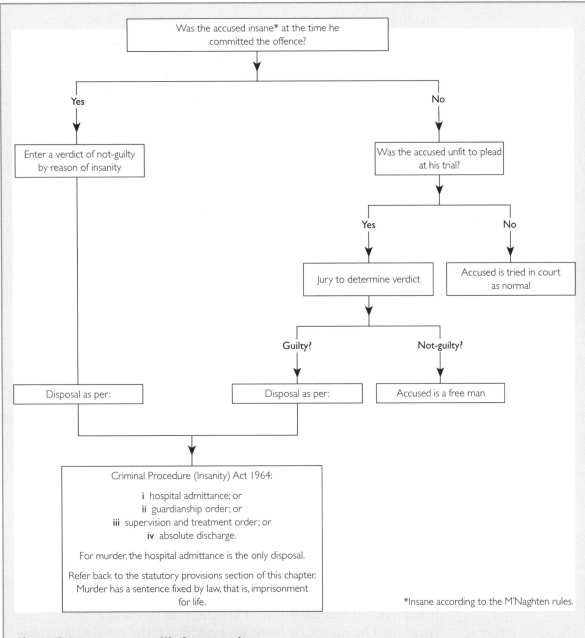

Figure 9.1
Insanity and unfitness
to plead

iii Automatism

The defence of insanity will only succeed if the disease of mind which led to the defect of reason was caused by internal factors. Where the defendant's actions were totally involuntary but caused by external factors, such as a blow to the head, the defence of automatism might be appropriate. Whereas the defence of insanity usually applies to those defendants who are suffering from such a medical condition which makes the possibility of recurrence of the involuntary action likely, with automatism the external event is usually a unique or novel event which is not prone to recurrence. When a jury decides that insanity is not the correct defence it may then consider automatism as a possible defence. It must be stressed that the loss of control of the defendant's actions must be total; if any degree of control is retained then the defendant was not acting like an automaton. Thus in the case of *Broome* v. *Perkins* (1987) the defendant was unable to rely on the defence of automatism when he had driven home from work in a state of *hypo*glycaemia (low blood sugar level). He could remember nothing of the journey but other people had seen him manoeuvre the car. The fact that he could drive home meant that he had not lost total control of his actions. Note that hypoglycaemia is not regarded as insanity under the M'Naghten rules and so the defendant would have been trying to rely on the defence of automatism. This defence exists because of the general premise in criminal law that the *actus reus* of a crime must have been committed voluntarily.

iv Mistake

If the defendant made a mistake as to the facts in a situation then it may be possible for him to have the defence of mistake. This defence is generally not available for mistakes of law. The mistake may negate the *mens rea* part of the crime and the leading case is *DPP* v. *Morgan* (1976). This case established the extent of mistake as a defence to negate *mens rea* as summarised in Figure 9.2.

v Intoxication

The defendant may be able to raise the defence of intoxication if charged with a 'specific intent' crime but not if charged with a 'basic intent' crime. This premise was formulated in the leading case of *DPP* v. *Majewski* (1987). The underlying principle is that if the defendant was incapable of forming *mens rea* at the time of the crime then he cannot be guilty of the crime. If the defendant, however much intoxicated, could still form the necessary *mens rea* for the crime, then intoxication would be no defence, and it would make no difference whether the defendant was voluntarily or involuntarily intoxicated. Unfortunately, it is not easy to determine which crimes are 'specific intent' crimes and which are 'basic intent' crimes. It seems that it is not possible to say that an offence

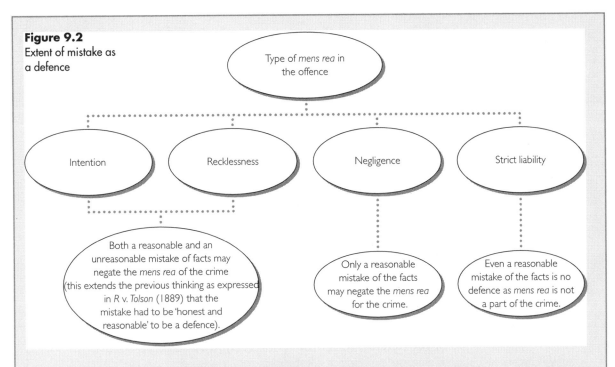

Figure 9.2
Extent of mistake as a defence

Type of *mens rea* in the offence

Intention

Recklessness

Negligence

Strict liability

Both a reasonable and an unreasonable mistake of facts may negate the *mens rea* of the crime (this extends the previous thinking as expressed in *R* v. *Tolson* (1889) that the mistake had to be 'honest and reasonable' to be a defence).

Only a reasonable mistake of the facts may negate the *mens rea* for the crime.

Even a reasonable mistake of the facts is no defence as *mens rea* is not a part of the crime.

will be one or the other in advance; rather, it is necessary to wait until an offence has been before the courts to see how the offence is classified. In Smith & Hogan's *Criminal Law*, 8th edition, J. C. Smith states that the classification of offences into 'specific intent' crimes seems to be determined by 'policy' decisions rather than by principle. He lists the following crimes (*inter alia*) as requiring 'specific intent':

Murder, Wounding or causing GBH with intent, Theft; Robbery, Burglary with intent to steal, Handling stolen goods; Criminal damage where only intention is alleged.

He also lists the following crimes (*inter alia*) as not requiring 'specific intent':

Manslaughter (all forms), Rape, Assault occasioning ABH; Malicious wounding or inflicting GBH, Common assault, Criminal damage where intention or recklessness, or only recklessness, is alleged.

Obviously, this is a difficult area of the law as it does not seem appropriate to let people escape responsibility for their actions just because they were so drunk that they did not know what they were doing. A line has to be drawn somewhere between those instances when it is appropriate to find the defendant not guilty

9

and those when it is appropriate to find the defendant guilty, and it seems that this line is drawn according to policy considerations. Consider the 'You Decide' cases which follow.

vi Self-defence

The essential feature of a crime involving violence is that the violence used against another is *unlawful*. It follows then that if the use of force is lawful, the person using the force has not committed an offence. In some crimes of violence the word unlawful or unlawfully appears in the definition so that it is obvious that if the accused used force lawfully he has not committed the offence. An example is in the common law definition of murder which is defined as an unlawful killing of another human being with malice aforethought. Thus when surgeons operate on a patient and the patient dies, this is regarded as lawful killing. However, it is not necessary for the word unlawfully to appear in the definition of a crime involving violence for the defence of lawful action to apply.

When is the use of force lawful?

The law recognises lawful use of force as follows:

i private defence – the common law defence of self-defence, which provides that a person may use such force as is reasonable in the circumstances, as the person believes the circumstances to be, and whether this belief in the circumstances is or is not a reasonable belief, in order to protect himself, another, his property or the property of another;

ii public defence – as provided to prevent crime and arrest offenders in section 3 Criminal Law Act 1967 (see statutory provisions on page 229).

The jury or the magistrates determine whether or not the force used by the defendant was reasonable in the circumstances as he perceived them to be. These private and public defences overlap because if a person uses force against an attacker, as well as defending himself (self-defence) he is obviously also preventing a crime (the use of force by the attacker which could have amounted to an assault occasioning actual bodily harm or even murder). In practice then it does not usually matter which of these defences is relied upon except in those instances where they do not overlap, for instance, when the attacker is incapable of committing a crime because he is aged under 10 years, is insane or is in a state of automatism. In these instances the defence of prevention of a crime would not be available and so the defendant would have to rely on self-defence.

It is not necessary for the defendant to wait until he has been attacked before retaliating if the attack upon himself is imminent and it is not necessary for the defendant to have first made an attempt to run away from the attacker. The jury will decide on how reasonable the defendant's behaviour was in all the circumstances. In doing so they will take account of the fact that the defendant quite often has to make a decision as to what to do in a split second and in a state of some anxiety. It must be noted that if the defendant successfully pleads self-defence then his actions are regarded as lawful and he is a completely free man. Consider the case below and the questions which follow.

R v. Owino (1996)

In this case the defendant was convicted of assaulting his wife occasioning actual bodily harm contrary to section 47 of the Offences Against the Person Act 1861. He had tried to rely on the defence of self-defence in that his actions were necessary to restrain his wife and to prevent her from assaulting him. He appealed against his conviction arguing that the test of whether or not the force used was reasonable was a 'subjective' test and that the judge had not directed the jury in this way. In the Court of Appeal:

Collins J.:

Mr Mendelle [for the appellant] essentially submits that [the trial judge] failed to direct the jury, as he ought to have done, that any force used must be unlawful ... more than was reasonable for self-defence; and further, that the test of what was reasonable was subjective ... He relies on the authority of Scarlett to support that proposition ...

Before I come to the case of Scarlett specifically, it is our view that the law does not go so far as Mr Mendelle submits that it does. The essential elements of the self-defence are clear enough. The jury have to decide whether a defendant honestly believed that the circumstances were such as required him to use force to defend himself from an attack or a threatened attack. In this respect a defendant must be judged in accordance with his honest belief, even though that *belief may have been mistaken. But the **jury** must then decide whether the force used was reasonable in the circumstances as he believed them to be ...*

What Mr Mendelle relies upon in the case of Scarlett is a passage ... where Beldam L.J. giving the judgment of the Court, said this:

'... They ought not to convict him unless they are satisfied that the degree of force used was plainly more than was called for by the circumstances as he believed them to be and, provided he believed the circumstances called for the degree of force used, he is not to be convicted even if his belief was unreasonable.'

*So far as the second half of the sentence is concerned, ... What he was not saying, in our view (and indeed if he had said it, it would be contrary to authority) was that the **belief, however ill-founded, of the defendant** that the degree of force he was using was reasonable, will enable him to do what he did. As Kay J. indicated in argument, if that argument was correct, then it would justify, for example, the shooting of someone who was merely threatening to throw a punch on the basis that the **defendant** honestly believed, although unreasonably, and mistakenly, that it was justifiable for him to use that degree of force.*

That clearly is not, and cannot be, the law.

Appeal dismissed.

9

Certain words are shown in bold. Can you see the significance of this? Who should decide on whether the use of force was reasonable in the circumstances, the jury or the defendant? If the defendant is allowed to make this decision then the test is a subjective one and as such it might be way out of proportion to what someone else might think was reasonable. Thus, defendant A might think it reasonable to shoot a pick-pocket whereas defendant B might think it only reasonable to punch a pick-pocket. The *jury* has to make this decision on what is reasonable in the circumstances according to what a reasonable man, placed in the circumstances which existed, would have considered reasonable force. If the defendant was allowed to determine what he thought was reasonable in the circumstances then the test would be subjective and this is what counsel was arguing in the case. However, this proposition was denied by Collins J. as shown above.

vii Duress

There are now two types of duress: duress by threats and duress of circumstances. See Figure 9.3.

When duress by threats is raised as a defence, the defendant admits that he commited the crime in question but claims that he only did so because of some immediate threat to kill or seriously harm him or his family or even a stranger. The defendant is saying that he would not have commited the crime but for the threats. Thus, the typical scenario would be where the 'real criminal' says to the defendant, 'Rob the bank or else I will kill your wife and children.' The defendant has to make a choice and whether or not the defence of duress succeeds will be determined with reference to the two-part test as laid down in the case of *R* v. *Graham* (1982):

i did the defendant act as he did because he feared that if he did not so act death or serious physical injury would result?

ii if so, would a sober person of reasonable firmness sharing the characteristics of the defendant have so acted?

The fact that the defendant's will to resist has been eroded by the voluntary consumption of drink or drugs, or both, is not relevant to this test.

When duress of circumstances is raised the defendant is saying that he only commited the crime because of the threatening circumstances in which he found himself, when either himself or his family or even a stranger were threatened with death or serious harm. Quite often the defendant commits the act which amounts to the crime (for instance, driving off recklessly) in order to escape those people who constitute the threat.

Refer to Figure 9.4 for relevant cases for each of these types of duress.

Figure 9.3

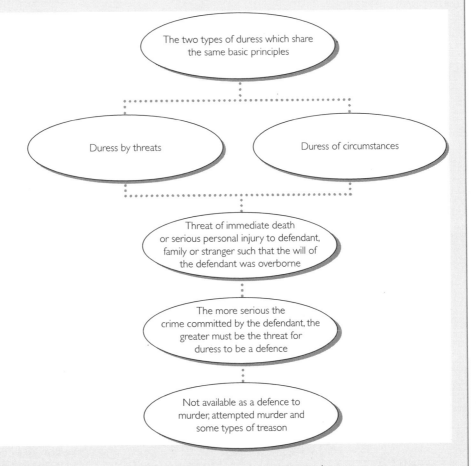

9

Duress by threats	Duress of circumstances
R v. Graham (1982) Formulates the two-part test for duress – see ante. Graham was a homosexual who lived with his wife and another homosexual. The two men strangled Graham's wife with a flex and Graham said that he only took part because of threats from the other man who was violent. Although this was a murder case, the Crown conceded that duress could be raised as a defence. (Note that this case was before *R v. Howe* [1987] which decided that duress was not available as a defence to murder.) The Court of Appeal held that the threats by the other man had not been sufficient to ground the defence of duress in this case anyway and the fact that Graham acted after having taken drugs and drink was irrelevant – the test was to be as for a sober man. *R v. Hudson & Taylor* (1971) Extends the concept of immediacy of the threat – the threat is immediate enough if it is 'operating on the accused's mind'. Thus, these two teenage girls had their convictions for perjury quashed – they had been the main witnesses at a trial but failed to identify the accused as they had been threatened by a gang member before the trial and a gang member was in the court. Despite the fact that they could have told the police or the court of the threats, the Court of Appeal held that the defence of duress should have been left to the jury as should the issue of whether or not they should have sought police protection before the trial. *R v. Sharp* (1987) Decides that when a person voluntarily joins a criminal organisation or gang which he knows might bring pressure on him to commit offences, and he was an active member of the gang when put under such pressure, he cannot use duress as a defence. Sharp had voluntarily joined a gang of robbers who carried out a series of robberies on sub-post offices in the last of which a sub-postmaster was shot dead. He claimed he had only taken part in this robbery as a gang member had put a gun to his head and threatened to blow it off if he did not take part. The Court of Appeal held that the defence of duress was not available to him as stated above. *R v. Cole* (1994) Decides that there has to be a nexus (a bond or connection) between the threat to the accused and the crime he commits. In this case the accused and his family had been threatened with violence by money lenders if they did not pay the monies due. The accused undertook a robbery to get the money but as the money lenders had not specified that the that the accused should commit an offence to raise the money, he could not rely on duress as a defence. The money lenders had not said, 'Rob the bank on the High Street this Tuesday.' Thus, the accused had determined the offence himself. *R v. Howe* (1987) Decides that the defence of duress is not available for a murder charge whether the accused was the principal offender or a secondary party. See ante. *R v. Gotts* (1992) Decides that the defence of duress is not available for attempted murder. In this case a 16-year-old boy had attempted to murder his mother on the instructions of his father who had threatened to kill the boy if he did not do as he asked. The boy stabbed his mother intending to kill her but she did not die. The House of Lords held that the defence of duress was not available for attempted murder – see ante. In this case the boy was given three years' probation as the circumstances mitigated against a more severe sentence.	*R v. Willer* (1986) Extends defence of duress to duress of circumstances. In this case the accused had driven his car over a pavement and into a shopping precinct. He only did so as he was surrounded by a gang of youths who were shouting threats to him and his passenger. At trial the assistant recorder had said that the defence of necessity was not available to him and so he pleaded guilty and appealed. The Court of Appeal said that the appropriate defence was duress and should have been left to the jury – hence the conviction was quashed. Note that this type of duress does not involve any direct threat from the aggressors – they had not said, 'Commit this crime or else'. Rather they put the accused in threatening circumstances from which he could only escape by committing an offence. *R v. Conway* (1989) Also involved reckless driving. Conway was charged with reckless driving after he drove off when approached by two men whom he believed were about to attack him and his passenger. In fact the two men were plain clothes policemen. He was convicted and appealed. The Court of Appeal held that the conviction should be quashed as the defence of duress of circumstances ought to have been left to the jury. This was the first time the defence had been referred to in this way. The Court of Appeal said that it would be subject to the same limitations as duress by threats. *R v. Martin* (1989) In this case the accused had driven his car while disqualified as his suicidal wife had threatened to kill herself if he did not drive his stepson to work. He was convicted and appealed. The Court of Appeal held that the defence of duress of circumstances should have been left for the jury to detemine and that the test for the defence was exactly the same as for duress by threats except as regards how the threat arises. *R v. Pommell* (1995) Extends the defence of duress of circumstances to all crimes except murder, attempted murder and some forms of treason. See below for discussion of case.

Figure 9.4

A leading case for the defence of duress and how it applies to a murder charge is *R* v. *Howe and Others* (1987). Consider the extracts from this case which are shown below.

R v. *Howe and Others* (1987)
House of Lords
In this case Howe and others had participated in the killing of two victims for which they were convicted.
Lord Hailsham of Marylebone L.C.: *[The first of the three questions certified by the Court of Appeal is as follows:]*

(1) 'Is duress available as a defence to a person charged with murder as a principal in the first degree (the actual killer)?' ... In my opinion, this must be decided on principle and authority, and the answer must in the end demand a reconsideration of the two authorities of DPP for Northern Ireland v. Lynch and Abbot v. The Queen ...

If duress is available as a defence to some crimes of the most grave why, it may legitimately be asked, stop at murder, whether as accessory or principal and whether in the first or second degree? But surely I am entitled to believe that some degree of proportionality between the threat and the offence must, at least to some extent, be a prerequisite of the defence under existing law. Few would resist threats to the life of a loved one if the alternative were driving across the red lights or in excess of 70 m.p.h. on the motorway. But ... it would take rather more than the threat of a slap on the wrist or even moderate pain or injury to discharge the evidential burden even in the case of a fairly serious assault. In such a case the 'concession to human frailty' is no more than to say that in such circumstances a reasonable man of average courage is entitled to embrace as a matter of choice the alternative which a reasonable man would regard as the lesser of two evils. Other considerations necessarily arise where the choice is between threat of death or **a fortiori** *of serious injury and deliberately taking an innocent life. In such a case a reasonable man might reflect that one innocent human life is at least as valuable as his own or that of his loved one. In such a case a man cannot claim that he is choosing the lesser of two evils ...*

During the course of argument it was suggested that there was available to the House some sort of halfway house between allowing these appeals and dismissing them. The argument ran that we might treat duress in murder as analogous to provocation, or perhaps, diminished responsibility, and say that, in indictments for murder, duress might reduce the crime to one of manslaughter. I find myself quite unable to accept this. The cases show that duress, if available and made out, entitles the accused to a clean acquittal, without, it has been said, the 'stigma' of a conviction.

Lord Griffiths:

[A]re there any present circumstances that should impel your Lordships to alter the law that has stood for so long and to extend the defence of duress to the actual killler? My Lords, I can think of none. It appears to me that all present indications point in the opposite direction. We face a rising tide of violence and terrorism against which the law must stand firm recognising that its highest duty is to protect the freedom and lives of those that live under it. The sanctity of human life lies at the root of this ideal and I would do nothing to undermine it, be it ever so slight ...

If the defence is not available to the killer what justification can there be for extending it to others who have played their part in the murder. I can, of course, see that as a matter of commonsense one participant in a murder may be considered less morally at fault than another. The youth who hero-worships the gang leader and acts as a lookout man whilst the gang enter a jeweller's shop and kill the owner in order to steal is an obvious example. In the eyes of the law they are all guilty of murder, but justice will be served by requiring those who did the killing to serve a longer period in prison before being released on licence than the youth who acted as lookout ... It is therefore neither rational nor fair to make the defence dependent upon whether the accused is the actual killer or took some other part in the murder ... I am not troubled by some of the extreme examples cited in favour of allowing the defence to those who are not the killer such as the woman motorist being hijacked and forced to act as getaway driver, or a pedestrian being forced to give misleading information to the police to protect robbery and murder in a shop. The short, practical answer is that it is inconceivable that such persons would be prosecuted; they would be called as the principal witnesses for the prosecution.

9

As for attempted murder it was held in the case of *R* v. *Gotts* (1992) that the defence of duress was not available. Lord Jauncey of Tullichettle:

'... I can therefore see no justification in logic, morality or law in affording to an attempted murderer the defence which is withheld from a murderer. The intent required of an attempted murderer is more evil than that required of a murderer ... A man shooting to kill but missing a vital organ by a hair's breadth can justify his action no more than can the man who hits that organ.It is pure chance that the attempted murderer is not a murderer and I entirely agree with what Lord Lane C.J. [1991] 1 Q.B. 660,667 said: that the fact that the attempt failed to kill should not make any difference ...'

Some of the arguments for and against duress being allowed as a defence to murder are to be found in *Criminal Law*, Smith and Hogan, 8th edition on pages 241 and 242, and are also summarised below.

Arguments against allowing the defence of duress for murder may be found in the speeches in the case of *R* v. *Howe* (1987) as follows:

i the ordinary man of reasonable fortitude, if asked to take an innocent life, might be expected to sacrifice his own;
ii when someone takes the life of an innocent person they cannot claim that they are choosing the lesser of two evils;
iii Parliament had not thought it appropriate to legislate to make duress available as a defence to murder, despite Law Commission recommendations to this effect;
iv not all people acting under duress will be prosecuted and, if they are, there is flexibility in the indeterminate sentence for murder for early release by the Parole Board.

Smith and Hogan submit that none of these reasons is convincing, arguing against each as follows:

i if the defence were available it would apply *only* when a jury thought a person of reasonable fortitude *would* have given in to the threat. The criminal law should not require heroism;
ii it could well have been the lesser of two evils to kill one innocent person if the lives of the defendant and all of his family were threatened;
iii the Government, for whatever reason, has not given Parliament the opportunity to legislate on the matter;
iv if prosecuted and found guilty of murder, for want of the defence of duress, the person bears the stigma of being a convicted murderer even if let out of prison after a very short

period of time. On such an important issue it does not seem right that the Crown Prosecution Service have the discretion to decide whether or not to prosecute a person who acted under duress; it would be better to take this decision from them and to create clear legal rules for such cases.

viii Necessity

There is some uncertainty as to the scope of the defence of necessity in English law. The essence of the defence is that the accused acted as he did out of necessity, he committed a crime because of *external* or objective factors which arose at the time (the circumstances). The accused claims that he committed the crime to avoid a greater evil that would have transpired had he not so acted – thus his action was the lesser of two evils. This is known as the balancing of harm principle. The overriding fear is that should this defence become *generally* available it could be used as a defence to just about any crime – you could say that you only stole the food from the supermarket because you were hungry (hence it was necessary) or that you only broke into the house in order to keep warm (hence it was necessary) and so forth. In other words, your conduct was 'justified'.

9

In the discussion which follows you will discover that it is generally accepted that a *general* defence of necessity, based on *justification* of behaviour, is unlikely ever to be accepted as a principle of English law. However, you will also discover that the defence of necessity has at least been recognised explicitly in the courts and inroads have been made in respect of the duress of circumstances cases. In such cases it is probably more accurate to say that the defence so framed *'excuses'* rather than 'justifies' behaviour. As such the law is not encouraging proactive behaviour, that is, for example, it is not encouraging a person to go into a shop and steal food because such behaviour is justified to feed the person's children. Rather, it is saying that if someone commits a crime and such behaviour *was* necessary in the limited circumstances which the law will allow, then, *in hindsight*, this behaviour can be excused.

The topic of necessity can appear wide ranging and unwieldy and so, for clarity, it will be dealt with under the following headings:

i cases which deny that there is a general defence of necessity;

ii cases where the defence of necessity has been allowed for 'specific' offences;

iii cases where a narrow general defence of necessity has been allowed;

iv cases where the defence of necessity has been disguised as duress of circumstances;

v a discussion of how wide the current defence of necessity is;

vi a discussion of whether the defence of necessity should be allowed in murder cases.

i Cases which deny that there is a general defence of necessity

Under this heading we will consider the cases of:

Buckoke v. *GLC* (1971)
London Borough of Southwark v. *Williams* (1971)
Cichon v. *DPP* (1994)

In *Buckoke* v. *GLC* (1971) Lord Denning stated:

During the argument I raised the question: Might not the driver of a fire engine be able to raise the defence of necessity? I put this illustration: A driver of a fire engine with ladders approaches the traffic lights. He sees 200 yards down the road a blazing house with a man at an upstairs window in extreme peril. The road is clear in all directions. At that moment the lights turn red. Is the driver to wait for 60 seconds, or more, for the lights to turn green? If the driver waits for that time, the man's life will be lost. I suggested to both counsel that the driver might be excused in crossing the lights to save the man. He might have the defence of necessity. Both counsel denied it. They would not allow him any defence in law. The circumstances went to mitigation, they said, and did not take away his guilt. If counsel are correct – and I accept that they are – nevertheless such a man should not be prosecuted. He should be congratulated.

This is an interesting quote which nicely poses the problem. It is also a quote which is often used in examinations (as is the one which follows) to encourage discussion of the topic of necessity. It must be noted that drivers of fire engines, police cars and ambulances are now allowed to regard red traffic lights as warnings to give way in emergency situations.

In *London Borough of Southwark* v. *Williams* (1971) Lord Denning stated:

> [I]f hunger were once allowed to be an excuse for stealing, it would open a way through which all kinds of disorder and lawlessness would pass. So here. If homelessness were once admitted as a defence to trespass, no one's house could be safe. Necessity would open a door which no man could shut. It would not only be those in extreme need who would enter. There would be others who would imagine that they were in need, or would invent a need, so as to gain entry. Each man would say his need was greater than the next man's. The plea would be an excuse for all sorts of wrongdoing. So the courts must, for the sake of law and order, take a firm stand. They must refuse to admit the pleas of necessity to the hungry and the homeless; and trust that their distress will be relieved by the charitable and good.

In *Cichon* v. *DPP* (1994) the defendant allowed his pit bull terrier to be in a public place while not wearing a muzzle, contrary to section 1(2) of the Dangerous Dogs Act 1991. He said that he had removed the muzzle because the dog had kennel cough and he regarded it as cruel to muzzle the dog in such circumstances. He was not allowed to rely on the defence of necessity because it was held that this offence was an absolute offence (where the prosecution need not prove *mens rea* or that the *actus reus* was committed voluntarily).

ii Cases where the defence of necessity has been allowed for 'specific' offences

In the seventeenth century some of the respected writers on English law (Bracton, Coke and Hale) noted when necessity could be a defence to specific offences, such as to pulling a house down when it was on fire in order to prevent the fire from spreading, to escaping from jail when it was on fire (despite a statute to the contrary) and to throwing cargo overboard in order to save lives when a ship was in a storm. More recently, the defence has been mentioned by way of *obiter dicta* (not binding precedent) to the effect that a police constable may direct other persons to disobey traffic regulations where it is reasonably necessary for the protection of life and property.

9

iii Cases where a narrow *general* defence of necessity has been allowed

In the case of *Re F.* (*mental patient: sterilisation*) (1990) Lord Goff expressly dealt with the issue of necessity as a defence. In this case the House of Lords held that it was lawful for a mental patient to be sterilised, to prevent her getting pregnant, despite the fact that she could not consent to the operation. It was shown that if she had got pregnant the condition would have had severe consequences for her mental well-being. In the House of Lords Lord Goff stated that there were three groups of cases when necessity could be allowed as defence:

Lord Goff:

> *That there exists in common law a principle of necessity which may justify action which would otherwise be unlawful is not in doubt. But historically the principle has been seen to be restricted to two groups of cases, which have been called cases of public necessity and cases of private necessity. The former occurred in the Great Fire of London in 1666. The latter cases occurred when a man interfered with another man's property in the public interest ... for example, when he entered upon his neighbour's land without his consent, in order to prevent the spread of fire onto his own land.*

> *There is, however, a third group of cases, which is also properly described as founded upon the principle of necessity and which is more pertinent to the resolution of the problem in the present case. These cases are concerned with action taken as a matter of necessity to assist another person without his consent. To give a simple example, a man who seizes another and forcibly drags him from the path of an oncoming vehicle, thereby saving him from injury or even death, commits no wrong ...*

> *We are concerned here with action taken to preserve the life, health or well-being of another who is unable to consent to it. Such action is sometimes said to be justified as arising from an emergency.... Emergency is however not the criterion or even a pre-requisite; it is simply a frequent origin of the necessity which impels intervention. The principle is one of necessity, not of emergency.'... in these cases of necessity ... to fall within the principle, not only (1) must there be a necessity to act when it is not practicable to communicate with the assisted person, but also (2) the action taken must be such as a reasonable person would in all the circumstances take, acting in the best interests of the assisted person.*

iv Cases where the defence of necessity has been disguised as duress of circumstances

Students should look back to the cases on duress of circumstances and should consider the case of *R* v. *Pommell* (1995). In this case Pommell was convicted of possessing a prohibited weapon without a firearm certificate but, on appeal, the conviction was set aside because the Court of Appeal held that the question of duress of circumstances should have been left to the jury. The incident in question took place in 1993. Pommell was visited by someone at his home at about 1 am. The visitor had with him a loaded gun which he intended to use to shoot some people who had killed his friend. Pommell managed to persuade the visitor to leave the gun with him, thus avoiding any more killings. Rather than take the gun to the police station during the night, he kept the gun in the bed beside him intending to take it to the police station in the morning. However, the police broke into the house at 8 am and he was arrested and charged with possession of a weapon without a firearm certificate. The fact that the Court of Appeal set aside his conviction on the basis that the question of duress of circumstances should have been left to the jury sent shock waves through the legal world. This is due to the fact that the Court held that the defence of duress of circumstances could apply to all crimes except for murder, attempted murder and some forms of treason. In the *Pommell* case it can be seen how there was a balancing of harm – it was a lesser evil to hold the gun illegally than let the visitor take it and shoot people (thus causing serious physical harm). The threat in this case was not directed against Pommell but against third parties to whom Pommell had no direct relationship yet the implication is that this would have been acceptable for the defence of duress of circumstances. It is arguable that this case is more analogous to the third group of cases described by Lord Goff in *Re F.* (*mental patient:sterilisation*) (1990) mentioned above. In which case the defence could have been described as one of necessity. We can apply the two tests put forward by Lord Goff to the *Pommell* case; it was not practicable to communicate with the assisted persons (those the visitor intended to shoot) and it is likely that the jury would have come to the conclusion that a reasonable person, in all the circumstances, would have done the same, acting in the best interests of the assisted persons. The main problem here could be the time delay; if it was necessary to take the gun off the visitor at 1 am, was it necessary to retain the gun throughout the night? It may well have been necessary in all the circumstances.

9

v A discussion of how wide the current defence of necessity is

Is it possible to say that there is now a general defence of necessity albeit disguised as the defence of duress of circumstances? The answer is probably no. This is because the defence of duress of circumstances is limited because it incorporates the principles which apply to duress by threats. Thus, duress of circumstances can only be a defence when the threat is of death or serious physical harm; for there to be a general defence of necessity it would surely have to be possible to plead the defence in relation to lesser threats. Also, the threat must arise from external or objective sources. That this limits the defence is illustrated in the case shown below which appeared in *The Times* on 30 July 1997 under the heading, 'Duress defence not available'.

R v. Rodger and Another
Court of Appeal (1997)
The defence of duress of necessity was not open to an offender where the causative feature in the commission of the offence was not extraneous to the offender.

The Court of Appeal, Criminal Division (Lord Justice Kennedy, Mr Justice Nelson and Sir Patrick Russell) so held on July 9 in a reserved judgment when dismissing the appeals against conviction of Andrew Rodger and Keith John Rose at Woolwich Crown Court (Judge Dunne and a jury) for the offence of breaking prison. Both appellants were serving life sentences for murder at Parkhurst Prison.

SIR PATRICK RUSSELL said that the authorities in the case of duress of necessity all had one feature in common, namely, the feature causative of the defendant committing the offence was extraneous to the offender, but in the present case the appellants broke prison because of their own suicidal thoughts, which was a subjective element.

Note the way in which the defence is described. It is not referred to as duress of circumstances or necessity, but duress of necessity. What is this defence? Does this not epitomise the dilemma of not providing for a general defence of necessity?

In addition, the defence of necessity can be excluded by statutory provision as shown in the case below which appeared in *The Times* on 8 December 1997.

L v. Bournewood Community and Mental Health NHS Trust (1997) Court of Appeal
Before Lord Woolf, Master of the Rolls, Lord Justice Phillips and Lord Justice Chadwick.
[Reasons December 2]

A hospital could informally admit a person for treatment for a mental disorder under section 131 of the Mental Health Act 1983 only with his consent. A person who had no capacity to consent or dissent, nor a guardian to consent on his behalf, had to be admitted under the statutory procedures in the 1983 Act, otherwise the hospital was detaining him. Since the common law principle of necessity was excluded by the statutory provisions, that detention was unlawful. The Court of Appeal so held ...

The appellant applied for judicial review, seeking to quash the trust's decision to detain him, a declaration that his detention was unlawful and *mandamus* and requiring his release forthwith. A writ of *habeas corpus*, and damages for assault and false imprisonment were also claimed.

Mr Justice Owen had refused judicial review on the ground that the appellant was free to leave. There would be no restraint until the appellant attempted to leave and steps were taken to prevent him from leaving. The appellant appealed.

THE MASTER OF THE ROLLS, giving judgment of the court ... Three issues were raised: (i) Was the appellant detained? If so (ii) Was that detention justified by the common law doctrine of necessity? If not (iii) What was the appropriate relief? ...

The right of a hospital to detain a patient for treatment for mental disorder was to be found in, and only, in the 1983 Act, whose provisions applied to the exclusion of the common law principle of necessity ... The trust had admitted the appellant and was detaining him for treatment for mental disorder without his consent and without the formalities required by the 1983 Act. It followed that they had acted and were acting unlawfully. The whole approach of the trust was based on the false premise that they were entitled to treat the appellant as an in patient without his consent as long as he did not dissent. That was wrong. They were only allowed to admit him for treatment if they complied with the statutory requirements.

The common law powers of necessity could be exercised by an individual to protect someone who was ill whether his illness was due to physical or mental causes. But where the 1983 Act covered the situation, no necessity to act outside the statute could arise.

9

However, Bournemouth Community and Mental Health NHS Trust appealed to the House of Lords. The case was heard in June 1998 and the appeal was allowed. It was held that the basis upon which a hospital was entitled to treat and care for such patients was the common law doctrine of necessity, which, where proved, had the effect of justifying actions which might otherwise be tortuous. This demonstrates a willingness to accept the common law defence of necessity 'despite' statutory provisions which widen the scope of the defence.

Finally, because the defence of necessity is based on common law principles, it is based on case law and previous cases have only gone so far in developing the defence. We have seen that it has been allowed in specific instances and in a narrow general defence; in no case has it been allowed as a broad general defence and it may or may not be deemed to be excluded as a defence by statute as shown in the case above. Thus, the defence of necessity is probably as wide a defence as allowed in the case of *R* v. *Pommell* (1995) disguised as duress of circumstances. In which case the defence need not cause great alarm or fear that the floodgates will open; the defence has strict limitations, not least of which is the fact that it seems to be restricted to instances where death or serious physical harm is part of the circumstances.

vi A discussion of whether the defence of necessity should be allowed in murder cases

The starting point for this discussion has to be the case of *R* v. *Dudley and Stephens* (1884) in which the defendants, after being shipwrecked for over a week without food or water, killed and ate the cabin boy. They were convicted of murder and their convictions were upheld on appeal as it was held that the defence of necessity was not available on a charge of murder. However, the mitigating circumstances lead to their sentence being commuted to just six months' imprisonment. In the case of *R* v. *Howe and Others* (1987) mentioned above in relation to duress by threats, the House of Lords approved the case of *R* v. *Dudley and Stephens* which could be taken as a clear indication that the defence of necessity will never apply to a charge of murder. However, Professor J. C. Smith, in *Justification and Excuse in the Criminal Law*, gives two illustrations to make one ponder whether it might be possible one day to have a general defence of necessity. The first illustration is concerned with the *Herald of Free Enterprise* ferry disaster which took place in Zeebrugge. The ferry sank before it had left the harbour and many lives were lost. During the disaster a group of people were trying to escape from the ferry by climbing up a rope ladder and were being helped by an army corporal. Unfortunately, one person on the ladder at the front of the others froze in fear and, despite shouts from the others, could not move. This put the lives of the others in grave peril. Accordingly, the army corporal told those people below the man to push him off the ladder. They did so and they managed to escape but the man pushed off the ladder was never seen again. No proceedings have been brought against the army corporal. The second illustration concerns a climber who is attached to another climber who falls off a mountain side. Should the climber who has not fallen cut the rope joining them together to save himself or should he wait until he is also pulled off the mountain side, probably to this death?

Do these illustrations fall within the scope of the defences of duress by threats or duress of circumstances? Obviously they do not fall within the scope of the former as no one is saying, 'Do this or else', and arguably they do not fall within the scope of the latter as in the circumstances there is no conscious threat from anyone; the frozen man on the ladder and the dangling climber are unconsciously endangering the lives of others but are not the perpetrators of a directed threat. Nor do these cases come within the scope of the two-part test of Lord Goff in the *Re F* case because in these illustrations the victims, upon whom the crime of murder is committed, are not saved from a greater evil to themselves because they die and it is very unlikely that they would have consented to sacrificing themselves had they been asked. Thus, as the law stands, the actions of the climber and the army corporal would amount to murder as there is no general defence of necessity. However, the mitigating circumstances would be recognised in sentencing, as in *R* v. *Dudley* and Stephens, although such recognition does not take away the stigma of a criminal conviction.

9

YOU DECIDE

Consider the cases below and answer the questions.
The answers are at the bottom of the page.

2 *Quick* (1973)

The accused, a nurse, was a diabetic who took his insulin but then forgot to eat; this caused him to suffer from *hypoglycaemia* (low blood sugar) during which time he attacked a patient.

Do you think this condition could amount to insanity according to the M'Naghten rules?

1 *R* v. *Hennessy* (1989)

The accused was a diabetic who forgot to take his insulin. This resulted in him suffering from *hyperglycaemia* (high blood sugar) during which time he took a vehicle without consent and drove when disqualified.

Do you think this condition could amount to insanity according to the M'Naghten rules?

3 *R* v. *Sullivan* (1984)

The accused suffered an epileptic fit during which he kicked out, without realising he was doing so, and struck a friend. He was charged with assault occasioning actual bodily harm.

Do you think an epileptic fit could amount to insanity according to the M'Naghten rules?

Answers

1 The condition of *hyperglycaemia* is regarded as insanity as the state of mind of the accused (his defective reasoning) is brought about by *internal* factors – the diabetes by itself caused the high blood pressure. In this case the defendant did not wish to be labelled insane and so (instead of using the defence of insanity and being found not guilty by reason of insanity) pleaded guilty to the charge and then appealed, but his appeal was dismissed and so the conviction stood.

2 The condition of *hypoglycaemia* is not regarded as insanity as the state of mind of the accused is brought about by *external* factors – the insulin introduced into the body. In this case the accused pleaded guilty at his trial (as the trial judge had indicted wrongly that insanity was the appropriate state of mind) and appealed and his appeal was allowed and so the conviction was quashed. You may wish to discuss this artificial way of approaching a defect of reasoning brought about by internal or external factors.

3 The House of Lords held that an epileptic fit does amount to insanity – it is an condition that itself leads to the defect of reasoning.

YOU DECIDE

Consider the cases below and decide the outcome. The answers are shown below.

1 Attorney-General for Northern Ireland v. Gallagher (1963)

In this case the accused decided to kill his wife but seemed to need 'Dutch courage' in order to do so. Therefore, he bought a bottle of whisky and drank most of it. He then killed his wife with a knife he had bought. Part of his defence was that at the time he killed his wife he was incapable of forming the *mens rea* for murder because he was so drunk.

Do you think the respondant (Gallagher) could rely on the defence of intoxication in this instance?

2 R v. Kingston (1994)

In this case, the defendant was 'set-up' by his colleagues who knew that he had paedophiliac tendencies. They laced his drinks while in the company of a 15-year-old boy. They intended to blackmail him. The defendant indecently assaulted the boy while drunk but claimed that he only did so because he was involuntarily drunk. However, he did say that at the time of the assault he had intended to do it.

Do you think involuntary intoxication would be a defence in this case?

3 R v. Hardie (1985)

In this case, when the appellant's relationship with a woman broke down, he took some of her Valium tablets in an attempt to calm himself down not realising what sort of effect they might have. While the woman was in the sitting room of the flat he started a fire in the bedroom. He was charged with criminal damage with intent to endanger life or being reckless as to whether life was endangered contrary to section 1(2) Criminal Damage Act 1971. In his defence he argued that the Valium had prevented him from having *mens rea* for the crime. He was convicted as he had voluntarily taken the drug. He appealed.

You decide the appeal.

Answers

1 The House of Lords held that the respondent could not rely on the defence of intoxication. Lord Denning said:
My Lords, I think the law on this point should take a clear stand. If a man, whilst sane and sober, forms an intention to kill and makes preparation for it, knowing it is a wrong thing to do, and then gets himself drunk so as to give himself Dutch courage to do the killing, and whilst drunk carries out his intention, he cannot rely on this self-induced drunkenness as a defence to a charge of murder, nor even as reducing it to manslaughter. He cannot say that he got himself into such a stupid state that he was incapable of an intent to kill.

2 The House of Lords held that at the time the offence was committed the respondent 'intended' the assault and so had requisite mens rea for the offence (as such it made no difference whether he was intoxicated voluntarily or involuntarily – he had *mens rea*.)

9

3 In the Court of Appeal, Parker L.J. stated that self-induced intoxication is not normally a defence to an offence such as in this case involving recklessness (a basic intent crime) because the self-administration of the drug or drink is reckless in itself when the person knows the likely effect of the drug or drink. However, it was possible to distinguish the present case because the appellant did not know that Valium could result in aggressive tendencies and so it was possible to argue that he had not been reckless in taking it. As such, his appeal was allowed (conviction quashed) because the trial judge had not directed the jury in this matter.

Applying principles to examination questions

Consider the question below and make notes of key points. Look back through the chapter to elicit relevant case law and statutory provisions. After you have done this look at the suggested answer.

Alan, a diabetic, was suffering a hyperglycaemic episode, during which time he formed the delusion that Brian was trying to kill him. Therefore Alan stabbed Brian and as a result Brian died.

Cheryl is in great pain due to a back problem and takes some strong pain killers to alleviate the problem. She reacts to the pain killers and becomes very aggressive. In this state she destroys the stereo system of a person with whom she shares a flat.

David recently joined a gang which he knew sometimes stole things from the shops in the town centre. The gang planned to steal money from a jeweller's shop and told David to act as the lookout. David did not want to do this as his uncle worked in the shop. However, he acted as lookout after the leader of the gang had threatened to beat up his sister if he did not.

Eileen went to the local fair with her boyfriend Fred. George, who had recently split up with Eileen, started to push Fred about. Eileen and Fred decided to leave the fair early and went to the car park to get into Eileen's car. Once they were inside the car George and his friends appeared and surrounded the car. They started to rock it and bang it with metal poles. Eileen was terrified and managed to start the car and drove off at speed. Two hundred yards down the road from the car park she was stopped by a police car for driving recklessly.

Consider what offences Alan, Cheryl, David and Eileen might be charged with and what, if any, defence they might be able to rely on.

Tips on how to approach such a question

Alan, a diabetic, was suffering a hyperglycaemic episode, during which time he formed the delusion that Brian was trying to kill him. Therefore Alan stabbed Brian and as a result Brian died.

Hyperglycaemia is regarded as insanity whereas hypoglycaemia is not. See the case of *R v. Hennessy* (1989). See the *M'Naghten rules* 1843.

Alan could plead not guilty by reason of insanity of though as this would result in committal to hospital, *Criminal Procedure (Insanity) Act 1964*, he may plead diminished responsibility.

Cheryl is in great pain due to a back problem and takes some strong pain killers to alleviate the problem. She reacts to the pain killers and becomes very aggressive. In this state she destroys the stereo system of a person with whom she shares a flat.

Did Cheryl know the pain killers might make her aggressive? She has voluntarily taken a drug and committed a basic intent crime – *see section 1(1) Criminal Damage Act 1971*.

Usually self-intoxication is not a defence to a crime of basic intent (*mens rea* here could be recklessness) but see the case of *R v. Hardie* (1985).

David recently joined a gang which he knew sometimes stole things from the shops in the town centre. The gang planned to steal money from a jeweller's shop and told David to act as the lookout. David did not want to do this as his uncle worked in the shop. However, he acted as lookout after the leader of the gang had threatened to beat up his sister if he did not.

David voluntarily joined the gang knowing of their criminal activities.

The threat here is of serious bodily harm to David's sister – would this be appropriate for duress by threats? Yes.

Could David plead the defence of duress by threats? Probably not – see *R v. Sharp* (1987).

Could David plead that he was only the lookout? No – he has acted as an accomplice and so is liable.

Eileen went to the local fair with her boyfriend Fred. George, who had recently split up with Eileen, started to push Fred about. Eileen and Fred decided to leave the fair early and went to the car park to get into Eileen's car. Once inside the car George and his friends appeared and surrounded the car. They started to rock it and bang it with metal poles. Eileen was terrified and managed to start the car and drove off at speed. Two hundred yards down the road from the car park she was stopped by a police car for driving recklessly.

George may have committed an offence against the person and/or criminal damage contrary to *section 1(1) or section 1(2) Criminal Damage Act (1971)*.

Could Eileen plead duress by threats? Not really as no one said, 'Do this or else'. But she might be able to plead duress of circumstances – see the cases of *R v. Willer* (1986), *R v. Conway* (1989) and *R v. Martin* (1989).

Eileen and Fred found themselves in circumstances in which they feared for their lives. It might have made a difference to the defence if Eileen was still driving recklessly two miles down the road as the threat would not be immediate.

Proposals for reform

Proposals for reform will be considered in light of *'Legislating the Criminal Code: Offences Against the Person and General Principles'* (Law Com. No. 218) published by the Law Commission in 1993. In this report the Law Commission included a Draft Criminal Law Bill which is in two parts: Part I deals with non-fatal offences against the person while Part II deals with general defences and other provisions. The whole point of the Draft Criminal Law Bill is to put the law concerned on a clear, statutory footing so that the criminal law becomes accessible and rational. Here we are concerned with Part II of the Draft Bill.

In Part II the common law defences of:

 i duress by threats;
 ii duress by circumstances; and
 iii use of force in public or private defence;

are put in statutory form so replacing their common law counterparts; indeed, in clause 36(2) of the Draft Bill these common law defences are specifically abrogated. However, the common law defence of necessity is specifically left untouched because its scope is not well enough defined to be put in statutory form. Necessity, and any other defences, would be considered in the future and if sufficiently developed, so as to avoid difficulties in statutory interpretation once enacted, could also be put on a statutory footing. At paragraph 27.8 and 27.9 in the report it says:

> *27.8*
> *... it is desirable that the courts should be free to develop or to expand on new defences to criminal liability, either to recognise changing circumstances or to piece out unjustified gaps in the existing defences.*

> *27.9*
> *At the same time, however, where a particular circumstance of defence arises frequently, and its limits have been worked out by the courts and can be stated with some confidence, it is right to make the position clear and accessible by stating it in statutory terms ...*

A major change as regards the two types of duress concerns the burden of proof which the report recommends be shifted from the prosecution (beyond all reasonable doubt) to the defendant (on the balance of probabilities). This is a big shift from the general rule in criminal law that the prosecution must prove the guilt of the accused beyond all reasonable doubt. Why has the onus been shifted onto the defendant? The report notes (at paragraphs 33.2 and 33.3) that shifting the burden of proof might make it easier to support the extension of duress as a defence to murder. At paragraph 33.5 it says:

It is no light matter to propose that the defendant bear the persuasive burden of proof, and that, moreover, not only in the case of murder, but in relation to all other offences, to which duress is already a complete defence, with the burden now resting on the prosecution to disprove it beyond reasonable doubt. Certainly we would not be recommending the change if we thought it might appear to undermine the important general rule that the prosecution must prove its case. On the contrary, we see the arguments for the change in the case of duress as wholly exceptional, depending on factors unique to that defence which distinguish it from all others.

The report goes on to say (in paragraphs 33.6 and 33.7) that duress is a defence like no other in that the accused relies on assertions that are particularly difficult for the prosecution to prove because the circumstances which the accused relies on occurred well before the actual commission of the offence in question. By contrast, for example, in self-defence, the circumstances giving rise to the defence occur at the same time as the offence is committed and this makes it easier for the prosecution to investigate all the circumstances. It is questionable whether this shifting of the burden of proof is fair on a defendant who genuinely acted under duress; the shift seems to be aimed at preventing members of criminal gangs concocting a false defence of duress.

9

As regards the justifiable use of force, the report says (at paragraph 36.3) that the most significant element in this part of the law is the present common law of self-defence. This law has a number of important features which form the basis of the statutory provision in the Draft Bill.

CHAPTER Summary

In this chapter we have considered the general defences of infancy, insanity, automatism, mistake, intoxication and self-defence in outline, and the defences of duress and necessity in more detail. Such an approach should help students prepare for both problem-solving questions and essay questions. The latter quite often focus on one particular defence, such as duress or necessity, and such a question is considered in the first consolidation section in Chapter 10. However, problem questions featuring any of the offences in the syllabus usually incorporate more than one of the general defences. For this type of question students need an outline knowledge of all of the general defences and such knowledge can be gained from a study of this chapter. Consent as a defence is dealt with in Chapter 11, on non-fatal offences against the person, as it is in relation to such offences that the defence is frequently used. A question dealing with the mental capacity of the accused may require an answer which mentions automatism, insanity, intoxication and diminished responsibility. All of these topics have been dealt with in this chapter, apart from diminished responsibility which is covered in Chapter 12, on homicide.

Consolidation

In this chapter you will be asked to answer two essay-type questions and two problem-solving questions. The questions feature offences against property (theft, burglary, robbery, criminal damage and the deception offences) and topics from the general principles section. When these topics were first dealt with in the appropriate chapters you were asked questions on them without the integration of any other topics. In the problem-solving questions which follow here, however, you will notice that now one question may contain many offences. It is up to you to ascertain which offences have been committed and if any general principles apply. For the essay-type questions which follow you will need to have detailed knowledge and understanding of either one particular aspect of an offence or one general principle. Thus, your examination preparation must be thorough. I have highlighted some key points which should be mentioned when answering these questions.

Essay-type questions

1 Give a critical evaluation of the law relating to duress and necessity.

(25 marks)

(Source: NEAB Law Advanced Paper II, 1995)

Suggested approach

1 First, you must note the key words in the title of the essay:

Critical evaluation   This tells you that it is not enough merely to write down all you know about duress and necessity; you have to critically evaluate the topic.

Duress and necessity   You have to know that these two words relate to two possible defences to crimes. Unless you have studied these in detail you should not attempt to answer this question.

2 Second, you must plan the structure of your essay paragraph by paragraph so that you can decide how much detail you can afford to

go into on any one aspect of the topic. In the examination you can do this briefly before you start writing the essay and then draw a line so that the examiner knows where your essay starts. You can then refer back to your essay structure as you progress through the essay to make sure that you have not omitted anything and to gauge how much time you have left. If you start to run out of time you will have to write less on each of the remaining topics as it is important to finish the essay and write a rounded conclusion. A suggested essay structure is given below.

Introduction

Start by stating that duress and necessity are possible defences to crimes and that there is some academic discussion as to whether necessity can be regarded as a 'general' defence to all or most crimes or whether it only applies in 'specific' instances. Then outline your approach to the essay, for example, that you are going to deal with duress first and then necessity, critically evaluating each of them in turn.

2nd paragraph

In this paragraph explain the defence of duress by:

- explaining that there are two types of duress: duress by threats and duress of circumstances;
- explaining the two-part test as laid down in *R* v. *Graham* (1982) which applies to both of them;
- quoting a selection of key cases with brief facts to explain duress by threats, such as: *R* v. *Hudson & Taylor* (1971), *R* v. *Sharp* (1987), *R* v. *Cole* (1994) and *R* v. *Gotts* (1992). The selection of cases will be determined by which ones you can remember and how fast you can write; do not attempt to write in great detail on all of the cases as you will run out of time. You could allocate 20 minutes for duress and 20 minutes for necessity.

3rd paragraph

In this paragraph discuss and critically evaluate whether the defence of duress by threats should be allowed as a defence to a charge of murder or attempted murder. This can be done by analysis of the cases of *R* v. *Howe* (1987) and *R* v. *Gotts* (1992) with arguments for and against duress by threats being allowed as a defence in such cases (see page 243–8 in Chapter 9, on general defences).

4th paragraph

In this paragraph explain duress of circumstances by tracing its development by reference to the cases of *R* v. *Willer* (1986), *R* v. *Conway* (1989) and *R* v. *Martin* (1989). You can then explain how the defence has been extended to all crimes except murder, attempted murder and some forms of treason by reference to the case of *R* v. *Pommell* (1995).

5th paragraph	In this paragraph trace the development of the scope of the defence of necessity under the following headings:

- cases which deny that there is a general defence of necessity;
- cases where the defence of necessity has been allowed for 'specific' offences;
- cases where a narrow general defence of necessity has been allowed;
- cases where the defence of necessity has been disguised as duress of circumstances.

Details for all of these headings can be found starting on page 250 in Chapter 9, on general defences.

6th paragraph   In this paragraph critically evaluate how wide the current defence of necessity is by reference to the cases of:

- *R* v. *Rodger and Another* (1997);
- *L* v. *Bournewood Community and Mental Health NHS Trust* (1998);
- *R* v. *Pommell* (1995).

At the end of this you could conclude that the defence of necessity still has limitations, not least of which is that it seems to be restricted to instances where death or serious physical harm is part of the circumstances and so there is no real fear that 'it will open the floodgates'.

7th paragraph   In this paragraph critically evaluate whether or not the defence of necessity should be allowed in murder cases by reference to:

- *R* v. *Dudley and Stephens* (1884);
- *R* v. *Howe* (1987);
- the views of Professor J.C. Smith on this matter.

Conclude that it is not available as a defence to murder at present.

Conclusion   In the conclusion to the essay you could mention the notions of justification and excuse as they apply to these defences, especially to necessity. You could also mention the Draft Criminal Law Bill which appears in *'Legislating the Criminal Code: Offences Against the Person and General Principles'* (Law Com. 218) which puts both types of duress on a statutory footing, leaving necessity as a common law defence. Finally, you could quote from Lord Denning in *London Borough of Southwark* v. *Williams* (1971), for instance:

> *If hunger were once allowed to be an excuse for stealing, it would open a way through which all kinds of disorder and lawlessness would pass. So here. If homelessness were once admitted as a defence to trespass, no one's house could be safe. Necessity would open a door which no man could shut.*

10

3 Consider the proposition that the concept of 'dishonesty' is too vague and uncertain to play a key role in property offences.   (*30 marks*)

(Source: NEAB specimen papers and mark schemes: Law 1998)

Suggested approach

1 First, you must note the key words in the title of the essay:

Consider

When you are invited to consider a proposition you have to show that you know what the proposition means and then you have to agree with it or disagree with it.

Dishonesty

Unless you have dealt with the topic of dishonesty in detail in relation to property offences, you should not attempt to answer this question. A general knowledge on the topic may be sufficient for problematic questions, but it would not prepare you for such an essay question.

Vague and uncertain

If something is vague and uncertain it is not clearly defined and understood. This could suggest that it needs to be clearly defined or that it is incapable of being so defined.

Key role

The suggestion is that the concept of dishonesty does play a key role in property offences, that it is vital to the whole topic. In this case, surely it should be clearly defined.

Property offences

There are several property offences and you have to know which ones are relevant for this essay.

2 Second, you have to plan the structure of your essay, paragraph by paragraph, so that you can allocate your time in the examination and so that you remember to include all the key points.

Introduction

Explain how the concept of dishonesty plays a key role in many property offences as defined in the Theft Act 1968 and the Theft Act 1978. Note that it does not appear in the statutory definition of criminal damage under the Criminal Damage Act 1971. Explain that the main reasons it is felt to be vague and uncertain are that it is left to the jury to determine and it is not actually defined in statutory form. Explain that you will look at these reasons in detail.

2nd paragraph

Start by demonstrating your general knowledge of property offences by listing some of the ones which make use of the concept of dishonesty in their definitions, such as:

► theft – section 1(1) Theft Act 1968;
► robbery – section 8 Theft Act 1968 as it incorporates theft;
► burglary – section 9 Theft Act 1968 when stealing is involved;
► abstraction of electricity – section 13 Theft Act 1968;
► handling stolen goods – section 22 Theft Act 1968;

> ► dishonestly retaining a wrongful credit – section 24A Theft Act 1968;
> ► the deception offences – as found in the Theft Acts 1968 and 1978 – which make use of the concept of dishonesty as well as the concept of deception.

Then explain that dishonesty is not actually defined in either of the Theft Acts other than in a negative way in section 2(1) of the Theft Act 1968. State that you intend to deal with the concept of dishonesty in relation to theft as it is generally held that dishonesty means the same thing throughout the Theft Acts.

3rd paragraph

Give the definition of theft according to section 1(1) of the Theft Act 1968, explaining that dishonesty is part of the *mens rea* of theft. Reiterate that dishonesty is only defined in negative terms as in section 2(1) of the Theft Act 1968. List the occasions when a person is not to be regarded as dishonest according to section 2(1):

> ► if he believes he has in law the right to deprive the other of it;
> ► if he believes he would have had the consent of the other person if they had known of the circumstances;
> ► if he believes that the owner of the property could not be found by taking reasonable steps.

Give everyday examples of the application of these occasions.

4th paragraph

Explain that if the accused's behaviour does not fall within the scope of section 2(1) this does not necessarily mean that the accused acted dishonestly. The matter of dishonesty will be determined by the jury. Explain that when the accused claims that he was not dishonest, the judge will direct the jury on the question of dishonesty according to the two-part test in *R* v. *Ghosh* (1982). Explain the two-part test.

5th paragraph

Analyse the two-part test. Explain that it has a subjective and objective part. Is this too complicated for the jury to deal with? Make reference to examples as given in the judgment of Lord Lane C.J. in *R* v. *Ghosh* (1982).

6th paragraph

Consider proposals for reform, noting that the Law Commission is undertaking a comprehensive review of the law of dishonesty. You may wish to mention the case of *R* v. *Preddy* (1996) and how the Law Commission's proposals to get rid of the lacuna in the law of theft created by the case were speedily acted upon, resulting in the insertion of section 15A and section 24A into the Theft Act 1968.

Conclusion

State whether you agree or disagree with the proposition in the title of the essay. It is probably easier to argue that the concept of dishonesty is too vague and uncertain at the moment but that, despite this, it nevertheless does play a key role in property offences.

10

It is generally left to the jury to determine whether or not someone acted dishonestly and until and unless we are allowed to analyse what goes on in the jury room, who is to say that juries find the tests in *R* v. *Ghosh* too complex?

Problem-type questions

1

John, a 17-year-old student, takes his father's cheque book, Visa card, driving licence and football club season ticket from his desk drawer.

Using the driving licence, John hires a car from Self Drive Cars Ltd. He pays by means of a cheque drawn on his father's account.

He spends the afternoon at a football match using the season ticket to gain entry.

Arthur, a violent criminal, discovers what John has done and threatens to tell the police and beat him up unless John obtains a cash advance of £100 from the bank's automatic dispensing machine using the Visa card.

Frightened, John obtains the £100 and gives the money to Arthur.

John is now worried that his father will find out what has happened and returns all the documents to the desk drawer and the car to Self Drive Cars Ltd.

What offences has John committed and what defences might he have?

(50 marks)

(Source: OCEAC specimen question papers and marking Schemes for Start of Teaching, September 1996: Law, Oxford)

2

Adam, aged 19, has recently spent two weeks in a psychiatric hospital. One week after his discharge from hospital he stopped taking his prescribed medication. He then began to develop a feeling that a music teacher from his former school had been plotting against him.

Adam decided that he would punish the teacher by breaking in and setting fire to the school piano. He persuaded his friend Ben to come and watch the piano burn 'for fun'.

Ben understood that Adam was simply going to use some matches and perhaps some paper to cause some minor damage to the piano. When they met outside the school Ben was horrified to see that Adam had a large can of petrol with him.

Ben said that it looked far too dangerous and that he was leaving. Adam appeared extremely annoyed and threatened to pour the petrol over Ben and set light to it if he did not break into the school with him. Ben was terrified and agreed.

Once inside the school hall Adam poured the petrol over the piano and set it alight. In the resulting fire the building was destroyed and Adam was seriously injured, although Ben managed to escape.

While in hospital Adam received further treatment from a psychiatrist who later concluded that although Adam was mentally ill, and had been so at the time of the fire, he was not unfit to stand trial.

Consider the criminal liability, if any, of Adam and Ben, and outline the options which might be available to a court in connection with the mental abnormality of Adam.

(30 marks)

(Source: NEAB specimen Papers and Mark Schemes: Law 1998)

10

Key points to mention when answering problem-type questions

1 Below, I have highlighted some key points and made reference to the statutory provisions. You should look back over the sections on property offences and general principles in order to add appropriate cases to back up the points you make. When you have done this you should attempt to write out the answer in a clear and logical manner, concluding that John might have committed some offences but that he might have a defence to one of the possible offences.

Is John's age relevant? He is old enough to commit a crime though his youth may be significant as regards his fear of Arthur.

Where was the desk? If in a study to which John was denied access, is this burglary? A study can represent a 'part of a building'– see *section 9 TA 1968*.

Did John use a cheque card to guarantee the cheque? Was the employee of the company deceived? Is this relevant if a cheque card was presented?

Is Arthur blackmailing John? See *section 21 TA 1968*.

If everything is returned did John have the intention of permanently depriving his father of the items?

Define and quote the statutory provisions for the offences of: Theft *section 1(1) TA 1968* and explain the provisions of section 6 Obtaining property by deception *section 15(1) TA 1968* Burglary *section 9(1) TA 1968* Obtaining services by deception *section 1(1) TA 1978* Explain the defences of: Duress Necessity/duress of circumstances.

John, a 17-year-old student, takes his father's cheque book, Visa card, driving licence and football club season ticket from his desk drawer.

Using the driving licence, John hires a car from Self Drive Cars Ltd. He pays by means of a cheque drawn on his father's account.

He spends the afternoon at a football match using the season ticket to gain entry. Arthur, a violent criminal, discovers what John has done and threatens to tell the police and beat him up unless John obtains a cash advance of £100 from the bank's automatic dispensing machine using the Visa card.

Frightened, John obtains the £100 and gives the money to Arthur.

John is now worried that his father will find out what has happened and returns all the documents to the desk drawer and the car to Self Drive Cars Ltd.

What offences has John committed and what defences might he have?

(50 marks)

(Source: OCEAC specimen question papers and marking Schemes for Start of Teaching, September 1996: Law Oxford)

These items represent 'property' for purposes of theft contrary to *section 1(1) TA 1968*. Did his father give him permission to take them? See *TA 1968 section 2(1)(b)*. Could the permission to take them have been with contraints e.g. for use in emergencies only?

Has John obtained property by deception? See *section 15(1) TA 1968*. By hiring the car has he obtained services by deception? See *section 1 TA 1978*.

How many matches are left in the season? Has the ticket any real value or worth left?

Can a machine be deceived? No, so no deception offence apply here. Theft is possible but has John a defence of duress?

Is John an innocent agent? Is robbery by Arthur possible?

Did John have the intention of permanently depriving the company of the car?

Note that you are not asked to consider what offences Arthur has committed, though you could mention assault, robbery/blackmail very briefly.

2 This question involves secondary parties, criminal damage, burglary, conspiracy to commit criminal damage, duress, assault and the issue of insanity. Read through the comments in the margins and then look back over the topics in the appropriate chapters to elicit the relevant case law and argument.

[...]am appears to have a [...]tory of mental illness. [...] this an insane delusion [...]used by internal factors? [...]e R v. Hennessy (1989).

Why did he stop taking his medication?

Unlikely to be automatism as no external, unique factor.

Adam, aged 19, has recently spent two weeks in a psychiatric hospital. One week after his discharge from hospital he stopped taking his prescribed medication. He then began to develop a feeling that a music teacher from his former school had been plotting against him.

[...]nspiracy to burgle? This [...]uld be burglary under [...]tion 9(1)(a) TA 1968.

Adam decided that he would punish the teacher by breaking in and setting fire to the school piano. He persuaded his friend Ben to come and watch the piano burn 'for fun'.

Conspiracy to commit criminal damage? Damage by fire is arson contrary to *section 1(3) CD Act 1971.*

[...] Ben a secondary party? [...] does not appear to have [...]ded, abetted, counselled [...] procured a crime, [...]ough it is possible to be [...] secondary party to a [...]nspiracy.

Ben understood that Adam was simply going to use some matches and perhaps some paper to cause some minor damage to the piano. When they met outside the school Ben was horrified to see that Adam had a large can of petrol with him.

What is the *mens rea* for criminal damage?

Ben had not contemplated such a drastic course of action.

Ben said that it looked far too dangerous and that he was leaving. Adam appeared extremely annoyed and threatened to pour the petrol over Ben and set light to it if he did not break into the school with him. Ben was terrified and agreed.

At this point has Ben withdrawn from the enterprise?

Has Adam assaulted Ben? Is Ben from this point on acting under duress?

[...]dam is the principal [...]fender. Did Ben just [...]and and watch? Is such [...]ssive acquiescence [...]fficient to make him a [...]condary party?

Once inside the school hall Adam poured the petrol over the piano and set it alight. In the resulting fire the building was destroyed and Adam was seriously injured, although Ben managed to escape.

Is this now criminal damage contrary to *section 1(2) CDA 1971*? Life could be endangered 'by' the damage/destruction.

[...]uld Adam form the [...]ecessary *mens rea* for the [...]imes he could be charged [...]ith?

While in hospital Adam received further treatment from a psychiatrist who later concluded that although Adam was mentally ill, and had been so at the time of the fire, he was not unfit to stand trial.

Note that legal insanity is different to medical insanity. For legal insanity consult the *M'Naghten rules* (1843)

[...]he defence of insanity [...]plies where the accused [...]as insane at the time of [...]e offence.

Consider the criminal liability, if any, of Adam and Ben, and outline the options which might be available to a court in connection with the mental abnormality of Adam.

(30 marks)

(Source: NEAB specimen Papers and Mark Schemes: Law 1998)

If found not guilty by reason of insanity Adam can be dealt with according to the *Criminal Procedure (Insanity) Act 1964.*

SECTION FIVE:
Offences against the person

The following topics are covered in this section:

Non-fatal offences

Common Law:
assault
battery

|

Statutory –
Offences Against the Persons Act 1861:
section 47
section 20
section 18

|

Statutory provisions

Offences Against the Person Act 1861
Criminal Justice Act 1988
Protection from Harassment Act 1997
Crime and Disorder Act 1998

|

Key cases

R v. Wilson (1955)
*Smith v. Chief Superintendent, Woking Police
Station* (1983)
Fagan v. Metropolitan Police Commissioner
(1969)
R v. Roberts (1971)
R v. Chan-Fook (1994)
R v. Savage and Parmenter (1955)
R v. Contanza (1997)
C (a minor) v. Eisenhower (1984)
R v. Burstow (1996)
R v. Brown (1955)
R v. Wilson (1996)
Laskey, Jaggard and Brown v. UK (1997)
A. v. UK (1998)

Fatal offences

Murder   Involuntary
| manslaughter
Voluntary manslaughter

Statutory provisions

Homicide Act 1957
Infanticide Act 1938
Infant Life (Preservation) Act 1929
Law Reform (Year and a Day Rule) Act 1996
Road Traffic Act 1988

Key cases

R v. Pagett (1983)
R v. Blaue (1975)
R v. Jordan (1956)
R v. Smith (1959)
R v. Cheshire (1991)
R v. Melcherek and Steel (1981)
Airedale NHS Trust v. Bland (1955)
R v. Byrne (1960)
R v. Tandy (1988)
R v. Gittens (1984)
R v. Hobson (1997)
R v. Acott (1997)
R v. Duffy (1949)
R v. Camplin (1978)
R v. Smith (Morgan) (1998)
R v. Morhall (1995)
R v. Aluwhalia (1992)
R v. Humphreys (1995)
R v. Thornton (1996)
R v. White (1910)
R v. Dear (1996)
R v. Ibrams (1973)
R v. Edwards (1973)
R v. Cato (1976)
R v. Dalby (1982)
R v. Church (1966)
R v. Dawson (1985)
R v. Watson (1989)
R v. Lamb (1967)
R v. Adomako (1995)
R v. Bateman (1925)

11 Non-fatal offences against the person

OVERVIEW

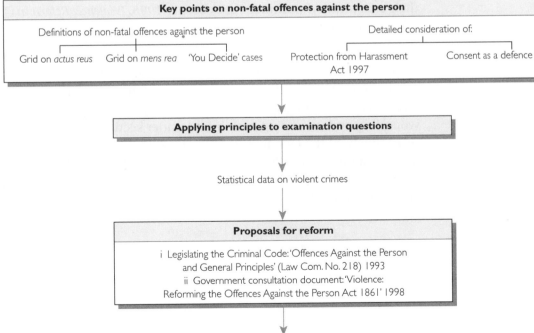

| **Terminology box** |
| Brief explanations of new legal terminology |

| **Statutory provisions** |
| Offences Against the Person Act 1861
Criminal Justice Act 1988
Protection from Harassment Act 1997
Crime and Disorder Act 1998 |

| **Setting the scene** |
| Four newspaper articles on the wilful transmission of the Aids virus,
plus introductory questions and answers |

| **Key points on non-fatal offences against the person** |

Definitions of non-fatal offences against the person

Grid on *actus reus*   Grid on *mens rea*   'You Decide' cases

Detailed consideration of:

Protection from Harassment
Act 1997   Consent as a defence

| **Applying principles to examination questions** |

Statistical data on violent crimes

| **Proposals for reform** |
| i Legislating the Criminal Code: 'Offences Against the Person
and General Principles' (Law Com. No. 218) 1993
ii Government consultation document: 'Violence:
Reforming the Offences Against the Person Act 1861' 1998 |

| **Chapter summary** |

The topic of non-fatal offences against the person warrants comprehensive coverage because it is a very important area of the criminal law which is presently in a state of some uncertainty. It has several shortcomings, most of which stem from the fact that the major part of this law is found in the antiquated and often confusing Offences Against the Person Act 1861. There is confusion as to what is meant by the word 'assault' and judges have recently extended the notion of assault to cover the growing nuisance of 'stalking'. However, as will be shown, this common law extension of the law has probably been superceded by the enactment of the Protection from Harassment Act 1997. This chapter gives a sound overview of the whole topic of non-fatal offences against the person while the following topics are considered in detail:

whether or not the wilful transmission of the Aids virus should be made a criminal offence;

the extent to which consent by the victim can or should amount to a defence in this area of the law;

the Protection from Harassment Act 1997;

the possible replacement of the Offences Against the Person Act 1861 with a new statute, either as proposed by the Law Commission in *'Legislating the Criminal Code: Offences Against the Person and General Principles'* (Law Com. No. 218) or as proposed by the Government in their consultation document of February 1998, *'Violence: Reforming the Offences Against the Person Act 1861'*.

In this chapter we will be looking at the common law offences of assault and battery (which can be charged under section 39 Criminal Justice Act 1988 as if they were statutory offences) and the statutory offences of assault occasioning actual bodily harm, malicious wounding and wounding with intent under sections 18, 20 and 47, respectively, of the Offences Against the Person Act 1861. The words used to define these offences lie at the heart of the problem with the law in this area as their definitions are by no mean certain. Students should read the definitions given below.

TERMINOLOGY: Non-fatal offences against the person

Assault	Where the accused intentionally or recklessly causes the victim immediate and unlawful personal violence. The degree of immediacy is somewhat uncertain since the cases of *R v. Burstow* (1997) and *R v. Constanza* (1997).
Battery	Where the accused unlawfully touches the body or clothing of the victim, either intentionally or recklessly.
Assault occasioning ABH	Where the accused carries out either an assault or battery on the victim which results in the victim suffering actual bodily harm (ABH), that is, some minor physical injury or some clinically proven psychiatric injury.
Malicious wounding	Where the accused unlawfully and maliciously wounds or inflicts grievous bodily harm (GBH) on the victim with or without a weapon.
Wounding with intent	Where the accused unlawfully and maliciously by any means wounds the victim or causes GBH to the victim with intent to do GBH or to resist lawful arrest.
Harassment	The Protection from Harassment Act 1997 introduces the word harassment but offers no definition of it. Some guidance is provided in the Private Member's Bill of 1996.

11

Statutory provisions

Offences Against the Person Act 1861

18 Whosoever shall unlawfully and maliciously by any means whatsoever wound or cause any grievous bodily harm to any person . . . with intent . . . to do some. grievous bodily harm to any person, or with intent to resist or prevent the lawful apprehension or detainer of any person, shall be guilty of an offence, and being convicted thereof shall be liable . . . to imprisonment for life.

20 Whosoever shall unlawfully and maliciously wound or inflict any grievous bodily harm upon any other person, either with or without any weapon or

---

instrument, shall be guilty of an offence, and being convicted thereof shall be liable . . . to imprisonment for a term not exceeding five years.

47 Whosoever shall be convicted upon an indictment of any assault occasioning actual bodily harm shall be liable . . . to be imprisoned for any term not exceeding five years.

Criminal Justice Act 1988

39 Common assault and battery shall be summary offences and a person guilty of either of them shall be liable to a fine not exceeding level 5 on the standard scale, to imprisonment for a term not exceeding six months, or to both.

Protection from Harassment Act 1997

1 Prohibition of harassment

(1) A person must not pursue a course of conduct –
    (a) which amounts to harassment of another; and
    (b) which he knows or ought to know amounts to harassment of the other.

(2) For the purposes of this section, the person whose course of conduct is in question ought to know that it amounts to harassment of another if a reasonable person in possession of the same information would think the course amounted to harassment of the other.

(3) Subsection (1) does not apply to a course of conduct if the person who pursued it shows –
    (a) that it was pursued for the purpose of preventing or detecting crime,
    (b) that it was pursued under any enactment or rule of law . . .
    (c) that in the particular circumstances the pursuit of the course of conduct was reasonable.

2 Offence of harassment

(1) A person who pursues a course of conduct in breach of section 1 is guilty of an offence.

(2) A person guilty of an offence under this section is liable on summary conviction to imprisonment for a term not exceeding six months, or a fine not exceeding level 5 on the standard scale, or both.

(3) In section 24(2) of the Police and Criminal Evidence Act 1984 (arrestable offences), after paragraph (m) there is inserted –

'(n) an offence under section 2 of the Protection from Harassment Act 1997 (harassment)'.

4 Putting people in fear of violence

(1) A person whose course of conduct causes another to fear, on at least two occasions, that violence will be used against him is guilty of an offence if he knows or ought to know that his course of conduct will cause the other so to fear on each of those occasions.

(2) For the purposes of this section, the person whose course of conduct is in question ought to know that it will cause another fear that violence will be used against him on any occasion if a reasonable person in possession of the same information would think the course of conduct would cause the other so to fear on that occasion.

(3) It is a defence for a person charged with an offence under this section to show that –
  (a) his course of conduct was pursued for the purpose of preventing or detecting crime,
  (b) his course of conduct was pursued under any enactment or rule of law . . .
  (c) the pursuit of his course of conduct was reasonable for the protection of himself or another or for the protection of his or another's property.

(4) A person guilty of an offence under this section is liable –
  (a) on conviction on indictment, to imprisonment for a term not exceeding five years, or a fine, or both, or
  (b) on summary conviction, to imprisonment for a term not exceeding six months, or a fine not exceeding the statutory maximum, or both.

(5) If on the trial on indictment of a person charged with an offence under this section the jury find him not guilty of the offence charged, they may find him guilty of an offence under section 2.

7 Interpretation of this group of sections

(1) This section applies for the interpretation of sections 1 to 5.

(2) References to harassing a person include alarming the person or causing the person distress.

(3) A 'course of conduct' must involve conduct on a least two occasions.

(4) 'Conduct' includes speech.

Crime and Disorder Act 1998

32 Racially aggravated harassment

(1) A person is guilty of an offence under this section if he commits –
  (a) an offence under section 2 of the Protection from Harassment Act 1997 . . . or
  (b) an offence under section 4 of that Act which is racially aggravated . . .

11

Setting the scene

In order to set the scene for this topic and to highlight some of its problems we will consider the issue of Aids and the wilful transmission of the disease. As you will see from the extracts from newspaper articles which follow, in the UK there is at present no offence which covers the act of knowingly transmitting the disease. All of the extracts concern the case of Janette Pink who was given the Aids virus by her Cypriot lover, Pavlos Georgiou. Georgiou was prosecuted in Cyprus under a little-used Cypriot law which had been introduced in 1957 to prevent the spread of typhoid, cholera and venereal disease on the island. Read the extracts and then answer the questions which follow. When you have done this, refer to page 317 where consideration is given to the present Government's attitude to this problem.

Article 1

This extract is taken from *The Times* dated 1 August 1997 and is from an article written by Michael Theodoulou.

Judge sentences Cypriot fisherman who gave Briton Aids to 15 months in jail, reports Michael Theodoulou

A CYPRIOT fisherman who is dying of Aids was jailed for 15 months yesterday for knowingly infecting a British divorcee, Janette Pink, with HIV. Pavlos Georgiou looked stunned at the severity of the sentence as lawyers had predicted that he would receive a suspended sentence. He had planned a party last night to celebrate the end of his trial.

Georgiou swayed on his feet in the dock as Judge Antonis Liatsos told him that he had not only failed to tell his lover that he had Aids but also 'avoided all protection, injecting her with death for months on end'. He stared in disbelief at the judge as he was told that he had escaped the maximum two-year sentence only because he had four children, including a son aged four who is infected with the virus, and 'because you have only a short time to live...'

The judge had complained that the 50-year-old law introduced to the island by the British to stop the spread of cholera needed stiffer penalties 'to protect the public which is at risk from this terrible disease'. The judge said: 'I would have expected of him, knowing his condition, that he would have taken all the precautions when having sex. His negligence led another person to death. Cyprus society must be protected, seeing that so many tourists come to the island.'

Source: *The Times*, 1 August 1997

Article 2

This article is taken from *The Times* dated 30 July 1997 and was written by Daniel McGrory.

Britain urged to copy tough Swedish line

Janette Pink's MP, Sir Teddy Taylor, is backing her call for those in this country who negligently transmit HIV to their partners to be prosecuted, writes Daniel McGrory

Her body was so ravaged by Aids that Janette Pink barely had the strength to tell British detectives in September 1996 about the death sentence her Cypriot boyfriend had knowingly infected on her.

While there was sympathy for her, the British authorities told Mrs Pink they had no jurisdiction to prosecute Pavlos Georgiou. She admits that her desire to see this country adopt a law to deal with those who negligently pass on Aids has helped her to survive.

Thwarted in Britain, she pleaded with her cousin, Sharon Keefe, to go to Cyprus to pursue her campaign there. Mrs Keefe said: 'At first, the doors were shut in my face. They didn't want the reputation of the holiday island to suffer.'

Then the Foreign Secretary, Malcolm Rifkind, urged the Cypriot authorities to act, as did Mrs Pink's MP, Sir Teddy Taylor. As a result

the island's Attorney-General, Alecos Markides, agreed to mount a test case, using an obscure 1957 law introduced by the British and intended to prevent the spread of typhoid, cholera and venereal disease on the island.

The case has provoked debate about how Britain should deal with Aids carriers who negligently spread the condition. Both Mrs Pink and Sir Teddy, Tory MP for Southend East, back the tough line taken by Scandinavian countries. In Finland earlier this month, Steven Thomas, a 36-year-old American-born nightclub bouncer, was jailed for 14 years for knowingly infecting at least 17 women with Aids. He was found guilty of attempted manslaughter. The records on the case will be sealed for 40 years to protect the women's identities. Finland has the lowest incidence of HIV in Europe. A government spokesman said: 'We will deal harshly with such behaviour to ensure we control this disease.'

During the Pavlos Georgiou trial, Mrs Pink and her family pursued their efforts for Britain to adopt a

similar approach. The Law Commission is investigating a proposal from Sir Teddy to use the 1861 Offences Against the Person Act.

Mrs Pink has also asked ministers to study Sweden's example, where those who test positive for HIV are obliged to obey rules of personal behaviour or are locked up in the grounds of a hospital near Stockholm. They are held in what is known as the 'yellow villa', a secure ward where they can be detained for up to three months with only an hour's recreation a day.

In Sweden and Denmark, HIV-positive males convicted of not telling their partners they they have the virus have been receiving prison sentences of two to three years.

Sir Teddy said: 'There is a lot to be said for this system. We must take a more determined view about how to deal with those who transmit this disease so others are not forced to suffer the same fate as Janette.'

Source: *The Times*, 30 July 1997

11

Article 3

This extract is taken from *The Times* dated 1 August 1997 and is from an article written by Daniel McGrory.

Ministers may make deliberate infection a criminal offence

BY DANIEL McGRORY

The Government said last night that it was considering making it a criminal offence to infect a person intentionally with a disease.

In a move opposed by Aids charities, Jack Straw, the Home Secretary, said in a Commons written answer that he would be consulting on the issue later this year. Janette Pink, backed by her local Tory MP, Sir Teddy Taylor, has urged a change in the law.

There is no specific offence covering the transmission of HIV, or other diseases, although someone who tried to pass on HIV out of malice could be charged with grievous bodily harm with intent. Mr Straw said new proposals would be included in a consultation paper setting out a draft bill for a wider reform of the 1861 Offences Against the Person Act.

Aids charities criticised the decision to jail Pavlos Georgiou and said they did not want British courts to adopt similar punishments. Derek Bodell, director of the National Aids Trust, said: 'Cases will be difficult to prove, the law could be misused for vengeance, and it could discourage people from finding out the results of an HIV diagnosis as then they could plead ignorance.

'It will be very dangerous if we try to introduce similar laws to those in Cyprus. All the work we have done to bring Aids and HIV out into the open will be halted.'

Source: *The Times*, 1 August 1997

Article 4

This extract is taken from *The Times* dated 4 March 1997 and is from an article written by Frances Gibb.

Romance turned to tragedy when Janette Pink met the man of her dreams in Cyprus

...In 1992, Kenneth Clarke, then Home Secretary, ruled out creating a criminal offence of knowingly transmitting HIV, arguing there were difficulties of both principle and practice.

'I am not persuaded,' he said, 'that these difficulties have been overcome in other jurisdictions.'

His decision followed a review of the law that year, set up when it was discovered that a Birmingham man with Aids had allegedly infected several women. Mr Clarke echoed the views of lawyers such as John Spencer, Reader of Law at Cambridge University, who has argued that the criminal law already covered such behaviour; and that civil claims for damages might also be possible, so new laws were not needed.

Abroad, the law has moved more quickly. Several Australian states have a specific offence which covers deliberate transmission of the virus. In Western Australia, those who knowingly infect others face fines of up to £8,000. In America the courts have held that the existing law on assault, in particular assault with a deadly weapon, can be held to cover deliberate transmission of HIV. Some American states outlaw sexual intercourse for people who know they have sexually transmissible diseases and Colorado and Indiana allow health officials to place restrictions on people with HIV who expose others to risk.

In Britain, in theory, charges of murder or manslaughter could be considered. But the prosecution faces the problem of proving the necessary *mens rea*; that the accused intended to cause the death of the victim. Lesser offences could be considered. There was a landmark ruling in 1888 called Clarence, in which a husband infected his wife with gonorrhoea. It was thrown out by the courts on the ground that his behaviour did not amount to an 'assault' on his wife, nor constitute 'inflicting harm'.

In today's changed social circumstances, lawyers agree courts might take a different view. The law remains unclear, however. The law on assaults dates back to the 1861 Offences Against the Person Act, which includes offences of causing or inflicting grievous bodily harm. The act is muddled and the Law Commission...proposed in 1993 an overhaul of the law and drafted a Bill that creates a new definition of injury. This would extend to cover intentional or reckless inflicting of serious injury – including illness or disease. To date the Government has not responded.

Source: *The Times*, 4 March 1997

Questions

1 An offence against the person may be fatal (the victim dies), in which case the offence may be murder or manslaughter. At the other extreme, an offence against the person may involve only slight physical harm and, indeed, as you will see further on in this chapter, an offence against the person may be committed without the necessity for the body of the victim to be physically touched. On such a scale of offences against the person one could have expected that the wilful transmission of Aids could be an offence against the person. However, as the articles above demonstrate, this is not necessarily the case. Look back over the articles and extract quotes supporting the proposition that the current law on offences against the person:

   i does not cover the wilful transmission of Aids;
   ii could be made to cover the wilful transmission of Aids;
   iii already covers the wilful transmission of Aids.

2 Pavlos Georgiou was convicted for wilfully transmitting Aids to Janette Pink in Cyprus. State what law he was convicted under and comment on whether or not you think this law is adequate.

3 Give some arguments for and against making the wilful transmission of Aids a criminal offence as expressed in the extracts.

Answers

1   i The following quotes support the view that the current law on offences against the person in England and Wales does not cover the wilful transmission of Aids:

Article 3

'The Government said last night that it was considering making it a criminal offence to infect a person intentionally with a disease.'

'There is no specific offence covering the transmission of HIV, or other diseases...'

Article 4

'...In 1992, Kenneth Clarke, then Home Secretary, ruled out creating a criminal offence of knowingly transmitting HIV, arguing there were difficulties of both principle and practice.'

ii The following quotes support the proposition that the current law on offences against the person could be made to cover the wilful transmission of Aids:

Article 2

'The Law Commission is investigating a proposal from Sir Teddy to use the 1861 Offences Against the Person Act.'

Article 3

'The Government said last night that it was considering making it a criminal offence to infect a person intentionally with a disease. In a move opposed by Aids charities, Jack Straw, the Home Secretary, said in a Commons written answer that he would be consulting on the issue later this year.'

'Mr Straw said new proposals would be included in a consultation paper setting out a draft bill for a wider reform of the 1861 Offences Against the Person Act.'

Article 4

'...the Law Commission...proposed in 1993 an overhaul of the law and drafted a Bill that creates a new definition of injury. This would extend to cover intentional or reckless inflicting of serious injury – including illness or disease.'

iii The following quotes support the proposition that the current law on offences against the person already covers the wilful transmission of Aids:

Article 4

'Mr Clarke echoed the views of lawyers such as John Spencer, Reader of Law at Cambridge University, who has argued that the criminal law already covered such behaviour; and that civil claims for damages might also be possible, so new laws were not needed.'

'In Britain, in theory, charges of murder or manslaughter could be considered. But the prosecution faces the problem of proving the necessary *mens rea*: that the accused intended to cause the death of the victim. Lesser offences could be considered.'

2 Pavlos Georgiou was convicted in Cyprus under a 50-year-old law which was introduced to prevent the spread of typhoid, cholera and venereal disease, that is, infectious diseases. The existence of this law at least meant that Georgiou could be prosecuted and punished for wilfully infecting Janette Pink with the Aids virus but because the law is so old it only has a maximum sentence of two years' imprisonment. Is this sufficient to deter others from wilfully transmitting the disease? Arguably not. The judge in the Georgiou case, as reported in article 1, complained that the law needed stiffer penalties to protect the public from this terrible disease. In article 2 we are told that in Finland a man was convicted of attempted manslaughter for knowingly infecting at least 17 women, for which he received a prison sentence of 14 years, and that in Sweden and Denmark HIV-positive males who have not told their partners that they have the disease can receive a prison sentence of two to three years. What is such a law attempting to acheive? It is not really aiming to punish the offender who is already living in fear of imminent death. Rather, the law should be attempting to deter HIV-positive people from wilfully or negligently infecting others with the disease for the protection of society as a whole. It is better for society if the law prevents the event rather than punishes the offender after the event. In this respect the maximum term of imprisonment must be for a long enough period so that potential offenders are deterred from acting because of the fear of spending their last few years of live in prison. This can be a deterrent, given that modern drugs can prolong the life expectancy of Aids sufferers for many years.

3 Some of the arguments for making the wilful transmission of Aids a criminal offence are:

i to protect the public from the terrible disease (article 1);

11

ii the victim is, in effect, given a death sentence by the accused, as death will follow the commission of the would-be offence by an indeterminate number of years (article 2);

iii it is already a criminal offence in Scandinavian countries and Finland has the lowest incidence of HIV in Europe which suggests that their approach is a successful deterrent (article 2). In Australia and America several states have made use of the criminal law to deal with the problem (article 4);

iv today (as opposed to in the nineteenth century) the courts might be more inclined to use the criminal law against those who knowingly spread the disease and so it would make sense to incoporate the criminalisation of such activity in the current modernisation of offences against the person (article 4).

Some of the arguments against making the wilful transmission of Aids a criminal offence are:

i Aids charities do not want it to happen (article 3);

ii cases could be very difficult to prove. How could you prove that the victim did not know his or her partner was infected with the virus? How could you prove that the victim did not already have the disease; or that they contracted it from another person? And so on (article 3);

iii the law could be used for vengeance in that a spurned lover might accuse someone of infecting them (article 3);

iv it could discourage people from taking HIV tests or collecting the results of such a test because then, if accused of 'wilfully' infecting someone else, they can plead they did not know that they were carrying the disease (article 3);

v criminalising the wilful spread of Aids could make it harder for the authorities to monitor the extent of the disease and control the disease as people might be less willing to admit that they are carrying the disease if there is a chance that someone might accuse them of wilfully transmitting the disease. In which case the law would have scored an own goal – it would achieve the exact opposite of what it was setting out to do (article 3).

Key points on non-fatal offences against the person

Typical examination questions approach the topic of non-fatal offences against the person in two ways. In the typical problem-solving question a variety of assaults might appear in a scenario which also involves burglary and/or theft and/or criminal damage. In order to answer such a question the student requires general knowledge of the key principles of the non-fatal offences against the person so that these principles can be applied to the assaults in question. In contrast, the typical essay-type question tends to focus on one topical issue, most frequently the issues of whether consent by the victim can act as a defence to the accused and the extension of the concept of assault to include acts which are neither immediate nor physical in relation to the victim. Additional topics for essay-type questions are likely to be the reform of the Offences Against the Person Act 1861 (see proposals for reform, page 314) and the criminalisation of the wilful transmission of the Aids virus (already comprehensively covered in 'Setting the Scene'). In order to accommodate these eventualities a general overview of the non-fatal offences against the person is provided by means of statistical data, grids (see Figures 11.1, 11.2 and 11.3) and consideration of key cases. The topics of consent by the victim, the extension of the concept of assault and the impact of the Protection from Harassment Act 1997 on the criminal law of non-fatal offences against the person are discussed in more detail.

Definition of the non-fatal offences against the person and key cases

Brief definitions of the non-fatal offences against the person are shown in Figure 11.1 which also highlights key cases. You will notice that the offences are found both in the common law (common assault and battery) and in statute, in the Offences Against the Person Act 1861 (OAPA 1861). In the Criminal Justice Act 1988 (CJA 1988), by section 39, common assault and battery are deemed to be summary offences and this has led to some confusion as to whether this makes them statutory offences. It is suggested that they remain common law offences although it is possible to bring a charge under section 39 CJA 1988. Brief details of the key cases are given in the text and in the 'You Decide' cases. Your ability to identify and apply these offences to a factual

11

Figure 11.1 Non-fatal offences against the person. Offences in ascending order of 'seriousness'

Source of the law	Type of offence	Type of harm	Maximum sentence	Definition of offence	Key cases
Common law – though can be charged under section 39 CJA*	Assault	Fear of personal violence	Summary offences as per section 39 CJA* 1988. Maximum of £5,000 fine and/or up to 6 months' imprisonment	The accused intentionally or recklessly causes the victim to apprehend immediate and unlawful personal violence	R v. Wilson (1955); Smith v. Chief Superintendent, Woking Police Station (1983); Fagan v. MPC (1955)
	Battery	Unlawful touching of victim or victim's clothes		The accused intentionally or recklessly inflicts unlawful personal violence on the victim	
Statute: Offences Against the Person Act 1861 (OAPA)	Section 47 assault occasioning actual bodily harm (ABH)	Either of the above plus minor physical injury or clinically proven psychiatric injury	TEW offence Maximum of 5 years' imprisonment	Any assault occasioning actual bodily harm	R v. Roberts (1971); R v. Chan-Fook (1994); R v. Savage & Parmenter (1991); R v. Ireland (1996); R v. Constanza (1997)
	Section 20 malicious wounding or inflicting grievous bodily harm (GBH)	Wound: breaking of the skin GBH: serious physical injury or serious psychiatric injury if clinically proven	TEW offence Maximum of 5 years' imprisonment	The accused unlawfully and maliciously wounds or inflicts GBH on the victim with or without a weapon	C (a minor) v. Eisenhower (1984); R v. Burstow (1997)
	Section 18 malicious wounding or causing GBH with intent		Indictable only Maximum of life imprisonment	The accused unlawfully and maliciously by any means wounds the victim or causes GBH to the victim with intent to do GBH or to resist a lawful arrest	

Notes:

1 Section 47 and section 20 have the same maximum penalty yet a section 20 offence is much more serious than a section 47 offence.

2 In section 20 the word *inflicts* is used while in section 18 the word *causes* is used. Since the case of *R v. Burstow* (1997) there is no difference between these words in this context and so it is possible to inflict GBH without an assault on the victim taking place.

3 The *mens rea* for these offences is outlined in **Figure 11.2**.

*CJA – Criminal Justice Act 1988

situation is tested in applying principles to examination questions on page 312. The *actus reus* of non-fatal offences against the person is discussed first, followed by a grid outlining their appropriate *mens rea*.

The *actus reus* of assault, battery and section 47 assault occasioning actual bodily harm

Assault and battery are very closely related, as recognised by James J. in *Fagan* v. *Metropolitan Police Commissioner* (1969) when he said:

> Although 'assault' is an independent crime and is to be treated as such, for practical purposes today 'assault' is generally synonymous with the term 'battery' and is a term used to mean the actual intended use of unlawful force to another person without his consent.

He went on to say:

> On the facts of the present case the 'assault' alleged involved a 'battery'. Where an assault involves a battery, it matters not, in our judgment, whether the battery is inflicted directly by the body of the offender or through the medium of some weapon or instrument controlled by the action of the offender.

In other words, in ordinary every usage judges and other people often use the term 'assault' to cover either common law assault or battery. However, in the following text, common law assault and battery will be dealt with as separate offences.

For the section 47 offence, the assault part can be committed by commission of either common law assault or battery. As such, developments in the law regarding common law assault and battery directly affect the section 47 offence which is really an aggravated form of the two common law offences in that, in addition to the assault and/or battery, the victim actually suffers some form of bodily harm. Actual bodily harm (ABH) is not defined in the statute but is generally thought not to require much harm at all. We will now consider assault and ABH in more detail.

When is there a common law assault?

The traditional view of when an assault has been committed is expressed in *Fagan* v. *Metropolitan Police Commissioner* (1969) which was affimed in *R* v. *Savage & Parmenter* (1991):

11

the accused intentionally or recklessly causes the victim to apprehend immediate and unlawful personal violence.

Other traditional cases are *Smith* v. *Chief Superintendent, Woking Police Station* (1983) and *R* v. *Wilson* (1955) (see the 'You Decide' cases which follow). However, this traditional view of when there is an assault has, in recent years, been extended beyond what would seem to be the natural boundaries of assault. This has happened so that the courts can deal with the problem of 'stalking' which has become an increasing problem in society. The leading cases are *R* v. *Ireland* (1997) which went to the House of Lords (on joint appeal with *R* v. *Burstow*) and *R* v. *Constanza* (1997). (See below for full details of these cases.) In the first case the appellant had run a campaign of silent telephone calls at night to a woman living on her own such that the woman suffered psychiatric illness. He was convicted at trial of three counts under section 47 OAPA 1861. His appeal against conviction was dismissed by the Court of Appeal and by the House of Lords where Lord Steyn said:

> *It was not feasible to enlarge the generally accepted legal meaning of what was a battery to include the circumstances of a silent caller who caused psychiatric injury.*
>
> *The crucial question was whether a silent caller might be guilty of an assault. The answer seemed to be: 'Yes, depending on the facts'. There was no reason why a telephone caller who said to a woman in a menacing way: 'I will be at your door in a minute or two' might not be guilty of an assault if he caused his victim to apprehend immediate personal violence. Accordingly, an assault might be committed in the particular factual circumstances.*

In *R* v. *Constanza* (1997) the appellant had stalked the victim over a period of two years and was convicted under section 47. On appeal the appellant argued that his actions could not amount to an assault according to the classic definition (as set out in *Fagan* v. *Metropolitan Police Commissioner* [1969] which was affirmed in *R* v. *Savage & Parmenter* [1991] in the House of Lords) as his victim did not fear 'immediate' personal violence. The appeal was dismissed on the grounds that it was sufficient for an assault for the prosecution to prove 'a fear of violence at some time not excluding the immediate future'.

These two cases have put the law regarding assaults in an uncertain position, as succinctly expressed by Allen, *Textbook on Criminal Law*, 4th edition 1997, pages 297–8:

A number of points are left in doubt.

First, as the psychological symptoms from which the victims suffered only developed after a number of telephone calls had been made, at what point did such calls become assaults?

Secondly, has the requirement of immediacy for 'normal' assaults been removed such that a fear of a future battery would be sufficient?

Thirdly, could indecent suggestions made over the telephone constitute indecent assault?

Fourthly, as Parliament has recently passed the Protection from Harassment Act 1997 which is specifically designed to deal with stalking and includes a new offence under section 4 of putting people in fear of violence, will the extensions to the law of assault in Ireland and Constanza be ignored in practice?

Clearly there are no answers to these questions but it is highly undesirable that an area of the law which was previously fairly clearly settled should be left in such a state of uncertainty.

See below for a detailed study of the Protection from Harassment Act 1997.

Assault and bodily harm by telephone call

Regina v Ireland
Regina v Burstow
Before Lord Goff of Chieveley, Lord Slynn of Hadley, Lord Steyn, Lord Hope of Craighead and Lord Hutton
[Speeches July 24]
The making of silent telephone calls which caused psychiatric injury to the victim amounted, in law, to have inflicted bodily harm and an assault. An offence of inflicting grievous bodily harm, in law, could be committed where no physical violence was applied directly or indirectly to the body of the victim.

The House of Lords so held dismissing the appeals by the defendants. Robert Matthew Ireland and Anthony Christopher Burstow.

Ireland appealed from the dismissal by the Court of Appeal, Criminal Division (Lord Justice Swinton Thomas, Mr Justice Tucker and Mr Justice Douglas Brown) (*The Times* May 22, 1996, [1997] QB 114) of his appeal against conviction on February 6. 1995 at Newport (Gwent) Crown Court (Judge Prosser, QC).

Ireland, having pleaded guilty to three counts of assault occasioning actual bodily harm contrary to section 47 of the Offences against the Person Act 1861, was sentenced to a total of three years imprisonment on March 10, 1995.

Burstow appealed from the dismissal by the Court of Appeal, Criminal Division (Lord Bingham of Cornhill, Lord Chief Justice, Mr Justice Owen and Mr Justice Connell) (*The Times* July 30, 1996; [1997] 1 Cr App R 144) of his appeal against conviction on March 4, 1996 in Reading Crown Court (Judge Josh Lait and a jury).

Burstow, having pleaded guilty to unlawfully and maliciously inflicting grievous bodily harm contrary to section 20 of the 1861 Act. was sentenced to three years imprisonment.

Mr Malcolm Bishop, QC and Mr Philip Richards for Ireland.

Mr Christopher Liewellyn-Jones. QC and Mr Roger V. Griffiths for the Crown.

Mr Peter Feinberg. QC and Mr Andrew Turion for Burstow; Mr Bruce Houlder. QC and Mr Paul W. Reid for the Crown.

11

LORD STEYN said that it was easy to understand the terrifying effect of a campaign of telephone calls at night by a silent caller to a woman living on her own.

It would be natural for the victim to regard the calls as menacing. What might heighten her fear was that she would not know what the caller might do next.

The spectre of the caller arriving at her doorstep bent on inflicting personal violence on her might come to dominate her thinking. After all, as a matter of common sense, what else would she be terrified about? The victim might suffer psychiatric illness.

Harassment of women by repeated silent telephone calls, accompanied on occasions by heavy breathing, was apparently a significant social problem. That the criminal law should be able to deal with the problem, and so far as was practicable, afford effective protection to victims was self evident.

To examine whether the law provided effective criminal sanctions for such cases one must turn to the 1861 Act. In descending order of seriousness the familiar trilogy of sections provided.

"18 Whosoever shall unlawfully and maliciously by any means whatsoever…cause any grievous bodily harm to any person…with intent…to do some grievous bodily harm to any person…shall be guilty of felony…"

"20 Whosoever shall unlawfully and maliciously…inflict any grievous bodily harm upon any other person. either with or without any weapon or instrument, shall be guilty of a misdemeanour…"

"47 Whosoever shall be convicted upon an indictment of any assault occasioning actual bodily harm shall be liable [to imprisonment …]"

An ingredient of each of the offences was bodily harm to a person. In respect of each section, the threshold question was therefore whether a psychiatric illness, as testified to by a psychiatrist, could amount to bodily harm.

If the answer to the question was "Yes", it would be necessary to consider whether the persistent silent caller, who terrified his victim and caused her to suffer a psychiatric illness, could be criminally liable under any of the sections.

Similar problems arose where the so-called stalker pursued a campaign of harassment by more diffused means. He might intend to terrify the woman and succeed in doing so, by relentlessly following

her, by unnecessarily appearing at her home and workplace and so forth.

The correct approach was to consider whether the words of the 1861 Act considered in the light of contemporary knowledge covered a recognisable psychiatric injury.

The proposition that the Victorian legislator when enacting those sections would not have had in mind psychiatric illness was no doubt correct. Psychiatry was in its infancy in 1861. But the subjective intention of the draftsman was immaterial.

The only relevant inquiry was as to the sense of the words in the context in which they were used. Moreover the 1861 Act was a statute of the "always speaking" type: the statute must be interpreted in the light of the best current scientific appreciation of the link between the body and psychiatric injury.

Accordingly, "bodily harm" in the sections must be interpreted so as to include recognisable psychiatric illness: see R v. Chan-Fook ([1994] 1 WLR 689).

Counsel stressed that there was a difference between "causing" grievous bodily harm in section 18 and "inflicting" grievous bodily harm in section 20.

The question was whether as a matter of current usage the contextual interpretation of "inflict" could embrace the idea of one person inflicting psychiatric injury on another. One could, without straining the language in any way, answer that question in the affirmative.

For those reasons the certified question, namely: "Whether an offence of inflicting grievous bodily harm under section 20…can be committed where no physical violence is applied directly or indirectly to the body of the victim" would be answered in the affirmative.

It was necessary to consider whether making silent telephone calls causing psychiatric injury was capable of constituting an assault under section 47.

An assault was an ingredient of the offence under section 47. An assault might take two forms. The first was battery which involved the unlawful application of force by the defendant upon the victim. The second form was an act causing the victim to apprehend an imminent application of force upon her.

It was not feasible to enlarge the generally accepted legal meaning of what was a battery to include the circumstances of a silent caller who caused psychintric injury.

The critical question was whether a silent caller might be guilty of an assault. The answer seemed to be: "Yes, depending on the facts". There was no reason why a telephone caller who said to a woman in a menacing way: "I will be at your door in a minute or two" might not be guilty of an assault if he caused his victim to apprehend immediate personal violence.

Accordingly, an assault might be committed in the particular factual circumstances.

Lord Hope delivered a concurring opinion and Lord Goff, Lord Slynn and Lord Hutton agreed.

Solicitors: Evans & Ellis, Chepstow; Crown Prosecution Service, Gwent.

Hart Brown, Woking: Crown Prosecution Service, Reading.

Fear of violence sufficient

Regina v Constanza

In order to prove that an assault had been committed, it was enough to prove a fear of violence at some time not excluding the immediate future.

The Court of Appeal, Criminal Division. (Lord Justice Schiemann. Mr Justice Curtis, and Sir Neil Denison, QC, Common Serjeant) so held in a reserved judgment on March 6. when dismissing the appeal against conviction at Luton Crown Court (Judge Moss and a jury) of Gaetano Constanza of assault occasioning actual bodily harm for which he was sentenced to a three-year probation order.

LORD JUSTICE SCHIEMANN said the appellant's behaviour was unusual; it involved stalking the complainant over a period of almost two years.

The appellant argued that that behaviour did not constitute assault.

There was no immediacy, referring to the classic definition of assault as involving causing another to apprehend immediate and unlawful personal violence, and there had been no physical action against the complainant.

Their Lordships held that it was enough for the prosecution to prove a fear of violence at some time not excluding the immediate future, and that an assault could be committed by words alone.

When is there a common law battery?

For common law battery, the slightest touching can suffice, even touching someone's clothing – see *R* v. *Roberts* (1971) in the 'You Decide' cases. However, common sense dictates that not all touching amounts to a battery, only unlawful touching. Thus, when you bump into someone while walking down the street, this is unlikely to amount to a battery as people accept the hurly burly of everyday living. Quite often a battery follows in time after an assault because if someone swings a stick towards you and you fear that you are about to be hit, this is an assault, and if the stick then in fact hits you, you have suffered a battery. A battery may take place without an assault, however, for instance, where the attacker attacks you from behind, in which case you have not seen the blow coming and so have not feared the attack.

What can amount to ABH for the section 47 offence?

The traditional thinking was that ABH referred to some degree of physical harm to the victim. However, in the case of *R* v. *Chan-Fook* (1994) it was held that pyschiatric harm could amount to ABH if supported by medical evidence, although hysterical and nervous conditions and mere emotions such as fear, distress or panic could not amount to pyschiatric injury. This proposition has been supported in more recent cases including that of *R* v. *Ireland* (1997) – see below – in which Lord Steyn said:

> . . . *Accordingly, 'bodily harm' in the sections [of the OAPA] must be interpreted so as to include recognisable psychiatric illness* . . .

Racially aggravated assaults

By section 29 of the Crime abd Disorder Act 1998 a person is guilty of a racially aggravated assault if he commits a common assault, a section 47 or section 20 offence which is racially aggravated. This demonstrates how the government is prepared to expand the law on non-fatal offences when it suits government policy.

YOU DECIDE

Read the cases shown below which are concerned with common law assault and battery and section 47 assault occasioning ABH, then answer the questions.

2 Smith v. Chief Superintendent, Woking Police Station (1983)

In this case the appellant had stared at a woman through the window of her ground floor bedsit flat at 11pm such that she feared violence from him. It was held by the magistrates that this could amount to an assault. The accused appealed.

You decide the appeal.

1 Fagan v. Metropolitan Police Commissioner (1969)

In this case the appellant had unintentionally driven his car onto a policeman's foot. When asked to move the car he refused to do so for some time. He was convicted of assaulting a police officer in the execution of his duty and appealed arguing that the initial act of driving onto the foot was not an assault as it was unintentional and that his refusal to move the car immediately was not an assault because it amounted to an omission rather than an act.

You decide the appeal.

3 R v. Wilson (1955)

In this case the accused shouted the words, 'Get out the knives'. On appeal Lord Goddard stated *obiter dicta* (not binding) that such words in themselves would be an assault.

You decide the appeal.

5 R v. Chan-Fook (1994)

In this case the accused thought that the victim had stolen his fiancee's ring and so dragged him to an upstairs room and locked the door. The victim felt humiliated and distressed and feared physical violence from the accused. Therefore, the victim tried to escape through a window but fell fracturing his wrist and damaging his pelvis. The accused was charged under section 47, not for the physical injuries, but for the fright, humiliation and distress of the victim. The accused was found guilty at trial and appealed.

You decide the appeal by deciding whether the victim had suffered actual bodily harm as charged.

4 R v. Roberts (1971)

In this case the accused had given a lift to a girl late at night and made sexual advances towards her and touched her clothes. The girl feared he was going to rape her and so jumped out of the moving car injuring herself. The accused was convicted under section 47 and appealed arguing that he had not intended to cause her any injury.

Given that the touching of the skirt was held to amount to a battery, do you think it was necessary to prove that the accused intended or was reckless as to whether injury would result from his advances?

11

Answers

1 The appeal was dismissed and the conviction upheld. James J. delivered the judgment of the Divisional Court: *'To constitute the offence of assault some intentional act must have been performed: a mere omission to act cannot amount to an assault . . .'* However, he qualified the position by saying: *'In our judgment a distinction is to be drawn between acts which are complete . . . and those acts which are continuing.'* The court held that although the initial battery was not criminal as there was no intention, an assault took place when Fagan formed the intention to assault the policeman as the battery was continuing.

2 The appeal was dismissed and the conviction upheld. Note that there was a closed window between the appellant and the victim which you might have thought would negate the aspects of the definition of assault in the *Fagan* case requiring apprehension of immediate personal violence.

3 Yes; the decisions in *R* v. *Ireland* (1997) and *R* v. *Constanza* (1997) support this. In the latter Lord Justice Schiemann said: '. . . that an assault could be committed by words alone'.

4 It was held that it was only necessary to prove that the accused had intended to carry out the assault or battery and that this caused the victim's injuries. The chain of causation would only be broken between the assault and injury if the victim had reacted in a way that no reasonable man could have foreseen.

5 The appeal was allowed and the conviction quashed. It was held that bodily harm was not limited to harm to the skin, flesh and bones of the body but also extended to psychiatric harm caused by injury to the nervous system and brain. However, mere emotions such as fear, distress or panic were not included; the psychiatric harm has to be of an identifiable clinical condition. Fear, distress and panic are probably covered by common assault anyway.

The *actus reus* of section 20 and section 18 offences against the person

In both of these offences two types of injury are referred to, that is, a wound and GBH. What is the difference between the two? It has been established by many cases, such as *C (a minor)* v. *Eisenhower* (1984), that for there to be a wound the whole skin must have been broken. In this case the accused had fired an air gun and a pellet hit the victim in the eye, causing ruptured blood vessels and internal bleeding. It was held that this was not a wound. A bruise would not be a wound either, although it could amount to ABH. What is GBH? This covers situations where the skin is not broken but the victim has suffered some serious or really serious harm, such as a broken arm or leg. Since the case of *R* v. *Burstow* (1997) in the House of Lords it is now possible for GBH to include psychiatric injury. While the case was in the Court of Appeal (1996) the Lord Chief Justice said:

> *. . . Had the question been free from authority, their Lordships would have entertained some doubt whether the Victorian draftsman of the 1861 Act intended to embrace psychiatric injury within the expressions 'grievous bodily harm' and 'actual bodily harm'.*
>
> *. . . But there was clear and, in their Lordships' court, unchallenged authority that actual bodily harm was capable of including psychiatric injury: R v. Mike Chan-Fook (1994) . . .*
>
> *There could in that respect be no meaningful distinction between actual bodily harm and grievous bodily harm . . .*
>
> *The question posted at the outset of the judgment had, accordingly, to be answered by their Lordships on the premise that 'grievous bodily harm' could include psychiatric injury.*

Thus, when the case reached the House of Lords in 1997 it was accepted that psychiatric injury was included in GBH and the appeal centred on the question of whether 'inflicting' GBH could take place without there being an assault (see below). The seriousness of the harm done to the victim is a question of fact to be determined by the jury.

In both these offences the words 'unlawfully' and 'maliciously' are used. The latter refers to the *mens rea* of the offences and is dealt with below. The word 'unlawfully' emphasises that in some instances it may be lawful to be the instigator of a wound or serious physical harm to another person, such as when a surgeon operates on a patient or when a person acts in self-defence.

The two offences differ in terms of the fact that:

i in the section 20 offence the GBH has to have been *inflicted*;
ii in the section 18 offence the GBH has to have been *caused*;
iii in the section 18 offence the GBH has to have been caused *with intent*.

At one time (the leading case being *R* v. *Clarence* [1888]) it was held that the accused could only be convicted of *inflicting* GBH if an assault had taken place. In this case the accused was suffering from gonorrhoea yet had intercourse with his wife, infecting her with the disease. It was held that he was not guilty under section 20 because this offence required an assault and he had not assaulted his wife as she had consented to intercourse. In this way the section 20 offence had a narrower application than the section 18 offence. However, it is now the case that it is not necessary to prove an assault in order to

11

convict someone under section 20. The leading case is *R* v. *Burstow* (1997) (see above) in which in the House of Lords, it was held that:

> *An offence of inflicting grievous bodily harm, in law, could be committed where no physical violence was applied directly or indirectly to the body of the victim.*

Thus, if the Clarence case came before the courts today it would be possible for the accused to be found guilty of the section 20 offence. It would seem, therefore, that there is no difference between the words 'cause' and 'inflict' for the purposes of these two offences.

The main difference between the two offences centres on the fact that the section 18 offence is regarded as more serious because it requires the intent to cause GBH.

The *mens rea* for non-fatal offences against the person

Figure 11.2

The *mens rea* for non-fatal offences against the person is outlined in Figure 11.2.

Offence	Mens rea for the offence	Comments
Assault	Intention or recklessness* as to causing apprehension of immediate unlawful personal violence	*In **all** of the non-fatal offences against the person recklessness is judged subjectively, that is, according to *Cunningham* recklessness. (see Chapter 2 on *mens rea*.)
Battery	Intention or recklessness* as to the infliction of unlawful personal violence	
Section 47 assault occasioning ABH	Intention or recklessness* as to the assault or battery part of the offence	It is not necessary to prove that the accused intended ABH or was reckless as to whether any ABH would result from the assault or battery so long as the assault or battery caused the ABH. See *R* v. *Roberts* (1978) in the 'You Decide' cases.
Section 20 unlawfully and maliciously wounding or inflicting GBH	Covered by the word 'maliciously' in the statutory definition which means that the accused intentionally or recklessly* caused **some** physical harm to the victim	You would have expected that the accused had to intentionally or recklessly cause some *serious* harm to the victim but in *R* v. *Mowatt* (1968) Lord Diplock stated: *'It is quite unnecessary that the accused should have foreseen that his unlawful act might cause physical harm of the gravity described in the section i.e. a wound or serious injury. It is enough that he [foresaw] … that some physical harm to some person, albeit of a minor character, might result.'*
Section 18 unlawfully and maliciously wounding or causing GBH with intent to do some GBH or resist arrest	There are two parts to the *mens rea* for the section 18 offence: i 'maliciously' which is described above; ii 'intention' to do some GBH or resist arrest	The ulterior intention part of the *mens rea* for section 18 makes this offence more serious than the section 20 offence. The intention part is as applied in the *mens rea* for murder – that the accused intended the consequences of his actions or knew that the consequences of his actions were a *virtual certainty* (in which case the jury *may* infer that the accused intended the consequences of his actions).

Statistical data on violence against the person

Having considered the substantive non-fatal offences against the person it is a useful excercise to consider the incidence of such offences. This helps to put the topic into perspective and provides additional material for the essay-type questions mentioned above and for questions which focus on statistics. The data below is taken from *Criminal Statistics England and Wales 1996* which is a publication of the Government Statistical Service.

In 1996 5.0 million notifiable offences were recorded by the police. Of these, 4.6 million or 92% were crimes against property; 345,000 or 7 per cent were crimes against the person; and the remaining 56,000 were other types of crime. In this chapter, we are interested in the 345,000 crimes against the person. It is interesting to note that because crimes against property represent such a large percentage of recorded crimes, *trends* in total recorded crime are almost entirely a reflection of those in property crime (paragraph 2.22). Figure 11.3 is taken from paragraph 2.23.

Figure 11.3
Violent crimes* recorded by the police, 1996

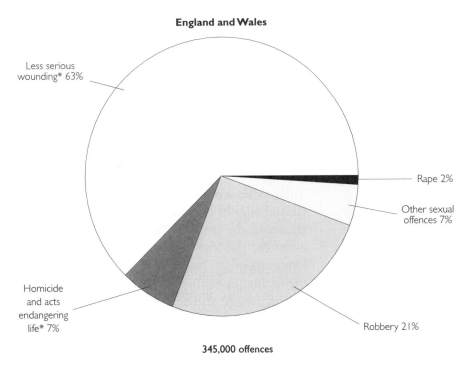

England and Wales

Less serious wounding* 63%

Rape 2%

Other sexual offences 7%

Robbery 21%

Homicide and acts endangering life* 7%

345,000 offences

*violent crimes include violence against the person, sexual offences and robbery.

11

It should be noted at this point that not all offences are notifiable. The term 'notifiable offences' broadly covers the more serious offences and, as such, most indictable and triable either way offences are included. A few summary offences are included although for the purposes of this chapter it is significant to note that since the Criminal Justice Act 1988 common law assault and battery became summary offences and are no longer included in notifiable offences. Thus, it is necessary to consider which non-fatal offences do feature in the statistics, and where.

▶ Included in the category of homicide and acts endangering life are the offences of murder, attempted murder, causing death by aggravated vehicle taking, and wounding with intent to do grievous bodily harm, etc. or to resist apprehension (that is, an offence under section 18 of the OAPA 1861).

▶ Included in the category of less serious wounding are offences of wounding or inflicting grievous bodily harm [inflicting bodily injury with or without a weapon] (that is, an offence under section 20 of the OAPA 1861) and assault occasioning actual bodily harm (that is, an offence under section 47 of the OAPA 1861).

In Figure 11.4 the offence of wounding with intent to do grievous bodily harm (section 18 offence) is shown in the offence column numbered 5 and it can be seen how the trend over the past 10 years has been for such offences to increase, with a big increase between 1995 and 1996. The offences of wounding or inflicting grievous bodily harm (section 20 offence) and assault occasioning actual bodily harm (section 47 offence) are shown in the offence column numbered 8 and the trend over the past 10 years has been for such offences to increase, especially between 1995 and 1996.

Thus, when considering the non-fatal offences against the person, we should bear in mind that the most common offences committed, as shown in the Home Office statistics, are the section 20 and section 47 offences. The incidence of common law assault and battery is no longer recorded but from the table in Figure 11.4 it can be seen that the incidence of these offences up to 1988 was much lower than for the section 20 and section 47 offences and the trend was for them to decrease.

England and Wales

Offence		Offences recorded											Number of offences	
													Offences cleared up 1996	
		1986	1987	1988	1989	1990	1991	1992	1993	1994	1995	1996	No.	%
1 Murder } 4.1 Manslaughter } 4.2 Infanticide	Homicide	661	688	624	641	669	725	687	670	726	745	681	635	93
2 Attempted murder		159	291	368	376	476	555	568	661	651	634	674	598	89
3 Threat or conspiracy to murder		1,340	1,785	2,730	3,579	4,162	4,712	5,487	5,638	6,844	7,044	8,533	7,112	83
4.3 Child destruction		–	2	8	2	–	2	–	3	7	8	2	2	(100)
4.4 Causing death by dangerous driving } 4.6 Causing death by careless driving when under the influence of drink or drugs }		232	292	339	393	419	416	277	292	278	242	320	309	97
37.1 Causing death by aggravated vehicle taking[1]		–	–	–	–	–	–	19	17	14	21	34	28	(82)
5 Wounding or other acts of endangering life		6,616	7,942	8,678	8,926	8,920	9,408	10,741	10,701	11,033	10,445	12,169	8,978	74
6 Endangering railway passenger		23	18	25	9	9	11	20	17	10	12	12	8	(67)
More serious offences		9,031	11,018	12,772	13,926	14,655	15,829	17,799	17,999	19,563	19,151	22,425	17,670	79
7 Endangering life at sea		–	–	1	2	1	–	–	–	–	–	–	–	–
8 Other wounding etc.		115,523	129,193	144,781	162,843	169,764	174,245	183,717	186,765	198,383	193,016	216,467	165,605	77
9 Assault[3]		798	686	503	–	–	–	–	–	–	–	–	–	–
12 Abandoning a child aged under two years		22	25	23	34	23	47	40	45	51	46	65	52	(80)
13 Child abduction		109	100	156	140	208	196	206	275	343	355	374	204	55
14 Procuring illegal abortion		3	3	3	5	5	3	1	2	3	5	7	8	(114)[2]
15 Concealment of birth		13	17	9	12	9	19	14	16	11	15	4	6	150[2]
Less serious offences		116,468	130,024	145,476	163,036	170,010	174,510	183,978	187,103	198,791	193,437	216,917	165,875	76
Total violence against the person		125,499	141,042	158,248	176,962	184,665	190,339	201,777	205,102	218,354	212,588	239,342	183,545	77

Notes:
[1] Offences introduced on 1 April 1992.
[2] Offences cleared up in current year may have been initially recorded in an earlier year.
[3] Following the Criminal Justice Act 1988 these assaults became summary offences and are no longer included in the notifiable offence series.
( ) Percentages in brackets are based on totals of less than 100.
Source: *Criminal Statistics England and Wales 1996 Office of National Statistics*

Figure 11.4 Notifiable offences of violence against the person recorded by the police by offence

11

A detailed look at the Protection from Harassment Act 1997 and how it affects the existing non-fatal offences against the person

This Act was introduced to deal with the problem of stalking and key parts of it are reproduced in the statutory provisions on page 277. It would be a good idea to read these again before continuing further. The Act has both criminal law implications and civil law implications. For the criminal law two new offences are created by sections two and four, while for the civil law a statutory tort of harassment is created by section three. For the purposes of this chapter we will concentrate on the two new criminal offences.

As has been mentioned already, the common law offence of assault has been extended, somewhat artificially, to cover stalking by the cases of *R* v. *Ireland* (1997) and *R* v. *Constanza* (1997). The new Act does not invalidate these cases and so they are good case law which can be relied on in future prosecutions. Additionally, there is already an offence of intentional harassment, created by section 154 of the Criminal Justice and Public Order Act 1994 (which inserted the offence as section 4A of the Public Order Act 1986). So why do we need the 1997 Act? The problem with intentional harassment is that the prosecution have to prove that the accused subjectively intended harassment and this has been difficult to do. However, with the 1997 Act the prosecution only have to prove harassment from the objective point of view of the reasonable man (see sections 1(2) and 4(2)) and so it should be easier for them to secure a conviction.

The first and less serious summary offence of harassment is provided for by section 2 of the Act. Read in conjunction with section 7, the offence is committed when a person harasses someone on at least two occasions and alarming a person or causing a person distress will suffice. Section 1(3)(a) should excuse police officers in their daily work on the streets while section 1(3)(c) provides a defence to anyone who can show that their conduct was 'reasonable'. Harassment as such is not defined and so it is up to the courts to determine the extent of the Act. Section 2 would appear to cover those situations where stalking takes place and where the accused does not fear violence but is, nevertheless, bothered by the conduct of the stalker. In the Private Member's Bill introduced in May 1996 by Janet Anderson MP, stalking was defined as:

> ...engaging in a course of conduct whereby a person:
> (a) follows, loiters near, watches or approaches another person
> (b) telephones (which for the avoidance of doubt shall include

> telephoning a person but remaining silent during the call), contacts by other electronic means, or otherwise contacts another person
>
> (c) loiters near, watches, approaches or enters a place where another person lives, works or repeatedly visits
>
> (d) interferes with property which does not belong to him and is in the possession of another person
>
> (e) leaves offensive, unwarranted or unsolicited material at a place where another person lives, works or regularly visits
>
> (f) gives offensive, unwarranted or unsolicited material to another person.

Probably all of the above types of conduct would be regarded as criminal harassment under the Act.

The second and more serious triable either way offence of aggravated harassment is provided for by section 4 of the Act where the harassment causes another to fear that violence will be used against him. Despite the fact that 'course of conduct' is defined in section 7 as meaning conduct on two occasions, in section 4 the phrase 'on at least two occasions' is used which could be interpreted as meaning that for section 4 the accused has to have carried out harassing conduct on four occasions; this will no doubt be clarified in the courts in due course. It is difficult to see how this aggravated form of harassment differs from common law assault, where the victim is made to fear unlawful personal violence, other than the fact that a prosecution can be brought for the latter after one occurrence of the conduct and that the new section 4 offence is a triable either way offence.

How is the new Act being used in the criminal and civil law?

The government anticipated that the Act would result in approximately 200 additional criminal cases a year which may be an underestimation when we consider how the Act is being used since it came into force on 16 June 1997. Some examples are given below:

i As reported in the *Daily Mail* on 22 October 1997 a bachelor aged 77 years was convicted of harassment under the new Act. After he split up with his girlfriend, aged 55 years, he sent her sordid letters, made abusive telephone calls, daubed derogatory graffiti about her on her new boyfriend's house and slashed a tyre on her car. He carried out this conduct for a period of eight months. He was fined £1,000 and ordered to pay compensation to his former girlfriend and her new boyfriend.

ii As reported in *The Times* on 31 December 1997 a man was arrested and charged under the new Act for singing '*Come Fly With Me*' at the top of his voice, throwing a ball about and erecting a one-eyed

11

plastic owl in his attempts to stop his neighbour's pigeons coming into his garden. After one court appearance the Crown Prosecution Service decided to drop the case. Police admitted that the new law was causing problems and that prosecutors were still 'finding their feet' with it.

iii As reported in *The Times* on 11 December 1997, the civil case of *Huntingdon Life Sciences Ltd* v. *Curtin and Others* as shown in the newspaper extract below.

Harassment Act misused over protesters

Huntingdon Life Sciences Ltd v Curtin and Others
Before Mr Justice Eady
[Judgment November 28]
The Protection from Harassment Act 1997 was not intended to be used to restrict those who were exercising their right to protest about a matter of public interest.

Mr Justice Eady so stated in the Queen's Benoh Division when allowing an application by the third defendants, the British Union for the Abolition of Vivisection, to vary an injunction, granted by Lord Justice Schiemann sitting in the Court of Appeal on October 15, 1997 restraining the third defendants among others from harassing the plaintiffs, by removing the third defendants' name from it.

Mr Peter Roth, QC and Miss Jessica Simor for the defendants;

Mr Timothy Lawson-Cruttenden, solicitor, for the plaintiffs.

MR JUSTICE EADY said that the plaintiffs, a company which undertook research on animals, had been granted an ex parte injunction against the defendants, among others, restraining them from any course of conduct amounting to harassment.

The plaintiffs had complained of a sustained and menacing anti-vivisection campaign directed at itself and its employees, which included many breaches of section 1 of the 1997 Act.

In the light of evidence adduced by the defendants for the first time at the inter partes hearing, the plaintiffs' allegations could not be sustained and the defendants' application would be granted.

His Lordship went on to say that

the legislators of the Act would no doubt be surprised to see how widely its terms were perceived to extend by some people.

The 1997 Act was clearly not intended by Parliament to be used to clamp down on the discussion of matters of public interest or upon the rights of political protest and public demonstration which was so much a part of our democratic tradition.

His Lordship had little doubt that the courts would resist any wide interpretation of the Act as and when the occasion arose.

It was unfortunate that the terms in which the provisions of the Act were couched were seen to sanction any such restrictions.

Solicitors: Mr John Cooper, Southwark; Lawson-Cruttenden & Co.

Consent and non-fatal offences against the person

In November 1995 the Law Commission published a Consultation Paper (No. 139) entitled 'Consent in the Criminal Law'. The paper was circulated for comment and criticism with an extended deadline for receipt of this of 31 December 1996. The fact that the consultation paper is nearly three hundred pages long demonstrates the importance of the topic of consent in the criminal law. Although the paper considers consent in the wider sense of the criminal law, for the purposes of this book we will concentrate on consent in relation to the non-fatal offences against the person.

At the heart of this debate is the question of whether or not and to what extent a person can or should be able to consent to injury being inflicted upon themselves. The extent to which a person may consent to injury to themselves marks the point when the perpetrator of the harm has a defence to a charge under the existing/proposed law on non-fatal offences against the person. The Law Commission recognised the philosophical arguments pertinent to such a debate and devoted appendix C of the paper to such arguments. The Law Commission recognised that philosophical inquiry into the moral limits of the criminal law could be divided into three competing perspectives, briefly explained as follows:

i liberalism
 – only to interfere in people's lives if *harm* is caused to others – to respect the autonomy of individuals – minimal state intervention;
ii paternalism
 – the 'state knows best' and can interfere in people's lives for their own good;
iii legal moralism
 – use the law to enforce morals – pass laws against immorality even if no harm is being done to anyone.

A detailed consideration of such philosophical perspectives has already taken place earlier in this book. Students should refer back to this in order to fully appreciate the problem of criminalisation of any aspect of human behaviour. In paragraph 2.2 the Law Commission states that, although fully cognisant of the philosophical arguments it nevertheless,

felt constrained to take much greater account of what we believe to be the contemporary approach of members of both Houses of Parliament to issues of criminalisation, even if they do not fit coherently into any consistent pattern of modern philosophy.

And in paragraphs 2.13, 2.14 and 2.15 it says:

As we have seen, on the one hand there were many individual and group respondents, particularly among those who advocated the de-criminalisation of sado-masochistic practices, who adopted a distinctly liberal approach. On the other hand there were those with very considerable experience of the practical side of law enforcement who adopted an approach which is determinedly paternalist. [2.13]

In these circumstances, for this second consultation exercise we consider it best if we adopt an essentially pragmatic approach [a practical, businessnesslike approach]. It is obvious to us that if our eventual recommendations do not follow what we perceive to be the grain of contemporary majority attitudes within Parliament to questions of

11

criminalisation they are unlikely to be taken at all seriously by those who are ultimately responsible for taking decisions about the future shape of the criminal law. [2.14]

The decisions that have been made by Parliament or Parliamentary committees in recent years appear to us on examination to be redolent [strongly suggestive] of a paternalism that is softened at the edges when Parliament is confident that there is an effective system of regulatory control, whether this is created by a licensing regime, by the standards or ethics of a profession, or by a series of self-regulation in which Parliament has trust. [2.15]

To what extent can a person consent to harm to themselves under current law?

In the Consultation Paper (No. 139) the Law Commission states that the law in this area has developed piecemeal and unprincipled over the years, the most recent cases being those of *R* v. *Brown* (1994), which reached the House of Lords, and *R* v. *Wilson* (1996). In the *Brown* case it was held that the consent of the injured party does not provide a defence to a person charged with assault occasioning ABH or more serious injury. The case then went to the European Court of Human Rights (*Laskey, Jaggard and Brown* v. *United Kingdom*, Case No.109/1995) and in February 1997 the court held that the prosecution and subsequent convictions in *R* v. *Brown* did not constitute an unjustifiable interference with their right to respect for their private lives, contrary to article 8 of the European Convention on Human Rights. In other words, the courts in the UK could criminalise injury at the level set in *Brown* despite the consent of the injured parties. (See below for details on these cases.)

However, the common law has allowed certain exceptions to this general principle so that injury which amounts to ABH or worse might *not* be criminal if it occurred:

  i during the course of properly conducted sports* or games;
  ii as part of lawful correction;
  iii while undergoing hospital surgery;
  iv during rough and undisciplined horseplay;
  v in dangerous exhibitions;
  vi as male circumcision;
  vii as religious flagellation;
viii tattooing**; or
  ix ear piercing.

* including boxing;
** see *R* v. *Wilson* (1996) below.

To avoid such unprincipled future development, the Law Commission stated (in paragraph 1.11) that it sought to identify those principles which *ought* to underpin the criminal law in this area and to recommend law reform as necessary to bring the law into line with those principles.

What provisional proposals were made by the Law Commission?

The Law Commission made the following provisional proposals and invited responses to them (Part XVI). These proposals concerning consent are put forward in light of the new hierarchy of non-fatal offences against the person as provided for in the Law Commission's draft Criminal Law Bill which appears in their consultation document, '*Legislating the Criminal Code: Offences Against the Person and General Principles*' (Law Com. 218). It would benefit students to refer quickly to this draft Criminal Law Bill, as shown on page 315, before reading the proposals below.

Seriously disabling injury

Para 2. *Intentional* causing of seriously disabling injury
We provisionally propose that the intentional causing of seriously disabling injury (as defined below) to another person should continue to be criminal, even if the person injured consents to such injury or to the risk of such injury.

Para 3. *Reckless* causing of seriously disabling injury
We provisionally propose that –
(1) the reckless causing of seriously disabling injury (as defined below) should continue to be criminal, even if
the injured person consents to such injury or to the risk of such injury; . . .

Para 4. Secondary liability for consenting to seriously disabling injury
We provisionally propose that, where a person causes seriously disabling injury to another person who consented to injury or to the risk of injury of the type caused, and the person causing the injury is guilty of an offence under the proposals in paragraphs 2 and 3 above, the ordinary principles of secondary liability should apply for the purpose of determining whether the person injured is a party to that offence.

11

Other injuries

Para 5. *Intentional* causing of other injuries

We provisionally propose that the intentional causing of any injury to another person other than seriously disabling injury as defined at paragraph 7 below (whether or not amounting to 'grievous bodily harm' within the meaning of the OAPA 1861 or to 'serious injury' within the meaning of the Criminal Law Bill) should not be criminal if, at the time of the act or omission causing the injury, the other person consented to injury of the type caused.

Para 6. *Reckless* causing of other injuries

We provisionally propose that the reckless causing of any injury to another person other than seriously disabling injury as defined in paragraph 7 below (whether or not amountin to 'grievous bodily harm' within the meaning of the OAPA 1861 or to 'serious injury' within the meaning of the Criminal Law Bill) should not be criminal if, at the time of the act or omission causing the injury, the other person consented to injury of the type caused, to the risk of injury or to the act or omission causing the injury.

Para 7. Definition of seriously disabling injury

We provisionally propose that for the purposes of paragraphs 2–6 above 'seriously disabling injury' should be taken to refer to an injury or injuries which –

(1) cause serious distress, and

(2) involve the loss of a bodily member or organ or permanent bodily injury or permanent functional impairment, or serious or permanent disfigurement, or severe and prolonged pain, or serious impairment of mental health, or prolonged unconsciousness;

and, in determining whether an effect is permanent, no account should be taken of the fact that it may be remediable by surgery.

Para 8. Meaning of consent

We provisionally propose that for the purpose of the above proposals –

(1) 'consent' should mean a valid subsisting consent to an injury or to the risk of an injury of the type caused, and consent may be express or implied;

Comments:

1 Note that in paragraph 7 the injury has to cause serious distress *and* one or more of the things listed.

2 In paragraphs 5 and 6 the threshhold of consent as a defence to injury has been raised (up to *seriously disabling injury*) so that, contrary to the decision in *R* v. *Brown* (1994), it could be possible to plead consent as a defence even if GBH had been caused. Is this a triumph for the liberalists? Not completely, as stated in the Law Commission's Thirtieth Annual Report 1995 (Law Com. No. 239) at paragraph 4.26 where it states on this point:

> *We believe that to allow a competent adult to consent to the causing of injury, or the risk of it, up to but not including seriously disabling injury, would be to steer a sensible middle course between the rival approaches of the liberal, whose proposals would go far beyond what public opinion would tolerate, and the legal moralist, who would propose a far greater level of state intervention than would, in our view, be either desirable or practicable in society today.*

3 Note that the word 'cause' is used throughout as opposed to a combination of the words 'cause' and 'inflict'. Look back to the case of *R* v. *Burstow* (1997) in which the judgment of the House of Lords meant

that there was no real difference between the words 'cause' and 'inflict' for the purposes of section 20 and section 18 of the OAPA 1861.

4 Note in paragraph 8 that consent can be implied from conduct so it is not necessary to actually say, 'I consent'.

Key cases

We will now consider the key cases of:

R v. *Brown* (1994)

R v. *Wilson* (1996)

Laskey, Jaggard and Brown v. *United Kingdom* (Case No. 109/1995) reported 2/1997

R v. *Brown* (1994)

For the facts of this case see *Laskey, Jaggard and Brown* v. *UK*, on the following page.

LORD TEMPLEMAN: ... In the present case each of the appellants intentionally inflicted violence upon another (to whom I refer as 'the victim') with the consent of the victim and thereby occasioned actual bodily harm or in some cases wounding or grievous bodily harm. Each appellant was therefore guilty of an offence under section 47 or section 20 of the Act of 1861 unless the consent of the victim was effective to prevent the commission of the offence or effective to constitute a defence to the charge.

In some circumstances violence is not punishable under the criminal law. When no actual bodily harm is caused, the consent of the person affected precludes him from complaining. There can be no conviction for the summary offence of common assault if the victim has consented to the assault ...

In earlier days some other forms of violence were lawful and when they ceased to be lawful they were tolerated well into the nineteenth century. Duelling and fighting were at first lawful and then tolerated provided the protagonists were voluntary participants ... Duelling and fighting are [now] both unlawful and the consent of the protagonists affords no defence to charges of causing actual bodily harm, wounding or grievous bodily harm in the course of an unlawful activity ...

The question of whether the defence of consent should be extended to the consequences of sado-masochistic encounters can only be decided by consideration of policy and public interest. Parliament can call on the advice of doctors, psychiatrists, criminolo-gists, sociologists and other experts and can also sound and take into account public opinion ... Counsel for some of the appellants argued that the defence of consent should be extended to the offence of occasioning actual bodily harm under section 47 of the Act of 1861 but should not be available to charges of serious wounding and the infliction of serious bodily harm under section 20. I do not consider that this solution is practicable ...

Counsel for the appellants argued that consent should provide a defence to charges under both sections 20 and 47 because, it was said, every person has a right to deal with his body as he pleases. I do not consider that this slogan provides a sufficient guide to the policy decision which must now be made. It is an offence for a person to abuse his own body and mind by taking drugs. Although the law is often broken, the criminal law restrains a practice which is regarded as dangerous and injurious to individuals and which if allowed and extended is harmful to society generally. In any event, the appellants in this case did not mutilate their own bodies. They inflicted bodily harm on willing victims ...

I am not prepared to invent a defence of consent for sado-masochistic encounters which breed and glorify cruelty and result in offences under sections 47 and 20 of the Act of 1861 ... Society is entitled and bound to protect itself against a cult of violence. Pleasure derived from the infliction of pain is an evil thing. Cruelty is uncivilised. I would answer the certified question in the negative and dismiss the appeals of the appellants against conviction.

11

Lord Jauncey of Tullichettle and Lord Lowry also dismissed the appeals while Lord Mustill and Lord Slynn of Hadley allowed the appeals; thus, the appeals were dismissed by a majority of 3:2. In the extract above it might be an idea for you to pick out phrases which you consider to support the philosophical arguments of the liberalists and paternalists. Can you find any moral philosophical arguments?

Laskey, Jaggard and Brown v. *United Kingdom* (Case No 109/1995/615/703–705)

The following extract is taken from the *Independent* newspaper dated 19 February 1997, written by Paul Magrath, Barrister.

The prosecution of members of a group of sado-masochistic homosexuals for offences of assault and wounding, despite the fact that in each case the 'victims' had consented to the deliberate infliction of pain, did not consitute an unjustifiable interference with their right to respect for their private lives, contrary to article 8 of the European Convention on Human Rights, since such interference was 'necessary in a democratic society' for 'the protection of health'.

The European Court of Human Rights unanimously held that there had been no violation of article 8 of the Convention in the cases of Colin Laskey, Roland Jaggard and Anthony Brown.

The applicants were members of a group of homosexual men who took part in sado-masochistic activities, involving maltreatment of the genitals, ritualistic beating and branding. These activities were consensual and took place in private between men of full age. The infliction of pain was subject to certain rules, including the use of a codeword to call a halt to any activity, and no permanent injury or infection was caused.

The group's members made videos of these events for private use, and some of the tapes fell into the hands of the police. The applicants were charged with various offences including causing bodily harm and wounding contrary to sections 47 and 20 of the Offences Against the Person Act 1861.

After the judge rejected their argument that their consent to the assaults provided them with a defence to the charges, they pleaded guilty and were sentenced to between one and three year's imprisonment. The Court of Appeal ((1992) QB 491) upheld the convictions but reduced their sentences. The House of Lords ((1994) 1 AC 212) by a majority also dismissed their appeals, taking the view that a victim's consent was no defence to a charge under the 1861 Act and that it would not be in the public interest to create an exception for sado-masochistic activity.

The applicants contended that their convictions constituted a violation of rights guaranteed by article 8 of the Convention, which provides:

1. Everyone has the right to respect for his private and family life, his home and his correspondence.
2. There shall be no interference by

a public authority with the exercise of this right except such as is in accordance with the law and is necessary in a democratic society in the interests of national security, public safety or the economic well-being of the country, for the prevention of disorder or crime, for the protection of health or morals, or for the protection of the rights and freedoms of others.

The European Court of Human Rights said it was common ground that the criminal proceedings against the applicants constituted an 'interference by a public authority' with their right to respect for private life, that the interference was 'in accordance with the law' and that it pursued a legitimate aim, namely that of 'protection of health of morals'. The only issue was whether the interference was 'necessary in a democratic society'. The state was unquestionably entitled to regulate the infliction of physical harm through the criminal law. The determination of the tolerable level of harm where the victim consented was primarily a matter for the state's authorities.

The court was not persuaded that the applicants' behaviour belonged exclusively to the sphere of their private morality and so fell outside the scope of the state's intervention. It was evident that the applicants' activities involved a significant degree of injury and wounding. Furthermore, state authorities were entitled to consider not only the actual harm but also the potential for more serious injury inherent in the activities.

There was no evidence to support the allegation that the authorities were biased against homosexuals. The mojority of the House of Lords had based their decision on the extreme nature of the practices.

The reasons given by the national authorities to justify the interference were relevant and sufficient. Nor, given the degree of organisation involved, the limited number of charges finally included in the prosecution case, and the reduced sentences imposed on appeal, could the interference be regarded as disproportionate.

The national authorities were entitled to consider the interference 'necessary in a democratic society' for the protection of health and there had been no violation of the convention.

Source: *Independent*, 19 February 1997

R v. *Wilson* (1996)
Court of Appeal

In this case a woman asked her husband to brand his initials on her buttocks with a hot knife. He did so and after the branding was discovered by a doctor, he was charged with and convicted under section 47 of the OAPA 1861. He appealed.

RUSSELL. L.J.:

...Mrs Wilson not only consented to that which the appellant did, she instigated it. There was no aggressive intent on the part of the appellant. On the contrary, far from wishing to cause injury to his wife, the appellant's desire was to assist her in what she regarded as the acquisition of a desirable piece of personal adornment, perhaps in this day and age no less understandable than the piercing of nostrils or even tongues for the purposes of inserting decorative jewellery...

In our judgment R v *Brown is not authority for the proposition that consent is no defence to a charge under section 47 of the Act of 1861, in all circumstances where actual bodily harm is deliberately inflicted. It is to be observed that the question certified for their Lordships in R v Brown related only to a 'sado-masochistic' encounter. However, their Lordships recognised in the course of their speeches, that it is necessary that there must be exceptions to what is no more than a general proposition...*

Does public policy or the public interest demand that the appellant's activity should be visited by the sanctions of the criminal law?...we are firmly of the opinion that it is not in the public interest that activities such as the appellant's in this appeal should amount to criminal behaviour. Consensual activity between husband and wife, in the privacy of the matrimonial home, is not, in our judgment, normally a proper matter for criminal investigation, let alone criminal prosecution... In this field, in our judgment, the law should develop upon a case by case basis rather than upon general propositions to which, in the changing times in which we live, exceptions may arise from time to time not expressly covered by authority.

11

The appeal was allowed and the husband's conviction was quashed. Note the phrases which have been emboldened. Russell L.J. is reiterating the fact that, at present, there is a common law proposition (assumption or generally held view) that consent of the 'victim' is no defence to the perpetrator of actual bodily harm or worse injury, as confirmed in the case of *R* v. *Brown*. He also notes that the common law has allowed exceptions to this general proposition over the years where neither public policy nor public interest demand that the behaviour in question should be made criminal, as regards actual bodily harm inflicted during properly conducted sports, games, surgery, tattooing, etc. This line of argument is exactly the line of argument which is criticised in the Law Commission's Consultation Paper, 'Consent in the Criminal Law' (see above), and is why the Law Commission wishes to replace such an approach with an approach to consent and non-fatal offences to the person which is based on agreed *principles* rather than on vague notions of public interest and public policy. (See above for their proposals.)

Applying principles to examination questions

Consider the question posed below and make notes. Look back through the chapter to find relevant statutory provisions and case law. Tips on how to approach such a question are given below but you should attempt the question for yourself initially. Students might find it useful to consider the grid provided in the chapter summary on page 320.

John is besotted with Carla who works at the same place as him. He decides to follow her home one night and stands outside her house trying to see what she is doing inside. At work he watches her in the canteen and has recently started making silent telephone calls to her at home.

Carla is now very distressed and alarmed due to John's actions.

Michael has recently bought a laser pen from a stationery shop. On his way home from school he shone it into the face of the bus driver who said that it was an annoyance and that he felt discomfort.

The bus driver's son, Chris, is angry with Michael and, later that night, head butts him, breaking Michael's nose.

Consider the criminal liability of John, Michael and Chris under the Offences Against the Person Act 1861 and/or under the Protection from Harassment Act 1997 and any common law offences.

Tips on how to approach such a question

nsider whether hn could be arged for mmon law sault – there pears to be no ttery. State the assic' definition assault as in agan v. MPC 969) under hich John might ot be liable. But te the cases of *R Ireland* (1997) d *R v. Constanza* 997) which have tended the ncept of assault, d *Smith v. Chief perintendent. oking Police ation* (1983)

uld John be arged under ction 2 of the PHA 77? Probably he uld as there is a ourse of conduct' d it is not ecessary to prove ar of violence.

as there been a attery? No, there as been no uching of the ctim – see *R v. oberts* (1971). Has e driver suffered hysical harm hich amounts to BH? Probably ot.

an a broken nose nount to a ound or GBH nder either *section* 0 or section 18 of APA 1861? Yes – a ound if the skin broken (probably cluding the inner kin of the nose) nd bleeding ccurs – and GBH serious injury) if e skin is not roken.

John is besotted with Carla who works at the same place as him. He decides to follow her home one night and stands outside her house trying to see what she is doing inside. At work he watches her in the canteen and has recently started making silent telephone calls to her at home.

Carla is now very distressed and alarmed due to John's actions.

Michael has recently bought a laser pen from a stationery shop. On his way home from school he shone it into the face of the bus driver who said that it was an annoyance and that he felt discomfort.

The bus driver's son, Chris, is angry with Michael and, later that night, head butts him, breaking Michael's nose.

Consider the criminal liability of John, Michael and Chris under the Offences Against the Person Act 1861 and/or under the Protection from Harassment Act 1997 and any common law offences.

OAPA = Offences Against the Person Act
PHA = Protection from Harassment Act

Carla is distressed and alarmed but does she actually fear personal violence at some time not excluding the immediate futuer? This is what is required to prove an assault as decided in *R v. Constanza* (1977).

If Carla did fear personal violence, and there was an asault, could John be charged under *section 47 OAPA 1861*? Has Carla suffered actual bodily harm? See the case of *R v. Chan-Fook* (1994) – her fear and distress would not amount to ABH.

Could John be charged under *section 4 of the PHA 1997*? Only if Carla feared violence.

Has there been a common law assault? There could be – Michael was acting either intentionally or recklessly and as it is now known that laser pens can cause damage to eyes, the driver could have feared personal violence.

Did Chris 'intend' to cause GBH? If he did he could be charged under *section 18 OAPA 1861* – if he did not he could be charged under *section 20 OAPA 1861*.

Proposals for reform

In this part of the chapter we will consider:

i   the proposals put forward by the Law Commission to reform the law on non-fatal offences against the person;

ii the proposals put forward by the Government to reform the law on non-fatal offences against the person.

Proposals of the Law Commission

In *'Legislating the Criminal Code: Offences Against the Person and General Principles' (Law Com. No. 218)*, hereafter Law Com. No. 218, the Law Commission builds on its Consultation Paper (No. 122) of similar title, hereafter LCCP 122, by producing a Criminal Law Bill dealing with non-fatal offences against the person and certain defences. In Law Com. No. 218 (para 1.1) the Law Commission recognises that codification of English criminal law is urgently needed as it is presently found in a complex and often confusing and antiquated mixture of common law and statute. The ultimate aim of the Law Commission is to create a series of Bills, each reforming a particular area of the criminal law and each formulated on similar lines so that they could, in the future, be consolidated into a single, unified, criminal code for England and Wales. The Law Commission selected non-fatal offences against the person as the subject of the first Bill as it is generally agreed that this area of the criminal law is in need of urgent attention. In this chapter we have already seen how the law needs reforming to take account of the wilful transmission of diseases, such as the Aids virus, and how the law on assaults has been 'stretched' to accommodate harassment and stalking.

We can set the scene for reform of the non-fatal offences against the person by reference to paragraph 4.1 of Law Com. No. 218:

> *Law that is muddled, irrational, unclear, or simply difficult of access, is almost certain to produce injustice. The need to take steps to avoid such injustice is especially great if it is the criminal law that suffers from such defects, since this part of our law embraces the vital matter of the exercise and control of coercive state power against the citizen. In this Report we show how the present law of offences against the person suffers from all those defects. In the interests of justice it ought to be replaced by a clearer and more precise set of rules.*

The following are extracts from the draft Criminal Law Bill in Law Com. No. 218.

Part I

Non-fatal Offences Against the Person

Offences of causing injury, assault, etc.

2 (1) A person is guilty of an offence if he intentionally causes serious injury to another.

3 (1) A person is guilty of an offence if he recklessly causes serious injury to another.

4 A person is guilty of an offence if he intentionally or recklessly causes injury to another.

6 (1) A person is guilty of the offence of assault if –

(a) he intentionally or recklessly applies force to or causes an impact on the body of another –

(i) without the consent of the other, or

(ii) where the act is intended or likely to cause injury, with or without the consent of the other; or

(b) he intentionally or recklessly, without the consent of the other, causes the other to believe that any such force or impact is imminent.

(2) No such offence is committed if the force or impact, not being intended or likely to cause injury, is in the circumstances such as is generally acceptable in the ordinary conduct of daily life and the defendant does not know or believe that it is in fact unacceptable to the other person.

18 In this Part 'injury' means –

(a) physical injury, including pain, unconsciousness, or any other impairment of a person's physical condition, or

(b) impairment of a person's mental health.

Part III

36 (1) The following common law offences are abolished –

(a) common assault;

(b) battery;

....

Schedule 2
Prosecution and Punishment

(1) Provision creating offence	(2) Nature of offence	(3) How triable	(4) Punishment
2	Intentional serious injury	Only on indictment	Life
3	Reckless serious injury	Either way	On indictment: 3 years Summarily: 6 months or a fine not exceeding the statutory maximum, or both
4	Intentional or reckless injury	Either way	As for section 3
6	Assault	Only summarily	6 months or a fine not exceeding level 5 on the standard scale, or both

11

Notes

1 Sections 18, 20 and 47 of the OAPA 1861 would thus be replaced by clauses 2, 3 and 4 of the Draft Criminal Law Bill and common assault and battery would be abolished to be replaced by clause 6 assault.

2   Clauses 2 and 3 above deal with 'serious' injury intentionally or recklessly caused to another, whereas section 4 deals with 'injury' intentionally or recklessly caused. Thus, a hierarchy of seriousness of offences has been created: clause 2 is more serious than clause 3 which is more serious than clause 4 which in turn is more serious than clause 6. Under clause 6 no 'injury' has to be proved, only the application of force or an impact.

3   Clause 18 defines 'injury' but 'serious injury' is deliberately not defined. At paragraph 15.8 in Law Com. No. 218 it states that it should be left to the jury in each case to decide whether a particular harm is serious.

4   At paragraph 15.7 in Law Com. No. 218 the Commission states its belief that the deliberate or reckless infection of others with life-threatening conditions, including the HIV virus, should not be beyond the reach of the criminal law as restated by clauses 2 to 4 of the Criminal Law Bill.

5   In clause 18 there is reference to 'impairment of a person's mental health'. The Commission states at paragraph 15.28 that the word 'health' is significant because it will probably require a court having to seek medical advice to see if the condition in question has passed beyond the line that divides anxiety or distress from damage to 'health'.

Government proposals

In February 1998 the Government published a consultation document entitled, 'Violence: Reforming the Offences Against the Person Act 1861', in which they included a draft Offences Against the Person Bill which, if enacted, would be cited as the Offences Against the Person Act 1998. The Government asked for views on the consultation document by 15 May 1998. We will now see to what extent the Government's draft Bill reflects that of the Law Commission in Law Com. No. 218.

The following are extracts from the draft Offences Against the Person Bill in the Government's consultation document of February 1998:

Draft Offences Against the Person Bill

Injury and assault

1 (1) A person is guilty of an offence if he intentionally causes serious injury to another.

2 (1) A person is guilty of an offence if he recklessly causes serious injury to another.

3 (1) A person is guilty of an offence if he intentionally or recklessly causes injury to another.

4 (1) A person is guilty of an offence if –
  (a) he intentionally or recklessly applies force to or causes an impact on the body of another, or
  (b) he intentionally or recklessly causes the other to believe that any such force or impact is imminent.

   (2) No such offence is committed if the force or impact, not being intended or likely to cause injury, is in the circumstances such as is generally acceptable in the ordinary conduct of daily life and the defendant does not know or believe that it is in fact unacceptable to the other person.

15 (1) In this Act 'injury' means –
  (a) physical injury, or
  (b) mental injury.

   (2) Physical injury does not include anything caused by disease but (subject to that) it includes pain, unconsciousness and any other impairment of a person's physical condition.

   (3) Mental injury does not include anything caused by disease but (subject to that) it includes any impairment of a person's mental health.

   (4) In its application to section 1 this section applies without the exceptions relating to things caused by disease.

23   The following common law offences are abolished –
  (a) common assault;
  (b) battery; . . .

How does this draft Bill compare with that of the Law Commission in Law Com. No. 218?

The first thing to notice is that the Government's draft Bill (as regards non-fatal offences against the person) is very similar to that of the Law Commission so that there is almost a direct parallel between clauses 2, 3, 4, 6, 18 and 36 of the Law Commission's draft Bill and clauses 1, 2, 3, 4, 15 and 23 of the Government's draft Bill.

In the document, the Government stated that its main purpose was to replace the outdated offences contained in the Offences Against the Person Act 1861. It did not intend to make the law either tougher or more lenient, but to make it clearer and easier to use. It made great reference to the work of the Law Commission in this area but has then produced a draft Bill which is structured rather differently from the Law Commission's although it largely reflects the policies and principles adopted by the Commission. In clauses 1 to 4 the Government replaces the existing offences of grievous and actual

11

bodily harm and assault with a set of simple and straightforward new offences which they hope are clear and easy to understand, being based on a combination of *motivation* and *outcome*. The Government accepted the Law Commission's proposal that it was appropriate to have a subjective rather than an objective definition of recklessness for offences against the person. Although the Government uses almost indentical language when setting out these offences, their scope is slighty different as shown below.

Intentional serious injury Cl 1

Reflects the proposal of the Law Commission to replace section 18 OAPA 1861 including the proposal that liability can be imposed for omissions to act where a person omits to do an act which he has a duty to do at common law, for instance, a vehicle maintenance engineer who deliberately omits to mend faulty brakes on a vehicle intending serious injury to result.

Reckless serious injury Cl 2

Reflects the proposal of the Law Commission to replace section 20 OAPA 1861 but raises the maximum penalty to seven years' imprisonment, compared with five years at present. This is to reflect the fact that under the new offence the prosecution would have to prove that the defendant had a more blameworthy *mens rea* as they would have to prove that he foresaw a risk of *serious injury* as opposed to mere *harm* as at present (*R* v. *Mowatt* [1968]). The offence is thus more serious than the present section 20 offence.

Intentional or reckless injury Cl 3

Reflects the proposal of the Law Commission to replace section 47 OAPA 1861 but raises the maximum penalty to five years' imprisonment, compared with the Commission's proposal of three years maximum. This is to refect the fact that the offence is more serious than the present section 47 offence because the prosecution have to prove that the defendant had a more blameworthy *mens rea* because he either intended to commit injury or was reckless as to whether injury would result.

Assault Cl 4

Reflects the proposals of the Law Commission but whereas the Law Commission included the effect of consent by the victim, the Government's proposals do not refer to consent as they are awaiting the outcome of their study of consent in the criminal law.

How do these proposals impact on the transmission of illness and disease?

This is particularly significant in relation to transmission of the AIDS virus. The Law Commission recommended that the new non-fatal offences could be used to prosecute for either the intentional *or reckless* transmission of illness or diseases. However, the Government proposes that only *intentional* transmission of illness or diseases should be criminalised. It acknowledges that this is a very sensitive issue, especially as regards the Aids virus which has ramifications beyond the criminal law into the areas of social and public health policy. At paragraph 3.16 it says:

> *The Government is particularly concerned that the law should not seem to discriminate against those who are HIV positive, have Aids or viral hepatitis or who carry any kind of disease. Nor do we want to discourage people from coming forward for diagnostic tests and treatment, in the interests of their own health and that of others, because of an unfounded fear of prosecution.*

The Government also states at paragraph 3.17 that the criminal law already extends into this area although it has not been used and, at paragraph 3.19 states:

> *It is important to emphasise that this proposal does not reflect a significant change in the law. Prosecutions for the transmission of disease are very rare for very good reasons. Any criminal charge has to be supported by evidence and proved to a court beyond reasonable doubt. It is very difficult to prove both the causal linkage of the transmission and also to prove that it was done intentionally. To do so beyond reasonable doubt is even more difficult. The Government does not expect that the proposed offence will be used very often, but considers that it is important that it should exist to provide a safeguard against the worst behaviour.*

Thus, by clause 15, only those who transmit disease with intent to cause serious injury will be criminally liable under clause 1. (If you look back to the newspaper articles on the transmission of the Aids virus on page 280–83 you might see how the Government has arrived at this stance.)

11

CHAPTER Summary

The topic of non-fatal offences against the person is currently undergoing change as reflected by the new Protection from Harassment Act 1997 and the growing impetus for replacement of the Offences Against the Person Act 1861. The unsatisfactory status of the law in this area has been recognised by the Law Commission and the Government for years and is typified by the apparent loophole in the law as regards prosecution of those who wilfully transmit the Aids virus. The Government published a consultation document in February 1998 which included a draft Offences Against the Person Bill and we have seen how this builds on the draft Criminal Law Bill of the Law Commission. In this chapter 'consent' as a defence to a charge of a non-fatal offence has been considered in detail as it is often the subject of essay questions in examinations. To put present and possible future prosecution options into perspective see Figure 11.5.

Figure 11.5 Present and possible future prosecution options for non-fatal offences against the person

Effect of accused's behaviour on the victim	Current prosecution options			Possible future prosecution options as outlined in:	
	PHA 1997	**Common Law**	**OAPA 1861**	**Law Com. 218 1993**	**Govt's draft OAP Bill 1998**
Distress/annoyance	Section 2	–	–	–	–
Fear of personal violence	Section 4	Assault	–	Cl 6(1)(b)	Cl 4(1)(b)
Touching of victim/ victim's clothes	–	Battery	–	Cl 6(1)(a)	Cl 4(1)(a)
Actual bodily harm	–	–	Section 47	Cl 4	Cl 3
Wound or grievous bodily harm	–	–	Section 20/ section 18	Cl 2(1)/Cl 3(1)	Cl 1/2

PHA = Protection from Harassment Act
OAPA = Offences Against the Person Act

12 Homicide

OVERVIEW

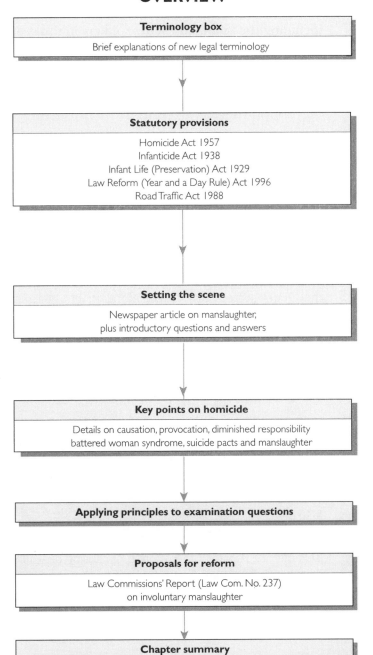

Terminology box

Brief explanations of new legal terminology

Statutory provisions

Homicide Act 1957
Infanticide Act 1938
Infant Life (Preservation) Act 1929
Law Reform (Year and a Day Rule) Act 1996
Road Traffic Act 1988

Setting the scene

Newspaper article on manslaughter,
plus introductory questions and answers

Key points on homicide

Details on causation, provocation, diminished responsibility
battered woman syndrome, suicide pacts and manslaughter

Applying principles to examination questions

Proposals for reform

Law Commissions' Report (Law Com. No. 237)
on involuntary manslaughter

Chapter summary

12

Homicide means the killing of a human being, which may be lawful or unlawful. As unlawful homicide may occur in a variety of circumstances there are serveral homicide offences, including murder, manslaughter, infanticide, child destruction and causing death by dangerous driving. For the purposes of most A-level syllabuses usually only the study of murder and manslaughter is required and, therefore, this chapter will consider these two types of homicide in detail. The other types of homicide will be mentioned only briefly. Homicide may be lawful, and so not a criminal offence, in situations including the killing of enemy soldiers in times of war and killing in self-defence.

Read the terminology box below which gives brief explanations of some of the new terminology for this chapter.

TERMINOLOGY: Homicide

Murder	Murder is the unlawful killing of a human being during the Queen's Peace with malice aforethought.
Malice aforethought	The accused either intended to kill the victim or intended to cause the victim serious bodily harm.
Voluntary manslaughter	Voluntary manslaughter is the unlawful killing of a human being during the Queen's Peace with malice aforethought which is *not* regarded as murder because the accused successfully pleads one of the three defences under the Homicide Act 1957, that is, diminished responsibility, provocation or suicide pact.
Involuntary manslaughter	Involuntary manslaughter is the unlawful killing of a human being during the Queen's Peace *without* malice aforethought.
Infanticide	This may be the offence the accused is charged with or it may be pleaded as a defence to a charge of murder. It is only applicable to women as it relates to the killing of an infant by the mother of the infant after the infant has been born but before it has reached the age of 12 months. On conviction the mother is guilty of manslaughter. It is provided for under section 1 of the Infanticide Act 1938. See the statutory provisions part of this chapter.
Causing death by dangerous driving	This offence replaced the offence of causing death by reckless driving. It is provided for under section.1 of the Road Traffic Act 1988. See the statutory provisions part of this chapter.

Child destruction   This covers the situation where a child is killed before it has an existence of its own independent of its mother. Thus, it covers those situations where a child is still in the mother's womb or is in the process of being born. It is provided for under section 1 of the Infant Life (Preservation) Act 1929. See the statutory provisions part of this chapter.

Statutory provisions

Homicide Act 1957

2   (1) Where a person kills or is a party to the killing of another, he shall not be convicted of murder if he was suffering from such abnormality of mind (whether arising from a condition of arrested or retarded development of mind or any inherent causes or induced by disease or injury) as substantially impaired his mental responsibility for his acts and omissions in doing or being a party to the killing.

    (2) On a charge of murder, it shall be for the defence to prove that the person charged is by virtue of this section not liable to be convicted of murder.

    (3) A person who but for this section would be liable, whether as a principal or as accessory, to be convicted of murder shall be liable instead to be convicted of manslaughter.

    (4) The fact that one party to a killing is by virtue of this section not liable to be convicted of murder shall not affect the question whether the killing amounted to murder in the case of any other party to it.

3   Where on a charge of murder there is evidence on which the jury can find that the person charged was provoked (whether by things done or by things said or by both together) to lose his self-control, the question whether the provocation was enough to make a reasonable man do as he did shall be left to be determined by the jury; and in determining that question the jury shall take into account everything both done and said according to the effect which, in their opinion, it would have on a reasonable man.

12

4 (1) It shall be manslaughter, and shall not be murder, for a person in pursuance of a suicide pact between him and another to kill the other or be a party to the other ... being killed by a third person.

(2) Where it is shown that a person charged with the murder of another killed the other or was a party to his ... being killed, it shall be for the defence to prove that the person charged was acting in pursuance of a suicide pact between him and the other.

(3) For the purposes of this section 'suicide pact' means a common agreement between two or more persons having for its object the death of all of them, whether or not each is to take his own life, but nothing done by a person who enters into a suicide pact shall be treated as done by him in pursuance of the pact unless it is done while he has the settled intention of dying in pursuance of the pact.

Infanticide Act 1938

1 (1) Where a woman by any wilful act or omission causes the death of her child being a child under the age of twelve months, but at the time of the act or mission the balance of her mind was disturbed by reason of her not having fully recovered from the effect of giving birth to the child or by reason of the effect of lactation consequent upon the birth of the child, then, notwithstanding that the circumstances were such that but for this Act the offence would have amounted to murder, she shall be guilty of felony, to wit of infanticide, and may for such offence be dealt with and punished as if she had been guilty of the offence of manslaughter of the child.

Law Reform (Year and a Day Rule) Act 1996

1 The rule known as the 'year and a day rule' (that is, the rule that, for the purposes of offences involving death and of suicide, an act or omission is conclusively presumed not to have caused a person's death if more than a year and a day elapsed before he died) is abolished for all purposes.

2 (1) Proceedings to which this section applies may only be instituted by or with the consent of the Attorney General.

(2) This section applies to proceedings against a person for a fatal offence if –
   (a) the injury alleged to have caused the death was sustained more than three years before the death occurred, or
   (b) the person has previously been convicted of an offence committed in circumstances alleged to be connected with the death.

Infant Life (Preservation) Act 1929

1 (1) Subject as hereinafter in this subsection provided, any person who, with intent to destroy the life of a child capable of being born alive, by any wilful act causes a child to die before it has an existence independent of its mother, shall be guilty of felony, to wit, of child destruction, and shall be liable on conviction thereof on indictment to penal servitude for life.

Road Traffic Act 1988

1 A person who causes the death of another person by driving a mechanically propelled vehicle dangerously on a road or other public place is guilty of an offence.

Setting the scene

Read the extract below, taken from *The Times* dated 24 April 1998, and answer the questions.

Soldier jailed for killing lover

By Russell Jenkins

A FORMER soldier who once saved shoppers' lives by carrying a live bomb out of a crowded department store in Northern Ireland was jailed for 4¹/₂ years yesterday at Mold Crown Court for killing his lover.

Hefin Jones, 45, a Royal Welch Fusilier, stopped taking medication to combat chronic depression three weeks after moving in with his lover, Elaine Topham, 41, a mother of two, in her flat in Colwyn Bay, Clwyd.

Jones, a chronic alcoholic who had been in and out of hospital for his psychiatric disorders over two decades, said he threw his drugs down the toilet at the suggestion of his lover. Later he killed her after a quarrel developed from a drinking session, breaking bones in her neck and face. Mrs Topham, who had 31 separate injuries to her body, died from internal bleeding after a heavy blow to her stomach. Jones denied murdering Mrs Topham, but his plea of guilty to manslaughter due to diminished responsibility was accepted by the prosecution. Jones told the court that he remembered nothing of the attack on Mrs Topham.

Mr Justice Thomas told him that he had beaten the dead woman horrifically, punching, kicking and using a belt on her. He said: "What happened that night was a result of both drinking heavily and you not taking medication and was a tragedy, particularly so for her two children."

The court was told that Jones suffered post-traumatic stress disorder after serving three tours in Northern Ireland with the fusiliers in the 1970s. He had been admitted voluntarily 20 times over more than 20 years at the former North Wales Hospital for Nervous Disorders, in Denbigh, where he was treated for depression.

Alex Carlisle, QC, for the defence, told the court that Jones had been unable to cope with his experiences following his military experience in the Province.

On one occasion, contrary to accepted practise, he carried a bomb out of a Woolworths store in Londonderry and threw it over a fence into a field.

Even more traumatic was an incident when a friend and fellow fusilier was blown up in front of him. Jones was given the responsibility of collecting his friend's remains and arranging for them to be sent for autopsy.

Mr Carlisle said there had been some kind of quarrel in which Jones had uncharacteristically exploded. The future risk of any repetition was remote, he said.

Michael Farmer, QC, for the prosecution, said that it was clear that she had been dead for some time before the alarm was raised. He said that, although Jones had stopped accepting psychiatric help, there was no way that he could be compelled to take treatment.

Source: *The Times*, 24 April 1998

12

Questions

1 Why is this case concerned with homicide?

2 Why do you think Hefin Jones denied murder?

3 Why do you think that he pleaded guilty to manslaughter due to diminished responsibility?

4 Diminished responsibility is a defence specific to a murder charge (it is not available for any other offences) but it has to be proved by the defence on a balance of probabilities. What does this tell us about the burden and standard of proof for this defence?

5 For diminished responsibility the defendant has to be suffering from an 'abnormality of mind' and it is for the jury to determine whether the defendant was so suffering. In this case what factors do you think would have led the jury to decide that Hefin Jones was suffering from an abnormality of mind?

6 Why do you think it was significant that Hefin Jones was a 'chronic' alcoholic?

7 Do you think that most homicides are committed by acquaintances or by strangers?

Answers

1 This case is concerned with homicide as homicide relates to the killing of a human being by another human being during the Queen's Peace. This homicide is an unlawful homicide as none of the conditions for making it a lawful homicide exist.

2 Hefin Jones could have denied the murder charge for several reasons. On conviction for murder he would have received an automatic sentence of life imprisonment. The judge has no discretion in this although the trial judge would be able to set the 'tariff' or minimum time Hefin would have had to spend in prison (as retribution for the offence) before his case could be reviewed by the Parole Board. On release from prison Hefin would not be a free man; he would only be released 'on licence' as was the case with Private Lee Clegg who was convicted of the murder of a woman in Northern Ireland at a road check-point. To be convicted of murder the prosecution have to prove that the defendant intended to kill the victim or intended to cause the victim serious bodily harm. Hefin might have denied any such intention. However, if the murder charge had been pursued in court the jury might not have believed his story and might have convicted him of murder and so it might have seemed the lesser of two evils to plead guilty to manslaughter due to diminished responsibility. This plea was accepted by the prosecution because in a murder trial it is the responsibility of the defence to raise this plea and defence.

3   Hefin Jones might have pleaded guilty to manslaughter due to diminished responsibility due to some of the factors mentioned above and due to the fact that if convicted of manslaughter the judge has more discretion when it comes to sentencing him; he would not automatically receive a life sentence. He could receive a hospital order under section 37 of the Mental Health Act 1983, a determinate or fixed term of imprisonment, probation order and so forth. The statistics shown at Figure 12.1, which are taken from *Criminal Statistics England and Wales 1996*, published by the Home Office, may help to demonstrate why Hefin Jones decided on his plea. Under the heading of 'other manslaughter' (part 2 of the table – which comprises diminished responsibility and suicide pact) it can be seen that on conviction the majority of defendants receive a sentence of between four to 10 years or under four years. This has to be 'better' than a life sentence.

4   Normally in a criminal trial the prosecution have to prove beyond all reasonable doubt that the defendant committed the offence. Thus, the burden of proof is normally on the prosecution and the standard of proof is a high one, *beyond all reasonable doubt*. However, with diminished responsibility, the defence bear the burden of proving that the defendant was suffering from diminished responsibility at the time of the killing. Because this is a reversal of the normal burden of proof in criminal trials, the defence only have to prove that the defendant was so suffering to a lesser standard of proof, *on the balance of probabilities*, which is the usual standard of proof in civil cases. Thus, in this case, the defence satisfied the jury that Hefin Jones was probably suffering from an abnormality of mind at the time he killed his lover.

12

5   In this case Hefin Jones was a chronic alcoholic who had been in and out of hospital for his psychiatric disorders for over 20 years. He was also a chronic depressive and he suffered from post-traumatic stress disorder after serving three tours in Northern Ireland . Thus, there was plenty of medical evidence on which the jury could determine that Hefin Jones was, on the balance of probabilities, suffering from an abnormality of mind at the time he killed his lover.

England and Wales

Sentence[2]	Male suspects										Female suspects										Total suspects									
	1987	1988	1989	1990	1991	1992	1993	1994	1995	1996	1987	1988	1989	1990	1991	1992	1993	1994	1995	1996	1987	1988	1989	1990	1991	1992	1993	1994	1995	1996
Murder																														
Life imprisonment[3]	206	180	190	179	186	195	216	206	240	136	9	9	8	7	10	19	8	20	9	8	215	189	198	186	196	214	224	226	249	144
Section 2 manslaughter																														
Immediate imprisonment:[4]																														
Life[3]	8	4	8	9	12	7	4	9	7	5	2	—	—	—	1	—	—	—	—	—	10	4	8	9	13	7	4	9	7	5
Over 10 years (excluding life)	1	1	—	1	—	—	—	—	—	—	—	—	—	—	—	—	—	—	—	—	1	1	—	1	—	—	—	—	—	—
Over 4 and up to 10 years	7	13	9	8	11	19	6	7	6	8	—	—	1	—	—	1	1	—	1	—	7	13	10	8	12	19	7	7	7	8
4 years and under	10	4	9	6	3	7	4	6	4	1	1	2	4	1	—	3	—	3	—	—	11	6	13	7	3	10	4	9	4	1
Fully suspended sentence	—	1	—	—	1	—	1	1	—	—	—	—	—	—	—	—	—	—	—	—	—	1	—	—	1	—	1	1	—	—
Hospital/Restriction Order	25	30	19	25	26	28	26	30	16	12	4	1	5	5	5	4	7	3	2	4	29	31	24	30	31	32	33	33	18	16
Hospital order	9	4	9	10	3	2	3	4	9	3	4	4	1	—	—	2	2	1	3	—	13	8	10	10	3	4	5	5	12	3
Probation/Supervision	4	5	7	3	5	5	4	2	1	—	2	4	9	2	7	1	3	2	4	1	6	9	16	5	12	6	7	4	5	1
Other sentence	—	—	1	—	—	—	—	—	1	—	1	—	—	—	—	—	—	—	—	—	—	—	1	—	—	1	—	—	1	—
Total	64	62	62	62	62	68	49	59	44	29	14	12	21	8	14	10	13	9	10	5	78	74	83	70	76	78	62	68	54	34

Number of persons

Figure 12.1A
Suspects convicted of homicide by type of homicide and sentence[1] (Source: *Criminal Statistics England and Wales 1996*, Home Office)

England and Wales — Number of persons

Sentence[2]	Male suspects										Female suspects										Total suspects									
	1987	1988	1989	1990	1991	1992	1993	1994	1995	1996	1987	1988	1989	1990	1991	1992	1993	1994	1995	1996	1987	1988	1989	1990	1991	1992	1993	1994	1995	1996
Other manslaughter																														
Immediate imprisonment:[4]																														
Life[3]	4	–	1	6	5	1	6	7	6	3	–	–	1	–	2	–	–	1	–	–	4	–	2	6	7	1	6	8	6	3
Over 10 years (excluding life)	6	6	2	1	1	3	1	3	8	4	1	–	–	–	–	1	–	–	–	4	7	6	2	1	1	4	1	3	8	4
Over 4 and up to 10 years	78	79	77	75	82	90	98	84	88	69	8	7	5	4	4	13	9	5	8	4	86	86	82	79	86	103	107	89	96	73
4 years and under	87	81	66	66	93	70	76	69	76	32	8	15	6	6	7	6	5	9	16	7	95	96	72	72	100	76	81	78	92	39
Fully suspended sentence	6	9	4	6	7	3	4	3	3	2	2	5	2	2	4	3	1	1	–	–	8	14	6	8	11	6	5	4	3	2
Hospital/Restriction Order	4	–	–	–	–	–	–	–	–	2	–	–	2	–	–	–	–	–	–	–	4	–	2	–	–	–	–	–	–	2
Hospital order	–	1	1	–	1	–	–	1	1	–	–	–	–	–	–	1	–	–	–	–	–	1	–	–	1	1	–	1	1	–
Probation/Supervision	9	8	–	8	5	5	3	4	4	2	3	10	7	7	12	7	4	4	2	2	12	18	7	15	17	12	7	8	6	4
Other sentence	4	–	3	2	–	1	–	1	–	–	–	–	–	–	–	–	–	–	–	–	4	–	3	2	–	1	–	1	–	–
Total	198	184	154	164	194	174	188	171	186	114	22	37	22	19	29	30	19	20	27	13	220	221	176	183	223	204	207	191	213	127
Infanticide																														
Hospital/Restriction Order	*	*	*	*	*	*	*	*	*	*	–	–	–	–	–	–	–	–	–	–	–	–	–	–	–	–	–	–	–	–
Hospital Order	*	*	*	*	*	*	*	*	*	*	8	7	1	4	4	4	5	3	2	3	8	7	1	4	4	4	5	3	2	3
Probation/Supervision	*	*	*	*	*	*	*	*	*	*	–	1	–	–	1	2	–	–	–	–	–	1	–	–	1	2	–	–	–	–
Total	*	*	*	*	*	*	*	*	*	*	8	8	1	4	5	6	5	3	2	3	8	8	1	4	5	6	5	3	2	3
Total	468	426	406	405	442	437	453	436	470	279	46	66	52	38	58	65	45	52	48	29	514	492	458	443	500	502	498	488	518	308

Notes:

1 As at 1 August 1997; figures are subject to revision as cases are dealt with by the police and by the courts, or as further information becomes available.

2 The results of appeals have been taken into account in compiling the table.

3 Including detention during Her Majesty's Pleasure under section 53(1) Children and Young Persons Act 1933 and custody for life.

4 Including detention under section 53(2) Children and Young Persons Act 1933 partly suspended sentences and young offender institution.

Figure 12.1B Suspects convicted of homicide by type of homicide and sentence[1] (continued) (Source: *Criminal Statistics England and Wales 1996*, Home Office)

12

England and Wales	Number of offences																													
Apparent circumstances[2]	Acquaintance										Stranger[3]										All relationships									
	1987	1988	1989	1990	1991	1992	1993	1994	1995	1996	1987	1988	1989	1990	1991	1992	1993	1994	1995	1996	1987	1988	1989	1990	1991	1992	1993	1994	1995	1996
Quarrel, revenge or loss of temper	234	208	215	239	286	292	215	229	269	249	62	65	51	57	73	60	52	57	86	84	296	273	266	296	359	352	267	286	355	333
In furtherance of theft or gain	23	14	16	19	18	12	15	14	19	11	37	32	27	24	25	29	25	34	34	24	60	46	43	43	43	41	40	48	53	35
Attributed to acts of terrorism[4,5]	–	–	–	–	–	–	–	–	–	–	7	2	11	3	1	5	3	–	–	2	7	2	11	3	1	5	3	–	1	2
While resisting or avoiding arrest[6]	–	–	–	–	–	–	–	–	–	–	2	1	–	1	3	1	2	1	–	–	2	1	–	1	3	1	2	1	1	–
Attributed to gang warfare, feud or faction fighting	1	4	2	3	4	1	4	3	2	–	4	2	4	2	3	–	4	6	10	3	5	6	6	5	7	1	8	9	12	3
The result of offences of arson	2	4	8	–	5	3	3	6	10	5	3	6	3	1	1	2	2	2	6	6	5	10	11	1	6	3	5	8	16	11
Other circumstances[7]	41	32	41	25	27	32	40	41	25	40	28	24	20	14	18	13	15	18	23	30	69	56	61	39	45	45	55	59	48	70
Not known: Suspect committed suicide[8]	43	42	29	33	48	36	30	38	–	–	15	1	6	2	3	3	–	4	–	–	58	43	35	35	51	39	30	42	–	–
Suspect mentally disturbed	18	20	26	32	18	11	31	38	27	20	5	–	2	2	1	1	3	8	10	7	23	20	28	34	19	12	34	46	37	27
Other[9]	26	37	13	25	14	16	33	34	51	54	48	53	50	73	75	66	89	102	90	92	74	90	63	98	89	82	122	136	141	146
Total	338	361	350	376	420	401	371	403	403	379	211	186	174	179	203	180	195	232	260	248	599	547	524	555	623	581	566	635	663	627

Figure 12.2 Offences currently[1] recorded as homicide by apparent circumstances and relationship of victim to principal suspect (Source: *Criminal Statistics England and Wales 1996*, Home Office)

6   It was significant that Hefin Jones was a 'chronic' alcoholic as intoxication is not usually allowed as a defence to a criminal charge. However, when the defendant is a chronic alcoholic his condition is more akin to a disease of the mind and is a permanent condition. Occasional intoxication through drink or drugs is not permanent nor a disease of the mind. Hefin Jones was also a chronic depressive.

7   Most homicides are committed by acquaintances as the table in Figure 12.2 clearly shows. Thus, of the 627 homicides committed in 1996, 379 were committed by acquaintances and only 248 by strangers. This table also reveals that most homicides are the result of a quarrel, revenge or loss of temper.

Key points on homicide

▶   In this chapter only the homicide offences of murder and manslaughter will be considered.

▶   There are two types of manslaughter: voluntary and involuntary, and their relationship with murder is shown in the diagram at Figure 12.3.

▶   It can be seen from the definitions given in the terminology box at the beginning of this chapter that murder and both types of manslaughter have the same *actus reus*, that is, the unlawful killing of a human being during the Queen's Peace. This definition is based on the definition of murder put forward by Coke in the seventeenth century. It is important to stress that this definition of murder is a common law definition; the definition of murder does not appear in the Homicide Act 1957. The *actus reus* of homicide will be discussed below in more detail.

▶   The *mens rea* for murder is malice aforethought which has been discussed at length in Chapter 2, on *mens rea* and *actus reus*. Thus, the *mens rea* for murder is either intention to kill the victim or intention to cause the victim serious bodily harm. The key word is *intention*. Refer back to the discussion on this topic before proceeding through this chapter.

12

▶ The *mens rea* for voluntary manslaughter is the same as for murder and the accused would be convicted of murder were it not for the existence of three defences as provided for in the Homicide Act 1957, that is: diminished responsibility; provocation; and suicide pacts. These defences are discussed in more detail below.

▶ For involuntary manslaughter the unlawful killing of a human being is effected *without* malice aforethought. As such the *mens rea* is different to that of murder and voluntary manslaughter.

There are two types of involuntary manslaughter: first, there is 'unlawful and dangerous act manslaughter' which is also known as constructive manslaughter; and second, there is 'gross negligence manslaughter'. Both of these are discussed in detail below. For unlawful and dangerous act manslaughter the *mens rea* is the same as for the unlawful act which brought about the death. For gross negligence manslaughter it is arguable that there is no true *mens rea* at all as gross negligence is an objective test.

▶ The relationship between murder and the two types of manslaughter is shown in Figure 12.3 which clearly shows how both murder and voluntary manslaughter share the same *mens rea* of intention to kill or cause serious bodily harm.

▶ Until the Law Reform (Year and a Day Rule) Act 1996 for these homicide offences the death of the victim had to occur within a year and a day of the *actus reus*. However, this no longer applies; see the statutory provisions part of this chapter. The advent of life-support machines means that victims are being kept alive beyond a year and a day and so homicide charges could not be brought against the accused if the victim then died after this time. Now the only *caveat* on initiating homicide proceedings is as provided for in section 2 of the Act. Thus when death occurs more than three years after the injury or if the accused has already been convicted of another offence for the injury (which has now resulted in death) the permission of the Attorney-General has to be obtained before the prosecution can take place.

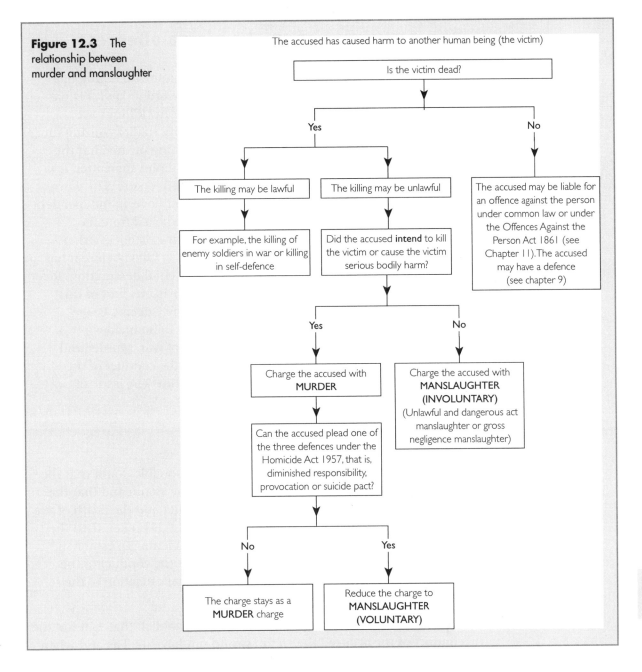

Figure 12.3 The relationship between murder and manslaughter

The accused has caused harm to another human being (the victim)

Is the victim dead?

Yes / No

Yes:

The killing may be lawful → For example, the killing of enemy soldiers in war or killing in self-defence

The killing may be unlawful → Did the accused **intend** to kill the victim or cause the victim serious bodily harm?

No: The accused may be liable for an offence against the person under common law or under the Offences Against the Person Act 1861 (see Chapter 11). The accused may have a defence (see chapter 9)

Did the accused intend...? Yes / No

Yes: Charge the accused with **MURDER**

↓

Can the accused plead one of the three defences under the Homicide Act 1957, that is, diminished responsibility, provocation or suicide pact?

No / Yes

No: The charge stays as a **MURDER** charge

Yes: Reduce the charge to **MANSLAUGHTER (VOLUNTARY)**

No: Charge the accused with **MANSLAUGHTER (INVOLUNTARY)** (Unlawful and dangerous act manslaughter or gross negligence manslaughter)

12

The *actus reus* of the homicide offences

The *actus reus* of the homicide offences is the unlawful killing of a human being during the Queen's Peace. The word unlawful is part of the definition as it serves as a reminder that some killings are regarded as lawful, such as the killing of enemy soldiers during times of war or killing in self-defence. The word killing means that the victim was alive at the time of the incident and dies thereafter. It is generally accepted that by 'dead' is meant 'brain dead'. The words 'human being' mean that the being killed must have an independent existence, thus a baby must have been fully expelled from its mother's body in order to have an independent existence. Other offences deal with the situation where a child is killed before it has an existence independent of the mother, such as child destruction. Refer back to the terminology box and statutory provisions part of this chapter for more details. The words 'during the Queen's Peace' remind us that these homicide offences relate to homicides committed in peacetime as opposed to times of war. Murder and manslaughter are result crimes and, as such, the conduct of the accused must have *caused* the death of the victim. The issue of causation will now be considered in detail.

Causation

The prosecution have to prove beyond all reasonable doubt that the conduct of the accused caused the death of the victim and that the *chain of causation* between the accused's conduct and the death of the victim was not broken; if the chain of causation is broken then the accused will not be liable for the death of the victim. To establish causation the prosecution must establish that the conduct of the accused amounted to both the factual and legal causation of the victim's death.

Factual causation – the prosecution must establish that 'but for' the conduct of the accused the victim would not have died as and when they did. See *R* v. *White* (1910) in the 'You Decide' cases which follow.

Legal causation – the prosecution must also establish that the conduct of the accused was the legal cause of the victim's death. Legal causation can be discussed under the following headings:

  i the *de minimis* principle;
  ii the *thin skull* principle;
iii intervening acts.

i The *de minimis* principle

Under this principle the accused will not be held to have caused the death of the victim if the conduct of the accused only amounted to a minimal cause of death. It is not clear when the conduct of the accused is to be regarded as more than a minimal cause of death and this is an issue which has to be determined by the jury. In the case of R v. *Pagett* (1983) (see below for details) Lord Goff L.J. said: '... *the accused's act need not be the sole cause, or even the main cause, of the victim's death, it being enough that **his act contributed significantly to that result**.'* It will be apparent that this principle could have significance when a doctor administers pain-relieving drugs to terminally ill patients.

ii The *thin-skull* principle

Under this principle the accused cannot escape liability by relying on the attributes of the victim which, unknown to the accused, made the victim more likely to die as a result of the accused's conduct. Thus, if the victim dies because of a pre-existing medical condition, mental condition or religious belief which made him more susceptible to death as a result of the accused's conduct then such conditions will not afford the accused a defence to a homicide charge. In the case of R v. *Blaue* (1975) the victim of a stabbing refused vital surgery and a blood transfusion because she was a Jehovah's Witness. Such medical treatment could have saved her life but because she refused the treatment she died. The accused was convicted of manslaughter which was upheld on appeal as it was held that assailants must take their victims as they find them.

iii Intervening acts

The accused may argue that, between his conduct and the death of the victim, some intervening act occurred, a *novus actus interveniens*, which broke the chain of causation, in which case the accused should not be held liable for the death. This is shown in Figure 12.4.

12

Figure 12.4 Causation and intervening acts

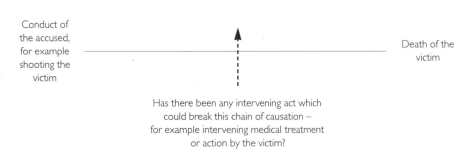

This problem will be considered through the cases of *R* v. *Jordan* (1956), *R* v. *Smith* (1959), *R* v. *Cheshire* (1991), *R* v. *Melcherek & Steel* (1981) and *Airedale National Health Service Trust* v. *Bland* (1993). See also *R* v. *Dear* (1996) in the 'You Decide' cases which follow.

R v. *Jordan* (1956)

In this case the accused had stabbed the victim who died eight days after the wound had been stitched. The accused was convicted of murder. However, on appeal the conviction for murder was quashed. It was revealed that at the time of death the wound had healed and that death was due to the fact that the victim had been given a second injection of an antibiotic to stop infection despite the fact that he had reacted badly to the first injection of this antibiotic. Moreover, the victim had been given abnormally large quantities of liquid intravenously and this had waterlogged his lungs causing pneumonia from which he died. It was held that *normal* medical treatment of injuries did not break the chain of causation between the conduct of the accused and the victim's death but that *palpably wrong* medical treatment did. In this case the medical treatment was regarded as palpably wrong. It will be shown that this case was unusual as medical treatment does not normally break the chain of causation.

R v. *Smith* (1959)

In this case soldiers were fighting in a barrack block and the victim was stabbed twice with a bayonet. The soldier who carried him to the medical centre dropped him twice and on arrival at the medical centre the medics failed to notice that one of his lungs had been pierced by the bayonet and that he was haemorrhaging, that is, bleeding heavily. The medics gave the victim saline solution, oxygen and artificial respiration but the victim died. This medical treatment was described as 'thoroughly bad' because the type of haemorrhage concerned can usually be stopped and, had there been a blood transfusion, then the victim would have had a good chance of recovery. The accused was convicted of murder at his trial and appealed against conviction, arguing that the treatment by the medics had broken the chain of causation between the stabbing and the death of the victim. He relied on the case of *Jordan* claiming that the medical treatment in his case was also abnormal. The appeal was dismissed – the conviction stood. Lord Parker C.J. said :

> ... *if at the time of death the original wound is still an operating cause and a substantial cause*, then the death can properly be said to be the result of the wound, albeit that some other cause of death is also operating. Only if it can be said that the original wound is merely the

setting in which another cause operates can it be said that the death did not result from the wound. Putting it another way, only if the second cause is so overwhelming as to make the original wound part of the history can it be said that the death does not flow from the wound ... in the opinion of the court [the facts of the case] can only lead to one conclusion: a man is stabbed in the back, his lung is pierced and haemorrhage results; two hours later he dies of haemorrhage from that wound; in the interval there is no time for a careful examination, and the treatment given turns out in the light of subsequent knowledge to have been inappropriate and, indeed, harmful. In those circumstances no reasonable jury or court could, properly directed, in our view possibly come to any other conclusion than the death resulted from the original wound. Accordingly the court dismisses this appeal.

R v. *Malcherek* **and** *R* v. *Steel* **(1981)**

These two cases came to the Court of Appeal together as they concerned the same point, namely, whether by turning off a life support machine a doctor broke the chain of causation between the acts of the accused and the death of the victim. In the *Malcherek* case the accused had stabbed his wife in the abdomen with a knife and in the *Steel* case the accused had attacked a girl, causing severe head injuries. Both victims were put on life support machines and after the doctors had carried out several tests which confirmed that the victims were brain-dead, the life support machines were turned off. At trial the two accused were convicted of murder. Their appeals were dismissed, the convictions for murder were upheld. Lord Lane C. J. said:

Where a medical practitioner adopting methods which are generally accepted comes bona fide and conscientiously to the conclusion that the patient is for all practical purposes dead, and that such vital functions as exist (for example, circulation) are being maintained solely by mechanical means, and therefore discontinues treatment, that does not prevent the person who inflicted the initial injury from being responsible for the victim's death. Putting it another way, the discontinuance of treatment in those circumstances does not break the chain of causation between the initial injury and the death.

12

R v. *Cheshire* **(1991)**

In this case the victim was shot in the leg and abdomen by the accused and underwent surgery which involved a tracheotomy – insertion of a tube into the windpipe in the neck – when the victim developed breathing problems. Two months after the original wounding, when the gunshot wounds were healed, and after the tracheotomy tube had been removed, the victim died as the medics had not properly diagnosed why he was having breathing problems. The accused was convicted of murder at trial and appealed. The appeal was dismissed, the conviction was upheld. Beldam L.J. said:

> When the victim of a criminal attack is treated for wounds or injuries by doctors or other medical staff attempting to repair the harm done, it will only be in the most extraordinary and unusual case that such treatment can be said to be so independent of the acts of the defendant that it could be regarded in law as the cause of the victim's death to the exclusion of the defendant's acts ... Even though negligence in the treatment of the victim was the immediate cause of his death, the jury should not regard it as excluding the responsibility of the defendant unless the negligent treatment was so independent of his acts, and it itself so potent in causing death, that they regard the contribution made by his acts as insignificant ... Even if more experienced doctors than those who attended the deceased would have recognised the rare complication in time to have prevented the deceased's death, that complication was **a direct consequence of the appellant's acts, which remained a significant cause of this death**. We cannot conceive that, on the evidence given, any jury would have found otherwise.

Airedale National Health Service Trust v. Bland (1993)

This case concerned Anthony Bland who was injured during the Hillsborough football stadium disaster such that he had irreversible brain damage and was left in a persistent vegetative state. Initially there was hope that he might recover and so it was felt to be in his best interests to feed him and ventilate him artificially in order to keep him alive. As such his doctors had a duty imposed on them to keep him alive by these methods. However, after being cared for in this manner for three and a half years with no signs of improvement, it was the considered medical opinion that there was no hope of Anthony ever recovering. As such the Heath Service Trust and the family applied to the High Court for a declaration that it would be lawful for life support treatment to be discontinued other than was necessary to allow Anthony to die comfortably. The Official Solicitor took the case all the way to the House of Lords, arguing that the withdrawal of life support would be a breach of the doctors' duty to care for the patient and so would amount to a criminal offence. The House of Lords upheld the decision of the High Court to grant the declaration that ending the life supporting treatment would not be unlawful. Lord Mustill justified the decision in terms of there being no general liability in the criminal law for omissions other than when, *inter alia*, there was a duty to act. Thus, in this case, whereas originally the doctors were under a duty to support Anthony's life artificially because it was in his best interests to do so as there was hope of recovery, when it became apparent that there was no hope of recovery it was not in Anthony's best interests to be kept alive artificially and so the doctors had no duty to keep him alive artificially. Thus, as the doctors were not under a duty to act they could not be held criminally liable for failing to act, for an omission. Although the House of Lords was acting in its civil capacity in this case the judgment will nevertheless be highly persuasive for any criminal case involving the termination of artificial life support, such as when the victim has been stabbed and needs artificial life support.

R v. *Pagett* (1983)

In this case the appellant had abducted a girl, Gail Kinchen, and armed police had surrounded the house. When the appellant tried to leave the house, using Gail Kinchen as a shield and firing shots at the police, Gail was killed by the instinctive return fire of the police. Lord Goff held that where the immediate cause of the victim's death was the act of a third party (in this case the police officers), the question of whether or not the accused is guilty of either murder or manslaughter is a question of causation and, in particular, of whether or not the actions of the third party amounted to a *novus actus interveniens*. Lord Goff held that the accused's act need not be the sole cause or even the main cause of the victim's death, it being enough that his conduct contributed significantly to that result. In this case it was obvious that the conduct of the appellant had contributed significantly to the death of the victim – but for his actions Gail would not have died. Lord Goff referred to the acclaimed work of Professors Hart and Honore, *Causation in the Law*, in which the authors suggest that involuntary conduct by a third party does not relieve the accused of criminal liability. Involuntary conduct included:

i a reasonable act performed for the purpose of self-preservation; and
ii an act done in performance of a legal duty.

In such instances the accused might be guilty of murder or manslaughter depending on whether the ingredients of the offences were proved. Lord Goff held that if police officers shot and killed an innocent bystander while acting in reasonable self-defence to a lethal attack, then on such facts it would have been open to the jury to convict the accused of either murder or manslaughter. In the present case, the appellant had committed two unlawful and dangerous acts: the holding of the girl as a shield and the shooting at police officers. Either of these acts could constitute the *actus reus* of manslaughter or

12

murder by the appellant even though the fatal shot was fired by a police officer.

Voluntary manslaughter

It can be seen from Figure 12.3 that voluntary manslaughter would be murder but for the fact that the accused can avail himself of one of the three defences specific to a murder charge which are found in the Homicide Act 1957. Thus the *actus reus* and *mens rea* of murder have been proven. The three defences which only apply to a murder charge are:

Homicide Act 1957	section 2	diminished responsibility;
	section 3	provocation;
	section 4	suicide pact.

Refer to the statutory provisions part of this chapter where these sections are shown in more detail. Each of these defences will now be considered in detail.

Diminished responsibility

This defence to a murder charge has to be raised by the defence which they have to prove on a balance of probabilities. Thus the normal burden of proof (that the prosecution has to prove its case beyond all reasonable doubt) is reversed, but to compensate for this the standard of proof is lower, the civil standard. Since this defence was introduced in 1957, insanity as a defence is rarely used in murder cases as diminished responsibility covers a wider range of mental disorders than insanity and allows for greater discretion on sentencing. The essence of the defence is that the accused was suffering from:

i an abnormality of mind;
ii which substantially impaired his mental responsibility;
iii for his acts or omissions at the time of the killing.

It is for the jury to determine whether the accused was suffering from an abnormality of mind but they can only do so on the basis of medical evidence. The problem is that what amounts to an abnormality of mind varies even between psychiatrists and, despite the guidance given in section two, that abnormality of mind may exist due to:

i arrested development of mind;
ii retarded development of mind;

iii any inherent causes;

iv when induced by disease; or

v when induced by injury.

In the case of *R* v. *Byrne* (1960) abnormality of mind was defined by Lord Parker C. J. as 'a state of mind so different from that of ordinary human beings that the reasonable man would term it abnormal'. In this case the phrases 'partial insanity' and 'being on the borderline of insanity' were approved as appropriate phrases which a judge could use when directing the jury. However, it must be noted that it is for the jury to determine whether or not the accused was acting with an abnormal mind at the time of the killing and quite often juries seem to base this decision on *moral* grounds. Thus, if the defendant has committed a 'mercy killing' of a terminally ill spouse, for example, while in a very depressed and anxious state, the jury might say that the defendant was suffering from an abnormality of mind. Likewise, a woman might be regarded as suffering from an abnormality of mind where she kills when suffering from pre-menstrual tension.

Generally, intoxication will not amount to an abnormality of mind unless it is shown that the defendant was suffering from long-term alcoholism or drug-taking which could be described as a disease – *R* v. *Tandy* (1988). If the killing took place when the defendant was suffering from an abnormality of mind caused partly by intoxication and partly due to inherent causes, then the jury have to consider the issue of diminished responsibility from the point of view of the inherent causes only – *R* v. *Gittens* (1984). The relationship between diminished responsibility and provocation is shown in the case of *R* v. *Hobson* (1997) in the newspaper extract on page 347. In some cases a woman suffering from battered woman syndrome (BWS), who killed her husband, might not have been able to rely on the defence of provocation (as there was a time lapse between the provocative act and the killing) but might have been able to rely on the defence of diminished responsibility. However, as is shown below, the courts now take a different view of provocation and women suffering from BWS who kill their husbands may be able to use the defence of provocation. Refer back to the setting the scene part of this chapter for more discussion on diminished responsibility.

Provocation

This defence is provided for by section 3 of the Homicide Act 1957 and it can be analysed by a close consideration of the words in the section. It will be seen how provocation involves a two-part test, one subjective and one objective, both of which are left to be determined

12

by the jury. The issue of battered woman syndrome will also be considered in this section.

i *Where on a charge of murder* – these words show that this defence only applies when the accused has been charged with murder.

ii *There is evidence* – there must be evidence of specific provocative acts or words before the jury can determine whether or not the accused was provoked. It is not necessary for the defence of provocation to have been raised by the defence, as if the judge decides that there is evidence raising the possibility of the defence of provocation, he must direct the jury on provocation. The need for specific provocative acts or words was shown in the case of *R* v. *Acott* (1997) in which the defence of provocation was held not to be available to the accused because there was no evidence of specific provocative acts or words. In this case a son was accused of murdering his mother and was convicted at trial. This conviction was upheld in the Court of Appeal and there followed an appeal to the House of Lords. Throughout the police investigation and at trial, the accused denied that he had killed his mother, saying that her injuries were caused by a fall. He said that his relationship with his mother was good and that she had done nothing to anger him. He maintained that he was innocent of any attack on his mother and should be acquitted. Thus, the accused denied the existence of any provocative acts by his mother. However, on appeal his counsel *suggested* that provocation should be left to the jury as, during cross examination at the trial, it was *suggested* that his mother provoked him and that this led to him attacking her and killing her. The House of Lords held that it would be wrong for the trial judge to direct the jury on provocation when there was only the *speculative possibility* of provocative acts or words by the victim; there had to be real evidence of such provocation.

iii *On which the jury can find that the person charged was provoked (whether by things done or by things said or by both together) to lose his self-control* – this is the subjective part of provocation. Where there is real evidence of provocation the jury must be directed on provocation and, first, decide whether or not *the accused* actually lost his self-control because of things done, said or both. Even a crying baby can amount to provocation as was the case in *R* v. *Doughty* (1986). The words spoken or actions do not have to be aimed at the accused; the crucial factor is whether or not the accused was actually provoked. Thus, provocation could be a defence where C is being verbally abused by B to such an extent that D loses his self-control and attacks and kills B.

> What is provocation? In *R* v. *Duffy* (1949) Devlin J. said that provocation, *'involved a sudden and temporary loss of self-control, rendering the accused so subject to passion as to make him or her for the moment not master of his mind'*.

This comment was *obiter dicta* but has been approved in later cases and so can be regarded as the test for provocation. Thus, if a period of time elapses between what provoked the accused and the carrying out of the unlawful act which results in death, it is less likely that provocation will be a defence as the unlawful act was not carried out in 'the heat of the moment'. See the 'You Decide' cases which follow. In some cases involving domestic violence, where the woman has been the subject of abuse over many years, this *history* of abuse might be relevant for the jury when determining whether the accused was actually provoked before killing the victim. The words or conduct of the victim which provoked the accused might seem trivial to others but to the accused at that time, with that history, it might have been the 'last straw'. However, the accused must, nevertheless, suddenly and temporarily lose self-control. Provocation can also be a possible defence where the accused has brought on the provocation – see the 'You Decide' cases which follow.

iv *The question whether the provocation was enough to make a reasonable man do as he did shall be left to be determined by the jury; and in determining that question the jury shall take into account everything both done and said according to the effect which, in their opinion, it would have on a reasonable man* – this is the objective part of provocation. The jury will only consider this second part of the test if in the first test they determined that the accused did lose his self-control. If he did not then this defence fails. If the jury determined that the accused did lose his self-control they then determine whether a reasonable man would have lost his self-control. The leading case is *R* v. *Camplin* (1978). In this case a 15-year-old boy was buggered by a man who then laughed at the boy. The boy lost his self-control and hit the man on the head with a chapati pan, killing him. He was convicted of murder at his trial as the judge directed the jury that when considering the objective test in provocation they should think of the reasonable man as an adult. The case reached the House of Lords where the Court of Appeal's substitution of the murder conviction with one of manslaughter was upheld.

12

> It was held that the reasonable man had to be regarded as having *the same sex and age* as the accused and sharing *the characteristics of the accused* which the jury felt would affect the gravity of the provocation on the accused.

It appears that characteristics such as race, sexual orientation, disabilities and physical features can be characteristics which can be attributed to the reasonable man. However, such characteristics will only be relevant if the provocation was concerned with such characteristics. Thus, if a person with big ears is taunted about his ears such that the provocateur is killed, the characteristic of big ears would be relevant to the issue of provocation. However, if the provocation had been about the accused's lack of skills as a footballer, then the fact that the accused has big ears is not relevant. Even distasteful characteristics such as glue sniffing can be a relevant characteristic (see below) but the fact that the accused was intoxicated at the time of the alleged provocation is not a characteristic which can be attributed to the reasonable man, which fits in with the general view of the criminal law that intoxication is not a defence.

> There are several cases which suggest that, in order for a characteristic of the accused to be attributed to the reasonable man, the characteristic needs to be *significant and permanent*.

Indeed, gender is usually permanent, as is race and sexual orientation, and physical features and disabilities may also be regarded as significant and permanent. Glue sniffing may be regarded as significant and permanent if it is of an *addictive* nature (*R* v. *Morhall* (1995]) rather than just an intermittent activity.

Battered woman syndrome (BWS)

BWS is a mental condition which occurs where a woman is subjected to either physical or verbal abuse or both over a period of time. Is BWS a characteristic which can be attributed to the reasonable man? From the foregoing discussion it should be the case that so long as the BWS is significant and permanent (which it would be if it had been suffered for years) and so long as the words or actions of the victim were connected to the BWS, then BWS could be regarded as a characteristic to be attributed to the reasonable man. However, *when BWS is raised in evidence for the defence of provocation it is usually the case that the victim was not provoking the woman about her BWS condition.* The man would be provoking the woman by abusing her.

Despite this lack of connection between the provocation and the characteristic of the woman, the Court of Appeal has affirmed that mental characteristics such as BWS, which is a type of post-traumatic stress disorder, are characteristics which could be attributed to the reasonable man.

This affirmation appeared in the cases of *R* v. *Aluwhalia* (1992), *R* v. *Dryden* (1995), *R* v. *Humphreys* (1995) and *R* v. *Thornton* (No. 2) (1996). Lord Goff disagrees with this premise and argues that mental conditions such as BWS should not be a relevant characteristic to be attributed to the reasonable man. However, in *R* v. *Parker* (1997) the Court of Appeal confirmed that the mental characteristics of the accused (in this case the accused was a chronic alcoholic with some brain damage) were relevant characteristics to be attributed to the reasonable man. In this case the trial judge had ruled that mental characteristics were not to be attributed to the reasonable man relying on a decision of the Privy Council in *Luc Thiet Thuan* v. *The Queen* (1996). However, the Court of Appeal said that it was not bound by previous decisions of the Privy Council and could choose to follow its own earlier decisions.

However, while such characteristics may be attributable to the reasonable man, the accused must still have experienced a sudden and temporary loss of self-control at the last provocative conduct of the victim. This requirement has been criticised by many people as being unfair to women in that a man who is provoked may have the physical strength to react to the provocation there and then, for example, by attacking the provocateur. However, as a woman suffering from BWS is usually physically inferior to her abuser and living in fear of him, attacking him there and then would probably be very foolish. In such situations a woman might wait and attack him when she stands more of a chance, such as when he is asleep or when she has armed herself with a knife. The problem then arises as to whether her actions were sudden enough.

BWS is a mental condition which was only included in the British classification of mental diseases in 1994. Thus, on a murder charge it is significant to both the defences of provocation and diminished responsibility. Several cases heard before 1994, which resulted in women being convicted of murder because BWS was not regarded as relevant to either of these defences, have since been to the Court of Appeal to raise BWS. In these cases the Court of Appeal may order a re-trial or substitute a conviction of manslaughter instead of murder. This is very significant as on conviction for murder the accused is given a mandatory life sentence, while on conviction for manslaughter the judge can award any sentence up to a maximum of

12

life imprisonment. Moreover, once released after a conviction for murder, the woman is never really free as she is released 'on licence'.

In *R* v. *Thornton* (1992) Sara Thornton was convicted of murdering her husband when, after years of abuse from her husband, and following an abusive incident, she went into the kitchen, sharpened a knife, and stabbed him to death. Despite the fact that the trial judge left the issue of provocation to the jury, she was convicted of murder. On appeal in 1995 it was held that BWS was a characteristic which could be attributed to the reasonable man in provocation and so a re-trial was ordered.

In 1985 Emma Humphrey was convicted of murdering her husband after she stabbed him to death. She had been subjected to years of physical and sexual abuse by her husband and fearing he was about to rape her, she slashed her wrists with a knife. Her husband laughed at her and said that she had not made a very good job of trying to kill herself. At this she stabbed and killed him. At trial the judge told the jury that when considering provocation they should only take note of the husband's jibes relating to the wrist slashing and not of the history of abuse. On appeal in 1995 the Court of Appeal substituted the murder conviction with one for manslaughter as the judge had misdirected the jury on provocation by telling them to ignore a psychiatric report which said that she was 'immature and attention-seeking'.

The relationship between BWS and the defences of provocation and diminished responsibility to a murder charge are shown in the case of *R* v. *Hobson* (1997) which is shown below. It can be seen how Lord Justice Rose stated that the trial judge had *'properly left provocation also for the jury's consideration'* despite the fact that it was self-defence which had been relied on. In other words, BWS was a characteristic to be attributed to the reasonable man.

Retrial after battered woman's syndrome diagnosis

Regina v. Hobson

Before Lord Justice Rose, Mr Justice Sedley and Mr Justice Keene

[Judgment May 23]

Where a woman had been convicted of the murder of her abusive and alcoholic partner before the condition known as "battered woman's syndrome" was included in the standard British classification of mental diseases, which might have enabled her to have claimed diminished responsibility for the killing in accordance with the provisions of section 2 of the Homicide Act 1957, her conviction could not be regarded as safe where fresh psychiatric evidence suggested that she might have been suffering from that syndrome.

The Court of Appeal, Criminal Division, so held in allowing an appeal by Kathleen Hobson against her murder conviction on October 19, 1992, at Liverpool Crown Court (Mr Justice Turner).

Miss Helena Kennedy, QC and Mr Paul R. Taylor, assigned by the Registrar of Criminal Appeals, for the appellant; Mr Stephen Riordan, QC, for the Crown.

LORD JUSTICE ROSE, giving the judgment of the court, said that the appellant stabbed to death her abusive and alcoholic partner. The defence was self-defence, although the trial judge, in his summing up, properly left provocation also for the jury's consideration.

Before their Lordships, Miss Kennedy submitted that it was not until 1994 that battered woman's syndrome was included in the standard British classification of mental diseases so that at the time of the appellant's trial in 1992 it would not have been a condition readily considered by many practising British psychiatrists.

However, two recent psychiatric reports showed that at the time of the killing the history of this appellant, and all the attendant circumstances, gave rise to the existence of battered woman's syndrome, which in turn was capable of giving rise to, and did in her case give rise to diminished responsibility for the killing in accordance with the provisions of section 2 of the Homicide Act 1957.

Mr Riordan relied on the medical report dated February 1997 of Dr Boyd, who at the time of trial had given reports to the defence in relation to the appellant's mental condition.

Dr Boyd's view was that, although a diagnosis of battered woman's syndrome could be made, in the light of what the appellant told him at the time her symptoms were not of a degree to give rise to an abnormality of mind such as to sustain a defence of diminished responsibility.

In the light of those submissions, their Lordships ruled that it would be proper to receive in evidence the current medical reports and, having considered that material, took the view that it was a matter of significance that battered woman's syndrome was not part of the British classification until 1994.

Accordingly, the appeal would be allowed, the conviction quashed and a retrial ordered.

Solicitors: Crown Prosecution Service, Mersey/Lancs.

Source: *The Times*

Suicide pacts

Since the Suicide Act 1961 it is no longer an offence to commit suicide. However, it is an offence to aid, abet, counsel or procure the suicide of another. With regard to suicide pacts, it is for the defence to show, on the balance of probabilities, that the accused also intended to die. If this is done then the accused will only be held liable for manslaughter.

12

YOU DECIDE

Read the cases below and answer the questions. The answers are given on the following page.

1 R v. White (1910)

In this case the accused put cyanide into his mother's drink intending to kill her. The mother drank about one quarter of the drink. She was later found dead and medical evidence showed that she had died of heart failure not of cyanide poisoning

Apply the 'but for' test to this case and decide whether or not the accused's actions were the factual cause of the death. What could he be charged with?

2 R v. Dear (1996)

In this case the victim had sexually assaulted the accused's 12-year-old daughter. As a result the accused had attacked the victim with a Stanley knife causing several disfiguring scars. The victim later either did not stop the wounds bleeding when they reopened or deliberately reopened the wounds himself in order to die. He died and the accused was convicted of murder and appealed against the conviction.

Do you think that the accused had caused the death of the victim or do you think that the actions of the victim amounted to suicide which broke the chain of causation? Decide the appeal.

3 R v. Ibrams (1981)

In this case the defendants were convicted of murder at trial. They had been terrorised by the victim for some time and a week after the last act of terrorism they killed him, having worked out a plan to do so. They appealed against their convictions.

You decide the appeal – should they have been able to rely on the defence of provocation to reduce the murder charge to one of manslaughter?

4 R v. Edwards (1973)

In this case the defendant had killed the man he was blackmailing. The defendant was demanding payment from the victim when the victim attacked the defendant with a knife. The defendant managed to get the knife from the victim and killed him with it in a fit of 'white hot' passion. At trial he was convicted of murder as the judge did not leave the issue of provocation to the jury. The defendant appealed.

You decide the appeal – as the attack on the defendant was self-provoked, does this mean that provocation was not available as a defence?

Answers

1 The accused was acquitted of murder as his actions were not the factual cause of the death of his mother – his mother died anyway. He was, however, charged with and convicted of attempted murder – his actions had gone beyond the merely preparatory stage of the crime of murder.

2 The appeal was dismissed and so the conviction for murder stood. It was held that the victim only acted as he did because of the wounds – thus, *but for* the actions of the accused which caused the wounds, the victim would not have died. It thus seems that the assailant may be held responsible for actions of the victim which result from the victim's reaction to the attack. In this case, if it could have been proved (which it was not) that the victim in effect committed suicide not because of how he felt about his disfigurement following the attack but because of his shame at assaulting a 12-year-old girl, then the chain of causation would have been broken.

3 They could not rely on the defence of provocation as too much time had elapsed between the last act of provocation and the killing. The fact that they had taken a week to devise a plan to kill the victim out of revenge demonstrated that they had not suffered a sudden temporary loss of self-control.

4 The defence of provocation can be available even if self-induced because this fact is just one which has to be weighed up by the jury when they are considering the defence. In this case the defence was allowed and a manslaughter conviction was substituted for the murder conviction.

Involuntary manslaughter

It can be seen from the diagram at Figure 12.3 that when the accused did not intend to kill the victim or cause the victim serious bodily harm then the most appropriate charge is one of involuntary manslaughter. The facts of the case might support a charge under either type of involuntary manslaughter and so the accused could be convicted on the basis of either type. Each type of involuntary manslaughter is considered below.

Unlawful and dangerous act involuntary manslaughter (constructive manslaughter)

This type of involuntary manslaughter is also known as constructive manslaughter but it is better referred to as unlawful and dangerous act manslaughter as this reminds us of the content of the offence. In order to give this type of manslaughter some structure the essential features of it are shown in the diagram at Figure 12.5. The definition of unlawful and dangerous act manslaughter is that the accused killed a human being during the Queen's Peace by an unlawful and dangerous act, and the unlawful and dangerous act must have *caused* the death. Thus it is a result crime which may be committed by the commission of any unlawful and dangerous act. It must be noted that the *actus reus* of this type of manslaughter *must* involve an act; an omission will not suffice. The requisite *mens rea* is as for the unlawful and dangerous act and thus the *mens rea* will vary. Sometimes recklessness will suffice and sometimes intention will be necessary. Relevant cases, with comments, are highlighted in the diagram.

Gross negligence involuntary manslaughter

If you look back to Chapter 2, on *mens rea*, you will see how the main types of *mens rea* which are required in order to impose criminal liability on someone are intention and recklessness. Negligence does not really describe a mental state by the accused as it is determined in accordance with an objective test to determine how the ordinary and prudent man would have behaved. As such, it should not form the basis of many crimes as the underlying concept of the criminal law is that a person will only be held to be criminally liable when the undesired conduct was brought about with a blameworthy state of mind. It seems alarming then that the word negligence appears in relation to such a serious offence as manslaughter which can result in imprisonment for a very long time, up to life. Negligence here is qualified by the word 'gross' but what does this mean? What is gross negligence? It has sometimes been equated with recklessness but this has been rejected. Unfortunately, gross negligence has not been defined because it is up to the jury to determine what conduct amounts to gross negligence and the judges do not wish to attempt to define the term. Thus, whether or not the accused is found guilty of gross negligence manslaughter is a very unsure area of the law; it will depend in large part on the interpretation given to gross negligence by the jury. This uncertainty in this area of the law is very unwelcome. So why do we have gross negligence manslaughter? Why do we not just have unlawful and dangerous act manslaughter? The reason gross negligence manslaughter exists is to cover those deaths which should be regarded as criminal and which do not fall under the head of unlawful and dangerous act manslaughter.

	Meaning	Application	Comments
Actus reus Killing of a human being during the Queen's Peace	As discussed for murder – note that it is a result crime and so the unlawful and dangerous act must have caused the death.	*R v. Goodfellow* (1986) demonstrates the need to establish the casual link between the act of the accused and the resultant death. Thus, in this case the appellant's conviction of manslaughter was upheld on appeal – he had set fire to his council house hoping to be rehoused and as a result of the fire two women and a child had died. It was his unlawful and dangerous act which had caused the deaths and there was no *novus actus interveniens* to break the chain of causation.	It is irrelevant that the unlawful and dangerous act was not actually directed at the victims (as was suggested in *R v. Dalby* (1982).
by an unlawful act	The unlawful act must be a criminal offence and it must be a positive act – omissions will not suffice.	This can be considered in the light of two contrasting drug cases: in *R v. Cato* (1976) two friends had spent the night injecting one another with heroin such that they became very ill. One of them died but Cato had survived and was convicted of unlawful manslaughter and administering a noxious substance contrary to section 23 OAPA 1861. On appeal the convictions were upheld. See comments. In *R v. Dalby* (1982) the facts were similar to those in *Cato* except that the possession of the drugs was legal as they were obtained on perscription. On appeal the conviction for manslaughter was quashed as *supplying* the drug, while unlawful, was not the *cause* of the death – the *taking* of the drug by the deceased was the cause of death and in this case the victim had injected herself.	Note, that it is an offence to supply heroin or to possess it but it is not an offence to take it or to administer it. In *Cato* the section 23 offence was the unlawful act which caused the death of the other – however it was stated *obiter dicta* that the conviction for manslaughter could have been upheld if the section 23 offence had failed – this must be wrong as mere possession of heroin by Cato was not *causally* linked to his friend's death. The need for a causal link is also stressed in *Dalby*.
which is also a dangerous act	The unlawful act must also be dangerous.	Whether or not an unlawful act is also dangerous is to be decided according to an objective test as laid down in the case of *R v. Church* (1966) in which Edmund Davies J. stated: *the unlawful act must be such as all sober and reasonable people would inevitably recognise must subject the other person to, at least, the risk of some harm resulting therefrom, albeit not serious harm.'* This objective test can be considered in light of two contrasting cases where the victim dies of a heart attack. In *R v. Dawson* (1985) the two defendants had robbed the victim's filling station wearing masks and wielding a replica gun and a pickaxe handle. Shortly after the robbery the victim, who had a heart condition, died of a heart attack. On appeal the convictions for manslaughter were quashed as the judge had not made it clear to the jury that under the test laid down in *Church* they could only ascribe to the sober and reasonable man knowledge gained as if he were himself at the scene of the crime. In this instance such a reasonable man would not have been able to tell that the victim had a heart condition and so would not have recognised that they were subjecting him to the risk of some harm. In *R v. Watson* (1989) the appellants lost their appeal against manslaughter convictions. It was held that the judge was correct in his direction that the reasonable man could be ascribed knowledge obtained during the whole duration of the crime. In this case the appellants had entered a house intent to steal and once inside noticed that the occupier was a frail old man who died of a heart attack after they left. A reasonable man at the scene of this crime would have realised that the victim was at risk of some harm.	In *Watson* what might the outcome have been had the occupant of the house been a young man who had a heart condition and later died? Probably this would not be dangerous and unlawful act manslaughter.
Mens rea Is the *mens rea* of the unlawful and dangerous act	Thus the *mens rea* for this type of manslaughter varies dangerous act and may be intention or recklessness	This is demonstrated in the case of *R v. Lamb* (1967) in which two friends were playing with a revolver which had two bullets in it. The accused did not realise that the bullets moved around when the gun was fired and so when he 'pretended' to shoot his friend the friend was really shot and died. At trial the accused was convicted but on appeal the conviction was quashed – the unlawful and dangerous act here would have been assault and/or battery for which the *mens rea* is subjective recklessness. As this was not established for the accused then no unlawful and dangerous act was proved and so there was no manslaughter under this heading.	

Figure 12.5 The key features of unlawful and dangerous act involuntary manslaughter (constructive manslaughter)

12

> Thus, gross negligence manslaughter covers deaths which are not caused by an unlawful act and which may result due to an omission.

> The essence of gross negligence manslaughter is that the accused owed the victim a duty of care and broke this duty such that the victim died. Whether or not the conduct of the accused, whether an act or omission, amounted to gross negligence has to be determined by the jury.

The relationship between negligence in civil law and in criminal law is discussed in the leading cases of *R* v. *Bateman* (1925), *Andrews* v. *DPP* (1937) and *R* v. *Adomako* (1995).

In *R* v. *Bateman Lord Hewitt C.J.* said:

In expounding the law to juries on the trial of indictments for manslaughter by negligence, judges have often referred to the distinction between civil and criminal liability for death by negligence. The law of criminal liability for negligence is conveniently explained in that way. If A has caused the death of B by alleged negligence, then, in order to establish civil liability, the plaintiff must prove (in addition to pecuniary loss caused by the death) that A owed a duty to B to take care, that that duty was not discharged and that the default caused the death of B. To convict A of manslaughter, the prosecution must prove the three things above mentioned and must satisfy the jury, in addition, that A's negligence amounted to a crime. In the civil action, if it is proved that A fell short of the standard of reasonable care required by law, it matters not how far he fell short of that standard. The extent of his liability depends not on the degree of negligence but on the amount of damage done. In a criminal court, on the contrary, the amount and degree of negligence are the determining question. There must be mens rea . . . the facts must be such that, in the opinion of the jury, the negligence of the accused . . . showed such disregard for the life and safety of others as to amount to a crime against the state and conduct deserving punishment.

In the *Andrews* case the House of Lords recognised the test for gross negligence manslaughter as expounded in *Batemen*. In the *Adomako* case, which also reached the House of Lords, the *Andrews* case was regarded as the authoritative case on gross negligence manslaughter. The facts of *Adomako* involved a patient dying on the operating table due to the conduct of the anaesthetist. During the operation the anaesthetist took nine minutes to notice that the tube supplying oxygen to the patient had become disconnected. As a result the patient suffered a cardiac arrest and died. Thus, the death of the patient was caused by what the anaesthetist failed to do, an omission, as he failed to realise what was causing the patient's distress and causing the monitors to sound alarms. What the anaesthetist did did not amount to an unlawful act and so the death could not be prosecuted as unlawful and dangerous act manslaughter. The anaesthetist's conviction for manslaughter was affirmed by the House of Lords and Lord MacKay of Clashfern stated:

> *Since the decision in Andrews was a decision of your Lordships' House, it remains the most authoritative statement of the present law which I have been able to find ... On this basis in my opinion the ordinary principles of the law of negligence apply to ascertain whether or not the defendant has been in breach of a duty of care towards the victim who has died. If such breach of duty is established the next question is whether that breach of duty caused the death of the victim. If so, the jury must go on to consider whether that breach of duty should be categorised as gross negligence and therefore as a crime. This will depend on the seriousness of the breach of duty committed by the defendant in all the circumstances in which the defendant was placed when it occurred. The jury will have to consider whether the extent to which the defendant's conduct departed from the proper standard of care incumbent upon him, involving as it must have done a risk of death to the patient, was such that it should be judged as criminal.*

(The highlighted sections in both extracts were added by the author.)

The interplay between the two types of involuntary manslaughter are demonstrated in the question which appears in applying principles to examination questions below. The interplay between murder and involuntary manslaughter is also demonstrated in the case of *R* v. *Khan* (1998) which is shown in the proposals for reform on page 356.

12

Applying principles to examination questions

Consider the question below and apply the principles you have learned in this chapter on homicide. Although the question appears in the format of a problem-solving question it really is more like an essay-type question on homicide. What you have to do is analyse the facts presented and apply the principles of homicide to it. A good approach is to see if murder is an appropriate charge and then if any type of involuntary manslaughter is appropriate.

Mike is a security guard in a cold storage depot. One night he fell asleep on duty and when he awoke and checked his video camera monitors, he saw two youths in the deep freeze area of the depot. He therefore triggered the locking system so that the youths could not get out of the deep freeze.

As he was still sleepy, Mike decided to leave the youths in the deep freeze and call the police a few minutes later. However, he fell asleep again.

When he awoke, he went down to the deep freeze but found the youths dead.

Discuss Mike's possible liability for homicide.

Source: NEAB June 1997, Law Advanced Paper II

Tips on how to approach such a question

This is not the type of problem question which is littered with numerous offences and possible defences. Rather it is quite precise as it relates to a homicide and all you are asked to do is discuss Mike's possible liability for homicide. Thus, unless you feel confident on all aspects of homicide you should not attempt such a question. You have not been asked to discuss Mike's liability for just murder or just manslaughter, which is an indication that you should discuss both.

Introduction   State that the two dead bodies make this a potential homicide as Mike could be facing a murder and/or manslaughter charge. Explain that you intend to analyse the facts in terms of the definition for murder and the two types of involuntary manslaughter. You could state that voluntary manslaughter is not an issue because even if a murder charge was found to be appropriate, none of the defences in the Homicide Act 1957 would seem to be appropriate.

1st paragraph   In this paragraph you could work through the common law definition of murder to see if it is appropriate. Look at the *actus reus* for murder – there is a killing of two human beings in the Queen's Peace and it would matter not whether the conduct of Mike was regarded as a positive act (the locking of the deep freeze) or as an omission (failing to open the deep freeze). Quote appropriate cases, such as *R* v. *Pittwood* (1902). The issue of causation should not be problematic either as but for the conduct of Mike, the two youths would not have died. But what about the *mens rea* part of murder?

2nd paragraph

State the *mens rea* for murder and quote appropriate cases, such as *R* v. *Nedrick* (1986), when explaining the difference between direct and oblique intent. Did Mike intend to kill the youths or cause them serious bodily harm? Probably not, but was death a virtual certainty as a result of his conduct? The jury might decide that it was and might infer intention from this, or they might not.

3rd paragraph

Move on to the first of the two types of involuntary manslaughter, unlawful and dangerous act manslaughter or constructive manslaughter, and apply the definition of each to the facts. What could be regarded as the unlawful act? The false imprisonment? False imprisonment is a crime but is usually dealt with in the civil courts. However, the *mens rea* for false imprisonment is that the accused unlawfully, either intentionally or recklessly, restrains the freedom of movement of a person from a particular place. Obviously Mike did intend to restrict the freedom of movement of the youths. But was it this unlawful act which *caused* the deaths or were the deaths caused by the cold? Discuss *R* v. *Cato* (1976) and *R* v. *Dalby* (1982).

4th paragraph

What conduct by Mike resulted in the deaths – the positive act of locking the deep freeze or his failure to open it – which was an omission? Note that omissions are not covered by this type of manslaughter. If the positive act of Mike is taken as causing the deaths, was it a dangerous act? Consider *R* v. *Church* (1966). Finally, note the *mens rea* and quote *R* v. *Lamb* (1967).

5th paragraph

Move on to the second type of involuntary manslaughter, gross negligence manslaughter. Note that this type of manslaughter does impose liability for omissions and does cover situations where there is no unlawful act. Consider the meaning of gross negligence manslaughter, quoting from *R* v. *Bateman* (1925) and *R* v. *Adomako* (1995). Quote the facts of *Adomako*. Apply the law to the facts – did Mike owe the two youths a duty of care? Did he breach this duty of care and as a result did the two youths die? Probably Mike did breach a duty of care to the youths and so caused their deaths and so the *jury* would have to determine whether such breach of duty (such negligence) should be regarded as criminal behaviour. The jury will have to decide if the behaviour amounted to *gross* negligence.

12

Conclusion

You could say that it is unlikely that a murder charge would be brought and that of the two types of involuntary manslaughter gross negligence manslaughter might seem most appropriate as the deaths were caused by an omission (failure to let the youths out of the deep freeze).

Arriving at what might be the 'correct' answer in this type of question is not that important. What is very important is that you demonstrate sound understanding of the law in question and apply it logically and analytically to the facts presented. You must remember to be discursive and talk around the various prosecution options. Do not fall into the trap of stating, for example, that this is a clear case of gross negligence manslaughter because if you do this you will lose lots of marks.

Proposals for reform

Does the law of homicide need reforming? This can be determined by summarising the problem areas, some of which have been identified in this chapter.

Murder

Problem areas

i *Mens rea*
- no definition of this in the substantive law which has led to problems when judges attempt to describe it to juries in complex directions, especially as regards oblique intent;

- is it justifiable to keep intention to cause serious bodily harm as part of the *mens rea* for murder when such intention suffices for a conviction under section 18 of the Offences Against the Person Act 1861? The accused is just as 'blameworthy' mentally whether the victim lives or dies yet, if the victim dies, on conviction, the accused faces an automatic life sentence as compared with a maximum life sentence if convicted for the section 18 offence.

   ii Automatic life sentence
     – the automatic life sentence for all types of murders (from domestic murders through to the most heinous murders involving torture) seems out out of date now – should judges be given more discretion in sentencing?

   iii Euthanasia
     – this topic is dealt with in Chapter 15.

Manslaughter

Problem areas

   i Unlawful and dangerous act manslaughter
     – unlawful and dangerous act manslaughter has the *mens rea* as for the unlawful act which does seem rather harsh – and the dangerous act is determined according to the test in *Church* which is an objective test involving the risk of only *some* harm, not serious harm.

   ii Gross negligence manslaughter
     – the problem here is that gross negligence sounds very much like recklessness and this type of manslaughter utilises tests for liability which are mainly used to impose civil liability for negligence and these difficult concepts are left for the jury to determine *criminal* liability.

   iii Corporate killing
     – this is dealt with in Chapter 15.

   iv Voluntary manslaughter
     – many problems exist with regard to the defence manslaughter of provocation because of the extension of which characteristics can be attributed to the reasonable man for the objective part of the defence – it now includes the mental characteristics of the accused – is there now an overlap between provocation, diminished responsibility and insanity?

The fact that so many problem areas can be identified with the law of homicide leads us to the conclusion that this area of the criminal law is badly in need of reform. It is essentially contained in the common law but it is probably true to say that reform will have to be by means of legislation from Parliament. Are any such reforms likely? That some are needed is aptly demonstrated in the case of *R* v. *Khan* (1998) shown in the extract below. This case shows the interplay between both types of involuntary manslaughter and murder.

12

Duty required in manslaughter by omission

Regina v Khan (Rungzabe)

Before Lord Justice Swinton Thomas, Mr Justice Rix and Mr Justice Astill

[Judgment March 18]

Manslaughter by omission was an example of manslaughter arising out of a breach of duty coupled with gross negligence and was not a free-standing category of manslaughter on its own.

Consequently in such cases the trial judge should make a ruling as to whether the facts were capable of giving rise to the relevant duty and the jury should be directed in relation to that issue.

The Court of Appeal, Criminal Division, so held in a reserved judgment allowing the appeal of Rungzabe Khan against his conviction on July 1, 1997 at Birmingham Crown Court (Mr Justice McKinnon and a jury) of manslaughter, charged in the indictment as murder, and supplying a controlled class A drug to another, possessing a controlled class A drug with intent, to which pleas of not guilty were entered, and conspiracy to prevent burial of a dead body to which a guilty plea was entered.

Mr Babir Singh, assigned by the Registar for Criminal Appeals, for the appellant; Mr John Mitting, QC, for the prosecution.

LORD JUSTICE SWINTON THOMAS said the appeal related solely to the jury's findings that the appellant was guilty of manslaughter. The facts were unusual.

The appellant sold heroin to a prostitute Lucy Birchell, aged 15. It was the first time she had tried heroin and the appellant gave her a dose which was twice the amount which would be taken by an experienced heroin user.

The girl went into a coma on the appellant's premises. Later the appellant left and several hours later she died alone.

It was established that if medical assistance had been requested at any time before Lucy Birchell's death she would have been saved. Originally the appellant was indicted on a charge of murder but following conclusion of the evidence called by the crown the trial judge withdrew that charge as no reasonable jury could conclude the appellant had the requisite intent for murder.

The prosecution did not put their case on the basis of manslaughter by gross negligence and the trial judge ruled that it was not manslaughter as the result of an unlawful or dangerous act on the authority of *R* v. *Dalby* [(1982) 1 WLR 425) as explained by *R* v. *Goodfellow* ((1986) 83 Cr App R 23). The trial judge did not have *Attorney-General's Reference No 3 of 1994* ([1997] 3 WLR 421) before him.

His Lordship reviewed the law of manslaughter and *R* v. *Stone* ([1977] QB 354), *Airedale National Health Trust* v. *Bland* ([1993] AC 789,893), *R* v. *Adomako* ([1995] 1 AC 171,187). *R* v. *Dalby* and *R* v *Miller* ([1983] 2 AC 161). He concluded that manslaughter by omission was but an example of manslaughter arising by breach of duty coupled with gross negligence.

The trial judge had not made any ruling as to whether the facts were capable of giving rise to the relevant duty and had failed to give any direction to the jury in relation to that issue. Accordingly, the appeal against manslaughter would be allowed.

To extend the duty to summon medical assistance to a drug dealer who supplied heroin to a person who subsequently died would undoubtedly enlarge the class of person to whom, on previous authority, a duty could be owed.

It might be correct to hold that such a duty did arise. However, before such a situation could occur a judge should first make a ruling as to whether the facts proved were capable of giving rise to such a duty.

Solicitors: Murria, Birmingham; Crown Prosecution Service, Birmingham.

Source: *The Times*, 7 April 1998

That reform of the law of homicide is needed is also reflected by the comments of many leading academics and lawyers, and during the latter part of 1997 there were several letters to the editors of national newspapers calling for such reform. These letters were prompted by the fact that, at the time, Tony Blair was considering signing up to Protocol 6 of the European Convention on Human Rights which would end the death penalty in the UK for the offences of treason, piracy and certain military offences. The death penalty for murder was abolished in 1965.

The letter below is typical of the time:

Call for a modern law of homicide

From Sir Louis Blom-Cooper, QC, and Professor Terence Morris

Sir, ... Much more important is the question of what to do with the law of homicide. In July, in an outstanding judgment of Lord Mustill, the House of Lords pronounced in a case of the margins between murder and manslaughter.

> *One could expect a developed system to embody a law of murder clear enough to yield an unequivocal result on a given set of facts, a result which conforms with apparent justice and has a sound intellectual base. This is not so in England, where the law of homicide is permeated by anomaly, fiction, misnomer and obsolete reasoning*

Attempts to abolish the mandatory life sentence for murder and to provide for greater flexibility in sentencing have so far met with no success. The time has now surely come for a reforming Government to put forward proposals for a modern law of homicide that both meets the requirements of justice and accords with the social and moral realities of our time.

Source: *The Times*, 10 October 1997

Proposals for reform of the law of involuntary manslaughter have been put forward by the Law Commission. In April 1994 they published a consulation paper (*'Criminal Law: Involuntary Manslaughter'* (1994), Consultation Paper No. 135) because the Commission noted that involuntary manslaughter is one of the few remaining common law offences and the law as it stands is uncertain and in some respects anomalous. The Commission's report on the consultation paper was published in March 1996, *'Legislating the Criminal Code: Involuntary Manslaughter'*, (1996) Law Com. No. 237. In the Law Commission's thirtieth Annual Report 1995 (Law Com. No. 239) it says at paragraph 4.2:

> *Our recommendations are based on the principle that criminal liability ought to depend primarily on the extent to which the defendant is at fault – that is, the consequences that he intends, or foresees, or ought to have foreseen – rather than on the consequences that happen to result. It follows from this principle, and we recommend in our report, that a person ought not to be guilty of manslaughter merely because he commits a minor assault which, through some unforeseeable mischance, results in death ... we recommend that the offence of involuntary manslaughter should be replaced by two new offences, one of 'reckless killing' and one of 'killing by gross carelessness'.*

12

The Law Commission is still awaiting the Government's response to its recommendations. In Law Com. No. 237 the Law Commission put forward a Draft Involuntary Homicide Bill 1995, highlights of which are shown below.

DRAFT INVOLUNTARY HOMICIDE BILL 1995

1. Reckless killing
(1) A person who by his conduct causes the death of another is guilty of reckless killing if –
(a) he is aware of a risk that his conduct will cause death or serious injury; and
(b) it is unreasonable for him to take that risk having regard to the circumstances as he knows or believes them to be.
(2) A person guilty of reckless killing is liable on conviction on indictment to imprisonment for life.

2. Killing by gross carelessness
(1) A person who by his conduct causes the death of another is guilty of killing by gross carelessness if –
(a) a risk that his conduct will cause death or serious injury would be obvious to a reasonable person in his position;
(b) he is capable of appreciating that risk at the material time; and
(c) either –
   (i) his conduct falls far below what can reasonably be expected of him in the circumstances; or
   (ii) he intends by his conduct to cause some injury or is aware of, and unreasonably takes, the risk that it may do so.
5. A person guilty of killing by gross carelessness is liable on conviction on indictment to imprisonment for a term not exceeding [ ] years.

CHAPTER Summary

In this chapter statistical data on homicide has been considered along with detailed discussion of the substantive law which is essentially still found in the common law. The problem areas of the law of homicide have been identified and the Law Commission's proposals for reforming involuntary manslaughter have been discussed. The topics of euthanasia and corporate killing are dealt with in Chapter 15.

Consolidation

In this chapter you will be asked to answer two essay-type questions and two problem-solving questions. The questions will feature offences against the person (assault, battery, offences under the Offences Against the Person Act 1861 and homicide) and topics from the general principles section. When these topics were first dealt with in the appropriate chapters you were asked questions on them without the integration of any other topics. In the problem-solving questions which follow you will notice that one question often covers many offences; it is your task to ascertain which offences have been committed and if any general principles apply. In the essay-type questions which follow you will need detailed knowledge and understanding of either one particular aspect of an offence or one general principle. Thus, your examination preparation must be thorough. I have highlighted some key points which should be mentioned when answering these questions.

Essay-type questions

1   Explain and comment on the proposition that the offences of conspiracy and attempt are too broad in that they criminalise behaviour where no harm has been done. (*25 marks*)

(Source: NEAB Law Advanced Paper II, 1993)

Suggested approach

1   First, you must note the key words in the title of the essay:

Explain and comment   You have to demonstrate sound knowledge of the offences in the title – conspiracy and attempt – and you have to provide critical analysis of them in light of the proposition below.

Proposition   The proposition put forward is that the offences of conspiracy and attempt involve no harm to society. Do you agree with this proposition? Are these offences too broad? What lines demarcate how broad they are?

Conspiracy and attempt

You have to recognise that conspiracy and attempt are two of the inchoate offences, the third one being incitement. Unless you have studied these offences in detail you should not attempt this question.

Criminalise behaviour where no harm has been done

You have to comment on the fact that the essence of the inchoate offences is that the substantive crime has not been committed. Thus, the behaviour of a person in society which is being made criminal falls short of the commission of the substantive offence in question. If the substantive offence has not been committed then, arguably, no harm has been done to society, so why do we have the inchoate offences? However, you have to consider the definition of 'harm'.

2   Second, you must plan the structure of your essay paragraph by paragraph so that you can decide how much detail you can afford to go into on any one aspect of the topic. In the examination you can do this briefly before you start writing the essay and then draw a line so that the examiner knows where your essay starts. You can then refer back to your essay structure as you progress through the essay to make sure that you have not omitted anything and to gauge how much time you have left. If you start to run out of time you will have to write less on each of the remaining topics to ensure that you finish the essay and write a rounded conclusion. A suggested essay structure is given below.

Suggested essay structure for the question on conspiracy and attempt

Introduction

Start by saying that you know that conspiracy and attempt are two of the inchoate offences, the other one being incitement. Explain that the inchoate offences exist in order to protect society from 'potential harm' and that a line has to be drawn demarcating criminal thoughts in someone's head (not criminal) and behaviour which goes beyond mere thoughts to 'overt actions' on the way to the implementation of a crime. The criminal law has drawn this line at the point where the inchoate offences come into being. Do you think that this line has been drawn in the correct place? The proposition in the title suggests that the line has been drawn too intrusively into human behaviour in society, the implication being that only behaviour which actually causes *harm* in society should be criminalised. You can then say that the validity of the proposition therefore rests on the definition of *harm* and that, throughout the essay, you will interpret harm as meaning harm caused by the commission of a criminal offence. However, you should also indicate that in the conclusion to the essay you will consider the definition of harm again.

2nd paragraph   In this paragraph explain the offence of conspiracy by:

- ▶ explaining that conspiracy only exists in relation to a substantive offence, that is, there is no such charge as pure conspiracy;

- ▶ demonstrating your knowledge of both common law and statutory conspiracy (see Figures 8.2 and 8.3 in chapter 8 which demonstrate this in chart format);

- ▶ explaining the impact of the Criminal Law Act 1977;

- ▶ explaining the effect of the case of *R* v. *Gibson* (1990) on conspiracy to outrage public decency;

- ▶ explaining the *mens rea* of conspiracy.

3rd paragraph   In this paragraph comment on conspiracy by considering factors which support the proposition and factors which do not.

It could be regarded as too broad for the following reasons:

- ▶ since the Criminal Law Act 1977, common law conspiracy, still allows a person to be charged with conspiracy for conspiring to commit non-criminal behaviour, that is, in relation to fraud and corruption of public morals. Is it right that *conspiring* to do something which is non-criminal can be regarded as criminal behaviour when, *if* the behaviour conspired to was carried out, it would not be criminal behaviour?

- ▶ the existence of common law conspiracy to defraud is only really justified because the legislature cannot keep pace with the speed at which new types of fraud appear. Should common law conspiracy exist just to fill in such a shortfall in the law?

- ▶ for statutory conspiracy, as provided for by section 1(1) of the Criminal Law Act 1977, a person can be charged with conspiring the commission of an offence which is impossible to commit;

- ▶ for conspiracy to corrupt public morals there is no maximum sentence.

It could be regarded as acceptable for the following reasons:

- ▶ most conspiracies are now statutory conspiracies which concern conspiracies to commit *crimes*;

- ▶ since the case of *R* v. *Gibson* (1990) conspiracy to outrage public decency is really statutory conspiracy and conspiracy to defraud can now be charged as either common law or statutory conspiracy;

13

▶ the *actus reus* of conspiracy cannot be committed when there are only two conspirators and one of them is the spouse of the other, is under the age of criminal responsibility or is an intended victim of the conspiracy (section 2 Criminal Law Act 1977);

▶ in relation to the *mens rea* for conspiracy, a person can be charged with conspiracy even if they do not intend to take part in the commission of the crime. Unless this was the case gang leaders would be immune from criminal prosecution – quote the case of *Yip Chiu-Cheung* v. *R* (1994) – surely the gang leader is in a position to effect a lot of harm (criminal offences) in society? Why wait until the criminal harm has been carried out? Does not the criminal law have a duty to 'protect' citizens from 'potential' harm?

▶ for common law conspiracy it is a defence if the conspiracy concerned behaviour which was impossible to commit – *Haughten* v. *Smith* (1975) and *DPP v. Nock* (1978).

4th paragraph

In this paragraph explain the offence of attempt by:

▶ explaining that attempt only exists in relation to a substantive offence, that is, there is no such charge as pure attempt;

▶ explaining that attempt is now a statutory offence governed by the Criminal Attempts Act 1981;

▶ discussing the *actus reus* of attempt in relation to key cases such as *R* v. *Geddes* (1996), *R* v. *Campbell* (1991) and *R* v. *Tosti and White* (1997);

▶ explaining the general rule as regards the *mens rea* for attempt.

5th paragraph

In this paragraph comment on attempt in light of the proposition in the essay title by considering factors which support the proposition and factors which do not.

It could be regarded as too broad for the following reasons:

▶ the substantive offence in question has not been fully carried out;

▶ the test for what amounts to 'acts more than merely preparatory' for the *actus reus* of attempt is particularly vague, hence the existence of contrasting cases such as *R* v. *Geddes* (1996) and *R* v. *Tosti and White* (1997);

▶ on consideration of the *mens rea* for attempting crimes which involve *mens rea* as to the circumstances of the offence – discuss *R* v. *Khan* (1990);

▶ by section 1(2) and (3) of the Criminal Attempts Act 1981 it is possible to attempt the impossible – discuss the case of *R* v. *Shivpuri* (1987);

▶ the maximum sentence is usually the same as for the substantive offence.

It could be regarded as acceptable for the following reasons:

▶ for the *actus reus* of attempt the acts of the accused have to be 'more than merely preparatory' which means' that the accused had started to commit the offence – quote *R* v. *Geddes* (1996);

▶ since the Criminal Attempts Act 1981 it is generally only possible to be charged with attempting an indictable or triable either way offence;

▶ the *mens rea* for attempt is generally specific intention even when the *mens rea* for the substantive offence is recklessness – use the example of the *mens rea* for attempted murder;

▶ discuss the case of *R* v. *Husseyn* (1977) and conditional intent.

Conclusion

In the conclusion revisit the issue of defining 'harm'. What is meant by harm? If we say that harm to society means harm affected by the commission of a criminal offence such that property or persons are harmed, then arguably the offences of conspiracy and attempt are too broad. However, if we say that harm means harm in the sense of corruption of others or the lowering of standards of acceptable behaviour in society, then arguably the offences of conspiracy and attempt are not too broad. The latter approach considers harm in terms less 'physical' than the former approach which is surely more acceptable now given the developments in the law on non-fatal-offences against the person where psychiatric injury and severe psychiatric injury can amount to actual bodily harm and grievous bodily harm, and where harassing behaviour has been criminalised.

2 How satisfactory is the criminal law regarding euthanasia?

(Source: NEAB Advanced Law Paper II, 1995)

Before attempting to answer this question students should refer to the topic of euthanasia in Chapter 15.

Suggested approach

1 First, you must note the key words in the title of the essay:

How satisfactory

The word satisfactory suggests that this topic is one for which opinion is divided and this is true. Thus, you must be able to write

13

critically on the topic of euthanasia, giving arguments which either support the satisfactory state of the law or support the dissatisfactory state of the law. You should choose an argument.

Criminal law

This reminds you that euthanasia is governed by principles of criminal law. You should state where the line is currently drawn, explaining what homicide means, both lawful and unlawful. You should also mention where the British Medical Association (BMA) stands on this issue. You should also mention morality and the autonomy of the individual.

Euthanasia

This term must be defined and critically evaluated in light of the other key words.

2 Second, you must plan the structure of your essay paragraph by paragraph so that you can decide how much detail you can afford to go into on any one aspect of the topic. In the examination you can do this briefly before you start writing the essay and then draw a line so that the examiner knows where your essay starts. You can then refer back to your essay structure as you progress through the essay to make sure that you have not omitted anything and to gauge how much time you have left. If you start to run out of time you will have to write less on each of the remaining topics to ensure that you finish the essay and write a rounded conclusion. A suggested essay structure is given below.

Suggested essay structure for the question on euthanasia

(This topic is comprehensively covered in Chapter 15 and so the structure below is the general outline to be followed.)

Introduction

Start by defining euthanasia. Then say that euthanasia is a dilemna in society for doctors treating terminally ill patients and also for others, such as relatives. Say whether you think the law is satisfactory or not and then write your essay to your argument.

2nd paragraph

In this paragraph define lawful and unlawful homicide:

▶ explain that if a doctor administers a lethal injection he has committed murder;

▶ explain what a doctor can *legally* do to hasten the death of a terminally ill patient;

▶ discuss the disadvantages of this approach for the patient and the patient's family.

3rd paragraph	In this paragraph explore the possibility of a doctor being allowed to administer a lethal injection:

- could this be achieved by a computer? Computer-aided death was experimented with in Australia whereby the patient was asked several questions by the computer, which required an answer *yes* or *no* from the patient, such that the computer would, following a *yes* instruction, then operate the mechanism for the patient to be given a lethal injection;
- could we expect such experiments in the UK?

4th paragraph	In this paragraph explain the attitude of the UK Government and courts towards euthanasia:

- mention the issue of living wills and the attitude of the Lord Chancellor;
- contrast this attitude with more liberal approaches, such as in Holland;
- explain the attitude of the BMA on euthanasia;
- discuss the case of Ms S (1998) who was forced to undergo hospitalisation and a caesarian section against her wishes.

5th paragraph	In this paragraph consider the case of Anthony Bland in detail – *Airedale NHS Trust* v. *Bland* (1993) and mention the case of Annie Lindsell – see the newspaper article on page 394 for details of the latter.
6th paragraph	In this paragraph consider the issues of consent and morality.
Conclusion	Conclude by saying whether you think the current state of the criminal law deals satisfactorily with the issue of euthanasia. Note how fine a line there is between the legally acceptable practices of administering pain-relieving drugs or switching off a life-support machine and the legally unacceptable practice of administering a lethal injection. Note also how the issue is closely associated with morality.

13

Problem-type questions

1 Consider the question below and note down your ideas which you can then incorporate into a properly structured essay.

> John was driving behind Sanjay on the motorway. John was frustrated because he thought that Sanjay was not driving fast enough. When Sanjay turned off the motorway into the service area, John followed and both men parked their cars.
>
> John ran over to Sanjay's car and began to shout at Sanjay in an abusive manner through the closed window of the car.
>
> Sanjay suddenly opened his car door and, in order to avoid being hit by the door, John jumped backwards. Unfortunately, John jumped into the path of another car which was driven by Emma, well in excess of the speed limit.
>
> As a result, John suffered a broken leg as well as cuts and bruises.
>
> Discuss the criminal liability of Sanjay and Emma for John's injuries.

2 The following question relates to homicide and in particular to murder and voluntary manslaughter.

> Deborah and Eric have been married for three years. They have two children, aged one and three. Eric has had numerous sexual encounters with other women during their marriage, and has always boasted of them to Deborah. He has also been violent to her on some occasions, especially during her pregnancies.
>
> Deborah feared that she might be pregnant and that she would again be subjected to violence. She decided that the only way out of the situation was to kill Eric, and attacked him with a knife, causing serious injury.
>
> During emergencey treatment in hospital Eric is given a new drug

which is undergoing a properly conducted clinical trial. He proves to be allergic to the drug and dies almost at once.

Deborah is charged with murder. While on remand in prison she discovers that she is not pregnant, but is prescribed sedatives by the prison doctor who describes her as 'a shell-shocked and traumatised young woman'.

Consider Deborah's criminal liability for murder and the issues which may be raised in answer to that charge. Include in your answer comments on the appropriateness of the law in such circumstances.

1 Suggested approach:

John was driving behind Sanjay on the motorway. John was frustrated because he thought that Sanjay was not driving fast enough. When Sanjay turned off the motorway into the service area, John followed and both men parked their cars.

John ran over to Sanjay's car and began to shout at Sanjay in an abusive manner through the closed window of the car.

Sanjay suddenly opened his car door and, in order to avoid being hit by the door, John jumped backwards. Unfortunately, John jumped into the path of another car which was driven by Emma, well in excess of the speed limit.

As a result, John suffered a broken leg as well as cuts and bruises.

> Possibly common law assault by John if Sanjay feared immediate personal violence – the closed window is irrelevant – see *Smith* v. *Chf Supt Woking Police Station* (1983).

> Why did Sanjay suddenly open the car door? If fearful of John surely he could have locked the doors and windows? Was this therefore some form of an non-fatal offence against the person by Sanjay, the door amounting to a weapon? See below.

> Cuts amount to wounds as the skin is broken – see *C (a minor)* v. *Eisenhower* (1984). Bruises are not wounds but can be actual bodily harm.

> Sanjay is unlikely to be able to use the defence of self-defence. Could he plead duress of circumstances? Unlikely as he could have avoided the danger he might have felt to be in by locking the doors of the car – mention cases of *R* v. *Conway, Willer & Martin*.

> If the skin is not broken this amounts to GBH and if the skin is broken it can also amount to a wound.

13

Discuss the criminal liability of Sanjay and Emma for John's injuries.

John's injuries constitute harm which can be categorised under sections 47, 20 and 18 of the Offences Against the Person Act 1861 and so these offences must be defined and applied:

section 47 – the *mens rea* is satisfied as Sanjay either intentionally or subjectively recklessly (*Cunningham* recklessness) opened his car door in such a way that a reasonable man would have foreseen that John would try to jump out of the way – thus the chain of causation between John's injury (bruises are enough for section 47) would probably not be broken by Emma's careless driving – see *R* v. *Roberts* (1971).

section 20 and – John has sustained wounds and GBH and
section 18 Sanjay has the *mens rea* even if he only foresaw that John might suffer some harm however minor – see *R* v. *Mowatt* (1968) – section 18 is the more serious offence which requires proof that the accused acted 'with intent' – probably Sanjay did not intend to wound John or cause him GBH even using oblique intent as per *R* v. *Nedrick* (1986) – for section 20 it is clear that Sanjay has maliciously wounded John (the cuts) and if the car door is regarded as a weapon he could be said to have *inflicted* GBH - even if he is not held to have inflicted GBH he could be said to have *caused* it because since *R* v. *Burstow* (1997) it is probably the case that there is no difference between between the words cause and inflict – thus note the probable irrelevance of *R* v. *Clarence* (1888).

– has Emma's careless driving broken the chain of causation? Probably not – use the 'but for' tests – Emma could be liable for careless driving under section 3 of the Road Traffic Act 1988 which is a 'conduct' crime as opposed to a 'result' crime.

2 Suggested approach:

This 'history' of events may well be relevant for Deborah if she wished to rely on the defence of provocation under section 3 of the Homicide Act 1957 But note that there must be evidence of specific provocative acts or words by Eric just before the attack – quote *R* v. *Acott* (1997).

Deborah and Eric have been married for three years. They have two children, aged one and three. Eric has had numerous sexual encounters with other women during their marriage, and has always boasted of them to Deborah. He has also been violent to her on some occasions, especially during her pregnancies.

Deborah has committed the *actus reus* of wounding with intent contrary to *section 18 of the OAPA 1861* and she has the necessary *mens rea* as she intended not merely to wound him but to kill him.

Deborah feared that she might be pregnant and that she would again be subjected to violence. She decided that the only way out of the situation was to kill Eric, and attacked him with a knife, causing serious injury.

It is probable that the chain of causation has not been broken by the acts of the medics, that is, there is probably no *novus actus interveniens*.

Has the treatment by the medics broken the chain of causation between the stabbing by Deborah and Eric's death? Consider the case of *R* v. *Jordan* (1956) and contrast it with the cases of *R* v. *Smith* (1959) and *R* v. *Cheshire* (1991).

During emergency treatment in hospital Eric is given a new drug which is undergoing a properly conducted clinical trial. He proves to be allergic to the drug and dies almost at once.

Is diminished responsibility a possible defence under *section 2 of the Homicide Act 1957*? Note the shift in the burden of proof and note the cases of *R* v. *Byrne* (1960) and *R* v. *Hobson* (1997).

Has Deborah in fact been suffering from Battered Woman Syndrome all these years? If this is established then it is relevant to the defence of provocation as it is now classified as a mental disease – discuss the cases of *R* v. *Thornton* (1996) and *R* v. *Humphreys* (1995) – but was Deborah provoked just before the stabbing so that she suffered from a sudden and temporary loss of self-control? If she did not so suffer then the defence of provocation is not available to her.

Deborah is charged with murder. While on remand in prison she discovers that she is not pregnant, but is prescribed sedatives by the prison doctor who describes her as 'a shell-shocked and traumatised young woman'

Consider Deborah's criminal liability for murder and the issues which may be raised in answer to that charge. Include in your answer comments on the appropriateness of the law in such circumstances.

Why is the defence of provocation not available if the woman has not lost self-control at the last minute? Note that it is up to the jury to decide if she was suffering from an abnormality of mind. If Eric had lived, despite having the *mens rea* of murder, Deborah would only have been charged under *section 18 of the OAPA 1861*.

13

SECTION SIX:
Sentencing and other topical issues

The following topics are covered in this section:

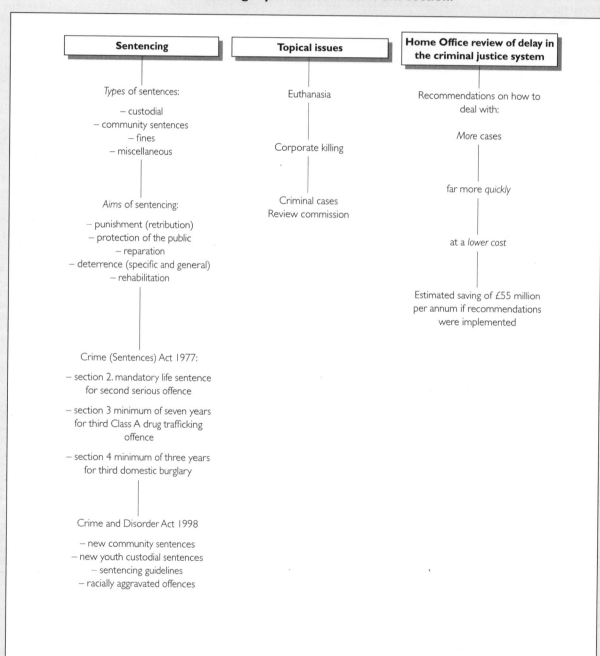

| **Sentencing** | **Topical issues** | **Home Office review of delay in the criminal justice system** |

Sentencing

Types of sentences:
- custodial
- community sentences
- fines
- miscellaneous

Aims of sentencing:
- punishment (retribution)
- protection of the public
- reparation
- deterrence (specific and general)
- rehabilitation

Crime (Sentences) Act 1977:
- section 2. mandatory life sentence for second serious offence
- section 3 minimum of seven years for third Class A drug trafficking offence
- section 4 minimum of three years for third domestic burglary

Crime and Disorder Act 1998
- new community sentences
- new youth custodial sentences
- sentencing guidelines
- racially aggravated offences

Topical issues

Euthanasia

Corporate killing

Criminal cases Review commission

Home Office review of delay in the criminal justice system

Recommendations on how to deal with:

More cases

far more *quickly*

at a *lower cost*

Estimated saving of £55 million per annum if recommendations were implemented

Sentencing

In this chapter sentencing is considered in terms of the types of sentences available to sentencers in the Magistrates' Court and Crown Court, the aims or objectives of each type of sentence, the Crime (Sentences) Act 1997 and the Crime and Disorder Act 1998. A more detailed consideration of penal policy in the twentieth century and extracts from the Crime (Sentences) Act 1997 are to be found in the *English Legal System* text in this Key Issues in A-level law series.

Types of sentences available to sentencers

As was noted in the first section of the text, trials take place in either the Magistrates' Court (for all summary offences and those TEW offences when summary jurisdiction is elected) or in the Crown Court (for all indictable offences and those TEW offences when trial by jury is elected). In the former court the sentence is passed by the magistrates, either a bench of (usually) three lay magistrates or one stipendiary magistrate. In the latter court the sentence is passed by the judge.

Magistrates' powers of sentencing are restricted to six months' imprisonment for one offence, 12 months' imprisonment for two or more offences and/or a fine up to a maximum of £5,000. They cannot pass a sentence greater than the maximum laid down in any appropriate statute. Given all of this, magistrates do have some discretion when sentencing offenders, although they do take heed of the sentencing guidelines provided for each type of offence in *The Magistrates' Association Sentencing Guidelines* last issued in April 1997. See Figures 14.1 and 14.2 for examples of these guidelines.

Until the Crime (Sentences) Act 1997 came into force, judges in the Crown Court had no restrictions on the sentence they could pass other than the maximum laid down in any appropriate statute. However, since this Act came into force judges in the Crown Court have to take heed of section 2 and section 3 of the Act (see below for a discussion of this Act) and judges do also take note of Court of Appeal guidelines on sentencing and Home Office statistical data on crime. Other than this, judges in the Crown Court have wide discretion when sentencing offenders.

Offences Against the Person Act 1861 s.47 Triable either way – see Mode of Trial Guidelines Penalty: Level 5 and/or 6 months	Assault — Actual Bodily Harm

CONSIDER THE SERIOUSNESS OF THE OFFENCE
(INCLUDING THE IMPACT ON THE VICTIM)

GUIDELINE: ➤

IS COMPENSATION, DISCHARGE OR FINE APPROPRIATE?
IS IT SERIOUS ENOUGH FOR A COMMUNITY PENALTY?
IS IT SO SERIOUS THAT ONLY CUSTODY IS APPROPRIATE?
ARE MAGISTRATES' COURTS' POWERS APPROPRIATE?

 CONSIDER AGGRAVATING AND MITIGATING FACTORS

for example
  Racial motivation
  Deliberate kicking or biting
  Extensive injuries (may be psychiatric)
  Group action
  Offender in position of authority
  Premeditated
  Victim particularly vulnerable
  Victim serving public
  Weapon

  Offence committed on bail
  Previous convictions and failures to respond
  to previous sentences if relevant
  This list is not exhaustive

for example
  Impulsive action
  Minor injury
  Provocation
  Single blow
  This list is not exhaustive

CONSIDER OFFENDER MITIGATION

for example
  Age, health (physical or mental)
  Co-operation with the police
  Voluntary compensation
  Remorse

CONSIDER YOUR SENTENCE

Compare it with the suggested guideline level of sentence and reconsider
your reasons carefully if you have chosen a sentence at a different level.
Consider a discount for a timely guilty plea.

DECIDE YOUR SENTENCE

NB. COMPENSATION – Give reasons if not awarding compensation

Remember: These are GUIDELINES not a tariff

© *The Magistrates' Association*   *Issue April 1997*

Figure 14.1

Theft	Theft Act 1968 s.1 Triable either way – see Mode of Trial Guidelines Penalty: Level 5 and/or 6 months

CONSIDER THE SERIOUSNESS OF THE OFFENCE
(INCLUDING THE IMPACT ON THE VICTIM)

GUIDELINE: ➤ *IS COMPENSATION, DISCHARGE OR FINE APPROPRIATE?*
IS IT SERIOUS ENOUGH FOR A COMMUNITY PENALTY?
IS IT SO SERIOUS THAT ONLY CUSTODY IS APPROPRIATE?
ARE MAGISTRATES' COURTS' POWERS APPROPRIATE?

 ## CONSIDER AGGRAVATING AND MITIGATING FACTORS

for example
  High value
  Planned
  Sophisticated
  Adult involving childrent
  Organised team
  Related damage
  Vunerable

  Offence committed on bail
  Previous convictions and failures to respond
  to previous sentences, if relevant
  This list is not exhaustive

for example
  Impulsive action
  Low value
  This list is not exhaustive

CONSIDER OFFENDER MITIGATION

for example
  Age, health (physical or mental)
  Co-operation with the police
  Voluntary compensation
  Remorse

CONSIDER YOUR SENTENCE

*Compare it with the suggested guideline level of sentence and reconsider
your reasons carefully if you have chosen a sentence at a different level.
Consider a discount for a timely guilty plea.*

DECIDE YOUR SENTENCE

GUIDELINE FINES		
LOW INCOME	AVERAGE INCOME	HIGH INCOME
£135	£340	£810

NB. COMPENSATION – Give reasons if not awarding compensation
Remember: These are GUIDELINES not a tariff

© *The Magistrates' Association*   *Issue April 1997*

Figure 14.2

14

What types of sentences are available to the magistrates and judges?

A wide range of sentences is available to magistrates and judges as provided for by various statutes, most notably the Criminal Justice Acts of 1948, 1967, 1972, 1988, 1991 and 1993, the Criminal Justice and Public Order Act of 1994, and the Crime and Disorder Act 1998. The trend is for the range of sentences available to the sentencers to increase to meet varying Government needs (see below). At present, the following types of sentences are available for adult offenders, that is, offenders aged 21 years or more:

- ▶ custodial sentences;
- ▶ community sentences;
- ▶ fines;
- ▶ conditional discharge;
- ▶ absolute discharge;
- ▶ binding over;
- ▶ miscellaneous orders.

The most significant statute as regards sentencing is the Criminal Justice Act 1991 (CJA 1991) which established a hierarchy of sentences as shown in Figure 14.3.

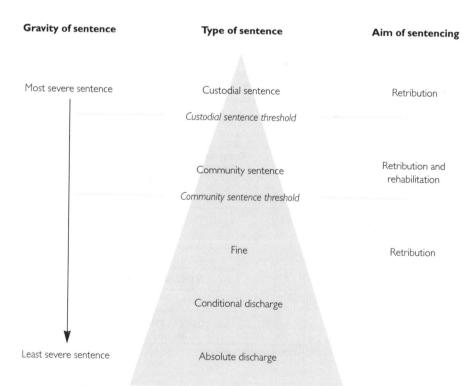

Figure 14.3   Sentencing framework introduced by the Criminal Justice Act 1991

Modifications were made to the CJA 1991 by the Criminal Justice Act 1993 and by the Criminal Justice and Public Order Act 1994.

Custodial sentences

A custodial sentence means that the offender is sent to prison. By virtue of section 1(2) of the CJA 1991 a court:

> shall not pass a custodial sentence on the offender unless it is of the opinion –
> (a) that the offence, or the combination of the offence and one or more offences associated with it, was **so serious** that only such a sentence can be justified for the offence; or
> (b) where the offence is a violent or sexual offence, that only such a sentence would be adequate to protect the public from serious harm from him.

The requirement for the sentencer to consider the seriousness of the offence or offences in question is said to create a **custody threshold** as shown in Figure 14.3. This section of the CJA 1991 was greatly criticised because it took away the sentencer's discretion to look at past criminal behaviour. This discretion was in part restored by the 1993 CJA and, in a 1993 Court of Appeal guideline case (*R* v. *Cox*), sentencers were given the following advice – that the phrase '*so serious that only a custodial sentence can be justified*' applies to an offence '*if it is such as to make right-thinking members of the public, knowing all the facts, feel that justice would not be done by the passing of anything other than a custodial sentence*'. However, in the case of *R* v. *Howells and related appeals* (1998) the Court of Appeal stated that the test in *R* v. *Cox* was not helpful. Instead it stated that:

> ...the court would bear in mind that criminal sentences were invariably intended to protect the public, by punishment, reformation or deterrence, but should be no longer than necessary to meet their penal purpose. The court would, **in borderline cases**, begin by considering **the nature and extent both of the defendant's criminal intention and of any injury to the victim**, so that where an offence was deliberate and premeditated and inflicted personal or mental injury it would usually be more serious than where it was spontaneous and unpremeditated and inflicted financial loss only.

A custodial sentence is usually *immediate* such that the offender is sent straight to prison from the court. However, where the custodial sentence is no greater than two years, the court can order that the custodial sentence be *suspended* for between one or two years (the operational period). This means that the offender is 'free' to leave the

14

court but if he commits an imprisonable offence during the operational period he can be sent to prison for the original term and for the term incurred by the most recent offence. The court can only pass a suspended sentence in exceptional cases.

When a custodial sentence is passed on an offender how much of it will actually be served in prison? It is unusual for a prisoner to serve the full amount of the sentence passed in court because of early release following 'good behaviour'. A prisoner may be released early only on licence (in which case he can be recalled if he re-offends) or may be released totally free, that is, unconditionally. The basic rules are as follows :

i   An offender sentenced to up to 12 months will be released automatically after serving half of the sentence *if of good behaviour*. This release is unconditional.

ii An offender sentenced to between 12 months and four years will be released automatically after serving half of the sentence *if of good behaviour*. This release is only on licence though.

iii An offender sentenced to more than four years will be released automatically and unconditionally after serving two-thirds of the sentence *if of good behaviour* although the Parole Board may consider release on licence at the half way point.

In other words, the sentence passed in court does not truly reflect the amount of time the offender will spend in prison. It is for this reason that Michael Howard, when Home Secretary under the Conservative Government, called for *'Honesty in Sentencing'* in his White Paper leading up to the enacting of the Crime (Sentences) Act 1997. Students should refer to the *English Legal System* text in this series for full consideration of this White Paper. More recently, in January 1998, the Lord Chief Justice, Lord Bingham of Cornhill, delivered a statement in court and on the internet, telling judges that when they pass a custodial sentence they have to explain in court how much of the sentence will actually be spent in prison, according to the basic rules shown above. It is hoped that such a move will help to restore confidence in the criminal justice system and help to remove many of the misconceptions over sentencing.

Community sentences

By section 6 of the CJA 1991 a community sentence consists of one or more of the following community orders (for those aged 21 or over):

i   probation order;
ii community service order;
iii combination order;
iv curfew order.

For those offenders aged under 21 years the court can also order a supervision order or an attendence centre order.

Since the CJA 1991 community sentences are viewed as a more serious sentence than they were previously. There is a *community sentence threshold* to cross before a community sentence can be passed. By section 6 CJA 1991 the court must not pass a community sentence unless:

(a) *the offence (or the combination of the offence and one or more associated offences) is serious enough to warrant it; and*

(b) *the court has considered which order or orders are most suitable for the offender; and*

(c) *the restrictions on the offender's liberty imposed by the order or orders are commensurate with the seriousness of the offence or the combination of the offence and one or more offences associated with it.*

Until section 38 of the Crime (Sentences) Act 1997 came into force on 1 October 1997, the court could only impose a community sentence with the consent of the offender. If the offender did not consent then the court could send the offender to prison. By virtue of section 38 of the Crime (Sentences) Act 1997 a community sentence can now be imposed without the consent of the offender. This is to reflect the fact that community sentences are now regarded as a more serious sentence, more of a punishment.

Probation orders may be imposed on an offender aged 17 years or more without his consent for a period of between six months and three years. The court may insist that the offender lives at a certain address during the period of probation. While under probation the offender has to report to a probation officer and be of good behaviour. As such the probation order impinges on the freedom of the offender and is thus a more serious punishment than a fine. If the offender breaches the terms of his probation or commits another offence during the probationary period, he will be brought back to the court and, in addition to being punished for the new offence, he might have the probation order for the original offence quashed and replaced with another sentence.

Community service orders may be imposed on an offender aged 16 years or more without his consent for a period of between 40 and 240 hours of community service. An offender aged 16 years can only be given a maximum of 120 hours. The offence in question must be an imprisonable one. A community service order is not usually given

14

without a pre-sentence report and under the order the offender has to undertake some form of work for the community, such as gardening, decorating and so forth, under the supervision of a probation officer. Thus, the community service order impinges on the offender's freedom and is seen as more of a punishment nowadays than merely rehabilitative. If the offender breaches the community service order he will be taken back to court and may be given a different sentence.

Combination order is a mixture (or combination) of a probation order and a community service order. The period of probation must be for at least 12 months and the community service part of the sentence must be between 40 and 100 hours. This type of order is used particularly for repeat vandals and burglars. It keeps them under supervision for at least a year and the community service could be detailed for times when they might be tempted to re-offend.

Curfew order is being used in certain parts of Britain in pilot schemes before it is introduced throughout the country. The order requires the offender to remain at a particular place, usually at home, for between two and 12 hours a day for up to six months. The order can be imposed without the consent of the offender. It is aimed at keeping offenders off the street at key times when they might re-offend and in some places it is monitored by electronic tagging. Again, such a sentence impinges on the freedom of the offender.

Fines

The sentencer can only impose a fine up to any maximum laid down in the statute concerning the offence in question and magistrates can only impose a fine up to a maximum of £5,000. In the Crown Court the judge can impose a fine up to any amount he thinks appropriate. A fine may be imposed in addition to other sentences or instead of other sentences, even instead of imprisonment. A fine is regarded as a less severe sentence than imprisonment and community sentences because it does not impinge on the freedom of the offender; it only impinges on his pocket. However, if the offender fails to pay his fine the court can send him to prison although the offender needs to have failed to pay several fines before this is resorted to. Since the Crime (Sentences) Act 1997 a fine defaulter (in certain pilot schemes) may now be given a community service order of between 20 and 100 hours or a curfew order with electronic tagging. It is likely that in these pilot areas the number of offenders on community service will therefore increase and, if such orders are given instead of sending the offender to prison, then the community service order has to be seen as a more severe sentence than it was previously.

Conditional and absolute discharge

A conditional discharge means that the offender receives no punishment immediately as he is free and will only be brought back before the court if he re-offends during the period of the conditional discharge which can last up to three years. The offender is not under the supervision of a probation officer and so his freedom is not impinged upon at all. If called back to court he can be given a different sentence for the original offence. An absolute discharge means that the offender is given no punishment at all and can go free from the court without any conditions. This might seem a strange sentence. Why bring the offender to court if, even if found guilty, he will not be punished? Such a sentence is available to cover situations where, although technically guilty of the offence in question, the court feels that punishment per se is inappropriate in all the circumstances. Offences of strict liability might be appropriate ones for such a sentence as in such offences the offender only committed the *actus reus* of the crime in question.

Binding over

The court might order the offender, or indeed anyone before the court, to be bound over to keep the peace and be of good behaviour. A sum of money has to be deposited with the court which will be forfeited to the court if the offender, or whoever, does breach the peace during the lifetime of the binding over. This type of sentence is particularly suitable for minor disturbances and, in many ways, acts as a warning to the parties concerned that should their behaviour continue, and maybe escalate, then the court might take a more severe line.

Miscellaneous orders

The court may also make use of the following orders, either instead of another sentence or in addition to another sentence: compensation orders, forfeiture orders and confiscation orders.

Compensation orders – magistrates can award compensation (money) for personal injury, loss or damage up to a total of £5,000 for each offence, while judges in the Crown Court can award compensation up to any amount. The compensation may relate to offences taken into consideration but do not normally extend to injury, loss or damage resulting from a road accident unless the offender is uninsured and the Motor Insurers Bureau will not cover the loss. The court should consider the award of a compensation order even when the victim has not applied for one and, even when such an order has been made, the victim may still pursue a claim for damages through the civil courts.

14

A victim of violent crime who is seriously injured is likely to be compensated under the Criminal Injuries Compensation Scheme. An offender can be ordered to compensate the victim up to a maximum of £1,000. This amount will be reduced by any amount the offender has already been ordered to pay by way of compensation to the victim.

The court has to have regard to the offender's ability to pay compensation and it might be payable over a period of time. Compensatory damages can be of two types: general damages, for the pain and suffering caused by the injury itself, and special damages, relating to financial loss sustained as a result of the injury, such as loss of earnings. The table shown at Figure 14.4 is taken from a Home Office Circular, issued in August 1993, which appeared in the Magistrates' Association Sentencing Guidelines of April 1997. The figures given are only a guideline and may be increased or decreased according to the circumstances of the case in hand.

Type of injury		Suggested award
Graze	depending on size	up to £50
Bruise	depending on size	up to £75
Black eye		£100
Cut: no permanent scarring	depending on size and whether stitched	£75–£500
Sprain	depending on loss of mobility	£100–£1,000
Loss of a non-front tooth	depending on cosmetic effect and age of victim	£250–£500
Other minor injury	causing reasonable absence from work (2–3) weeks	£550–£850
Loss of a front tooth		£1,000
Facial scar	however small – resulting in permanent disfigurement	£750+
Jaw	fractured (wired)	£2,750
Nasal	displaced fracture of the nasal bone	£750
Nasal	undisplaced fracture of bone requiring manipulation	£1,000
Nasal	not causing fracture but displaced septum requiring sub-mucous resection	£1,750
Wrist	simple fracture with complete recovery in a few weeks	£1,750–£2,500
Wrist	displaced fracture – limb in plaster for some 6 weeks; full recovery 6–12 months	£2,500+
Finger	fractured little finger; assuming full recovery after a few weeks	£750
Leg or arm	simple fracture of tibia, fibula, ulna or radius with full recovery in 3 weeks	£2,500
Laparotomy	stomach scar 6–8 inches long (resulting from exploratory operation)	£3,500

Figure 14.4 Guidelines for compensation in Magistrates' Courts

Forfeiture orders – only apply to the Crown Court and may be ordered where the offender is convicted on an indictable offence which can be punished with a term of imprisonment of two years or more. The offender can be ordered to forfeit (that is, to surrender to the court) any property which was in his possession or control at the time of apprehension which was to be used in committing or facilitating an offence. Thus, any tools used in a burglary or weapons used in an armed robbery could be forfeited, as could the getaway car.

Confiscation orders – also only apply to the Crown Court. By a confiscation order the proceeds of the crime may be confiscated. This is governed by the Proceeds of Crime Act 1995. Proceeds of drug trafficking are covered separately by the Drug Trafficking Offences Act 1994. In a White Paper entitled *Tackling Drugs to Build a Better Britain* published in April 1998, it was suggested that assets seized from convicted drug barons should be used to fund treatment for drug addicts and education programmes for children. The courts seize about £5 million a year in assets and it is unusual for any of this to be earmarked for specific expenditure – it simply goes into treasury funds.

New sentences under the Crime and Disorder Bill 1998

Various new sentences have been introduced in the Crime and Disorder Bill 1998 and these are discussed below.

Reforms aimed at improving consistency in sentencing

The CJA 1991 was an attempt to bring some structure to sentencing but this Act had to be modified in 1993 and in 1994. There is still a lack of consistency in sentencing and, currently, two developments are underway which may lead to greater consistency.

The Law Commission is attempting to consolidate the sentencing powers of the court and has engaged a consultant, a former member of the Parliamentary Counsel Office, to undertake this. Dr David Thomas QC (Hon), editor of *Current Sentencing Practice* has agreed to help with this project.

The Crime and Disorder Act 1998 also aims to promote greater consistency in sentencing. By section 80 the Court of Appeal is to review existing sentencing guidelines and to produce sentencing guidelines for areas of law where they do not already exist. Apart from achieving consistency in sentencing, the Court of Appeal has to be aware of the need to promote public confidence in the criminal justice system when undertaking this task. Under the Act, a Sentencing Advisory Panel will be appointed by the Lord Chancellor.

14

This panel will consult with the police, probation service and victims and then give advice to the Court of Appeal. See below for more details of section 80.

The need for consistency in sentencing is demonstrated in the two extracts shown below. The first is from the Magistrates' Association *Sentencing Guidelines* of April 1997 and appears at the front of the guidelines:

> *I think it most important that, within discretionary limits, Magistrates' Courts up and down the country should endeavour to approach sentencing with a measure of consistency, and I have no doubt that these guidelines will contribute powerfully to that end.*
> **The Rt. Hon. The Lord Bingham of Cornhill,**
> *Lord Chief Justice of England*

The second extract (*R* v. *Street* 1997) is taken from the Law Report section of *The Times* dated 31 March 1997:

Consolidation of sentencing provisions sought

Regina v. Street

Before Lord Bingham of Cornhill, Lord Chief Justice, Mr Justice Ognall and Mr Justice Forbes [Judgment March 7]

It was the clear duty of counsel to familarise themselves with the court's relevant sentencing powers and, where appropriate, to direct the judge's attention to them and, in particular, to the relevant legislation if the judge passed a sentence which did not take account of the appropriate maximum penalties.

Sentencing judges faced extreme difficulty, having regard to the dispersal of sentencing powers through different provisions in different Acts. An attempt to consolidate sentencing provisions in one comprehensive statute would be greatly welcomed.

The Court of Appeal, Criminal Division, so stated when sitting at Liverpool and varying sentences imposed on Arthur Street who had been convicted in Chester Crown Court (Judge David, QC) on pleas of guilty to six counts in respect of offences under sections 14(1) and 15(1) of the Sexual Offences Act 1956 committed between 1967 and 1981.

The Sexual Offences Act 1985, which came into force on September 16, 1985, amended certain maximum penalties which might be imposed under the 1956 Act. The judge's attention had not been drawn to the fact that the offences had been committed before the amendment took effect and, in sentencing the defendant on the offences under section 14(1), he had not given effect to the lower maximum penalties in force at the relevant time.

Since the defendant was only liable to be sentenced to the previous maximum the sentences imposed on those counts had therefore to be varied accordingly.

Mr Stephen Hesford for the defendant.

THE LORD CHIEF JUSTICE said that the court had emphasised on a number of previous occasions and now wished to re-emphasise in unambiguous terms that it was the clear duty of both counsel, counsel for the Crown and for the defendant to familiarise himself or herself with the relevant sentencing powers of the court, to direct the judge's attention to those powers where it was appropriate to do so and, in particular, to the relevant legislation if the judge passed a sentence which did not take account of appropriate maximum penalties.

The court was mindful of the extreme difficulty which sentencing judges faced, having regard to the state of the statute book and the dispersal of sentencing powers through different provisions in different places in different Acts, and would greatly welcome an attempt to consolidate sentencing provisions in one convenient and comprehensive statute.

That was not however the state of the law and the court would emphasise the importance of drawing the judge's attention at the time to all relevant provisions to avoid errors such as undoubtedly occurred in relation to the last four counts of the present indictment.

Solicitors: Abson Hall Loring, Macclesfield.

The aims or objectives of sentencing

When a sentencer passes a particular sentence on an offender, do they aim to achieve something by passing that sentence? What are the aims or objectives behind each type of sentence? It will be shown that this question can only be answered in relation to a particular time frame; the aim of passing a custodial sentence today might not be the same as it was 50 years ago. Thus, whereas in the mid 1900s long prison sentences were thought desirable to allow an offender to be rehabilitated, in the 1990s long prison sentences are thought to be desirable in order to protect the public from the offender and in order to punish the offender. Such changes in penal policy are instigated in large part by government policy. A full consideration of this topic is provided in the *English Legal System* text in this series. The general aims or objectives of sentences are discussed below. How these aims are linked to particular types of sentences is part of the penal policy discussion.

There are several aims or objectives in sentencing:

- ▶ punishment of the offender – retribution;
- ▶ protection of the public;
- ▶ deterrence;
- ▶ rehabilitation;
- ▶ reparation;
- ▶ denunciation.

Punishment of the offender – retribution

Some elements of some types of sentences are included in order to punish the offender for his wrongdoing. The punishment element of a sentence is often referred to as the 'tariff' part of the sentence. The tariff relates to the offence committed and not to the offender himself. Thus, when the offender is convicted of murder and receives a life sentence, the trial judge will state what the tariff is to be, that is, the

14

number of years the offender has to spend in prison (as a punishment) before his case can come before the Parole Board for consideration of release on licence. The concept of punishment is not appropriate for sentences such as conditional and absolute discharge, although it can play a part in fines, community sentences and custodial sentences. How large a part it plays in these sentences is linked to penal and government policy.

Protection of the public

All crimes represent anti-social behaviour against the state and thus the public. As such it is part of the job of the criminal justice system to protect the public from such behaviour. The best way to protect the public from criminals is to remove the criminals from society. In the nineteenth century this was done by sending the worst criminals to oversees destinations, most notably Australia. Once this practice ceased, criminals could only be taken out of society by sending them to prison. As such, the number of prisons and the prison population have grown enormously in the twentieth century. A custodial sentence is regarded as the most severe type of sentence available to the criminal courts and this sentence is reserved for the most serious types of offences. Thus, this aim of sentencing is not linked to the offender but to the crime committed. The prevalence of custodial sentences is linked to penal policy and government policy.

Deterrence

The aim of some sentences is to deter the commission of crimes in the future, either by the offender before the court (specific deterrence) or by others (general deterrence). Thus, it could be that the offender receives what appears to be a somewhat severe sentence for the crime committed. In this respect the particular offender before the court is being made 'an example of' to show what will happen to those who behave in this particular manner. Such a tactic might be used when the courts are trying to eradicate a particular nuisance in an area, such as joy-riding or drug abuse. In this respect the deterrence element of a sentence is not concerned with the particular offender although it is concerned with the particular offender if the court only wishes to deter that particular offender from re-offending. Deterrence thus operates on the basis of instilling dread of the possible punishment if convicted of certain crimes.

Rehabilitation

If the sentence aims to rehabilitate the offender it aims to make the offender see the error of his ways so that he is less likely to re-offend. In many ways this aim of sentencing is the opposite of aiming to punish the offender. An offender might be punished for committing a crime and then continue to re-offend, whereas it is hoped that an offender who has undergone some rehabilitative programme is less likely to re-offend. The types of sentences most usually associated with rehabilitation are the community sentences. However, as has been noted above, the community sentences are now taking on a more punitive role. This is due to shifting penal and government policy. When rehabilitation is the aim of sentencing, the sentencer is concerned more with the offender himself rather than with the crime committed.

Reparation

Reparation involves the offender in giving something back to society and to the victim to amend for his wrongdoing. Such an aim of sentencing can easily be linked to rehabilitation and is most readily associated with community sentences and compensation orders. Reparation is becoming more prominent in sentencing and in some areas for some crimes (such as domestic burglary), the offender is brought face to face with his victim to see the suffering caused to the victim by the crime. Such techniques are widely used in Australia and are being studied by those involved in the criminal justice system in England and Wales. Reparation concerns the offender and the crime.

Denunciation

Denunciation involves showing society's disapproval of the behaviour in question. In some ways it establishes what is morally acceptable in society. Thus, it is possible that denunciation could be a dominant aim in sentencing sex offenders. As such, denunciation is linked to the crime committed rather than to the offender.

Recidivism

People who habitually commit crimes are known as recidivists. Despite the fact that they may already have been processed through the criminal justice system, they continue to commit further crimes. For such people the criminal justice system has a cyclical nature as shown in Figure 14.5. Thus, for recidivists, the type of sentence awarded and the aim of the sentencer in awarding the sentence are

14

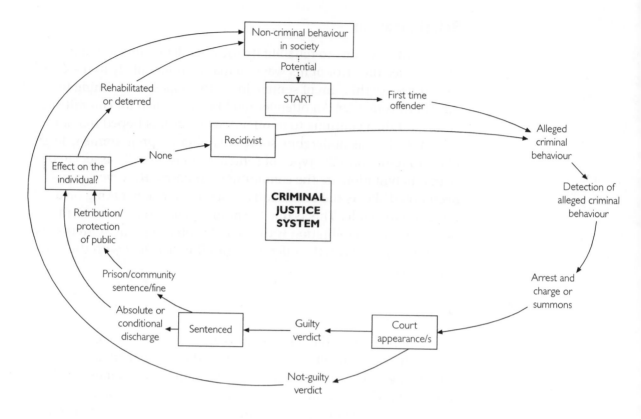

Figure 14.5 Diagram showing the cyclical nature of the criminal justice system for recidivists and the potential within the criminal justice system for criminals to be rehabilitated or deterred from criminal behaviour

ineffective in preventing future criminal activity. It follows logically that the only way to prevent recidivists from committing crimes for any period of time is by awarding them a custodial sentence.

Crime (Sentences) Act 1997

The Crime (Sentences) Act 1997 aroused great interest and debate because it introduced a mandatory life sentence for an offence and two mandatory minimum sentences. Until this Act only murder attracted a mandatory or automatic life sentence. Most other offences attract a maximum sentence as laid down in statute and the sentencers in court have the discretion to pass a sentence up to this maximum as they feel is appropriate in all the circumstances. The key words here are *maximum* and *discretion*. When a statute lays down a minimum sentence for an offence or a mandatory life sentence, the sentencer in court has no discretion at all as regards sentencing. Why is this a problem? The debate concerns the position of the three arms of Government relative to one another. The executive is supposed to propose new laws, the legislature is supposed to enact new laws and the judiciary is supposed to apply those laws. It is supposed to be part of the job of judges and magistrates in the criminal courts to determine the appropriate sentence in each case. If the legislature stipulates a mandatory life sentence or a minimum sentence, it is, in effect, taking on the sentencing role of the judiciary. Due to the heated debate surrounding the passage of this Act through Parliament, the final form of the offending sections of the Act, sections 2 to 4, were amended to allow the sentencers some discretion to avoid the mandatory or minimum sentences in exceptional or unjust circumstances. It will be interesting to see whether sentencers avoid the mandatory and minimum sentences most of the time or only in rare instances.

Section 2 of the Act provides that the court must impose a life sentence on an adult convicted of a serious offence for the second time, unless there are exceptional circumstances for not doing so. A serious offence is defined so as to include offences such as attempted murder, conspiracy to commit murder, manslaughter, wounding or causing GBH and rape.

Section 3 of the Act provides that the court must impose a minimum custodial sentence of seven years on an adult convicted for the third time of a Class A drug trafficking offence, unless it would be unjust to do so in all the circumstances.

Section 4 of the Act provides that the court must impose a minimum custodial sentence of three years on an adult convicted for the third time of a domestic burglary unless it would be unjust to do so in all the circumstances.

Sections 2 and 3 of the Act came into force on 1 October 1997 and section 4 is due to come into force in December 1999.

Crime and Disorder Bill 1998

The Crime and Disorder Act 1998 aims to amend parts of the Crime (Sentences) Act 1997 and some of the key clauses with regards to sentencing are shown below.

New sentences:

14

Section 58

This empowers a court to impose a sentence on a sexual or violent offender which includes an extended period of post-release supervision. In other words, the offender is released 'on licence'. This is to be effected by inserting a new section 44 into the CJA 1991. This has been introduced to prevent, for instance, paedophiles being released into the community at the end of a fixed (determinate) sentence when they have not been rehabilitated and therefore continue to pose a threat to society.

For sexual offenders the licence can be up to 10 years and for violent offenders the licence can be up to five years.

Section 61

This empowers a court to make a 'Drug Treatment and Testing Order' of between six months and three years on a convicted offender aged 16 years or over when the court is satisfied that the offender is dependent on drugs or has a propensity to misuse drugs and that the offender is susceptible to treatment.

Section 67

This empowers a court to make a 'Reparation Order' for a convicted young offender. It requires the offender to make reparation to either the person or persons specified or to the community at large. The reparation order should not require the offender to work more than a total of 24 hours or to make reparation to any person without that person's consent.

Section 69

This empowers a court to make an 'Action Plan Order' for a convicted young offender. This requires the offender to comply with an action plan for a period of three months. The action plan contains a list of requirements with respect to the offender's actions and whereabouts during the period of the order, places the offender under supervision for the period and requires the offender to comply with any directions given by the supervisory officer with a view to implementation of the plan.

Section 73

This empowers a court to pass a 'Detention and Training Order' on a convicted young offender where the offence is one which would be punishable by imprisonment in the case of a person aged 21 years or over. Such an order will only be passed on an offender under the age of 15 at the time of conviction if the offender is a persistent offender, and for an offender under the age of 12 at the time of conviction if a custodial sentence is the only adequate way to protect the public from further offending by him.

Section 80

This empowers the Court of Appeal to issue sentencing guidelines for a particular category of indictable offence when it is seised of an appeal against the sentence passed for an offence or it receives a proposal to issue sentencing guidelines for a particular category of offence from the Sentencing Advisory Panel which is to be set up under section 81. When framing or revising guidelines the Court is to have regard to:

i the need to promote consistency in sentencing;
ii the sentences imposed by courts in England and Wales for offences of the relevant category;

  iii the cost of different sentences and their relative effectiveness in preventing re-offending;

  iv the need to promote public confidence in the criminal justice system; and

  v the views communicated to the Court by the Sentencing Advisory Panel.

Section 82 Under this section when a court is considering the seriousness of an offence, if the offence was racially aggravated the court shall consider this as a factor that increases the seriousness of the offence. When it does so it is to announce in open court that the offence was so aggravated.

14

Topical issues

There are several topical issues to consider, some of which have already been dealt with in the appropriate chapter in the text, that is:

i the effect of *R* v. *Preddy* (1996) on the law of theft;

ii the effect of *R* v. *Powell and Daniels* and *R* v. *English* (1997) on the law of joint enterprise;

iii the effect of *R* v. *Geddes* (1996) on the law of attempt;

iv the effect of *R* v. *Pommell* (1995) on the defence of necessity;

v the effect of *R* v. *Ireland* and *R* v. *Burstow* (1997) on the section 20 and section 18 offences under the Offences Against the Person Act 1861;

vi the Protection from Harrassment Act 1997;

vii consent and non-fatal offences against the person;

viii the possible criminalisation of the wilful transmission of the Aids virus; and

ix battered woman syndrome (BWS).

The issues to be considered in this chapter are:

i euthanasia;

ii corporate killing;

iii the Criminal Cases Review Commission (CCRC).

These are issues which may appear in examination questions on the A2 paper and which stimulate discussion of the nature of the criminal law and the processes within the criminal justice system. For most A-level law syllabuses such issues will also be useful when studied in conjunction with the A1 paper as they will provide a depth of knowledge which should equip students to undertake a more critical analysis of the criminal justice system as a whole.

Euthanasia

Euthanasia describes the situation where a human being (usually a doctor) brings about the death of another human being (the patient) in circumstances where the patient is terminally ill; the doctor accelerates the death (usually by the administration of a large dose of pain-relieving drugs) in order that death will follow easily and gently to minimise the suffering of the person dying. The dilemma for society is whether or not such actions by the doctor amount to an unlawful killing and whether or not the doctor could actually do more than administer pain-relieving drugs in such a situation. For instance, could the doctor administer a lethal injection which would achieve the same result as the administration of a large dose of pain-relieving drugs, only more quickly? The problem is that administration of a lethal injection involves the doctor in conduct which has, as its purpose, the killing of a human being, whereas the administration of pain-relieving drugs involves the doctor in conduct which amounts to doing what is best for the care of the patient. The former course of conduct is pro-active in ending life, whereas the latter course of conduct is reactive to a life-threatening situation.

Remember that the *mens rea* for murder is *intention to kill* or cause serious bodily harm. If a doctor administered a lethal injection he would be intending to kill the patient and by doing so he would carry out the *actus reus* of murder. The attitude of the state to euthanasia varies from country to country. In the UK the Government has repeatedly stated that it will not allow euthanasia. By this the Government means that it will not tolerate pro-active euthanasia involving, for instance, the administration of a lethal injection. However, it does tolerate the administration of large dosages of pain-relieving drugs as this practice is widespread among doctors. In Holland, by contrast, the attitude of the state towards euthanasia is more liberal. Should the law on euthanasia be built up piecemeal by various individuals taking their case to court for adjudication on its lawfulness, or should the law be made in advance by Parliament? Such issues are discussed in the newspaper article shown below in Figure 15.1.

Some people fear that the government in the UK is moving towards a more liberal stance towards euthanasia because of a consultation paper which was issued in December 1997 entitled, 'Who Decides?', which proposes that people should be allowed to make 'living wills'. The purpose of a living will is to enable a person to make arrangements for themselves in the event that they become *mentally incapable*. Such arrangements could involve giving a relative the power of attorney to deal with the patient's money or to provide for the withdrawal of life-prolonging treatment. However, in the consultation paper, the government stresses that there should be no move towards the legalisation of euthanasia. The Lord Chancellor, Lord Irvine of Lairg, told the House of Lords:

15

Figure 15.1   Attitude of the British Government to euthanasia contrasted to the attitude of the Dutch Government

Lords warned over following Dutch road to euthanasia

By Philip Johnston, Home Affairs Editor

CONCERN that Britain could follow Holland along the road to widespread use of euthanasia was voiced in the House of Lords last night by one of the country's leading surgeons.

Lord McColl, the Professor of Surgery at Guy's Hospital, London, said there was evidence from the Netherlands to show that "the current practice of euthanasia is out of control".

Advocates of the "right to die" often point to Holland as a model for how doctor-assisted voluntary euthanasia for terminally-ill patients can work without abuse.

But Lord McColl said the system of regulation was not working and pointed out the dangers of Britain adopting similar practices under a review of the law now taking place in Whitehall.

Last month, Church leaders expressed concern that plans to make "living wills" legally enforceable marked a further step towards the acceptance of voluntary euthanasia. It is feared that the courts could be used

to make case law that would bypass Parliament and allow doctors to assist the deaths of mentally-incompetent patients.

Lord McColl said that as a result of lenient judgments by Dutch courts, accepted medical practice changed and euthanasia became acceptable. "By the time Parliament considered the matter in 1993, it was a case of attempting to shut the stable door after the horse had bolted," he said.

He claimed that attempts were being made in Britain to mirror the position in Holland and cited last year's High Court action brought by Annie Lindsell, who suffered from motor neurone disease.

The action was supported by the Voluntary Euthanasia Society ostensibly to establish the sort of treatment her family doctor was entitled to give. In the event, the case collapsed because the court ruled the palliative care proposed was already legal.

But Lord McColl said: "The purpose behind the Annie Lindsell case

was to try to obtain permission to give an unlimited and unspecified dose of diamorphine which could have resulted in her immediate death and would then have been hailed as the first legal case of euthanasia in this country.

"How can we be sure that what happens in Holland today will not happen in this country tomorrow?"

Although euthanasia and assisted suicide strictly remain illegal in Holland, doctors who help patients to die will not be prosecuted provided they follow certain guidelines.

Lord Irvine, the Lord Chancellor, is considering whether to introduce laws to give statutory force to living wills, whereby an individual states what sort of treatment they would want should they fall seriously ill.

He said last month: "The Government's opposition to euthanasia is settled, well-known and unqualified."

Source: *The Daily Telegraph*,
7 May 1998

Euthanasia is a deliberate intervention undertaken with the express intention of ending a life, at an individual's own request or for a merciful motive. The Government is absolutely opposed to euthanasia in any form.

He also said that: '*The blunt truth is that if a doctor took such action [deliberately ending life] he would be exposed to a charge of murder.*'

Where does the medical profession stand on the issue of euthanasia? Doctors have got to act within the law and, as stated above, the Government will not tolerate the legalisation of euthanasia. It seems that most doctors see their role as life-preserving, not life-ending. This life-preserving role is, however, tempered by the need to be aware of the *best interests of the patient*. As such, it may be necessary to administer a large dosage of a pain-relieving drug to a terminally ill patient when to do so would probably only hasten death by hours or days. Under such reasoning, the doctor would not be liable for murder as his intention would not be to kill the patient and the *de minimis* principle would also apply – look back to the notes on causation for murder. Also, it might be appropriate for a doctor to turn off a life-support machine (a withdrawal of care which amounts to an omission) when the patient has no hope of recovery, as when in a persistent vegetative state or when brain dead. Look back to the case of *Airedale National Health Service Trust v. Bland* (1993) – once it was established that Anthony Bland was not going to make a recovery the doctor *was relieved of his duty* to provide life-support and so, being under no duty to act positively for the patient, his *omission* to provide life-support was not criminal. See also the newspaper article in Figure 15.2.

Thus, as the law currently stands, a doctor may legally:

i administer a large dose of pain-relieving drugs to a terminally ill patient to relieve pain but which may hasten death by an indeterminate period of time while acting in the best interests of the patient;

ii withdraw life-support mechanisms when there is either no chance of the patient making a recovery or when the patient is already 'brain-dead';

but a doctor may not administer a lethal injection to bring about immediate death. It is a fine line indeed.

15

Figure 15.2   Attitude of the medical profession towards euthanasia

BMA rejects legal euthanasia

DOCTORS overwhelmingly opposed any idea of euthanasia yesterday after a debate in which they said they would use all their professional influence to oppose any attempt to make it legal for them to kill patients (Ian Murray writes).

Sandy Macara, chairman of the British Medical Association, summed up the emotional mood of its annual conference in Edinburgh: "Our patients rightly see us as saving life and not embracing death. We should do nothing to betray their trust in that vital function."

Surendra Kumar, a GP from St Helens, Merseyside, said doctors should not be regarded like a vet to put down sick animals. They must ease suffering and not end life.

Fay Wilson, a Birmingham GP, said: "Our function is not to dispose of people. Our function is to care for them and make their lives better. Changing the law would take us down the slippery slope to an expectation that our function is to kill those whose life is not worthwhile."

Michael Stuart, a GP from Southendon-Sea, Essex, who founded a hospice and helped to set up the Association of Palliative Care, said that during 30 years in practice he had patients who "asked me to finish them off". When he asked them if they really wanted him to come along with a syringe and end it all, they all changed their minds. He had treated patients who had been able to live for some time with a good quality of life after proper treatment to control their physical, mental and spiritual pain.

Dr Stuart said he was sometimes suspicious of the motives of relatives who asked for someone to be put out of their misery. Even though most were seriously concerned about the suffering of someone they loved, there were some who wanted to get their hands on an expected legacy.

Source: *The Times*, 4 July 1997

What is the *morality* of euthanasia? Could it be that in the two situations listed above where the doctor does not act illegally (does not practice euthanasia), his conduct is only regarded as legal because it would be morally wrong to punish the doctor in such situations and/or it would be morally wrong to prolong the 'life' of such a patient? From the moral standpoint is it thus the case that it would be morally wrong to allow a doctor to administer a lethal injection? If the doctor could legally administer a lethal injection, how would the law protect the old and infirm from doctors who decided to 'play God' and/or from relatives who wished to inherit the patient's fortune? When the patient is unable to speak for himself this could be a very difficult issue.

What about the issue of consent? Why cannot a terminally ill patient, in full command of his mental faculties, determine that he wishes to end his life? Suicide is no longer unlawful but it might be impossible for such a patient to commit suicide, in which case the patient would need assistance. In Australia 'computer-aided' euthanasia was experimented with, whereby the patient was asked at least three times by a computer if he wished to end his life. The patient had to respond positively to these questions and, after being reminded several times that death would follow if the programme was completed positively, if the patient so chose, the computer was connected to apparatus which, on the patient's command, injected the patient with a lethal injection. Could such a system not be introduced into the UK? The risks of exploitation of such a system are obvious. The usual position in the criminal law is that a person may only consent to common law assault and battery; a person cannot generally consent to the infliction of more serious bodily harm to themselves and so a person cannot consent to their own death. However, the criminal law should not be used to take away a person's autonomy to do as they wish with their own body. In 1996 Ms S was sectioned under section 2 of the Mental Health Act 1983 and so forced into hospital to have a baby by caesarian section, against her wishes. She took the NHS Trust, Mental Health Services Trust and social worker concerned to court for judicial review of their actions and, in the Court of Appeal (*St Georges Healthcare National Health Service Trust* v. *S, R* v. *Collins and others, ex parte S,* 1998), they were all held to have acted unlawfully. Lord Justice Judge, who delivered the judgment of the court, stated:

> ... *Even when his or her life depended on receiving medical treatment, an adult of sound mind was entitled to refuse it. That reflected the autonomy of each individual and the right of self-determination: see Airedale NHS Trust v. Bland (1993) ... She was entitled not to be forced to submit to an invasion of her body against her will, whether her own life or that of her unborn child depended on it. Her right was not reduced or diminished merely because her decision to exercise it might appear morally repugnant.*

Thus, the autonomy of the individual is recognised as paramount in some situations, even when such autonomy might result in the death of the individual and an unborn baby, and even when such a decision might seem morally wrong, yet, in the case of euthanasia, an individual is not allowed such autonomy even when to allow it would seem morally correct.

A possible essay title for euthanasia and suggested approach to answering it are provided in Chapter 13.

Corporate killing

In 'Legislating the Criminal Code: Involuntary Manslaughter' (1996) Law Com. No. 237, the Law Commission put forward a Draft Involuntary Manslaughter Bill – see Chapter 12 for more details. Clause 4 concerns corporate killing as shown below:

15

4. (1) A corporation is guilty of corporate killing if –
    (a) a management failure by the corporation is the cause or one of the causes of a person's death; and
    (b) that failure constitutes conduct falling far below what can reasonably by expected of the corporation in the circumstances.
  (2) For the purposes of subsection (1) above –
    (a) there is a management failure by a corporation if the way in which its activities are managed or organised fails to ensure the health and safety of persons employed in or affected by those activities; . . .
  (3) A corporation guilty of an offence under this section is liable on conviction on indictment to a fine . . .
  (5) This section does not preclude a corporation being guilty of an offence under section 1 or 2 above.

This new offence of corporate killing has been proposed by the Law Commission because of the public outrage at the inability to hold corporations to account when disasters happen, such as when the Zeebrugge ferry sank or when there are serious train crashes. The problem with the existing law on involuntary manslaughter, as regards such corporations, is that it is not easy to identify which particular person within the corporation should be held liable for the death or deaths which occur. Usually the directors are held to be the *directing mind* of a corporation but the safety officer for the corporation is usually someone much lower down in the structure of the corporation to whom no corporate liability can attach. The only successful prosecution of a corporation for gross negligence manslaughter was when four teenagers drowned in Lyme Bay in Dorset while on an activity holiday run by OLL Ltd. In this case the director was one man who ran the whole corporation and, as such, it was possible to prosecute him. He was sentenced to imprisonment. Under the new law it would be a lot easier to prosecute a corporation as it would not be necessary to identify the *directing mind* of the corporation.

Under the proposed Bill corporations found guilty on indictment can only be given a fine. Will this act as a deterrent? Will it be a punishment? Will corporations take more care in their activities, fearing the stigma of being branded corporate killers? And what about those corporations which are run by one director – will such individuals be prosecuted for corporate killing under clause 4 of the new law, facing only a fine, or will they be prosecuted for reckless killing or killing by gross carelessness under clauses 1 or 2 of the new law, facing possible imprisonment? This option is provided for by clause 4 (5).

The Criminal Appeal Act 1968 (as amended by the Criminal Appeal Act 1995) and the Criminal Cases Review Commission

The system of appeals in the criminal justice system

It has been said that the hallmark of a civilised society is demonstrated by the operation of its legal system. In the English legal system some of the hallmarks of the criminal justice system are that a person is presumed innocent until proven guilty and that provision is built in to ensure 'due process', whereby the individual is given certain rights to ensure that he is not overborne by the power of the state. Such rights include things such as the right to silence, protection afforded by PACE 1984 (Police and Criminal Evidence Act 1984) and the ability to appeal against conviction or sentence. Such rights should help minimise the occurrence of miscarriages of justice.

At this point in the text the ability of an individual to appeal against conviction or sentence will be considered in some detail in conjuction with consideration of the newly established Criminal Cases Review Commission which has as its remit the investigation of potential miscarriages of justice.

The grounds and procedures for appeal from the Magistrates' Court to the Crown Court, from the Magistrates' Court to the Queen's Bench Division (Divisional Court) and from the Crown Court to the Court of Appeal (Criminal Division) are shown in Figures 15.3, 15.4 and 15.5. The hierarchy of the criminal courts and appeal routes are shown in detail in Chapter 1 in Figures 1.2 and 1.3.

15

Route A

For a re-trial with different magistrates

By virtue of section 142 Magistrates' Courts Act 1980

In the 'interests of justice'

For example, if new evidence comes to light after the trial

Route B
If route A is not appropriate

The defence can appeal to the Crown Court on the facts or on a point of law or both

If convicted following a plea of **NOT GUILTY**

If convicted following a plea of **GUILTY**

The defence can appeal against conviction or sentence or both

The defence can generally only appeal against sentence

The procedure: within 21 days of the passing of the sentence, the defence must give *notice of appeal* to the Magistrates' Court Clerk

Note that there is no need for any leave to appeal and no filtering out of weak cases for appeal – thus, appeals cannot be refused

The appeal is heard by a Circuit Judge or Recorder (part-time judge) with usually two magistrates – no jury– they fully re-hear the case

Powers :
– confirm the decision of the magistrates;
– reverse the decision of the magistrates;
– vary the decision of the magistrates;
– award a smaller sentence;
– award a greater sentence up to the maximum of the magistrates.

Figure 15.3
Appeals from the Magistrates' Court to the Crown Court – for the DEFENCE ONLY on a point of fact or law or both

Figure 15.4
Appeals from the Magistrates' Court to the
Queen's Bench Division (Divisional Court) – for both
the PROSECUTION and DEFENCE on a point of
LAW only

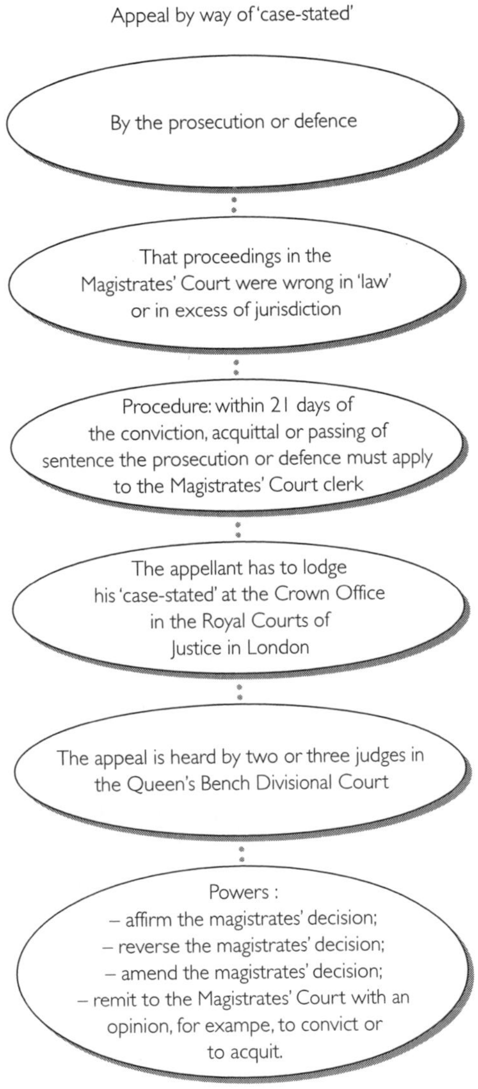

Appeal by way of 'case-stated'

By the prosecution or defence

That proceedings in the
Magistrates' Court were wrong in 'law'
or in excess of jurisdiction

Procedure: within 21 days of
the conviction, acquittal or passing of
sentence the prosecution or defence must apply
to the Magistrates' Court clerk

The appellant has to lodge
his 'case-stated' at the Crown Office
in the Royal Courts of
Justice in London

The appeal is heard by two or three judges in
the Queen's Bench Divisional Court

Powers :
– affirm the magistrates' decision;
– reverse the magistrates' decision;
– amend the magistrates' decision;
– remit to the Magistrates' Court with an
opinion, for exampe, to convict or
to acquit.

15

Figure 15.5

Appeals from the Crown Court to the Court of Appeal (Criminal Division) – generally only available to the DEFENCE

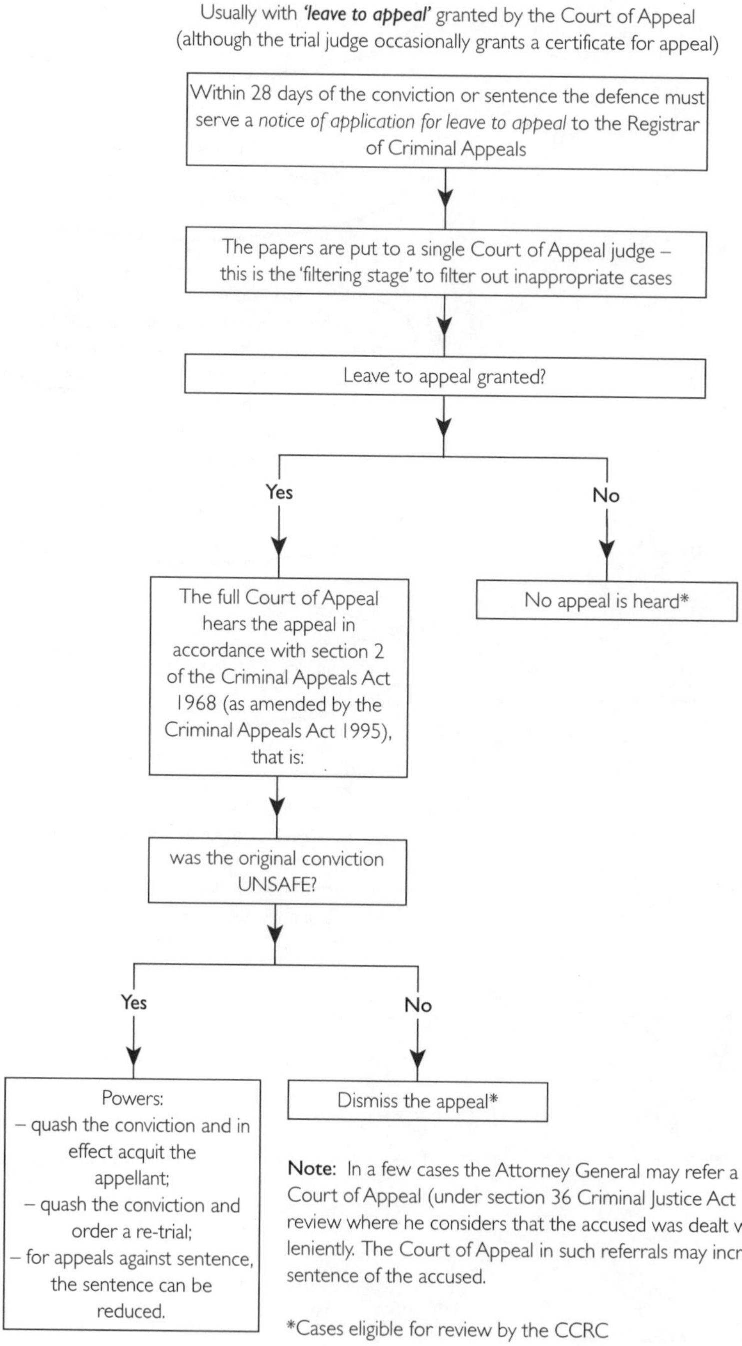

Usually with *'leave to appeal'* granted by the Court of Appeal
(although the trial judge occasionally grants a certificate for appeal)

Within 28 days of the conviction or sentence the defence must serve a *notice of application for leave to appeal* to the Registrar of Criminal Appeals

The papers are put to a single Court of Appeal judge – this is the 'filtering stage' to filter out inappropriate cases

Leave to appeal granted?

Yes

No

The full Court of Appeal hears the appeal in accordance with section 2 of the Criminal Appeals Act 1968 (as amended by the Criminal Appeals Act 1995), that is:

No appeal is heard*

was the original conviction UNSAFE?

Yes

No

Powers:
– quash the conviction and in effect acquit the appellant;
– quash the conviction and order a re-trial;
– for appeals against sentence, the sentence can be reduced.

Dismiss the appeal*

Note: In a few cases the Attorney General may refer a case to the Court of Appeal (under section 36 Criminal Justice Act 1988) for review where he considers that the accused was dealt with unduly leniently. The Court of Appeal in such referrals may increase the sentence of the accused.

*Cases eligible for review by the CCRC

The Criminal Appeal Act 1968 (CAA 1968) was amended by the Criminal Appeal Act 1995. With regard to the hearing in the Court of Appeal, in accordance with section 2 of the CAA 1968, the court will determine the appeal on the basis of whether or not the original conviction was *'unsafe'*. Prior to the CAA 1995 the integrity of the original conviction was determined according to whether it was *'unsafe or unsatisfactory'*. Does this mean that fewer appeals will be allowed? It could do, as it is possible for a conviction to be unsatisfactory but safe. This situation could arise when, for example, the Court of Appeal considers that the conviction is safe (they believe that the appellant committed the offence) though they believe that the conviction was unsatisfactory because of some 'bending' of the rules of evidence. This appeal would be dismissed now whereas, before the CAA 1995 it would have been allowed. If fewer appeals are allowed then it is possible that more cases will end up being referred back to the Court of Appeal by the newly formed Criminal Cases Review Commission which was also set up by the CAA 1995. This is discussed below.

Finally, an appeal can be made from the Court of Appeal (Criminal Division), by either the prosecution or defence, to the House of Lords. In order to do this the Court of Appeal must certify that the decision involves a point of law of general public importance and leave to appeal must have been granted by either the Court of Appeal or the House of Lords.

The Criminal Cases Review Commission

The Criminal Cases Review Commission (CCRC) was established under the CAA 1995 to investigate possible miscarriages of justice in England, Wales and Northern Ireland. This task was previously carried out by the Home Secretary. The CCRC came into being on the first of January 1997 and took on over 250 cases from the Home Office. If a case has been to appeal and failed or was refused leave to appeal then the CCRC may consider the case to see if a miscarriage of justice might have occurred and, if so, the CCRC can refer the case back to the Court of Appeal.

Why was the CCRC established?

The CCRC was established on the recommendation of the Royal Commission on Criminal Justice as a result of several cases of miscarriages of justice which received comprehensive media coverage, such as the Birmingham Six and the Carl Bridgewater case, and in order to establish an 'independent' review body. Hitherto cases

15

had been referred back to the Court of Appeal by the Home Secretary and confidence in this procedure was severely undermined.

How is the CCRC composed?

The CCRC is composed of 14 members of whom one third will be legally qualified and two thirds will have relevant experience in the criminal justice system. At least three members have to sit as a committee in order to refer a case back to the Court of Appeal.

On what basis can the CCRC refer a case back to the Court of Appeal?

The CCRC can refer a case back to the Court of Appeal in the following situations:

i where the CCRC considers that there is a *real possibility* that the conviction, finding or sentence would not be upheld if the case was referred; and

ii usually, other than in exceptional circumstances, only where either the case failed on appeal to the Court of Appeal or was refused leave to appeal.

There is a 'real possibility' that the *conviction, verdict or finding* might not be upheld where :

i an argument or evidence has not been raised during the trial or on appeal; or

ii there are 'exceptional circumstances'.

There is a 'real possibility' that the *sentence* might not be upheld where:

i an argument or point of law was not raised during the trial or on appeal.

The key phrases for the CCRC to consider, therefore, seem to be *real possibility* and *in exceptional circumstances*, both of which are rather ambiguous and undefined in the 1995 Act. In many ways this gives the CCRC wide discretion.

Can the CCRC be assessed as operating *better* than the Home Secretary in referring cases for review?

The CCRC is a body independent of Government which is:

i attempting to be as user friendly as possible, for instance, in the application procedure;

ii taking as many approaches as is felt necessary for the proper investigation of cases;

iii operating without too many financial constraints.

As such, it could be said to operate better than the Home Secretary did in this respect. However, the investigations are still carried out by the police which may be a disadvantage as many miscarriages of justice involve incorrect behaviour by the police involved in the particular case.

How successful has the CCRC been since it was established on 1 January 1997?

Up to 31 March 1998 it had received 1,348 applications in addition to the 252 cases handed over to it from the Home Office. How is its success to be determined? It only has any work to do if the criminal justice system has, possibly, previously operated unjustly and so if the CCRC is found to be successful, by suspected miscarriages of justice being rectified in the Court of Appeal, then this means that the criminal justice system is capable of frequently failing in its *raison d'etre* – to acheive justice. If the criminal justice system worked satisfactorily in the first place then the CCRC would not be necessary. Thus, it would be unwise to measure its success based on how many convictions were quashed by the Court of Appeal or on how many sentences were altered. Maybe a more appropriate benchmark of success would be how many applications for review it deals with in any one year and within what timescale. As the CCRC has only been in existence for a short period of time it is difficult to talk of its success if this is, indeed, something that should be attempted in the first place.

Some prominent cases have been referred back to the CCRC, including that of Derek Bentley (see Chapter 7) and Ruth Ellis. In the former case, at trial in December 1952, Derek Bentley was convicted of the murder of a policeman. He was convicted not as the principal offender, but as an accomplice. The principal offender, Christopher Craig, was also convicted of murder but as he was only 16 years old he was sentenced to detention at Her Majesty's pleasure and was released in 1963. As Bentley was 19 years old he was sentenced to death and was hanged at Wandsworth Prison in January 1953.

Bentley's case was presented to the CCRC on 1 April 1997 and on 6 November 1997 the CCRC referred the case back to the Court of Appeal. On 20 July 1998 the Court of Appeal started to hear the appeal and on 30 July 1998 judgment was given and Bentley's conviction for murder was quashed. The following extract is from the law report which appeared in *The Times* on 31 July 1998:

15

Regina v. Bentley

Before Lord Bingham of Cornhill, Lord Chief Justice, Lord Justice Kennedy and Mr Justice Collins. [Judgment July 30]

*Having regard to the evidence adduced at trial the jury, **if properly directed** [emphasis added] would have been entitled to convict Derek Bentley of murder as the offence was then constituted, before the abolition of constructive malice and the introduction of the defence of diminished responsibility.*

*However, since the trial judge in his summing-up failed to direct the jury on the standard and burden of proof, to give sufficient direction on the law of joint enterprise, or adequately to summarise the defence case, made prejudicial comments about the defendants and their defences, and indicated that the police officers' evidence, because of their bravery on the night in question, was more worthy of belief than that of the defendants, **Bentley was denied the fair trial to which he was entitled and his conviction was in consequence unsafe.***

Source: *The Times*, 31 July 1998

Ruth Ellis, aged 29 years, was the last woman to be hanged in Britain. She was executed at Holloway Prison in 1955 after being convicted of the murder of her racing-driver lover. Her case went before the CCRC in August 1998. It is hoped that the CCRC will refer the case back to the Court of Appeal and that Ellis's conviction for murder will be reduced to manslaughter on the basis that vital medical and other evidence was not heard at the trial.

Review of delay in the criminal justice system – A report by the Home office, February 1997 – 'The Narey report'

Although in recent years there have been several government reports concerning the criminal justice system, the Narey report is given special attention in this chapter. This is because it deals with many matters which constitute key parts of A-level law syllabuses. A knowledge of this report should aid students' understanding of the workings of the criminal justice system as a whole and should afford numerous discussion topics, many of which should serve to consolidate topics covered while studying the English legal system. Each of the nine chapters in the report is discussed, with commentary as appropriate. Students are advised where the recommendations in the report have subsequently been acted upon, such as by the Crime and Disorder Act 1998 and by the Glidewell Report of June 1998.

The Home Office reviewer, Martin Narey, began the review on 15 October 1996 with the following brief:

to identify ways of expediting the progress of cases through the criminal justice system from initiation to resolution, consistently with the interests of justice and securing value for money.

He stated in his preface to the report:

A small minority of people suggested to me that justice should not be managed, that somehow management and justice are incompatible. Others asserted that delay cannot be tackled without resorting to constitutional change, including a Ministry of Justice. I disagree. The criminal justice processs is a complex one involving different agencies at different stages. But almost everyone I talked to agreed that it can still be managed, and management of the process is very much the theme of this report. Managing each stage of the process can help bring offenders to justice and acquit the innocent more promptly.

Chapter one – Summary of main proposals

In this chapter it is stated that the recommendations in the report would enable:

i **more** cases to be dealt with;
ii far more **quickly**; and
iii at a **lower cost**.

It further stresses that there is greatest scope for bringing cases to the Magistrates' Court more quickly in respect of those involving a guilty plea.

Chapter two – the growing problem of delay

Indictable (including TEW) offences

The reviewer states that despite a drop in the number of cases coming before the criminal courts in recent years, there has been a deterioration in the speed at which cases are proceeded with from commission of the offence to completion of the case in the courts. This was demonstrated by Chart A as shown in Figure 16.1.

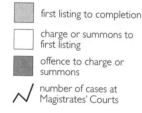

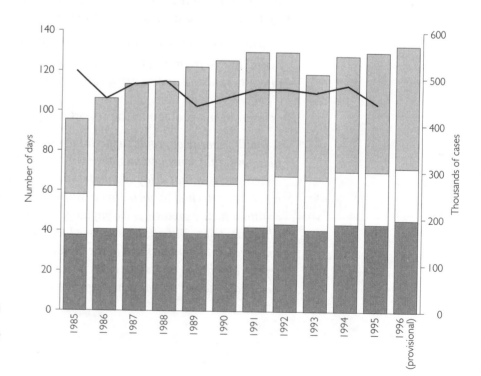

Figure 16.1
Chart A – Average time taken for indictable (including triable-either-way) offences at Magistrates' Courts.

In 1985 the number of prosecutions in the Magistrates' Court for Indictable (including TEW) offences was 520,000, while in 1995 this figure dropped to 464,000 (see Figure 16.1). However, during this period of a significantly falling caseload at the Magistrates' Court, the average time taken to complete indictable and triable either way cases, from the date of the offence, deteriorated from 98 days to 132 days. All stages of the process took longer, as shown in Figure 16.1, that is:

▶ the average time taken by the police to charge or summons a defendant (from the date of the offence) deteriorated from 38 to 45 days;

▶ the average time between charge or summons and first listing of the case at Magistrates' Courts deteriorated from 18 to 28 days;

▶ the average time between the first listing and the completion of the case at Magistrates' Courts deteriorated from 41 to 60 days.

Summary offences (non-motoring)

For summary offences (non-motoring) the situation was not as bad (as shown in Figure 16.2) because although the time taken to prosecute a case increased (compare column one for 1985 with column twelve for 1996) the total number of cases being prosecuted *rose* and so delay is more understandable.

- first listing to completion
- charge or summons to first listing
- offence to charge or summons
- number of cases at Magistrates' Courts

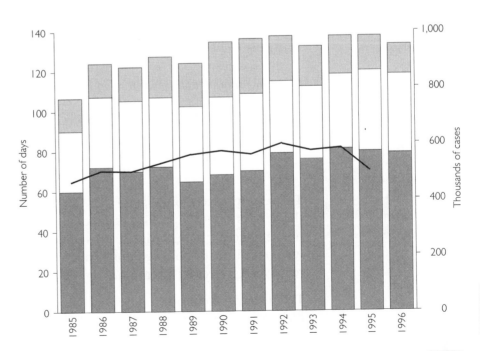

Figure 16.2
Chart B – Average time taken for summary (non-motoring) offences at Magistrates' Courts.

16

Adjournments

The reviewer states that the average number of adjournments for indictable (including TEW) offences was 2.6, with each adjournment lasting an average of 23 days. Obviously, the more adjournments there are, the more time it takes for a case to be completed.

Time taken between committal to the Crown Court and arraignment in the Crown Court

The reviewer states that the average waiting time in the Crown Court from committal to arraignment had dropped from 16.7 weeks in 1994 to 13.1 weeks in 1996.

Chapter three – managing the decision to prosecute

In the report the reviewer states:

> A significant number of people who wrote to me or who were interviewed suggested that increased delay in the criminal justice process was at least partly the fault of the Crown Prosecution Service which started work in 1986. The main complaint levelled at the CPS was that they did not deal promptly with the prosecution of straightforward cases.
>
> Although a few of those people sought the complete abolition of the CPS and a return to the 'good old days' of police prosecuting cases, most did not question the existence of an independent prosecuting service, agreeing with the Royal Commission that it was necessary for the preservation of:
>
> > 'the unambiguous separation of the roles of investigator and prosecutor'.
> >
> > The majority of the Chief Constables I spoke to also favoured the continuing existence of an independent prosecuting service, but called for it to be dismantled into locally managed units free from central direction.

The reviewer went on to state that the structure and organisation of the CPS as set up in 1986 was generally satisfactory. However, it was not satisfactory as regards the prosecutors in the 98 operational units who have little or no discretion. This was a problem which the reviewer felt needed attention.

The reviewer went on to state that there was, in some areas, a severe dislocation between the police and CPS causing police/CPS breakdown of co-operation due to the fact that preparing cases for prosecution involved two distinct parts – police file preparation (the charge) and CPS review of the charge. He stated:

> ...this two part system seems inevitably to be combative and time consuming. Until prosecution files can be sent electronically (still some time away) the simple process of transferring papers can take a number of days, is expensive, and seems to result in files sometimes being mislaid.

To overcome this problem the reviewer recommends that to cover likely guilty pleas, CPS prosecutors should have a permanent base at police stations to enable close police–CPS preparation of cases. Would this arrangement compromise the independence of the CPS? The reviewer thinks not and states:

> To paraphrase one defence lawyer I interviewed, 'independence is a state of mind'.

In respect of likely **guilty** pleas, cases could be dealt with as shown in Figure 16.3 over the page.

In order to prosecute such cases the day after the charge, the reviewer states that the CPS review of the file should be speeded up and it is suggested that this be achieved by amending the Code for Crown Prosecutors as follows:

Test One

evidential test – to stay the same;

Test Two

public interest test – if Test One is satisfied there should be an 'express presumption' that prosecution should take place. The ability to discontinue a case because the offence is not serious or likely to attract a small penalty should be removed.

The reviewer states:

> This change would not only speed CPS review of the prosecution file, but, more importantly in my view, it would remove the potential for conflict between police and prosecutors. The decision on what type of offending behaviour is suitable for prosecution would once again be one for the police and would allow Chief Constables to make decisions about the targeting of particular crimes, often involving petty criminality of an anti-social nature.

> One Chief Constable suggested that this change to the public interest test had the potential to renew police officers' confidence in the criminal justice system by returning to them – so long as evidential requirements were met – the decision whether or not to prosecute. This change would also provide an explicit recognition that locating CPS staff in police stations would not imply any role whatsoever for the CPS in the management of the investigative process and the decision to charge.

16

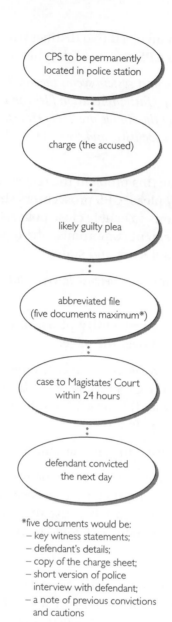

*five documents would be:
 – key witness statements;
 – defendant's details;
 – copy of the charge sheet;
 – short version of police
   interview with defendant;
 – a note of previous convictions
   and cautions

Figure 16.3   Procedure in respect of likely guilty pleas

These proposals were considered by Sir Iain Glidewell who undertook a review of the CPS and whose report was published in June 1998, 'The Glidewell Report'. The report contains many proposals including the following in relation to the prosecution process. It recommends that the CPS should take responsibility for:

▶ the prosecution process immediately following charge;
▶ arranging the initial hearing in the Magistrates' Court;
▶ witness availability, witness warning and witness care.

It also states that the police should remain responsible for the investigation of offences and for charging and for the preliminary preparation of case papers. But, to breach the gap between the police and CPS, it recommends the formation of 'Criminal Justice Units'. Such CJUs would, in effect, amalgamate the work presently done in police Administrative Support Units (ASUs) and file preparation and review which is done in CPS branches. Such CJUs would be located in or near the relevant police station. A senior police officer would need to be part of the unit so that the unit could call on the police to take action to in obtaining more evidence. The CJUs would deal with 'fast-track' cases (as mentioned in the Narey report) in their entirety and with simple summary cases. The CPS should be responsible for ensuring the speedy disposal of cases through the Magistrates' Court and share with the court one or more performance indicators related to timeliness. It is hoped that such speeding up via fast-track cases will lead to a shift in the centre of gravity of the CPS towards the Crown Court. In other words, the CPS will not spend as much of their time as at present on the more straightforward cases which are dealt with in the Magistrates' Courts. Rather, the mundane cases will be dealt with speedily by the fast-track procedure, leaving the CPS lawyers more time to work on the more complex and serious cases. This should have the knock-on effect of creating a more rewarding working environment for CPS lawyers who have been suffering from low morale. This change in working practices, coupled with increased rights of audience for CPS lawyers in the Crown Court, should mean that some of the more able solicitors feel inclined to join the CPS.

The increasing use of lay persons in the prosecution process

The reviewer recommends that lay persons should be able to review files as well as CPS lawyers. He further recommends that lay persons should be allowed to present guilty plea cases in the Magistrates' Court. The reviewer states that such use of lay persons to prosecute is already in existence for prosecutions undertaken by, for example, the

16

Health and Safety Executive, the Inland Revenue, Customs and Excise, Trading Standards, and so forth. These recommendations have come under criticism from both the Law Society and the Bar Council as highlighted in the newspaper articles below taken from *The Times*.

Lawyers lose role to CPS officials

By Richard Ford
HOME CORRESPONDENT

OFFICIALS in the Crown Prosecution Service are to be given the authority to deal with tens of thousands of cases in magistrates' courts, the Government is to announce tomorrow.

Jack Straw will tell MPs that lay presenters are to be allowed to present uncontested cases in an attempt to cut costs and free lawyers to focus on not guilty pleas.

Hundreds of administrators working in the Crown Prosecution Service will be given powers similar to those of staff working for Customs and Excise and the Health and Safety Executive in cases where a defendant pleads guilty. Some 734,000 – 81 per cent – of all cases dealt with in magistrates' courts in 1996–97.

The change, expected to be included in the Crime and Disorder Bill, is one of a package of measures outlined in a review of delays in the criminal justice system published by the Home Office in February. The Home Secretary's proposal is strongly opposed by the Law Society and the Bar, which fear that their professional status is being undermined.

An attempt in 1988 to allow files to be reviewed by CPS executive officers was ruled unlawful by the courts after the First Division Association challenged the move by the then Director of Public Prosecutions.

Plans for lay prosecutors attacked

By Frances Gibb
LEGAL CORRESPONDENT

PLANS for non-lawyers to prosecute routine "guilty plea" cases in the magistrates' courts were heavily criticised at the Bar conference on Saturday. Nigel Pascoe, QC, chairman of the Bar's public affairs committee, said: "If I go into hospital for standard surgery, on the whole I don't want it done by the administrator."

Kevin Goodwin, of the Association of First Division Civil Servants, said the plans would damage confidence in the Crown Prosecution Service. Robert Owen, QC, the Bar chairman, was "extremely uneasy" about the plans, seen by the Government as one way of reducing delays in the criminal justice system: "It is a cost-cutting measure which does not address the fundamental problems in the service."

But Jack Straw, the Home Secretary, said that it was a ridiculous waste of time for experienced, qualified lawyers to have to deal with lists of routine guilty pleas, such as those for parking offences. "In the old days, those kind of cases – which involve reading out some brief facts – were done by police inspectors."

This proposal has been taken forward by section 53 of the Crime and Disorder Act 1998 which enables the DPP to designate, for the purpose of exercising certain powers of Crown Prosecutors, members of staff of the CPS who are not legally qualified.

For contested case (not guilty pleas) the reviewer states that more time is needed for completion of the files by the police and the CPS and that in order to guarantee CPS advise to the police at all times about the charge (not just during weekdays) the CPS should be 'on-call' at all times, to cover weekday evenings, nights and weekends.

Chapter three is concluded as follows:

> *The recommendations in this chapter are not without controversy. Some CPS lawyers might object to work being delegated to administrative staff and argue that to locate staff in police stations would erode independence. Conversely, some police officers, and some Chief Constables, would be suspicious, suspecting that the CPS were intent on getting closer to the management of the investigation. But I believe the majority of Chief Constables would recognise these proposals as offering the potential for significant improvements to current arrangements.*

Chapter four – managing legal representation and legal aid

In this chapter the reviewer deals with the delay in the criminal justice system caused by the application for legal aid and associated adjournments. The recommendations are geared to speeding up the process of granting legal aid in respect of **guilty** pleas so that the proposals in Chapter Three are not thwarted.

Chapter five – managing cases in magistrates' courts

In this chapter the reviewer states that it is necessary for cases to be *'managed'* in their progress through the Magistrates' Courts to ensure that cases move forwards. He recognises that *stipendiary* magistrates are efficient at managing cases already but points out that *lay* magistrates are not so efficient, partly due to their lack of knowledge on law and procedure and partly due to the fact that between adjournments a different bench of magistrates may be constituted which is not familiar with the case. However, the reviewer rejects the idea of replacing lay magistrates with stipendiary magistrates, not

16

because of the financial implications, but because of the the fact that lay magistrates are *'intrinsic to our justice system'* and because *'the Lord Chancellor has made his commitment to lay magistrates abundantly clear'*.

So how can cases in the Magistrates' Courts be managed?

The reviewer recommends giving the justices' clerks (or other senior staff) the job of managing cases, leaving the lay magistrates to decide on verdict, sentence and bail matters. The reviewer notes that pre-trial review (PTR) of cases by justices' clerks already takes place in some Magistrates' Courts and that this does speed up court proceedings. However, there is no compulsion on the parties to attend these PTRs and the justices clerk has limited powers. The reviewer recommends the extension of the justices' clerk powers so that they should manage PTRs, putting cases before the magistrates only when ready for trial. The reviewer notes that such PTR would be very useful in contested (not guilty plea) cases especially. The reviewer also recommends the use of early administrative hearings (EAH). This is shown in Figure 16.4.

Figure 16.4   How EAH and PTR would work

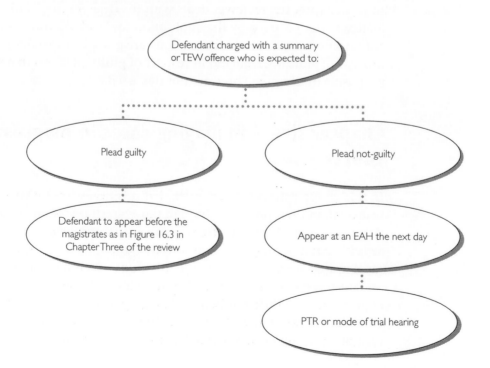

Such use of EAH and PTR should reduce the number of adjournments and so speed up the criminal justice process as in these proceedings many routine administrative decisions and simple procedural decisions are made, for example:

EAH – decisions concerning legal aid, bail, explaining court procedures, filling in forms, etc.

PTR – decisions concerning pre-sentence reports, dismissing cases for lack of evidence, remitting defendant to Crown Court for sentence etc.

These proposals have been taken forward by section 49 and 50 of the Crime and Disorder Act 1998.

Section 49

authorises a number of the powers of a Magistrates' Court to be exercised by a single Justice of the Peace and permits the Lord Chancellor to make provision, following consultation with the justices and justices' clerks for an area, for any of the listed powers (subject to certain modifications) to be exercised by justices' clerks in that area.

Section 50

provides for early administrative hearings at Magistrates' Courts to be conducted by a single Justice of the Peace or justices' clerk.

What do magistrates themselves think of these recommendations and enactments?

The commentary in the extract on the following page, from an article by Paula Davies, an inner London magistrate who frequently writes for *The Times*, is not directly aimed at the Narey report. However, given that the article appeared in *The Times* on 6 May 1997 (the Narey report was published in February 1997) and the nature of the commentary, it is suggested that it was written with the Narey report in mind. For instance, where the author states, 'cases are still said to take an average of 132 days to get through compared with 98 days ten years ago', direct reference can be made to Chapter Two of the Narey report and Chart A which is shown in Figure 16.1. In addition the commentary concerning justices' clerks managing bail matters and adjournments has direct relation to Chapter Five of the report – see the newspaper extract overleaf.

16

Justices may face erosion of powers

Many magistrates are apprehensive about likely changes to their role, writes **Paula Davies**

With a new Government elected, magistrates will be bracing themselves for more change. Change is likely in the law and in their role. Since 1989 legislation has poured out in Act after Act, requiring justices to follow a steep learning curve, which is particularly onerous on those who give their time and effort for no monetary reward. Yet they have embraced extra training with enthusiasm; it is only recently that an air of demoralisation has appeared. Rightly or wrongly, many of them feel they are being sidelined.

They are accused of being too slow, yet in my experience it is not so much the fault of the justices as in the paper-driven system forced on us by the so-called paperless society of the computer. It ought to work more efficiently but it does not, and cases are said to take an average of 132 days to get through compared with 98 days ten years ago. Then there is the attitude of some court users. Recently our bench discovered that witnesses had been "de-warned" on the assumption that we would grant an adjournment.

"It is," the representative of the Crown Prosecution Service said, "only the first trial date."

We insisted that the case go ahead, principally because of the age of the defendants–13 and 14 respectively – and because the next trial date could not be fixed for another three months. After all, it is for the justices alone to decide on an adjournment.

This situation may not last much longer. Recently, the Justices' Clerks Society has made suggestions about taking on what it claims are only administrative jobs designed to speed up justice. Yet if clerks can decide on such matters as adjournments, bail matters, fixing trial dates and discontinuing cases, they will be taking on roles previously held by the justices.

This problem of judicial and administrative boundaries is now being examined by a working party in the Lord Chancellor's Department. Nonetheless, lay magistrates are starting to believe that this is the thin end of the wedge and that their powers are likely to be eroded.

Chapter six – managing the distribution of cases between the courts

This chapter deals with two topics:

i the current right of the defendant to elect trial by jury (for TEW offences) in the Crown Court; and
ii the fact that all criminal cases start in the Magistrates' Court.

These will be considered in turn.

The current right of the defendant to elect trail by jury (for TEW offences) in the Crown Court

In this part of the chapter arguments for and against retention of the defendant's right to elect trial by jury for TEW offences are considered. The reviewer argues towards the recommendation that such a right should be abolished, that it should be for the magistrates to determine whether or not a TEW case should go to jury trial. As such, he argues, delay and expense in the criminal justice system would be reduced as in the year to September 1996, 24,170 defendants elected Crown Court trial which represents one quarter of the Crown Court workload.

Arguments 'for' the retention of the defendant's right to elect trial by jury

i This right has existed since *Magna Carta* in the Middle Ages.

ii A professional person of good character, charged with, for instance, a minor theft (a TEW offence) should be allowed to elect trial by jury to be able to protect his reputation.

iii Most solicitors and barristers and organisations representing a wider interest in the criminal justice system support retention of this right.

Arguments 'against' retention of the defendant's right to elect trial by jury

i The defendant's right to elect jury trial does not date back to *Magna Carta*. At least one eminent historian queries whether the phrase 'lawful judgement of peers' in *Magna Carta* should be interpreted as meaning trial by jury. Indeed, at that time the jury was not an independent tribunal but a group of local people selected because of their familiarity with the district and the accused. In some ways, therefore, the jury of that time resembled the modern day bench of three lay magistrates (local knowledge).

ii In the Middle Ages the criminal justice system afforded the defendant far fewer due process protections than he is afforded now. (Due process means that the defendant is protected against abuse by the state, for example, rights afforded to the defendant under the Police and Criminal Evidence Act 1984.) As such, the defendant nowadays need not rely solely on the fairness of the jury system to protect his rights against the state.

iii Few other jurisdictions had found it necessary or desirable to let the defendant have the right to elect trial by jury.

iv Some defendants only elect trial by jury to delay the court proceedings and so delay conviction and sentence where this is anticipated as the likely outcome.

v For defendants not likely to be given bail, custody before trial is likely to be in a local prison which allows the defendant to be close to family and friends and to have more visiting times. Such a reason for election is therefore nothing to do with the desire to be tried by a jury.

vi Some defendants elect trial by jury as they think that they are more likely to be acquitted by the jury. However, this reason must be queried as about two thirds of defendants who elect trial by

16

jury subsequently plead guilty once in the Crown Court. Hence, such defendants have no desire for a trial by jury.

vii The alternative way to reduce the number of cases going to the Crown Court for trial, by reclassifying some TEW offences as summary offences, would not be appropriate. For instance, if minor theft (up to say £90) was reclassified as a summary offence, then the defendant whose reputation was paramount to his livelihood would not be able to have a trial by his peers.

The reviewer recommended the removal of the defendant's right to elect jury trial for TEW offences. Magistrates would make this decision based on the defendant's reputation and past record, the seriousness of the offence, the complexity of the case and its likely effect on the defendant.

The fact that all criminal cases start in the Magistrates' Court

The reviewer recommends that indictable only cases should start in the Crown Court rather than in the Magistrates' Court where at present they spend half of their life, on average 87 days before committal for trial. In other words, the criminal court structure would be more like the civil court structure as, in the latter, not all cases start in the county court; some start in the High Court. The reviewer supports this recommendation by pointing out that the Crown Court could speedily decide if there was a case to answer because of case management through plea and direction hearings (PDHs). (See the notes on Chapter Seven of the review.) At such PDHs an early guilty plea would also attract a maximum sentence discount. An additional factor for this recommendation is that it could reduce prisoner escapes as most escapes occur when prisoners accused of the most serious offences are taken to the Magistrates' Court. See Figure 16.5.

These proposals are taken forward by sections 51 and 57 of the Crime and Disorder Act 1998 which state:

Section 51

(1) Where an adult appears or is brought before a Magistrates' Court ('the court') charged with an offence triable only on indictment ('the indictable only offence'), the court shall send him forthwith to the Crown Court for trial –

    (a) for that offence, and

    (b) for any either-way or summary offence with which he is charged which fulfils the requisite conditions (as set out in subsection 11 below).

Figure 16.5   Chart F – Escort escapes, March to December 1996.

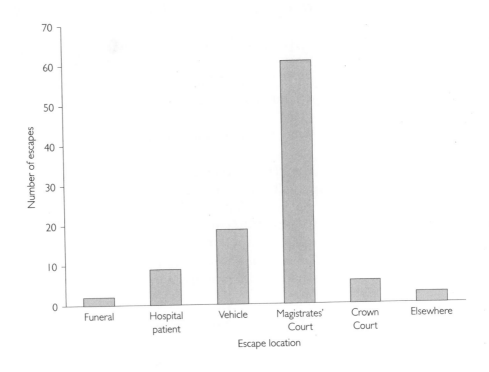

(11) An offence fulfils the requisite conditions if –

   (a) it appears to the court to be related to the indictable-only offence and

   (b) in the case of a summary offence, it is punishable with imprisonment or involves obligatory or discretionary disqualification from driving.

Section 57   (1) In any proceedings for an offence, a court may, after hearing representations from the parties, direct that the accused shall be treated as being present in the court for any particular hearing before the start of the trial if, during that hearing –

   (a) he is held in custody in a prison or other institution; and

   (b) whether by means of a live television link or otherwise, he is able to see and hear the court and to be seen and heard by it.

Thus, clause 54 aims to reduce the number of prisoners who escape custody while in transit from prison to court and back.

16

Chapter seven – managing pre-trial preparation at the Crown Court

PDHs were adopted in all Crown Court centres in January 1996. The PDH has to be held within four weeks of committal for a case where the defendant is held in custody and within six weeks when the defendant is bailed to appear in the Crown Court.

What is the purpose of the PDH?

The PDH is designed to avoid delay and thus expense when the case actually comes to trial and so it ensures that the case is fully ready for trial before it procedes to trial. However, some Crown Court judges feel that PDHs are unnecessary for straightforward cases and, in effect, waste court time. Thus, the reviewer recommends that the Trials Issue Group, currently looking at such issues, should consider whether PDHs should only be mandatory for the more complicated cases.

The reviewer further recommends that time and expense in the management of PDHs could be saved if CPS solicitors could conduct the PDH in the Crown Court instead of having to brief barristers who do not know the case well and who rely on CPS directions. At the time of the review CPS solicitors could only appear in the Crown Court for bail applications and in some areas for guilty pleas and appeals from the Magistrates' Court. However, since the review, CPS solicitors have gained wider rights of audience in the Crown Court. In March 1998 34 CPS solicitors were awarded higher courts rights of audience but, as of June 1998, they had not exercised such rights, awaiting the publication of the CPS's 'ethical statement' outlining how solicitors will exercise these rights, which is a legal requirement.

Chapter eight – managing the Youth Court

The reviewer recommends that a separate review of the Youth Court is needed because most of the people consulted in this review stated that the Youth Court was unsatisfactory. Delay was one area of concern, coupled with the fact that many people involved in youth justice were uncertain as to the purpose of the Youth Court – should it punish offenders or be concerned mainly with the welfare of the defendant? Also it was felt by many that for some offenders the court was toothless and could do nothing to deter them. However, the reviewer recommends that 17 year olds should be returned to the jurisdiction of the adult court and that stipendiary magistrates should be allowed to sit alone in the Youth Court. By section 48 of the Crime and Disorder Act 1998 metropolitan stipendiary magistrates may sit alone in the Youth Courts.

Chapter nine – cost Implications

The reviewer states that there was not time to estimate potential savings with any sort of rigour. However, he states that the recommendations suggested in the review could bring more offenders to court, more quickly, at a saving of about £55 million per annum.

16

Index